The Limits of the Legal Complex

The Limits of the Legal Complex

Nordic Lawyers and Political Liberalism

Edited by

MALCOLM FEELEY

University of California (Berkeley)

MALCOLM LANGFORD

University of Oslo

OXFORD
UNIVERSITY PRESS

OXFORD
UNIVERSITY PRESS

Great Clarendon Street, Oxford, OX2 6DP,
United Kingdom

Oxford University Press is a department of the University of Oxford.
It furthers the University's objective of excellence in research, scholarship,
and education by publishing worldwide. Oxford is a registered trade mark of
Oxford University Press in the UK and in certain other countries

First Edition published in 2021

Impression: 1

Published in the United States of America by Oxford University Press
198 Madison Avenue, New York, NY 10016, United States of America

British Library Cataloguing in Publication Data

Data available

Library of Congress Control Number: 2021939173

ISBN 978–0–19–284841–3

DOI: 10.1093/oso/9780192848413.001.0001

Printed and bound by
CPI Group (UK) Ltd, Croydon, CR0 4YY

To the future: Ari, Ariav, Elai, Liv, Maxine, Sam, Shai, Shelly, and Zev

Contents

Preface

This idea for the book arose over a lunch meeting at the University of California (Berkeley) between the two editors, while Malcolm (Langford) was a Visiting Scholar at the Center for the Study of Law and Society in Berkeley. Having just completed a second volume on the legal complex with Halliday and Karpik, the other Malcolm (Feeley) was wondering just how far the idea of lawyers' collective struggle for political liberalism could be extended. Langford offered Norway as a potential counter-example. It has a long-standing liberal tradition, but until recently its bar was small and its celebrated history of collective political engagement was limited. With this, we were off and running, and because of their common culture and intertwined political histories, we quickly expanded the project to all five of the Nordic countries—Iceland, Denmark, Norway, Sweden, and Finland.

The result is this book on the role of Nordic lawyers in struggling for political liberalism—basic civil rights and a moderate state. It seeks to expand geographically the study of legal complexes, while subjecting its underlying theories and empirical findings to critical inquiry. Full-length studies are provided on five new countries, which show the limits of the legal complex and provide a departure point for new theoretical inquiry.

Our greatest debt is to the contributors to this volume. We are deeply appreciative of these recognized, busy, and productive scholars' enthusiastic engagement with the enterprise. Their chapters—which span more than two hundred years—stand on their own as significant scholarly contributions, and taken together represent an impressive account of the development of Nordic legal professions. And, because they remained true to the spirit of the project on the Nordic legal complex, the collective result of their research is perhaps a useful model for conducting comparative historical sociology.

We cannot conclude without also acknowledging several people who have aided in this project. Lucien Karpik and Terry Halliday of course developed the theory, which we explore here in the Nordic states. In addition, they contributed insights and comments over the course of the development of this book, were active participants in both workshops, commented on successive drafts of chapters, and Terry read and offered detailed comments on the entire finished manuscript. In all this, they were generous with their time and gracious in their comments. The book is far better for their involvement.

In Oslo, we are very grateful to UiO:Norden at the University of Oslo for financing the first phase of the project and to its larger *Nordic Branding: Politics of Exceptionalism* project for shepherding the project to its conclusion. A special thanks to Tori Kirkebø, Sevda Clark, and Charlotte Aslesen for research and administrative assistance, together with the Norwegian Centre for Human Rights and Department of Public and International Law at the University of Oslo. In Berkeley, the Center for the Study of Law and Society hosted the second workshop, and its staff, Yvette Cooper and Erika Espinoza, were indispensable in making travel and housing arrangements and administering the funds that covered some of the project's costs. Thanks to John Smallman and Jamie Berezin at Oxford University Press and Ashirvad Moses and Mark Ajin at Newgen for shepherding this book through production.

Malcolm Feeley, Berkeley
Malcolm Langford, Oslo

List of Contributors

Malcolm M. Feeley is Claire Sanders Clements Dean's Chair, Professor of Law, Centre for the Study of Law and Society, University of California (Berkeley).

Ragnhildur Helgadóttir is Professor, Faculty of Law, Reykjavik University.

Johan Karlsson Schaffer is Associate Professor, University of Gothenburg and Research Professor, University of Oslo.

Esa Konttinen is Professor (emeritus), University of Jyväskylä.

Malcolm Langford is Professor, Faculty of Law, University of Oslo and Co-Director, Centre on Law and Social Transformation. He led the project *Nordic Branding: The Politics of Exceptionalism* 2017–2020.

Hans Petter Graver is Professor, Faculty of Law, University of Oslo.

Mikael Rask Madsen is Professor of Law and Director of iCourts, The Danish National Research Foundation's Center of Excellence for International Courts.

List of Abbreviations

CCF	Congress for Cultural Freedom
ECHR	European Convention on Human Rights
ECJ	European Court of Justice
ECtHR	European Court of Human Rights
FRU	*Fri- och rättighetsutredningen* (Liberties and Rights Commission, Sweden)
GLB	*Grundlagsberedningen* (Constitutional Commission, Sweden)
IADJ	International Association of Democratic Lawyers
ICJ	International Commission of Jurists
RF	*Regeringsformen* (Instrument of Government, Sweden)
SDP	Social Democratic Party
SLR	Scandinavian legal realism

1
Introduction

Malcolm M. Feeley and Malcolm Langford***

In the 1970s, a burgeoning revisionist body of scholarly work emerged to challenge the conventional understanding of the professions, and in particular the legal profession, which had traditionally enjoyed the status of a "high calling". Following the social unrest in Europe and the United States in the 1960s and the resistance of the organized bar to endorse and help implement legal services for the poor, a new generation of scholars characterized law as a tool of political repression, and lawyers as instruments of class and racial domination masquerading as neutral and disinterested servants of the public good (see e.g., Kairys 1982; Kennedy 1982; Rabinowitz 1987). What began in the United States quickly spread to England, Europe, and elsewhere.

In those heady times, it was easy to see self-evident truth in these revisionist claims. Law remained rooted in doctrines presented as neutral principles that in fact preserved privilege. In the legal academy, successive waves of critical and alternative scholarship emerged: critical legal studies (see e.g., Unger 1983), critical race scholarship (see e.g., Delgado and Stephancic 2001), and feminist legal studies (see e.g., Mackinnon 1983, 1987; Crenshaw 1989), which cumulatively revealed built-in class, racial, and gender biases that permeated the law. Parallel developments occurred in England and in Europe (see e.g., Dahl 1987; Fitzpatrick and Hunt 1987; Goodrich 1992).

The social unrest and its interlocutors had provided a natural experiment. Local and national bar associations in the United States, Great Britain, Western Europe, and elsewhere were rarely at the forefront of liberal politics and often resisted constitutional and legal innovation. However, the successive waves of the civil rights movement, the Great Society, student activism generated by the anti-Vietnam War movement, and a global wave of cause lawyering by a small cadre of lawyers and student law clinics in the 1960s and 1970s (in the United States and some European, African, and Latin American countries) only underscored the perception that

* Claire Sanders Clements Dean's Chair, Professor of Law, Center for the Study of Law and Society, University of California (Berkeley).

** Professor, Faculty of Law, University of Oslo and Co-Director, Centre on Law and Social Transformation. He led the project *Nordic Branding: The Politics of Exceptionalism* 2017–2020.

Malcolm M. Feeley and Malcolm Langford, *Introduction* In: *The Limits of the Legal Complex*. Edited by: Malcolm Feeley and Malcolm Langford, Oxford University Press. © Malcolm M. Feeley and Malcolm Langford 2021.
DOI: 10.1093/oso/9780192848413.003.0001

mainstream lawyering was out of touch with societal needs (see, e.g., Carlin, Howard, and Messinger 1967; Sarat and Scheingold 1998; Romano 2016).

To be sure, in the United States, the civil rights movement, the consumer movement, and the due process (criminal and administrative) revolution *eventually* had some transformative effects on the organized bar and judiciary, and as the chapters in this volume also reveal, the reverberations energized elsewhere in time to a certain degree the otherwise passive and deferential legal professions and judiciaries. Europe, amongst others, saw first the emergence of a domestic human rights movement from the 1980s and cause lawyering and legal student clinics expanded in the 1990s from a few countries to cover most by the 2000s (Romano 2016), which gradually inflected the *actual* work of bar associations. For example, the Council of Bars and Law Societies of Europe, founded in 1960, had the objective of "advancing the views of European lawyers and defending the legal principles upon which democracy and the rule of law are based", but only in the last two decades has it moved beyond questions of professional control over accreditation, legal ethics education, and transnational legal services to engage concretely on questions of the rule of law and human rights.[1]

Thus, with this backdrop, it was all but inevitable in the 1970s that a generation of scholars of the legal profession would arise to challenge the bromides and banalities about the legal profession that had been put forward until then by generations of advocates in the organized bar and on law faculties, and had been savaged by the mounting scholarship attacking conventional legal doctrine and method. The lodestone for this new approach was Magli Sarfatti-Larson's *The Rise of the Professions* (1979), an erudite history of the learned professions, which maintained that the constant concern uniting all professions was self-determination and monopoly control over their designated (and expanding) domains. In the United States, Richard Abel began his inquiry by examining informal dispute processes in so-called simple societies (1982), and then expanded his attention to the organized legal profession in more industrialized societies. He drew on Sarfatti-Larson's work after his observations of the English and American bar's tepid responses, if not opposition, to the establishment of a legal services program to provide free legal services to the poor (Abel 1979, 1981a, 1981b). This led him to organize studies of legal services and the legal profession around the world (Abel and Lewis 1988a, 1988b, 1989; Abel 1987).

Contemporaneously, in France, Pierre Bourdieu (1987) penned *The Force of Law: Toward a Sociology of the Juridical Field*, applying his theory of the field—how institutions operate in and manage their social-spatial arena and enhance their interests and status within it—to lawyers. His key assertion was that the "juridical field, like any social field, is organized around a body of internal protocols and

[1] https://www.ccbe.eu/about/who-we-are/

assumptions, characteristic behaviors and self-sustaining values—what we might informally term a 'legal culture'" (Bourdieu [Terdiman, trans and intro] 1987: 806). In turn, his work stimulated several focused studies on the legal profession by Yves Dezalay and Bryant Garth (see e.g., 1996), who focused on how lawyers organize to expand their expertise and enhance both wealth and status, especially in the age of globalism. This body of work has influenced vast numbers of critical legal scholars around the world, and stimulated the development to two closely related "realist" schools of scholarship, one which emphasized the protection of income (Abel 1979, 1981a, 1981b)[2] and the other which emphasized the protection of status (Dezalay and Garth 1996),[3] anchored almost wholly in materialist terms.

Alongside this and in contrast, Lucien Karpik (1988, 1998) and Terrence Halliday (1987, working independently and then together (Halliday and Karpik 1997; Halliday, Karpik, and Feeley 2007, 2012; Karpik and Halliday 2011),[4] found that a distinctive segment of lawyers clung to the idealism of the legal profession advanced in the classic works of Max Weber (1954; see also Turner 1994 and Talcott Parsons 1951), so that idealism as a motivating factor could not be discounted entirely. Both agreed in large part with the new realist theories of the legal profession, but they also maintained that lawyers, or at least some crucial component of the organized bar, viewed themselves as stewards of the law and consistently organized to fight for and to protect the rule of law, basic liberal rights, and features of the moderate state. This position did not flow so much as a deduction from any a priori theory about the functions of the law or lawyers in society, but from their observations that it was a patterned empirical reality in the historical studies of the organized legal profession in France and the United States that they and various collaborators found.

Intrigued by this, they joined forces, recruited other scholars, including eventually one of these authors—Feeley—and went on to produce three edited volumes consisting of several dozen accounts of lawyers' participation in political struggles in countries around the world (Halliday and Karpik 1997; Halliday, Karpik, and Feeley 2007, 2012). These studies found that at crucial moments in the struggle for political liberalism, lawyers in some combination and form regularly organized to press for the rule of law and political liberalism. Their actions in these situations went beyond representing clients or specific causes; they spoke "in the name of the law," and as stewards of values they understood as implicit in the very idea of the rule of law—even-handedness, due process, freedom of expression, political moderation, limited executive power. At times when liberalism was nascent or was in danger, groups of lawyers from various segments would join in what they called the

[2] See, e.g., Espeli, Næess, and Rinde (2008).
[3] See, e.g., Langford, Behn, and Lie (2017).
[4] The latter provides an synthesis and overview of the theory and findings.

legal complex, often forming coalitions with other civil society groups to press for political liberalism (for a summary of the project, see Karpik and Halliday 2011).

The theory, if that is what it is, is modest. It does not hold that the organized profession always mobilizes to fight for political liberalism, or that the legal profession is even a powerful counter-force to a repressive state. Rather, it reports that consistently some lawyers mobilize in the name of the law and often with some support from the organized bar, judges, government lawyers, and legal academics, as well as other civil society groups, to oppose repressive politics. At best, lawyers have a voice and can make powerful appeals; but in contrast, governments have generally a monopoly over violence and control the levers of the state. A powerful autocratic state can silence lawyers and close down law societies. Still, studies generated in this project have found that lawyers from various segments of the legal profession regularly coalesce into temporary legal complexes and form coalitions with other civil society groups to fight for political liberalism.

The theory is also not Panglossian, especially as to the impact of legal complexes. At times, liberal principles prevail and the efforts of the legal complex are vindicated. At other times, they are defeated, sometimes soundly. However, consistently this work reports, when struggles for the rule of law, limited government, and core liberal principles occur, one finds lawyers, the legal complex in various combinations and coalitions, participating in the struggle. Neither is the theory deterministic. The struggles of the legal complex are found repeatedly in a variety of times and places. The conditions that give rise to them are contingent, and are more salient under some circumstances than others. Nor does the theory dictate that lawyers always and everywhere are necessary ingredients in the formation and maintenance of the rule of law and the moderate state. Although, as the last chapter in this volume points out, there is some slippage as the general summaries of the research are sometimes more upbeat than the nuanced empirical findings.

It is this last issue that concerns us in this volume. We ask, are there decidedly liberal states, in which lawyers as members of the legal profession or the legal complex have played no appreciable role in establishing or maintaining in the face of illiberal movements? Admittedly, this question assumes at least a tentative answer before it is even asked, and the two of us had a short list of some readily available candidates before we began the search. The Nordics stood out, especially as the countries in the region top multiple indexes on rule of law and democracy (Langford and Schaffer 2014) but do not have a fabled history of lawyerly political engagement (Hirschl 2011). Our concern, though, was not to find a single counter-example to falsify the theory of the legal complex. The theory, at least as formally stated, is not deterministic and is far too open-ended and contingent to allow this. Still, we thought it valuable to pursue something of a deviant case analysis (Seawright and Gerring 2008) to help better clarify who, when, how, and why in the struggle for political liberalism. If not lawyers, who?

While the history of liberalism in the Nordic countries is well traversed, the political role of lawyers and judges has been the subject of little research. Much of the focus has been on selected celebrated moments—such as the Norwegian constitutional moment in 1814 and the breakthrough of judicial review in that proto-state in 1821. As Karlsson-Schaffer (forthcoming) has noted, courts get only two mentions in the Swedish Handbook on Political Science. Even the history of Nordic liberalism in English is limited—most discussions of the "Nordic miracle" deal almost exclusively with social welfare policies, especially those developed in response to the Great Depression and following World War II. Still, relative to other countries, they provided a good place to start our inquiry. We began with an initial historical question: how did the liberal politics emerge in the early to mid-nineteenth century? Who advanced them? What, if any, was the role of the legal complex? And how did lawyers engage in the years and events that followed?

To explore these and related questions, we pursued the strategy that had served Halliday, Karpik, and Feeley so well: Collect a group of single country experts, engage them in the same collective effort to answer the same set of questions, allow them time to do their research, and then bring them together for reports and the construction of a comparative analysis. Here, we turned to a group of noted scholars of legal history and the legal professions, one from each of the Nordic countries, with backgrounds in law, sociology, and political science, and asked them to join together to pursue a set of parallel issues in each of the five countries. All of them expressed enthusiasm for the project, and adjusted their schedules in order to participate.

Each author was tasked with conducting parallel surveys of the political history of their respective country, with a special focus on moments of intense internal political stress, times at which liberal institutions were in danger and all elements in the machinery of government and civil society were likely to have been activated. Moreover, where were the lawyers, judges, prosecutors, government lawyers, and legal academics during these periods of conflict? Still another task: Chart the growth and nature of legal education in their respective country, and the founding, growth, and functioning of lawyers' organizations.

We imposed no style or form for responding to our questions but we pushed our authors toward studying both the *longue durée* and *événements*. We had selected our contributors because they were experts, and each was likely to face distinct and different challenges with respect to issues and upheavals we asked them to address, and the period of time to be covered. However, we were confident that if they each looked at several transformational political events and identified major participants, they would locate lawyers if they played a distinctive collective role over time or in any of the significant events. It was also a deeply collective process, beginning with a workshop in Oslo where the contributors presented "think pieces," which were commented on generously by Karpik, Halliday, and the other participants. This was followed by a second and intensive workshop on full draft chapters in Berkeley. The opening chapter emerged from Feeley and Langford's reading and rereading of the contributions to search for commonalities and differences; while Langford developed his alternative theory of the legal complex into a concluding reflection.

There is no recipe for successfully pursuing expansive cross-national research, especially detailed comparative research that spans several locations and decades and centuries. While online databases provide an increasingly rich source of historical information on political governance and even social mobilization, they are limited to what others have chosen to collect and post. Our strategy, like that of Halliday and Karpik, was to have someone on the ground who knows not only the nature of the inquiry, but also the lay of the land. It worked. The process we followed in developing and executing this project gives us considerable confidence in its findings.

What do we find? In sum: lawyers acting collectively played virtually no role in the establishment of the modern liberal states in the Nordic countries in the late eighteenth and nineteenth centuries. The potential reasons are two-fold. First, a bricolage of other actors were central, vocal, and influential in the establishment of political liberalism during the course of the nineteenth century. Until well into the nineteenth century, legal training was not accorded the status of training in theology (Lutheran) and medicine. Liberalism in the Nordic countries was influenced by Enlightenment ideas advanced in France, Germany, and England; it was given momentum by the American and French Revolutions, and the embrace of the Rechtsstaat in Prussia and Russia. Politically, liberalism was advanced by members of the great Estates or families, whose male leaders were often trained in theology; literate and often wealthy peasants; and leading clergy from the Lutheran church, which emphasized individual responsibility and good works. It was embraced by the privileged who surrounded the crown in Stockholm and Copenhagen, who bent in light of the excesses of the French Revolution. Liberal policies were also endorsed by the strong civil service that staffed the expanding ministries. Later in the nineteenth century, the project was advanced by emerging political parties that had evolved from the Estates, organized peasants, and later labor unions in the expanding urban areas. The principal exception, though, was Norway (and later Finland) where lawyers were a dominant profession but, as the authors point out, organized themselves within different wings of the hegemonic political complex rather than as a separate profession and legal complex; or fleeting moments such as the Nordic criminal reform movement in as part of Nordic Legal Meetings in the 1880s.

This brief account hints at a second factor accounting for the relative absence of lawyers in the public arena. The Nordic legal professions were poorly organized until well into the nineteenth century, long after major strides were made in establishing political liberalism. Throughout the eighteenth century and most of the nineteenth century, there were few lawyers and law faculties. The growth of the

Rechtsstaat required law-trained officials, but their roles were largely seen in terms of civil service and public administration. Law schools did not expand dramatically until the later part of the nineteenth century, nor did they produce a cadre of graduates who formed a robust private bar. Judges in courts in smaller communities were almost all local notables without legal training, and in the larger cities, specialized judiciaries were developed within each ministry to handle cases within its jurisdiction, and these officials often assigned lawyers from within the ministry to argue both sides of a controversy before them. While law-trained university graduates began to replace those trained in theology in the civil service, they did not form a distinct legal cadre in the civil service any more than those trained in theology had formed a clerical cadre. Both were primarily civil servants. While this began to break down by the outset of World War I; by then the new public officials were not so much lawyers but the growing numbers of economists, psychologists, social workers, educators, and others trained in the human sciences. This trend accelerated during the inter-war years, and again after World War II. By then legal training had expanded dramatically, though a sizeable proportion of lawyers still moved into positions in the growing civil service right after completing their legal training, and the private bar remained modest and not well organized. As the individual studies in this volume indicate, the pace and details of this development varied by country, but the overall picture is uniform.

Lawyers within the civil service *might* have seen themselves as a distinct professional group and at times organized to develop and pursue common professional views. However, as the authors of the case studies who took pains to look for it emphasize, there is no evidence that they did. Of course, there were exceptions, but they were few, and they did not lead to any concentrated or continued developments.

Student unrest in the 1960s changed all this. Following their counterparts in Paris and the United States, young people in many Nordic countries opposed to the war in Vietnam and the failures of the civil rights revolution pressed to open up new fronts for law students and some of the younger law faculty members. Together they developed and staffed gradually clinical law programs, modelled partly after American legal clinics (Rønning and Hammerslev 2018), and championed the rights of student protestors, squatters, the Romani, guest workers, new immigrants, and the Sami, which eventually emerged into an approach to legal practice that has come to be known as "cause lawyering" (Scheingold and Sarat 2005; see in Norway, Mathisen 1997), but has also been viewed as a governmental outsourcing of legal aid given the number of routine cases (Rønning and Hammerslev 2018).

These developments were compounded by the unanticipated effects of international treaties signed by most of the Nordic countries, which bound them to rulings of the European Court of Justice and the European Court of Human Rights. Almost overnight, the Nordic countries were subject to judicial review imposed on them by the treaties. Human rights lawyers would take their cases to Luxembourg or Strasbourg for hearings in international courts, and then return home to try to secure enforcement in domestic courts. Not to be left out, domestic judges began applying international law to review domestic practices and laws. In Norway, as early as 1976, and slightly predating the Strasbourg shift, the Supreme Court signaled an openness to questions of judicial review (Kierulf 2018). Rights consciousness, cause lawyering, and concerns with the rule of law led to the rise of legal complexes to pursue issues here and there. The Nordic legal profession gradually joined the rest of Europe and most of the common law countries in supporting lawyers drawn to political causes. More members of the profession began arguably to see themselves as stewards of an autonomous system and defenders of political rights, and often found themselves in intense conflict with defenders of a strong version of parliamentary sovereignty and opponents of judicial review.

Each of the studies in this volume reports that the foundations of the liberal Nordic states were not erected with any appreciable effort on the part of the organized legal profession. Indeed, liberalism was institutionalized before the establishment of any well-organized bar. At most, our claim is modest, that a legal complex is not necessary for the successful establishment of a moderate state and the institutionalization of liberal principles. However, the case studies also reveal that Nordic liberalism was not as liberal as many might assume, and that in the 1970s onward the legal complex helped expand the embrace and defence of liberal principles. Thus, the book provides some strength to the idea of the Nordics as a deviant case in legal complex studies.

In the epilogue, however, Langford ponders the reverse implications of these findings. He asks what if the weak findings for the Nordics prompt the need to revisit findings elsewhere. Is there a risk that research has focused too much on choosing cases on the dependent variable—instances where lawyers might be expected to mobilize? Is it a case of Nordic exceptionalism or Franco-American exceptionalism?

Delving more deeply, Langford focuses on what the Nordic contribution says for the theory of *why* lawyers might mobilize for political liberalism. Focusing on cases where lawyers did and did not collectively mobilize, he suggests an alternative theory to that of Halliday and Karpik. While the latter draw on historical sociology and constructivism in positing that lawyers embrace a self-understanding as guardians of political liberalism, Langford draws more broadly on the social sciences and looks to a combination of agency and structure. He argues that rational choice and legal mobilization theory might better explain individual lawyer's choices in participating or not in struggles to advance or defend political liberalism—whether in the Nordics or any country. Decisions to mobilize are a function of the material and reputational costs and benefits, and mediated by views on whether the legal rather than political opportunity structures are more advantageous or disadvantageous. Taking this approach may provide a unifying theory of action and retreat, helping explain more clearly the mixed findings in previous legal complex studies. In this respect, we hope the book opens a greater focus on explanation in the ongoing scholarship on the legal complex.

Some readers of the draft of this manuscript noted with irony that our contributors discovered the late arrival in the Nordics of an active and organized liberal legal profession just as liberalism began to recede in many parts of the world, replaced by nativist authoritarian governments. They point to Russia, Hungary, and Poland, and developments in other former Soviet states and satellites. They also single out Turkey, Egypt, and other Middle Eastern countries where the Springtime of freedom quickly turned into a Winter of repression. Similarly, promising developments in China, Brazil, and still elsewhere have proved disappointing to advocates of the rule of law, and downright dangerous for those who attempt to pursue it. India, a stable and vibrant democracy long militantly committed to the rule of law, has succumbed to shrill calls of nativist nationalism and intolerance. Even the United States, France, and Great Britain have not been immune to such developments.

Some readers suggest that we are chasing a disappearing illusion; that the rule of law and political liberalism are contracting, and thus the role of political lawyers is diminishing. But we do not read developments or the theory of the legal complex this way. There is no question that powerful authoritarian and illiberal movements have captured control of governments in enough countries since the 2010s to conclude these are bad times for liberalism. Neither the study of the legal complex nor the existence of national or even international legal complexes outlines a recipe for the triumph of the rule of law and liberalism. The study of the legal complex focuses on features common to the legal profession, and more particularly its self-conscious and organized role in fighting for political liberalism. Neither our claims nor the theory of the legal complex maintains that political liberalism will triumph. Indeed, from the outset of the project, evidence adduced in the many studies of the legal complex reveals that political liberalism is tentative and unstable, and vulnerable to government intimidation. The modest claim of the theory is that lawyers in their many forms and the organized bar or parts of it have a strong propensity to fight for political freedom, and to form coalitions with civil society groups to enhance collective powers of resistance; and various theories seek to explain under what conditions this occurs.

Even a cursory glance at the continuing battles for political freedom in Hungary, Poland, Turkey, Hong Kong, China, India, and elsewhere reveals that vast numbers of lawyers have fought hard to protect the liberal gains that were achieved in the 1980s and 1990s. Since then, in Hungary, Poland, and Turkey hundreds of judges have been summarily dismissed and some jailed, and replaced by apparatchiks. In these and other countries, lawyers and their coalition partners have fought and lost battles, been dismissed from jobs and jailed in droves, but have regrouped to fight again. They have certainly lost battles, but it is too early to declare that they have lost the war. Still, whatever the outcomes in the 2010s and 2020s, the role of lawyers and judges in these settings supports the general theory of the legal complex and political liberalism.

References

Abel, Richard L. 1979. "Socializing the Legal Profession: Can Redefining Lawyers' Services Achieve Social Justice?" *Law & Policy* 1: 5–51.

Abel, Richard L. 1981a. "Toward a Political Economy of Lawyers," *Wisconsin Law Review* 117–118.

Abel, Richard L. 1981b. "Why Does the ABA Promote Ethical Rules?" *Texas Law Review* 59: 639–688.

Abel, Richard L. (ed.). 1982. *The Politics of Informal Justice*, Vol. 1, *The American Experience*; Vol. 2, *Comparative Studies*. New York: Academic Press.

Abel, Richard L. 1987. *The Legal Profession in England and Wales*. Oxford: Basil Blackwell.

Abel, Richard L. 1989. *American Lawyers*. New York: Oxford University Press.

Abel, Richard L., and Philip S. C. Lewis (eds.). 1988a. *Lawyers in Society, Vol. 1: The Common Law World*. Berkeley, CA: University of California Press.

Abel, Richard L., and Philip S. C. Lewis (eds.). 1988b. *Lawyers in Society, Vol. 2: The Civil Law World*. Berkeley, CA: University of California Press.

Abel, Richard L., and Philip S. C. Lewis (eds.). 1989. *Lawyers in Society, Vol. 3: Comparative Theories*. Berkeley, CA: University of California Press.

Bourdieu, Pierre. 1987. "The Force of Law: Toward a Sociology of the Juridical Field," *The Hastings Law Journal* 38: 805–853.

Carlin, Jerome, Jan Howard, and Sheldon Messinger. 1967. *Civil Justice and the Poor*. New York: Russell Sage Foundation.

Crenshaw, Kimberle. 1989. "Demarginalizing the Intersection of Race and Sex: A Black Feminist Critique of Antidiscrimination Doctrine, Feminist Theory and Antiracist Politics," *University of Chicago Legal Forum* 1989(1): 149.

Dahl, Tova. 1987. *Women's Law: An Introduction of Feminist Jurisprudence*. Oslo: Norwegian University Press.

Delgado, Richard, and Jean Stefancic. 2001. *Critical Race Theory: An Introduction*. New York: New York University Press.

Dezalay, Yves, and Bryant Garth. 1996. *Dealing in Virtue: International Commercial Arbitration and the Construction of a Transnational Legal Order*. Chicago, IL: University of Chicago Press.

Espeli, Harald, Hans Eyvind Næess, and Harald Rinde. 2008. *Våpendrager og Veiviser: Advokatenes Historie i Norge*. Oslo: Universitetsforlag.

Fitzpatrick, Peter, and Alan Hunt. 1987. "Critical Legal Studies: An Introduction," *Journal of Law and Society* 14: 1.

Goodrich, Peter. 1992. "Critical Legal Studies in England: Prospective Histories," *Oxford Journal of Legal Studies* 12: 1.

Halliday, Terrence. 1987. *Beyond Monopoly: Lawyers, State Crises, and Professional Empowerment*. Chicago, IL: University of Chicago Press.

Halliday, Terrence C., and Lucien Karpik (eds.). 1997. *Lawyers and the Rise of Western Political Liberalism: Europe and North America from the Eighteenth to the Twentieth Centuries*. Oxford: Oxford University Press.

Halliday, Terrence C., Lucian Karpik, and Malcolm M. Feeley (eds.). 2007. *Fighting for Political Freedom: Comparative Studies of the Legal Complex for Political Change.* Oxford: Hart Publishing.

Halliday, Terrence C., Lucian Karpik, and Malcolm M. Feeley (eds.). 2012. *Fates of Political Liberalism in the Post British Colony.* New York: Cambridge University Press.

Hirschl, Ran. 2011. "The Nordic Counternarrative: Democracy, Human Development, and Judicial Review," *International Journal of Constitutional Law* 9: 449–469.

Karpik, Lucien. 1988. "Lawyers and Politics in France, 1814–1950: The State, the Market, and the Public," *Law & Social Inquiry* 13: 707–736.

Karpik, Lucien. 1998. *French Lawyers: A Study in Collective Action, 1274–1994.* Oxford: Oxford University Press.

Karpik, Lucien, and Terrence C. Halliday. 2011. "The Legal Complex," *Annual Review of Law and Social Science* 7: 217–236.

Kairys, David (ed.). 1982. *The Politics of Law.* New York: Pantheon Books.

Kennedy, Duncan. 1982. "Legal Education and the Reproduction of Hierarchy," *Journal of Legal Education* 32: 591.

Kierulf, Anine. 2018. *Judicial Review in Norway: A Bicentennial Debate.* Cambridge: Cambridge University Press.

Langford, Malcolm, and Johan Karlsson Schaffer. 2014. "The Nordic Human Rights Paradox," University of Oslo Faculty of Law Research Paper No. 2013–25.

Langford, Malcolm, Daniel Behn, and Runar Lie. 2017. "The Revolving Door in International Investment Arbitration," *Journal of International Economic Law*, 20(2): 301–332.

MacKinnon, Catharine. 1983. "Feminism, Marxism, Method, and the State: Toward Feminist Jurisprudence," *Signs* 8: 635–658.

MacKinnon, Catharine. 1987. *Feminism Unmodified.* Cambridge, MA: Harvard University Press.

Mathisen, Thomas. 1997. *Retten i samfunnet: En innføring i rettssosiologi.* Oslo: Pax.

Parsons, Talcott. 1951. *The Social System.* Glencoe, IL: The Free Press of Glencoe.

Rabinowitz, Victor, and Tim Ledwith (eds.). 1987. *A History of the National Lawyers Guild: 1937–1987.* Philadelphia, PA: National Lawyers Guild.

Romano, Maria. 2016. "The History of Legal Clinics in the US, Europe and around the World," *Diritto & Questioni Pubbliche* 16: 27–39.

Rønning, Olaf Halvorsen and Ole Hammerslev (eds.). 2018. *Outsourcing Legal Aid in the Nordic Welfare States.* London: Palgrave MacMillan.

Sarat, Austin, and Stuart Scheingold. 1998. *Political Commitments and Professional Responsibilities.* Oxford: Oxford University Press.

Sarfatti-Larson, Magli. 1979. *The Rise of Professionalism: A Sociological Analysis.* Berkeley, CA: University of California Press.

Schaffer, Johan Karlsson. Forthcoming. "Rättvisans entreprenörer: Mobilisering för tillgång till rättvisa I civilsamhället." In Wallerman Ghavanini, Anna and Sebastian Wejedal (eds.) *Tillgång till rättvisa i Skandinavien.* Stockholm: Santérus.

Scheingold, Stuart, and Austin Sarat. 2005. *Something to Believe in: Politics, Professionalism, and Cause Lawyering.* Stanford, CA: Stanford University Press.

Seawright, Jason, and John Gerring. 2008. "Case Selection Techniques in Case Study Research: A Menu of Qualitative and Quantitative Options," *Political Research Quarterly* 61(2): 294–308.

Turner, Stephen. 1994. *Max Weber: The Lawyer as Social Thinker*. London: Routledge.
Unger, Roberto Mangabeira. 1983. *The Critical Legal Studies Movement*. Cambridge, MA: Harvard University Press.
Weber, Max. 1954. *Max Weber on Law in Economy and Society*, edited and translated by Edward Shils. Cambridge, MA: Harvard University Press.

2
Nordic Exceptionalism and the Legal Complex

Malcolm M. Feeley and Malcolm Langford***

A "Golden Age for lawyers," asserts Michael Madsen in his discussion of nineteenth-century Denmark. "Lawyers, lawyers everywhere," writes Malcolm Langford about Norway in the same period. Across the Nordic region, the number of law graduates ballooned (in Norway there was an eight-fold increase), law faculties expanded in size, a new law faculty was established in Christiana (Oslo), and another law school, in Finland, was relocated from Turku to Helsinki to better supply the civil service. Everywhere, lawyers formed a central part of political, bureaucratic, and cultural elites. This change is partly accounted for by the dramatic increase in university students generally, but it was also a marked shift in preferences for subjects and career paths (Konttinen, this volume, Chapter 7, Section 10; Langford, this volume, Chapter 5, Section 3), as well as the needs of the civil service. At the turn of the nineteenth century, theology was the subject of choice; but by century's end, law and medicine reigned supreme.

During this same period, strong parliamentary governments displaced absolute monarchs. By mid-century, save for Finland (Russia), the last of the absolutist rulers had disappeared. Moreover, and central to this project, many of the core tenets of liberalism had found a place in law and increasingly in politics and practice. This confluence of the explosion of lawyers and the rise of political liberalism raises the natural question as to whether there is a causal relation—is the latter a function of the former? What role did lawyers play in this development of political liberalism?

The case studies in this volume show that it was, to use Letto-Vanamo's observation, "comparatively late that so called learned law and university-educated legal professionals started to have an impact on law-making and dispute resolution" (Letto-Vanamo 2021: 22), and even later (in the late nineteenth century) that legal professionals began to develop an independent legal profession, and when it did

* Claire Sanders Clements Dean's Chair Emeritus, School of Law, and Center for the Study of Law and Society, University of California (Berkeley).

** Professor, Faculty of Law, University of Oslo and Co-Director, Centre on Law and Social Transformation. He led the project *Nordic Branding: The Politics of Exceptionalism* 2017–2020.

Malcolm M. Feeley and Malcolm Langford, *Nordic Exceptionalism and the Legal Complex* In: *The Limits of the Legal Complex*. Edited by: Malcolm Feeley and Malcolm Langford, Oxford University Press. © Malcolm M. Feeley and Malcolm Langford 2021. DOI: 10.1093/oso/9780192848413.003.0002 it was slow to mobilize to press for core or first-generation liberal principles. The studies in this volume also show that those with legal training were active in politics, but they acted in their capacities as civil servants, parliamentarians, ministers, journalists, and statesmen, and not as spokespeople for a profession or "the law." Furthermore, they show that lawyers' positions ranged across the political spectrum. They were as likely to support entrenched monarchs as emerging parliaments, and to oppose the expansion of rights as support them.

Even in its so-called "golden era," those with legal training did not organize as a profession, and thus lawyers' groups played almost no role in mobilizing to press for moderate government or champion even the most basic features of political liberalism. For the most part when it did organize, the bar limited its activities to social functions and the occasional response to requests for technical assistance from parliamentary committees (Michalsen 2014). No Nordic bar associations proclaimed a declaration of rights—although did mobilize briefly on criminal law reform; and no groups of lawyers held forth in celebrated trials or other forums to challenge the authority of the state, though occasionally a solo lawyer spoke out. Norwegian and Icelandic courts occasionally exercised a weak form of judicial review in the nineteenth century, but it was not until well into the twentieth century that any of the Nordic high courts asserted a robust form of judicial review and struck down significant parliamentary actions in the name of constitutional rights. The modest Norwegian and Icelandic exceptions, both Langford (Chapter 5, Section 3.2) and Helgadóttir 2006, and Chapter 8, Section 2.2 of this volume) agree, it is partly attributable to the early and lasting influence of *Marbury v. Madison* (1803), the celebrated assertion of judicial review in the early years of the United States and American theories of judicial review that flowed from it (Helgadóttir 2006). For the most part both lawyers and judges were politically quiescent (Hirschl 2011). Indeed, apart from judges in the smaller communities, usually not law trained, who handled minor issues, judges were ensconced in the ministries and were not even afforded protection by the principle of the separation of powers. Therefore, we confront a seeming paradox: An age of lawyers during the formative period of liberalism's growth, but no collective action by lawyers to speak of, and no consistently robust independent judiciary.[1]

These accounts stand in sharp contrast to the initial study and many subsequent studies of lawyers elsewhere, which have reported that "lawyers more or less intensively fought in favor of civil and political rights and the moderate state" (Halliday 1987; Karpik 1999; Halliday and Karpik 1998; Halliday, Karpik, and Feeley 2007a; 2012; Rajah 2012; Massoud 2013; Gobe and Salaymeh 2015. For an overview of

[1] This collective portrait of the function of law and the role of lawyers in Nordic societies from the seventeenth to the twentieth century is reinforced by the several articles in Letto-Vanamo, Tamm, and Mortensen (2019). They too note the history of remote villages and local government, reliance on informal and non-lawyer dispute resolution, and communities guided by social welfare rather than rights concerns.

the study of legal complexes, see Karpik and Halliday 2011: 219). Drawing on historical observations, initially of practicing lawyers, later of a legal complex that can also include judges, prosecutors, civil servants, academics, and military lawyers, Halliday and Karpik later joined by Feeley, and others have identified legal professionals who periodically mobilize to act collectively in their self-appointed roles as the guardians and champions of political liberalism, and at times to form coalitions with other civil society groups. As individuals, lawyers are not likely to be powerful, but they may be so when they don the mantle of spokespersons for the law and for the public, when they hold forth in a court, and when they join to act collectively in the name of the bar and form coalitions with other civil society groups. While a determined autocrat or powerful state has any number of ways to crush the collective efforts of lawyers, the studies of the legal complex show that a few—at times many—lawyers regularly mobilize in the name of law and engage in struggles to protect political rights and the ideal of a moderate state.

The Nordic regions appears to be different. Certainly, "political liberalism" emerged, especially throughout the nineteenth century. The term is not easily translatable in the Scandinavian languages but it approximates to the notion of a liberal *rettstat* (Wessel-Aas 2011: 1; Smith 2015: 13)—a "liberal rule of law state." This requires limits to executive power, due process, and equality before the law (*rettsikkerhet*), and certain civil rights such as freedom of expression and association, habeas corpus, and protection from torture (Smith 2015: 14).[2] Yet, as the case studies in this volume report, until the latter part of the twentieth century there are only limited traces of political activism by lawyers, and rarely collective action by a wider legal complex in the Nordic counties. Only one case study reports one sustained collective (indeed, heroic) effort by judges to resist tyranny and fight for political liberalism—in Norway, during World War II. It was only in the late 1970s that the rights revolution entered the Nordic region, and gradually transformed the legal landscape—especially from the 1990s.

The explanation for these findings is contestable. It may simply confirm another case of Nordic *exceptionalism*, with the celebrated Nordic model of "consensus decision-making" smoothing and facilitating the liberal and social transformations of the state. Certainly, scholars of Nordic legal culture, refer to peasant or rural "one-norm societies," that blur the distinction between state and civil society that are defined by the close connection between the state and the Lutheran church, and emphasize pragmatic compromise of disputes over insistence on principle (Letto-Vanamo 2021: 23). Or it may be a case of the less-celebrated Nordic model of a "*strong state,*" which long prevented the emergence of an autonomous legal profession that could mobilize, such that political liberalism largely emerged

2 However, the above authors differ on the selection of rights. For example, unlike legal complex theorists, Merete Smith does not name rights to property and freedom of religion but does name rights to family life and free choice of residence and work. See further discussion below.

on the terms of the state rather than selected interests in civil society. Alternatively, the Nordics may be the exception that *disproves* the rule. This historical absence of lawyers in a mostly successful development of political liberalism may lead us to question different results about the extent and impact of collective lawyerly action found elsewhere. As we shall discuss, for both theoretical and empirical reasons, the answer is most likely a mix of all three of these explanations. The Nordic experience is distinctive, but the institutional and ideational conditions under which legal complexes emerge may help us shed new light on when and why lawyers mobilize elsewhere for political liberalism.

1. The Theory of the Legal Complex

Beginning in the 1970s, the view that the legal profession or some portion of it organized to protect the autonomy of law and fight for political liberalism and the idea of a limited state was dismissed by "realist" theorists, who held that professions organize to protect their material interests, their monopoly rights to certain types of business, their control of professional licensing, and their authority to establish minimum fee structures (Sarfatti-Larson 1977; Abel 1988, 1991). Others have expanded these concerns to include efforts to enhance lawyers' social status (Dezelay and Garth 1996).[3] According to these theories, public regardingness stances by the organized bar or segments of it are little more than public relations efforts or incidental activities undertaken as part of the larger collective project to enhance monopoly rights, material interests, and social status. These realists acknowledge that at times "cause lawyers" act on behalf of liberal causes, but they emphasize that cause lawyers see their legal actions not so much as an internalization of a sense of professionalism or part of their roles as stewards of the law, but as the use of their skills to further the political agendas they share with their clients.

However, since the 1980s a great many empirical studies have forced a modification of this view. The most significant challenge was mounted by Terence Halliday (1987) in the United States, and by Lucien Karpik (1999) in France. Both conducted independent studies of the history of the legal profession in the United States and France respectively, and found that historically the organized bar has long occupied a significant public role. The bar or some portion of it, acting in the name of the law or the legal profession, has consistently mobilized or attempted to mobilize to protect the autonomy of the law and protect basic political rights. These conditions, they assert, are minimal requirements for the rule of law, and as such are of distinctive interest to the legal profession, which takes seriously its role as a steward of the law. Since their independent work, Halliday and Karpik

[3] See the previous chapter for a longer discussion of these two theories.

have combined forces and overseen the production of a host of studies, which, with many variations, supported their position. One consistent finding: The legal profession or some significant segment of it regularly, though not invariably, mobilizes in the name of the law to resist encroachments on or to expand core principles of liberalism, including freedom of expression, judicial independence, and the moderate state. Sometimes they succeed in advancing their causes, and at other times, they experience setbacks or defeat. Advancement or retreat are contingent on a host of factors: the ability to mobilize a critical mass, the nature of the issues, the ability to act in concert with other civil society groups, and most importantly the strength and determination of opposition, often autocratic executives who wield immense state powers.

This approach advanced by Halliday and Karpik does not dispute altogether the claims of "realist" theories of the legal profession; that a principal concern of organized legal professions is to serve the interests of the propertied classes, and to enhance the material interests of members. But Halliday and Karpik return to an earlier, less materialist conception of professionalism (Weber 1946; Parsons 1951), which emphasized that legal professionalism contains an idealist element, and focuses on politics as well as markets. Lawyers, and cognate legal occupations, it holds, view themselves as protectors of the legal order, and are quick to react when their space is invaded. Research reveals that the legal profession is politically weak and vulnerable, and that at best only a tiny part of the profession ever organizes "in the name of the law." Still, lawyers can and do organize and make a difference, when speaking as lawyers and using distinctive legal platforms—trials, bar associations, legal opinions, the press—and in coalitions among themselves and with other groups in civil society (Halliday, Karpik, and Feeley 2007a). It is these small, evolving, and temporary groups of mobilized lawyers, together with other practicing legal occupations, that collectively constitute what Karpik and Halliday have termed the "legal complex."

This theory is neither deductive, normative, nor deterministic. It does not flow from first principles about the nature of law, the state, or the legal profession. Rather it is an empirically observed "regularity" of the behavior of lawyers and their professional institutions coupled with an inductively generated explanation (Halliday, Karpik, and Feeley 2007a). Study after study in various far-flung settings since the 1990s have revealed this general pattern. (For a review of these findings, see Karpik and Halliday 2011.)

For the most part, studies of the legal complex reveal lawyers on the whole to be conservative, defenders of entrenched legal rights and property interests, and as an organized group rarely if ever central in any progressive political vanguard. Indeed, they are usually reactive, mobilizing primarily in reaction to challenges of the rule of law, or encroachments on the core and limited principles of political liberalism. For these lawyers, "political liberalism [consists of] a limited set of specific civil rights such as equality before the law, freedom of political speech, personal security, property rights, and due process of law, the so-called first generation rights or basic freedoms" (Karpik and Halliday 2011: 219). In the twentieth century, this concern was not expanded as progressive movements consolidated and sought to secure an expanded set of social and political rights, curtail literary censorship, promote universal suffrage, and advance "positive rights" such as guaranteed housing, employment, education, and health care.

This narrow focus is shaped in part by lawyers' self-interest and sense of professionalism. It is also shaped by the pragmatic awareness that lawyers' solidarity is limited, and it will break down if a legal complex engages with contentious expansion of economic, social, and political rights. Hence the focus on the lawyer's specialty, process. This narrow set of liberal values fosters the autonomy of the bar and judicial independence in ways that make lawyers spokespeople for the people, civil society as opposed to the state (Karpik 1998; 1999; Halliday, Karpik, and Feeley 2007a: 30–32; Karpik and Halliday 2011: 220). This sensibility cuts across the various roles that that lawyers occupy in modern societies, lawyers in private practice, judges, civil servants, prosecutors, and legal academics, all of whom may be linked by a sense of legal professionalism. Still, these relations vary widely, depending on legal training, occupational segmentation, and support structures (Epp 1998).

At times, studies of the legal complex reveal, clusters of legal occupations have mobilized in spectacular and decisive fashion.[4] More typically, however, lawyers play only limited, though perhaps crucial, roles in larger political struggles. In addition, at times they do not respond to threats to political liberalism, and may even represent its very opposition. Almost always struggles are reactive, rest on fragile organizational capacities, are vulnerable to silencing and co-optation by political authority,[5] and are conditioned by prevailing legal discourse.[6] However, the findings of by now a great many empirical studies of the legal mobilization reveal that segments of the bar and bench and other legal occupations—the legal complex—regularly engage in struggles in the transition toward *or away* from political liberalism (Halliday, Karpik, and Feeley 2007b: 3). And, when a legal complex does not form and mobilize, it is often because the state has successfully suppressed or neutralized it.

As noted, the research on the legal complex focuses on various conditions under which various segments—lawyers, judge, legal academics, civil servants, and prosecutors—of the legal profession will or will not mobilize to protect three principles: the moderate state; a civil society outside the control of the state; and basic

[4] For example, in eighteenth-century France; 1990s in Pakistan; and the 1980s in Brazil, Zambia, and South Korea.

[5] See the analysis of effects in Halliday, Karpik, and Feeley (2007b). These studies and others such as Graver (2014) detail the complicity of some judges and lawyers in illiberal regimes.

[6] Karpik (1998: 117) highlights the power of disinterested discourse as highly credible in the nineteenth century, giving a particular ascendancy to the legal profession.

(negative) political freedoms protecting citizens from state tyranny. While the organized legal profession in any society is rarely unanimous on any issue, some segments of legal occupations regularly attempt to mobilize to support these objectives at given moments when core legal values are under stress. They do this, studies of the legal complex have found, from a sense of professionalism. They embrace the idea of law as an autonomous or quasi-autonomous form of social ordering, and believe that as lawyers, they are stewards of this autonomy. Thus, they resist absolutism, and uncircumscribed executive powers (see Halliday and Karpik 2012: 26–34). They take seriously Justice Joseph Story's observation that, "law is a jealous mistress."

However, as Karpik and Halliday (2011) emphasize, there is nothing inevitable about lawyers or a legal complex organizing to fight for political liberalism. Mobilization depends upon a host of contingent factors. At times, political divisions fragment and weaken the bar, and prevent meaningful collective action. At other times autocratic rulers ban or assume control over lawyers' organizations. And, as is some Latin American countries, the bar, bench, and other legal occupations are divided internally by political party affiliations, in ways that inhibit collective action (Halliday and Karpik 2011: 225). Still, the grounded theory of the legal complex associates the various legal professions with support for the moderate state and political liberalism that is often manifest in mobilization to support these values (Karpik and Halliday 2011: 225). Furthermore, as various accounts of such struggles reveal (Halliday and Karpik 2012), lawyers often fail because by themselves they are not a substantial political force, or because a determined autocratic state has an arsenal of weapons to defeat or neutralize it—taking over law societies, controlling membership in the bar, intimidating its leaders, and the like.[7] Nevertheless, investigations of the issue reveal that lawyers and other elements of a legal complex often mobilize or attempt to mobilize, and join with other groups in civil society to press for political liberalism, a pattern observed with surprising frequency across continents and centuries.

2. Lawyers and Political Liberalism in the Nordic States

Our concern is with the history of lawyers and political liberalism in the Nordic region.[8] These states present perhaps the greatest challenge to the theory and

[7] cf. Rajah (2012) on Singapore; and Liu and Halliday (2016) on China.

[8] This was previously, at least, not so common outside the study of the social welfare state: "A related similarity is that Nordic political science has not paid much attention to comparative research. This seems surprising as the Nordic countries should be rewarding objects for comparison: on the one hand they are similar enough to encourage comparisons from a methodological point of view; on the other they are dissimilar to an extent which guarantees variation and thus provides the basis for meaningful contrasts and comparisons. There are some truly comparative works, of course ... and comparative approaches to the study of Nordic politics have lately become more frequent in the research literature, but much of the work labelled comparative is in fact ethnocentric in the form of country-specific treatments

particularly its claims of "universal application" (Halliday, Karpik, and Feeley 2007a). Sitting atop most global indexes on core civil rights (not to speak of political and social rights), the Nordic states, at least on the surface, seem curiously devoid of an active and visible bench and bar that have a history of making bold pronouncements on public affairs of any sort.

According to Hirschl (2011: 458), the Nordic constitutional tradition has been based on "local and national democracy, popular sovereignty, parliamentary supremacy, and majority rule" together with "overall good governance," political and judicial restraint, relative social cohesiveness, traditional commitment to social democracy, and a well-developed welfare state combined with a vibrant market economy. His brief survey of Nordic political and legal developments over the eighteenth and nineteenth centuries argues that the rise of the celebrated twentieth-century welfare states occurred when the legal profession at the time was small and weak. As we shall see, this assertion requires significant nuance. Nonetheless, he is clearly right to ask whether lawyers were collectively *active* in the development of what he describes as the "Northern paradise" (Hirschl 2011: 468).

Thus, the Nordic political experience presents an interesting focus for an examination of the legal complex, whether construed narrowly in terms of private lawyers or more widely in terms of all practicing legal occupations inside or outside the state and market. In the nineteenth century, the Nordic states shed absolute rule, and developed robust parliamentary governments, embraced and institutionalized the rule of law, accepted the principle of limited government, and recognized basic rights. Yet none of these changes, as we find, was effected in any meaningful way by the sustained actions of an organized bar, or small segment of it, working in concert with the bench or other civil society institutions. By the late nineteenth century, all the Nordic states or proto-states[9] had parliamentary governments, were governed by principles of the Rechtsstaat, and had granted most citizens basic rights and liberties associated with the rule of law and the moderate state. None of them, save perhaps Sweden, experienced internal violent upheaval. And while independence in Finland from Russia in 1917 was followed by a brutal civil war, and Sweden snuffed out Norway's first drive for independence in a brief war, Norway's second attempt in 1905, ended successfully and peacefully. Since the early twentieth century, the Nordic countries have been near or at the apex of political liberalism by virtually any measure, and at first blush, there is no sign that an

of political phenomena. Comparisons between Nordic political systems and external political systems are rare" (Ancker 1987: 79).

[9] Norway was transferred from Denmark to a "union with Sweden" in 1809, and then gained full independence in the early twentieth century. Iceland was granted "home rule and parliamentarianism" by Denmark just after the turn of the century, in 1904. In 1814, Finland, long an integral part of Sweden, was suddenly transferred to Russia and accorded the status of an autonomous Grand Duchy. One hundred years later it secured full independence during the chaos of the Russian Revolution.

organized legal profession, or some group acting on its behalf, played any significant or enduring role in these developments.

This is not to deny that the Nordic states were sluggish in achieving political liberalism in particular areas and regressed seriously during some important historical junctures. The Nordic brand has its dark side (Langford and Larsen 2018; Larsen, Moss and Skjelsbæk 2021; Puyvallée and Bjørkdahl 2021). As some of the authors in this volume recount, Socialists and Communists, Jews, Catholics, Roma and Travelers, controversial literary figures, and detainees in police cells have all faced the heavy hand of the state over long periods of history. However, until recently, as the authors of the case studies hereshow, lawyers and judges were rarely the heroic actors that mobilized against these contradictions and reversals. Few lawyers organized and what occasional nascent action there was easily and quickly snuffed out, at least until the last third of the twentieth century. The most serious early threat from the legal complex came with the move toward a social welfare state in the late nineteenth and early twentieth century, when parliaments began to encroach on traditional property rights. Lawyers and courts raised feeble challenges, but the battle was lost before it got started. The deferential doctrine of Scandinavian legal realism was developed (Strang 2009) and complemented by deft court stacking as well as promises by ascendant social democratic parties to respect capitalism.

According to some scholars of judicial politics (Hirschl 2011), not only did practicing lawyers play no role in constructing the "Nordic miracle," neither did judges. If that is so, it may be, as Charles Epp (1998) has found elsewhere, because there was no legal support structure on which courts could rely, no critical mass of mobilized lawyers to formulate doctrine and bring cases, no robust lawyers' associations that might have provided a source of sustenance and countervail a civil service-based and oriented judiciary. Or it may be founded upon the relationship between judges and the executive—the Nordic tradition of judicial deference to the executive, a fragmented judiciary embedded in departments within separate ministries (Husa 2011), or a strategic response to strong states embedded in principles of majoritarianism and parliamentary supremacy (Rytter and Wind 2011). Certainly, neither judges nor lawyers, at least not until the late twentieth century, figured prominently in political developments in Nordic political life. Authors such as Hirschl (2011) suggest that the Nordic success may be *because* of such inaction. But, there are other possibilities: political liberalism emerged *despite* such lawyerly involvement; or lawyers found other less visible avenues to exert influence. As to the former, it is important to recall that throughout the seventeenth and eighteenth centuries most Nordic states strangled the development of an autonomous legal profession, in contrast to the United Kingdom's or France's tolerance of an independent bar. In other words, pre-conditions for robust lawyers' associations and the formation of legal complexes—namely a cohort of lawyers and a functioning bar—were largely lacking.

The second issue—that lawyers found other avenues to exert influence—deserves comment. The transformation from moderate autocracies to modern democratic and restrained states in the Nordic states occurred at different times in different places, but in all of them this process occurred while legal education was expanding and law graduates were recruited for positions in the higher civil service and other positions of influence. Certainly, they were well placed to draw on their technical training in drafting legislation and regulations, administering the rapidly growing bureaucracies, and managing an increasingly complex public service. However, as the case studies reveal, the impetus for the development of the modern state occurred before the dramatic increase in legal training, and was in large part was driven from within the Estates and prominent families who feared revolution. The later development, the rise of the welfare state, did take place once lawyers were well ensconced in government service, but as the case studies show, impetus for these developments came from organized labor and political parties. Here too lawyers played important roles in the civil service and political parties. Unlike the United States during the early days of the New Deal, where the organized legal profession was split into identifiable divisions (see e.g. Shamir 1995) , the legal profession in the Nordic countries was not well-enough organized to debate let alone take collective positions on the emerging welfare state. There were occasional celebrated controversies, and occasionally lawyers and legal disputes stood out, but as the authors of the case studies emphasize, these were not collective actions but isolated and limited cases.

So, this volume asks, where were the lawyers? For a period, particularly by the mid-nineteenth century, they seemed be everywhere. University-based legal training grew rapidly throughout the nineteenth century. Admittedly, it grew from a base of near zero, but by the end of the century, law constituted one of the largest faculties and student bodies at Nordic universities. So, where did the graduates go, and what did they do? In addition, where were they in the twentieth century? The contributors in this volume trace the expansion of legal training, the rise of the rule of law, and the construction of parliamentary democracy over the course of the nineteenth and twentieth centuries, and they do so with an eye on the role of lawyers and judges. They all report expanded legal training supplied the growing civil service, but did little to facilitate or foster an independent legal profession. A small minority of law graduates went into private practice, but when they did, they were slow to organize professional associations whose purpose was to enhance their collective professional interests.

To be sure, this assertion is over-drawn and obscures important details of the Nordic landscape. Everywhere those trained in the law held positions of importance. They dominated the "political complex." In many settings, they played significant roles, and in some places, they were more organized and active than others. In Norway in the 1850s, what might be termed the world's first "Lawyers Party" was proposed and partly formed in parliament—although it was more a parliamentary grouping and bears little resemblance to the institutionalized political parties that emerged from the 1880s. Moreover, occasionally a single lawyer took on a celebrated case. Still, almost always when lawyers engaged in the struggle for liberalism, they acted in their capacities as civil servants, parliamentarians, statesmen, spokesmen for elite families, professor-politicians, journalists, or activists in political parties, and not distinctively as members of the organized bar or some set of it speaking on behalf of "the law." In a concluding chapter, Langford elaborates on the possibility that the open political space may have obviated the need for such legal mobilization.

The case studies in this volume sketch out remarkably similar accounts of the development of the modern liberal state in each of the Nordic societies, and the marginal collective action by groups of lawyers in this process. Despite their differences in geography, political history, and pace of development, Sweden, Denmark, Finland, Norway, and Iceland followed roughly parallel paths. Each of the studies identifies a similar set of factors that account for this development of modern economies, robust democracies, and advanced welfare states. They all emphasize the dramatic increase in law training in the nineteenth century, but also emphasize that law training was training for public administration. No one suggests that law-trained civil servants consisted of a special group with shared interests in advancing a shared vision of the moderate state. And most point out that judges were civil servants located within individual ministries without the benefit of separation of powers, and that in many types of cases lawyers for both plaintiffs and defendants with business in the national, and at times community, courts were selected by and drawn from the ranks of the ministries. With the partial exception of Norway, the emergence of the Rechtsstaat was largely a top-down development, introduced by absolute monarchs and further expanded by emerging parliamentary governments. We explore this development in more detail below.

It is beyond the scope of the case studies in this volume to provide full accounts of political histories of each of the Nordic states. However, each of them does identify significant events and institutions that shaped the emerging contours of (and setbacks with) parliamentary democracy and the modern welfare state, and explore events that resulted in significant perturbations in political life that mobilized both public and civil society institutions. Working independently of each other, the authors nevertheless identify the same two sets of factors that laid the groundwork for modern Nordic political development: 1) the ancient and powerful Estates (or broad political groupings) that eventually transformed themselves into democratic parliaments and robust political parties—although often only after considerable mobilization by workers, women, and peasants; and 2) the Rechtsstaat that was largely established by imposition, initially by absolute monarchs in response to the Enlightenment values and concern about revolution. In showing how these two institutions developed and interacted, they also show how lawyers did not or could not develop as a profession in which segments of it could act collectively by mobilizing around core issues of political liberalism. Together the evolution of these two powerful institutions goes a long way toward explaining both Nordic political development in the nineteenth and early twentieth centuries and why the bar and bench remained at best bit players in the process—at least until the late twentieth century.

These historical and contemporary developments are examined in different ways in this volume, both in this crosscutting essay and in the case studies. Section 3 of this chapter draws on the case studies to explore political developments over the longue durée. It traces first the transformation of the Estates from informal advisory groups into parliaments with members selected through competition of political parties, explores the development of the Rechtsstaat and its transformation into the institution that manages the modern social welfare state, and examines how an independent bar failed to emerge until well into the twentieth century. Section 4 takes a different tack. It focuses on a series of *événements*, specific activities or processes that caused perturbations in political life (independence, constitutionalism, the rise of the social welfare state, and restrictions on freedom of expression and association), and led various sectors of civil society to mobilize. Within each trajectory, in Sections 3 and 4, we focus on the role of lawyers in order to determine what roles they played in these momentous developments. Following these sections, we examine two more periods that may have particular implications for the legal complex. Section 5 explores the impact of war and armed conflict, which often pose the greatest challenge to political liberalism and often represent a hard case for the legal complex. Section 6 traces the influence of the global rights revolution in the latter third of the twentieth century, when Nordic legal complexes eventually emerged.

3. The Longue Durée

3.1 The Estates

Well into the nineteenth century, and to put it simply, Nordic countries were overwhelmingly rural, with economies based on farming, fishing, and traditional crafts. The industrial revolution was late to the region. Small farming communities dotted the vast landscapes, and tiny fishing villages strung out along endless coastlines and countless islands. Mining and manufacturing came later. Its most powerful state, Sweden, had long ceded its grand European empire and spent most of the nineteenth century as a declining absolute monarchy. Denmark was significantly weakened after siding with France in the Napoleonic Wars. Nominally controlled from the center, governance in all the states was for all practical purposes confined to the local community. Local governments raised funds to maintain roads, appoint local law enforcement and judicial officials, operate public schools, and build and support local churches. Positions of authority and status were filled from among the local notables, farmers, doctors, teachers, artisans. More important positions were filled from within the nobility or landed elite, and only occasionally an official sent from the capital .

The aristocracy and landed elite had ties to the capitals; they served as advisors to and emissaries for the crown. They sent sons to serve as officers in the royal armies and navies, and to train for the clergy. The provinces were represented in the national governing structure through these Estates, formal and informal groupings representing the most powerful interests in society, the landholding aristocracy, the military, landowning and wealthy peasants, and the church. By the nineteenth century, the Nordic countries were distinctive from many other regions in Europe in one important respect: peasants were free, often owned their own land, and for the most part were literate and politically active, and in Norway, most had gained the right to vote by the mid nineteenth century. The reasons for the relative freedom of the Nordic peasantry are complex, ranging from the emancipatory effects of the black plague in Norway to the brief and revolutionary reforms of Denmark's Prime Minister Streunsee between 1770 and 1772, which ended serfdom. However, their influence probably owes most to the Lutheran church, which promoted literacy and self-reliance. As Bo Strath (2004: 9) has argued, the Nordic "figure of the peasant" was "not just a romantic fiction with no relation to the real world, but an increasingly active participant in economic and political processes." These Estates or groups varied in composition and strength from region to region, but everywhere were powerful and organized enough to provide a counterweight to the supposedly absolute monarchs in the capitals. Traditionally the nobility, the military, and the clergy were drawn from the same small number of families who were linked closely to the crown.

One of nationally organized pillar of Nordic societies was the Lutheran Church. Though highly decentralized, its leading theologians often resided in the capital cities and the clergy scattered throughout the countryside had been trained in the handful of faculties of theology in these same centers. From the seventeenth well into the nineteenth century, leading theologians and clergy were active in public affairs, shaping both policy and the law, and providing recruits for the growing civil service in ways that the law and the legal profession did not. On the historical roles of the church and theologians in Nordic societies (see Modeer and Vogt 2021).

Still, the interests of the Estates did not always coincide with those of the crown. Great landholders were not always willing to cough up tribute and taxes, or give blanket approval to military ventures. The Lutheran state church taught individualism, self-reliance, and education, qualities that did not foster passive acceptance of royal prerogatives. Furthermore, the church was partly decentralized, with no strong spiritual hierarchy at the center for the crown to cultivate and co-opt. Landowning and literate peasants adamantly protected their prerogatives and were wary about taxation and military conscription, however absolute in theory the monarch was.

In addition, throughout the nineteenth century, half of the Nordic region was governed at arm's length, by rulers who commanded little legitimacy. Finland was separated from Sweden by the Gulf of Bothnia, and at least among ordinary citizens, by language. Later as a Grand Duchy, it was separated from Russia by both culture and language. Norway was ruled by Denmark, but was separated by the Baltic and North Seas, and then while under Swedish rule, its population centers were in the far west while Stockholm was on Sweden's eastern coast. Iceland, of course, was far removed from Denmark, and for most practical purposes was self-governing throughout the long period of Danish rule.

Within each of these countries, powerful national identities and institutions developed long before independence. So, when independence finally came, it was anti-climactic; meaningful national autonomy had preceded it by decades. One reason for this is that in most of the countries, populations were widely scattered in rural areas and villages that were distant from one another. For centuries, the most meaningful government was local government and the most important government officials were those who were chosen locally. Kings did issue royal decrees and judges and occasional bureaucrats moved through the countryside dispensing justice and ordering affairs. But communities developed their own institutions with a minimum of oversight from central authorities. Each was likely to have its own local elite, local officials who mediated local affairs, approved of local tax rates, and represented the community in dealings with the national government.

Schaffer describes the local elites in Sweden as constituting part of the national Estates, which for centuries had been called together from time to time to serve as an advisory body to the king (Schaffer, Chapter 3, Section 2.3, this volume). Over time, they came to insist upon meeting on a regular basis whether or not called by the king and, by the early eighteenth century, they were in effect a proto-parliament, whose views at times conflicted with the king's. In the wake of Sweden's disastrous war with Russia in 1809, this group of "advisors" took matters into its own hands, forced the king to reconstitute them into something approaching a parliament, and then slowly but inexorably throughout the nineteenth century began to take control of the machinery of government, expanding and strengthening the Rechtsstaat, and creating a parliament through which the king ruled (Schaffer, Chapter 3, Section 2, this volume). Hardly democratic in the contemporary sense, nevertheless this body "represented" the interests of the several Estates, and consisted of members of the elite who set about major law reforms, which incorporated Enlightenment values. A series of liberal reforms over the nineteenth century, achieved after protracted political struggle, but without violence, strengthened the parliament, expanded and rationalized the Rechtsataat, and professionalized the judiciary. In all this, the legal profession played a significant role, not by litigating or organizing to publically champion liberal causes, but as appointed members of the government Law Commission and successive committees charged with revising the laws. In addition, as Schaffer suggests, motivated as much by their association with liberal movements as their professional commitments (Schaffer, Chapter 3, Section 2.4, this volume). In fact, many prominent members of the committees were also members of parliament or held distinguished positions in government ministries. The long struggle culminated in a full parliamentary democracy with only limited powers of the monarchy, in the early twentieth century. Schaffer attributes the confinement of the actions of the legal professionals to government committees rather than in the judicial arena to the "immaturity of the judicial apparatus and the legal profession," as well as their "dependency on state bureaucracy" (Schaffer, Chapter 3, Section 2.4, this volume). A more robust liberal parliamentary democracy eventually emerged in the early twentieth century following industrialization, urbanization, and the growth of organized labor and women's movements who pressed for expanding the franchise.[10] Political parties replaced the Estates, and popular elections replaced hereditary or traditional allocations of positions, and the monarch's powers were reduced to advisory.

Other case studies present a variation on this theme. In his review of nineteenth-century Danish political history, Madsen describes the construction of the Rechtsstaat, and the shift from hereditary representation in parliament to electoral competition among political parties. Norway's history is similar; although Langford emphasizes that its elite consisted of "one thousand academic families," more an intelligentsia than a landed aristocracy (see Myhre 2008). However, peasants were relatively well represented in the constitutional convention that wrote the liberal Norwegian constitution of 1814, and worked with members of the elite to keep Sweden at arm's length during this process, and by the mid-nineteenth century became a driving force behind the national Romantic Movement that precipitated new liberal reforms and eventually independence from Sweden.

Konttinen describes the establishment of a powerful new centralized bureaucracy following transfer to Russia in the early nineteenth century, and eventually the emergence of a powerful diet comprised of representatives of the Four Estates: the nobility, the clergy, the bourgeoisie, and powerful free peasants. He notes that from the outset, its members were *elected* from within these four groups (Konttinen, Chapter 7, Section 1, this volume). While its role was limited during the first half of the century, it emerged as a powerful political force after 1863, and was instrumental in the break with Russia after the disastrous war with Japan in 1904–05. Through the century, political parties emerged in both Russia and Finland, and in Finland at the turn of the century, the worker's party and elites groups formed coalitions to defend Finish autonomy against Russia's effort

[10] In the early twentieth century, the Nordics were among the first to recognize women's right to vote but were oddly amongst the last in Europe to recognize the rights of the extreme poor to vote (Larsen 2021: 34).

to restrict it. The worker's party went further and demanded greater democracy within the Grand Dutchy and within the diet (Konttinen, Chapter 7, Section 4, this volume). In 1917, the diet declared Finland's independence in the wake of the chaos of the Russian Revolution, but was unable to prevent the bloody civil war that immediately followed, a war that did not contest the declaration of independence, but did pit Bolshevik parties against other more moderate revolutionary parties. The civil war led to a political stalemate and then quiescence, followed by the upheaval of World War II. Following the war, democratic policies flourished, and in short order Finland developed a modern welfare state. Here, too, party politics and strong state institutions led the charge. Lawyers as a group were nowhere to be seen in advocating for political liberalism.

In recounting the transformation of the Estates into proto-parliaments, the establishment of modern representative legislatures, political parties, and electoral politics, the authors of the more sweeping case studies of Denmark, Norway, Sweden, and Finland all emphasize the importance of lawyers at each stage of development. So too does Ragnhildur Helgadóttir in her account of political development in Iceland since the late nineteenth century. Lawyers were active participants in the establishment and development of each of these modern democratic states. Indeed, they often played key roles. But each author emphasizes that lawyers were rarely important as representatives of the legal profession. Rarely, if ever, did lawyers, in the words of Lucien Karpik, "speak in the name of the law," or mobilize as a group to defend their roles as stewards of an autonomous legal order, or defenders of liberal rights. Rather, it was as members of parliament, government ministers, leaders of political parties, civil servants, journalists, publishers, and the like that they stood out. It may be that their law training facilitated the part they played; there is no evidence that they organized collectively and identified as lawyers to act in the name of the law. More telling, the authors repeatedly emphasize that law-trained political activists and politicians were arrayed on all sides of issues.

With two partial exceptions and one notable exception in Norway, up to the 1960s, none of the authors suggests that lawyers organized collectively to advance any sort of commonly agreed-upon position. They were consistently on all sides of the major political issues.

Let us take the first partial exception. Beginning in the nineteenth century and extending throughout the Nordic region, academic lawyers and later members of the tiny organized bar, would from time to time respond to ministerial or parliamentary requests for professional advice and technical assistance in drafting or reviewing drafts of regulations and proposed laws. This is a traditional role that lawyers, and particularly academic lawyers, embrace in all societies. But even here, there is no indication that the lawyers consulted saw the requests as invitations or opportunities to mobilize and act collectively to advance the cause of political liberalism or the moderate state. Rather, it was a standard sort of technical assistance that academic lawyers regularly perform, especially in countries with civil law systems. In Norway 30 percent of members of recently-appointed government-appointed expert commissions and 60 percent of their leaders are lawyers (Langford and Saevereide 2018). Indeed, the strong expert role of lawyers in Nordic states may have had the opposite effect on legal mobilization—providing opportunities for inside influence or disincentivizing oppositional action that threatened prestigious and lucrative appointments (see discussion on this in Chapter 9 from a theoretical perspective). This limit on their roles was shattered in the 1970s, in response to the rights revolution and the access to justice moments.

The other partial exception: In her book, Ragnhildur Helgadóttir (2006) traces the influence of *Marbury v. Madison* (1803) and American theories of judicial review on Nordic constitutional law, and reports their deepest influence on Norway and Iceland. The Norwegian lawyers who took the lead in drafting the liberal con stitution of 1814, were more in tune with English and American ideas of natural law than German positive law, which was the general model for the rest of Scandinavia. Iceland followed Norway's lead in embracing American constitutional theory (Helgadóttir 2006). The dramatic exception occurred in Norway during World War II. Hans Petter Graver (Chapter 6, this volume) reports that following the *coup d'état* in 1940 that established the Quisling Government, Norwegian judges met to assess their situation and collectively devised a course of action: trial court judges were to remain in place so that they could carry on since their work would rarely if ever involve sensitive political issues. In contrast, the justices on the Supreme Court were to resign en masse and join the resistance, thereby signaling to the Norwegians that the new regime was illegal and would not receive any recognition by the legitimate court (Graver, Chapter 6, Section 3, this volume). They were supported in this work by the bar association which moved many of its activities underground. Apart from these examples, there is little evidence that over the course of the turbulent century-and-a-half that Norwegian lawyers mobilized and acted collectively "in the name of the law" to fight for political liberalism and the moderate state.

If lawyers as a group did not mobilize to help shape any of the modern Nordic states, who or what did? The case studies identify two sets of factors: the Rechtsstaat and the Estates and their lineal descendants. In the Rechtsstaat, lawyers were absorbed into the civil service, and legal education was expanded to train civil servants. Lawyers were active in the Estates and later the parliaments, ministries, political parties, and allied institutions, but in ways that did not involve their mobilizing distinctly as lawyers and on behalf of the law.

3.2 The Emergence of the Rechtsstaat

"Rechtsstaat" translates literally as "rule of law state." It emerged as a consequence of the spread of Enlightenment values that celebrated man as the measure of all things, and unleashed revolutionary sentiments from Paris to Philadelphia, and throughout much of Europe. The Rechssstaat first appeared in Central Europe, where it was embraced by autocrats who were forced to grant concessions to mounting pressures fostered by the Enlightenment, and who also saw the Rechsstaat as a way to strengthen their own power.[11] In this doucle movement, the state guaranteed the rule of law, but then it also enacted the law. Indeed, the state constituted the law, and the law constituted the state. It was liberal in that subjects once ruled at whim were transformed into citizens with rights, which they could claim against the state. But, under this idea or historical practice of the Rechtsstaat, the state remained powerful in its ability to fashion, enforce, and adjudicate the law. In this latter sense, the Rechtsstaat was an incomplete form of liberalism, which made far bolder claims about the rights of man, and the separation of law and politics. To be sure, this varied widely. In France, England, and the nascent United States, the ideas of autonomous law and natural rights took hold, and fostered a more robust liberal tradition.

As studies of lawyers and the legal profession in Central and Eastern Europe reveal, liberals, often led by lawyers, were active in pressing for the Rechtsstaat. As Reuschemeyer (1997: 105; See also 2014) reports, in 1700 there was one lawyer for every two thousand residents in Prussia, a ratio not likely to be equaled anywhere else in Europe at the time, and while the relationship between the legal profession and the state was turbulent throughout the eighteenth century, lawyers nevertheless were active in pressing for and shaping the Rechtsstaat that was erected, beginning at the end of that century and continuing on into the next). Still, even in Prussia and elsewhere in the German states, as Reuschemeyer (2014: 207) shows, after its establishment, these states sought to curtail the independence of lawyers by limiting the numbers of those admitted to the bar and by intervening in the internal affairs of lawyers' associations.

The histories of the development of the Rechtsstaat in the Nordic states are different. When the administrative state began to emerge in Prussia, that state already had a long tradition of an independent legal profession, an association of lawyers who guarded their prerogatives jealously, and indeed a history of contention between lawyers and the state. Segments of the legal profession embraced the idea, some as groups within civil society pressing for change, and others as members of the nascent civil service trying to give shape to the new ideas. In contrast, the Nordic countries had no histories of a vibrant and independent legal profession. When the administrative states in Denmark and Sweden began to emerge in the 1600s, professional lawyers and legal training were also just emerging, and lawyers in Norway and Iceland were trained abroad if they received professional training at all, and Finnish legal education took in Turku. Changes were imposed from

[11] See e.g., Silkenat, Rickley, and Barenboim (2014).

the top down, not just by the crown since the crown constituted absolute rule in name only, but by members of the traditional Estates (particularly Sweden), which had long circumscribed the power of monarchs. As the case studies reveal, some of these transformations were by-products of abrupt historical events rather than slow and incremental changes. In addition, in all cases, save perhaps Norway, they occurred before there was an independent legal profession or organized bar, and indeed before universities even offered training in the law in any meaningful numbers. Consider, for example, in 1700 there was one lawyer for every two thousand inhabitants in Prussia; in Norway the ratio was one to every twelve thousand!

That said, the case studies in this volume show that the Nordic Rechtsstaat established gradually liberal regimes anchored in the rule of law. From the late eighteenth century, and especially the beginning of the nineteenth, royal pronouncements and parliamentary proclamations embraced the rule of law, lifted restrictions on movement (which in places, bound tenants to the land), guaranteed freedom of employment, liberalized free expression (within limits), expanded representative assemblies, and created a powerful and effective civil service. Ad hoc personalist administration by royal retainers gave way to law-trained officials selected on merit; and a mercantilist economy dominated by royal privileges was succeed by a market economy, although one guided by an effective civil service (Slagstad 1998).

The causes of these developments are many and varied, but foremost among them were monarchs' efforts to accommodate to the new order brought about by the Enlightenment and pressed on them by representatives of the powerful Estates, and who warned of revolution. In the Nordic region, this shift is seen most clearly and dramatically in Finland. With Finland an integral part of Sweden for centuries, Finnish nobility had provided the state with a disproportionate proportion of its of military officers. Their prowess had helped make Sweden one of the Great Powers of Europe in the late eighteenth century. With Sweden's defeat in the Swedish–Russian War of 1809, Finland was ceded to Russia and became a "Grand Duchy." In his study, Esa Konttinen describes the dilemma confronting the new Russian masters: how to manage a potentially hostile group of noblemen who has lost their high ranking positions as Swedish military officers (Konttinen, Chapter 7, Section 2, this volume)? In one bold stroke, Konttinen tells us, the Czar solved two problems at once. Russia dismantled the Finnish division of the Swedish army, and redirected ambitious young men to study law and move into the newly established civil service, the new Finnish Rechtsstaat. One form of profession, honor, income, and status was replaced by another; loyalty transferred from one autocrat to another. As Konttinen shows, this move worked. The national university was moved from the Swedish side of Finland to Helsinki, closer to the Russian border. The Finnish nobility was co-opted, and a powerful new bureaucracy was established. Indeed, the policy was an extension of the development of the fledgling Rechtsstaat already under way in Russia (Konttinen, Chapter 7, Section 2, this volume). The retooled Finnish nobility—from soldiers to lawyers—proved to be reliable and capable civil servants for the Russian-controlled Duchy for the next one hundred years (Konttinen, Chapter 7, Section 2, this volume).

Everywhere in the Rechtsstaat, the upper level of the civil service was dominated by law-trained university graduates, who were in turn kept on short leashes. In the case of Denmark (and by extension Norway and Iceland), this was a result of the state's long-standing monopoly of the emergent legal profession. After granting the right to practice as a lawyer in 1638, the state responded with a series of reforms—partly after popular outrage over lawyer's remunerative tactics—that effectively made the legal profession a creature of the state. Each ministry had its own administrative law system for adjudication, for which it supplied both advocates and judges.

In Sweden and Finland and elsewhere, the heads of separate ministries appointed civil servants for judicial service and moved them up the ranks. And, at times, they appointed advocates for the both parties appearing before these ministerial courts (Konttinen, Chapter 7, Section 2), and in Sweden well into the nineteenth century, Sweden operated under a system of corporative courts for distinct segments of society (Schaffer, Chapter 3, Section 2.3, this volume).

Madsen describes the state-building efforts of King Frederick VII of Denmark who assumed the throne in 1848. Influenced by developments in Germany and Russia, he set out to impose a Rechtsstaat both at home and in Iceland. The foundation for this was the Constitution of 1849, which provided for separation of powers, an expansive electoral franchise, and guaranteed freedom of expression and due process. The king was head of the executive branch, but the parliament, consisting of two chambers, was acknowledged as the law-making authority. Under this constitution, the civil service expanded, and requirements for entry shifted from training in theology to training in law. King Frederick established a new and powerful form of government, seemingly liberal in its concern for the rule of law, separation of powers, freedom of expression, and a guarantee of due process. But it was also much more powerful in its ability to act decisively. By the 1860s the liberal Rechtsstaat was in full bloom, though a subsequent military defeat and the loss of Schleswig-Holstein to a German principality weakened the state and led to a retrenchment of its liberal policies, which slowly returned over the balance of the century. Schaffer provides a similar account for Sweden, though changes occurred at a slower pace, as an increasingly powerful parliament not only established the Rechtsstaat but also propped up a weak monarchy.

Setting aside tiny Iceland, Norway probably least fits into this general model of the emerging Rechtsstaat. Separated by Denmark by the North Atlantic Ocean and the Baltic Sea, Norway's rural population was dispersed over a vast area and isolated by chains of mountains and steep valleys. Until the 1830s, its then largest city, Bergen, and its largest population centers were on the Atlantic coast, which had as much significant contact and intellectual exchanges with Scotland and England as with Denmark and Sweden. The ability of the 1814 Constitution-makers to lobby and mobilize the otherwise unsympathetic British parliament to discuss the "Norway question" is testament to these relationships. However, for all practical purposes its isolated and dispersed population was largely self-governing at the local level until well into the nineteenth century. Furthermore, it had a limited nobility or aristocracy; it was a nation of crofters and fishermen scattered over a vast area. Doctors, clergymen, and teachers constituted the elite in most villages, although literate, landowning peasants were also active in local affairs. Governors, bureaucrats, and lawyers were appointed by the Danish Crown (all trained in Denmark even if Norwegian-born) but their penetration of Norwegian society varied in breadth and depth. These various upper classes were large enough by the beginning of the nineteenth century to create an identifiable "elite" in Norway, distinctive as such because of their modest wealth, tradition of sending sons to university, and their formal roles in society (Langford, Chapter X, Section 3.2, this volume).

This review of the establishment of the Rechtsstaat goes a long way to help us understand Langford's nineteenth-4century puzzle: "lawyers, lawyers everywhere." Law training was preparation for public administration. Law faculties emerged and expanded not in order to produce lawyers, and certainly not an autonomous profession, but to staff the civil service. The expanding regulatory state extended its tentacles everywhere. Bureaucrats also staffed the courts as judges, prosecutors, and advocates. Students flocked to burgeoning law faculties as a way station on their journey to a secure position in government service.

Five of the six case studies trace the rapid expansion of legal education in the nineteenth century and link it to the development of the Rechtsstaat. Their accounts parallel each other, though timing, magnitude, and pace of development varied. Langford notes that in Norway, between 1820 and 1895, the number of law graduates increased nine-fold, from fifty in 1820, to nearly 450 in 1895 (Langford, Chapter 5, Figure 5.1, this volume).

Both the dramatic expansion of in university enrollments and the growing preference for law over theology reflected the needs of the expanding Rechtsstaat. In 1820, in Norway, 45 percent of all university students studied law, 45 percent studied theology, and the balance studied medicine. By the end of the century, the picture was entirely different. Medicine and law had grown; theology had dwindled. But Langford also notes that the formative step towards the liberal state took place before and not after or even during this expansion of legal education.

The rise of legal training must be understood in context. It was partly a consequence of shifting preferences amongst elites. Even before the development of the Rechtsstaat—since the mid-eighteenth century and earlier—university training in theology provided young men from well-to-do families entry positions in government service, and over time the preferred prerequisite shifted from theology to law. The contemporaneous and restrictive regulation of lawyer's activities in many

Nordic states paradoxically made the field more lucrative and prestigious. The Rechtsstaat accelerated this trend. Furthermore, this seemingly dramatic increase in legal training began from a low base so that even after three-quarters of a century of growth, the number of lawyers in the Nordic states remained comparatively small, and the profession ill-defined. Drawing on the scholarship of Letto-Vanamo (2014) and Pihlajamäki (2009) on legal education and law practice in Sweden (and Finland) in the eighteenth and early nineteenth centuries, Konttinen (this volume) notes that 'in the old Swedish System "no educational qualifications were required to act as an attorney," and "educated lawyers were particularly scarce in Finland." Similarly, Michalsen (2014) reports that until the middle of the eighteenth century, law faculties in the Nordic countries did not even impose examinations on their students. But, as he notes, once the curriculum was established and exams imposed, a degree in law "paved the way for a career in the law and public service" (2014: 4).

By the early nineteenth century, law training was a standard stepping-stone for the sons of the nobility and well-to-do into prestigious positions in the upper civil service. Indeed, over the course of the century, law training became a prerequisite for holding an increasing number of positions in the civil service. However, it had only marginal impact on the development of a private bar. By the end of the nineteenth century, the private bar in all the Nordic countries was tiny and remained largely unorganized—and partly intentionally so. None of the Nordic states had many lawyers in comparison, say, to Prussia or the larger German states, or to other advanced industrialized countries. Langford's report of a nine-fold increase in lawyers between 1820 and 1895 appears impressive until we note the fact that there were only 450 lawyers in Norway in 1820. Similarly, Konttinen (Chapter 7, Section 4, fn 11, this volume) reports that at the end of the nineteenth century, Finland had only one private lawyer for every fifty thousand people. Finally, to underscore points made earlier, at the beginning of the twentieth century, the number of lawyers in private practice in the Nordic states was miniscule, and the bar was not well organized. In addition, those trained in law were usually engaged in the civil service and public affairs, and usually acted in their capacities as civil servants, parliamentarians, advisers to the government, and publishers. Courts were lodged in separate ministries and staffed by civil servants. In some places in important matters of state, advocates for the separate parties were selected by the ministries. Until recently, those trained in the law did not mobilize as legal professionals around any set of issues.[12]

[12] Modernization in Japan followed a similar pattern. After the Meiji Restoration in 1868, the government promoted legal training for civil servants, and to this end sent hundreds of young men to study law in Germany, England, and the United States, with the expectation that they would return to Japan and assume positions in the rapidly expanding bureaucracy. The vast majority of them did, but a small number—especially those trained in England—had come to appreciate the idea of an independent legal profession, and when they returned home, established private practices, often against the will of the

However, it is important not to overstate the extent to which Nordic states were in fact liberal societies, with strong traditions of individual rights and robust limits on governments. Langford, for instance, partly understands the Norwegian struggle for autonomy not in terms of liberalism, but nationalism—an effort to create distance first from Denmark and then Sweden. With the rise of constitutionalism, Norwegian priorities were largely to throw off foreign rule. Parliamentary government and separation of powers was as much a means as an end. As we shall see, even as Nordic states transformed themselves into advanced welfare states in the 1930s, they lacked certain basic liberal protections common to France, England, the United States, and other liberal democratic states. Schaffer notes that despite its expansion of liberal policies throughout the nineteenth century, Sweden's monarchy continued to exercise substantial powers well into the twentieth century (Schaffer, Chapter 3, Section 3, this volume).

3.3 The Slow Emergence of the Organized Bar

All the case studies reveal an increase in the numbers of law graduates in the nineteenth century, and slow and uneven development of a legal profession and judiciary separate from and independent of the ministries.[13] What they do not find is a parallel development of an active association of lawyers and judges; neither an independent judiciary (except in Norway) nor an independent bar emerged in the nineteenth century. The first bar associations were formed at the very end of that century, and were organized to sponsor social functions. Recessions in the early twentieth century led some of them to engage in activities to foster economic well-being among members. With but minor exceptions, robust bar associations engaged in public issues did not appear until the late twentieth century.

The historical quiescence of the legal profession is arguably the result of three factors. First, although the numbers of law-trained men grew rapidly throughout the nineteenth century, expansion was built on a very low base. So, despite increases, the numbers of lawyers per capita in the Nordic states remained well below comparable figures for other European countries and the United States (Michalsen 2014; and others, this volume). In fact, in some of the Nordic countries in the early part of the twentieth century, the numbers of lawyers actually declined. Second, as noted above, the expansion of legal training in the early nineteenth century was explicitly designed to produce civil servants for the Rechtsstaat, and not private

government. As a consequence, the legal profession emerged as an institution with a built-in tension with the government, a relationship that can be seen today (see Feeley and Miyazawa 2007).

[13] Other recent studies of Nordic lawyers provide additional details about the relatively (as compared to elsewhere in Northern Europe and England) late development of the legal profession and organized bar. See, e.g., the chapters in, Ervo, Letto-Venamo, and Nyland (2021).

lawyers. Law schools were schools of public administration, and there was no organized bar to support an alternative model of private practice. Third, the state restricted directly and indirectly development of an independent bench and bar until well into the twentieth century. In the provinces, courts were rarely staffed by law-trained judges, and advocates appearing before them rarely had formal legal training.

A robust legal complex requires an active independent bar—a free profession—which is not constrained by ties to an employer or the state (Karpik and Halliday 2011). It requires lawyers who share the idea of the autonomy of law, and see themselves of stewards of that order. To be sure, other lawyers—academic lawyers, government lawyers, prosecutors, civil servants, judges—can also embrace this stance, but only to the extent that they see themselves as part of a "free profession"—members of a bar as well as government employees. But the case studies reveal that lawyers formed law societies relatively late as compared to lawyers in the United Kingdom, France, and even the strong civil service states of Prussia and other German states (Halliday and Karpik 1998) .

Konttinen reports that the first law firm in Finland was established in 1888, and that country's first national bar association was established twenty-one years later, in 1919. It was created, he tells us, in order to address issues of income, which had eroded due to continuing political instability and rising inflation following the political and economic crisis that erupted in 1905. At the outset, the association had a membership of 177, which probably constituted the vast majority of the country's practicing lawyers. By the early 1930s, its membership has increased to 500, but twenty five years later had dwindled to 350 despite the increased number of law graduates (Konttinen, Chapter 7, Section 8, this volume). This suggests the deeper institutionalization of lawyers within the welfare state, rather than a rights orientation of a liberal polity.

Sweden's national bar association was established in 1887, when a group of lawyers organized to protest a state-sponsored recommendation that specified who could call themselves an "advocate" and appear in the higher courts. Despite this promising effort at collective action, the association remained weak and ineffectual. It took over sixty years before the association was able to gain the authority to license advocates. Even then, it did not succeed in preventing unlicensed advocates from representing clients in court (Schaffer, Chapter 3, Section 2.4, this volume).

Langford also shows that the vast majority of law graduates went into the civil service, business, or politics (Langford, Chapter X, Section 3.2, this volume), but he also emphasizes the long tradition that "the cunning lawyer" has played in Norwegian lore, and notes the influence of English and American ideas on the practice of law in Norway. He reports that in the early nineteenth century, 14 percent of law graduates worked as private lawyers, a proportion that had more than doubled by 1900, to 35 percent. But, again, the absolute numbers were small, far smaller than the German states, France, and England (Langford, Chapter X,

Section 3.3, this volume). A bar association, though established in the 1880s, focused on social events in its early years. Langford does note several examples of individual lawyers mounting vigorous arguments in high-profile cases, but they were isolated defenses in selected causes and did not involve a mobilized legal community (Langford, Chapter X, Section 3.3, this volume). And like the authors of the other case studies, he notes that throughout the nineteenth century and up until the 1970s, law graduates were active in public affairs as members of parliament, political parties, labor unions, civil service groups, and the like, and with only two exceptions, they did not act collectively. The two exceptions, the first minor, the other notable: in the late nineteenth century, criminal lawyers joined together to press for reforms in the criminal law. The notable: during World War II lawyers and judges acted collectively in resisting the Nazi *coup d'état*, and later in the war to constrain Nazis appointed to the bench. Much later, during World War II, there was a third dramatic exception (see Graver, Chapter 6, Section 2, this volume; and Section 5, below).

The Danish Bar and Law Society was founded in 1919 by a group of lawyers holding the title "Advokat." The association, Madsen tells us, was established to enhance the profession's ethical standards and to administer the bar examination. Since then, its various committees have been also active in consulting with government officials regarding the development of legislation and regulations. Like the organized bar in other countries, it has worked with whatever government was in office and dealt with a wide variety of matters. Iceland, the then semi-autonomous dependency of Denmark, tracks that country closely until World War II. In her case study, Helgadóttir (Chapter 8, Section 2.2, this volume) reports that at the end of the nineteenth century, there were forty-eight lawyers in Iceland, all of whom had been trained in Denmark, and most of whom served as judges or held other positions in the civil service. At the time, only two of them were licensed to appear before the high court, though in 1905, two more lawyers were granted licenses to appear for defendants in criminal proceedings, a prerogative which previously had been assigned to civil servants (Helgadóttir, Chapter 8, Section 2.2, this volume). Local legal education was initiated in the early 1900s, and a bar association was established a short time later—for the purposes of "protecting the interests of its members, support their cooperation and ensure that they follow the same rules regarding remuneration" (Helgadóttir, Chapter 8, Section 2.2, this volume, quoting Pálsson (1981: 180). Since then, she maintains, there has been a small but robust independent bar that has included a handful of legal academics. Upon request, it has offered advice on legal drafting to successive governments, but until the 1980s it had not mobilized around any political issues. Helgadóttir does identify one possible exception to this quiescence. In the 1930s, lawyers—joined by judges, and most members of parliament, and the press—organized to challenge a proposal by the Minister of Justice to summarily dismiss and replace all the justices on the Supreme Court. Helgadóttir reports that the consensus among the varied group of notables was that an irascible official had finally gone too far, and so they quickly found a way to unseat him remove him from office.

None of the case studies thus presents a robust picture of any type of lawyers organization let alone a bar association able to mobilize from time to time to engage struggles to advance or preserve political liberalism—at least not until the 1970s. The authors describe the development of the law school-civil service pipeline, and provide accounts of law graduates moving into publishing, politics, and business, but with minor exception do not find lawyers in private practice and elsewhere forming robust law societies or occasionally some portion of them to fight for the rule of law. There is not even a long history of vibrant law societies. What few collective civic concerns they evinced were restricted to responding to ministerial requests technical advice. In short, bar associations came late to the Nordic countries, in contrast to lawyers' associations in France, England, Prussia, and elsewhere (Halliday and Karpik 1998), and when they did arrive they were small and inactive in public affairs.

Again, there are some partial exceptions, but very partial, prior to the 1960s. These exceptions usually involve one determined lawyer in one major case or series of cases. Langford describes the activities of a well-known conservative lawyer in Oslo. In the 1850s, he dropped everything for a short period to doggedly pursue a treason case against workers' representatives (Langford, Chapter X, Section 3.3, this volume), who he felt had been unfairly charged. Similarly, Madsen describes the activities of a Copenhagen cause lawyer before his time, who in the 1950s represented despised members of the Communist Party at the height of the Red Scare, and who later during the Cold War took up the defense of unpopular clients well into the 1960s (Madsen, Chapter 4, Section 4.2, this volume). In his chapter, Graver describes the heroic action of judges and lawyers in Norway during World War II. Apart from this study, accounts focus on particular issues pursued by individual lawyers. These exceptions seem to point to a rule, that the organized bar and bench were quiescent in the face of illiberal government actions at least until the 1970s, aside from, of course, the remarkable actions of the judges in Norway during World War II.

3.4 Conclusions on the Longue Durée

In their assessment of Nordic political developments over the longue durée, the authors of the case studies found that an independent legal profession anchored in civil society played almost no role in shaping or fighting for political liberalism. They noted and then explained a seeming paradox: An increasing number of men trained in the law, but no development of a legal profession that mobilized to advance the cause of the rule of law, political liberalism, and the moderate state. This anomaly, if that is what it is, was largely resolved by the fact that throughout the nineteenth century, law training in Nordic societies was slow or develop in comparison to other European states, and that it was designed to meet the demands of a growing civil service. Of course, as we saw, there were some exceptions, but they were limited.

However, this account does not end the inquiry. Although the authors of the case studies were charged with the task of keeping a sharp eye on the role of lawyers as they provided an account of political developments over the longue durée, they covered so much ground in their overviews that they might easily have missed crucial encounters or processes in which lawyers emerged to play a crucial role and then faded back into the political tapestry. As a way of guarding against this, the authors were also asked to identify events or processes that destabilized or disrupted the ordinary machinery of state and various institutions in civil society. We wanted to see if such disruptions led lawyers, however small in number to mobilize and to act collectively, even if briefly. The discussion below examines the potential emergence of legal complexes in such situations that were common to two or more countries. Here, too, with but one major exception, we do not find legal complexes until the late 1970s, when a rights revolution began to slowly transform the Nordic legal and political landscape. The one example of sustained collective action prior to this—by judges in Norway during World War II—is explored in Section 5 below.

4. *Evénements*

What might be invisible or only dimly perceived in an account of the longue durée can become visible in a focused inquiry of momentous events or perturbations in the political system that cause its major elements to mobilize. Each country has a different and contingent history; our aim was for the authors to select significant disruptive situations that were likely to have reverberations throughout the government and civil society in the countries on which they focused. They identified major events, traced their reverberations, and reported on what roles, if any, organized groups of lawyers played, either alone or in concert with other civil society groups. If members of a potential legal complex mobilized to fight for or protect basic political freedoms and the moderate state, we would expect to see them in at least some of these selected *événements*.

Not surprisingly, there was considerable overlap on issues in the several case studies. In most instances three or more of the authors identified similar issues, and we have organized our discussion of them around six clusters of issues: (1) independence movements, (2) constitutional moments, (3) crucial stages in the development of the welfare state, (4) freedom of expression and association, and (5) World War II and its immediate aftermath, and (6) the rights revolution of the 1970s. Not all the discussions presented in the case studies can be subsumed neatly into one or another of these categories, but enough can to allow us to be confident about the generalizations we tender in the concluding part of our discussion.

4.1 Independence Movements

For centuries, there were only two Nordic states, Denmark and Sweden. Finland was an integral part of Sweden for five hundred years until it was ceded to Russia in 1809 after Sweden's disastrous war with Russia. A century later, in 1905, after Russia was defeated in war by Japan, Finnish nationalists mounted a campaign for greater autonomy with the Dutchy. Twelve years later, the worker's party took advantage of the chaos brought about by the Russian Revolution in 1917 and succeeded in obtaining independence. Following the end of the Napoleonic wars in 1814, the Congress of Vienna approved the transfer of Norway from Denmark into a "union" with Sweden. The already budding nationalist movement in Norway sought to preempt this move by declaring independence and proclaiming a constitutional monarchy (to be headed by a Danish Crown Prince). Sweden enforced their Congress of Vienna-backed claim, but Norway managed to obtain an arm's-length union, and one hundred years later peacefully achieved full independence. Iceland was in union with or overseen by the three Scandinavian powers for almost a thousand years, and in 1904 was granted home rule and parliamentarianism by Denmark. In 1943 during the war, it declared full independence, when Denmark was occupied by Germany and Iceland was occupied by the Allied Forces (Helgadóttir, Chapter 8, Section 2.1, this volume).

In each case, independence came about—in the short or long run—after calamitous external wars, and long-standing but mostly non-violent internal struggles. Finns took advantage of war-weakened Russia after its defeat by Japan, and then the Russian Revolution; Norwegians took advantage of the post-Napoleonic War vacuum and cemented an autonomy that eventually helped facilitate a peaceful break in 1905; and Iceland took its last steps when Denmark was under German occupation. Indeed, Norway's liberal constitution adopted in 1814 is still the constitution. None of the movements occasioned a violent struggle for independence itself, though a bloody civil war did follow independence in Finland. And, of course, Denmark and Sweden lost their possessions due to defeats in wars.

Certainly, these were tumultuous times. One nation was ripped apart, others were moved about like chess pieces. The events fostered confusion, resentment, nationalism, resistance, and calls for autonomy and moderation. All the case studies indicate that lawyers were present and active in these various nationalist and independence movements. But the case studies reveal that lawyers rarely if ever organized as distinctive spokespeople for independence, political liberalism, or the moderate state as part of state formation. They did not mobilize as a group to advance the cause of liberalism and independence when moments of opportunities arose, nor did they provide rhetoric in the quest for independence. However, legally-trained men (they were all men) were present instead in their roles as representatives of Estates or the aristocracy, civil servants, parliamentarians, ministry officials, leaders of political movements, journalists, and the like; and not self-consciously as groups of lawyers.

Of the three countries that obtained independence during the period under investigation, only in one—Norway—is there any indication that lawyers and judges were active as a group in the process. Confronted by Sweden's post-Napoleonic claim, the successful drafting of the Norwegian 1814 constitution was owed in part to the adroitness, skill, and leadership of Norwegian lawyers and judges. This group led the drafting of a constitution that—despite being amended after Swedish intervention to acknowledge the "union" with Sweden—placed the authority of the Swedish king "under Parliament", guaranteed basic rights for its citizens, explicitly provided for limited government, and provided implicitly the possibility for judicial review as a check on royal power.

Even here, however, Langford is careful not to attribute too much autonomy to an organized group of lawyers and judges (Langford, Chapter X, Section 3.1, this volume). While a scattered handful of individual lawyers and judges did play important roles, he emphasizes that most of those centrally involved in this enterprise were members of elite families that had long dominated the state, market, and church.

The abrupt severance of Finland from Sweden and attachment to Russia might have precipitated a bitter struggle for Finnish nationalism, but Konttinen shows how in one fell swoop—as discussed above—the Czarist government co-opted potential opposition through the creation of the Rechtsstaat and the redirection of the Finnish nobility from the military into the new civil service, the Finnish administrative center from Turku to Helsinki. In so doing one potential source of opposition to Russian rule was quashed even before it might organize (Konttinen, Chapter 7, Section 2, this volume).

One hundred years later, following Russia's defeat by Japan in 1905, an increasingly weakened czar imposed limits on free speech and press throughout Russia and Finland. These actions in turn generated strong sentiments for reform and revolution. In Finland, labor organizations were the backbone of the independence movement; they organized demonstrations and strikes, demanded the restoration of rights, and when the time was right pressed successfully for independence. Konttinen tells us that few lawyers took part in these efforts. Indeed, there were very few private lawyers, and no organized law society in which such issues could be debated. Those lawyers who did engage, were not organize collectively as "lawyers," but acted in their capacities as civil servants, members of diet, political activists, or journalists. Following independence Finland descended into its own bloody civil war. The war, however, was not over independence—national consensus supported it. Rather it was which of two sides—opponents of the Russian Revolution or its supporters—should take control of the new Finnish state. In this struggle, lawyers played no significant role, though Konttinen does note that a handful of lawyers distinguished themselves by insisting, though with limited success, that the dominant White faction (anti-Russian) treat the opposing Reds (supporters of the Bolsheviks) as prisoners of war rather than murder them on the battlefield (Konttinen, Chapter 7, Section 5, this volume).

Between the thirteenth century until 1904, Iceland was at governed at arm's length by Denmark at which time it was granted "home rule." In an Act of Union in 1918, it was proclaimed a sovereign country in a personal union with Denmark (based on the Swedish-Norwegian Union). In 1944, Iceland declared itself a republic and severed all governmental ties with Denmark. Helgadóttir (Chapter 8, Section 2.1, this volume) offers no hint that either of these steps toward independence was aided by lawyers who mobilized to establish the Danish-Icelandic Act of Union of 1918, or again in 1944. The two separate acts were taken in large part by the Icelandic parliament, and were broadly supported by all segments of society. While both moves were clear assertions of national autonomy, the first in 1918, Helgadóttir shows, was by no means inspired by liberalism and political moderation. Conservative Icelandic farmers had long resented Danish-imposed rights that allowed paupers to marry, and landless peasants in the countryside to migrate to the city because they reduced the supply of cheap labor. Throughout the nineteenth century, the Icelandic movement for self-government was led by farmers and conservative parties. The movement was nationalist not liberal, and the question of the relationship with Denmark dominated political life. Full independence in 1944 occasioned no immediate controversy or struggle. Denmark was occupied by the Germans, and Iceland, occupied by Allied Forces, and there was no opposition when Parliament announced declared independence.

4.2 Constitutionalism

Over the course of two centuries, roughly from 1800 to 2000, each of the Nordic countries adopted at least one constitution. Norway's constitution, adopted in 1814, is still in place today (although it has been amended more than 150 times: Ginsburg 2011). The other countries have had a succession of constitutions or significant emendations. Depending on how one counts, Denmark has had four constitutions, and several other significant but failed efforts. Iceland has had up to seven constitutions if one includes the original understanding with Demark in 1376 (Helgadóttir, Chapter 8, Section 2.1 this volume), the four Danish constitutions, and restructuring following the two declarations of independence. Sweden has had three constitutions, or at least three great constitutional moments. Finland has adopted a constitution following independence, and then another heavily revised constitution in 2002.

Some of the constitutions and emendations were bold new statements on the structure of government, and others did little more than consolidate and codify a series of incremental actions that had been taken over preceding decades through parliamentary and executive actions. In all this, lawyers and jurists were important in establishing constitutional committees in parliaments, calling constitutional conventions, shaping and drafting proposed constitutions, and in promoting their adoption. Our concern here, however, is more focused: did members of distinct legal communities mobilize to press for liberal principles and political moderation during these constitutional moments? Again, with one possible exception, the answer appears to be "no." Lawyers and judges were "everywhere" and active in proposing, debating, and drafting the various constitutions, but their roles as participants were usually defined by other allied but nevertheless distinct roles. Academic lawyers offered technical assistance in drafting proposed constitutions and amendments. Lawyer-civil servants collated past laws into new forms that were introduced as constitutional amendments, and assessed proposed amendments for their implications. Along with others lawyers they served as spokespeople for political parties, government ministries, civil services, labor unions, the church, the aristocracy, and the like in advocating various provisions. In debates, lawyers were consistently found on all sides of the issues. Some argued for the preservation of aristocratic privileges such as hereditary upper chambers in parliaments or the monarch's prerogative to appoint ministers without the approval of parliament.

As suggested above, this limited role is not for lack of dramatic constitutional moments. The Danish Constitution of 1849 (Madsen, Chapter 4, Section 2, this volume), consolidated liberal legislative reforms of the previous quarter-century that significantly limited the powers of the monarch and strengthened the powers of the parliament. Madsen reports that if the shaping of this constitution could be attributed to any single group, it would be Lutheran theologians, and not lawyers, since it was theologians, and not lawyers, who had most actively pressed for liberal reforms throughout the first half of the nineteenth century (Madsen, Chapter 4, Section 2, this volume). Subsequent constitutional changes in Denmark were products of shifting parliamentary coalitions, and to the extent lawyers were involved, it was as members of parliament. However, here, as well as elsewhere in the Nordic countries, there was a tradition of academic lawyers providing technical drafting assistance to parliamentary committees and ministries.

As discussed earlier, Norway adopted a liberal constitution in 1814, which remains in place today, the world's second-oldest written constitution. Lawyers played an active role in writing it, Langford reports, but their roles were shaped more by their positions in the Norwegian elite and civil service than by their collective identity as lawyers. Still, as we have seen, Norwegian and Icelandic lawyers were deeply influenced by English and American natural law theories and the American doctrine of limited government and of judicial review. The 1814 Norwegian constitution reflected in different ways these ideas, and both the Norwegian and Icelandic courts have acted on them. Shortly thereafter, the Norwegian Supreme Court held in effect a law on licenses for copper mining to contravene the Norwegian constitution and, in 1866, it embraced formally judicial review.

This tradition was strong enough by 1918, to precipitate a major crisis; the Supreme Court appeared poised to strike down a law partially nationalizing hydroelectric power companies, a law passed in order to prevent a company from being purchased by foreigners. This decision was neatly avoided by the governing Social Liberal Party, which at the last minute packed the Court with enough new justices to assure a Government victory. (Langford, Chapter X, Section 4, this volume).

Similarly, Icelandic judges, influenced by both American and Norwegian developments, ruled on numerous occasions in the late nineteenth century that decrees from Denmark violated the Icelandic constitution and declared them void.

Following World War II, the Norwegian parliament added more rights (although a number were social and environmental rights). And of course, the most significant constitutional changes occurred in the wake of the Rights Revolution in the Nordic region of the 1970s. All the Nordic countries were forced to come to grips with the implications of the international human rights treaties they had signed. Some provisions in these treaties had quasi-constitutional status. They superseded domestic law, and many were subject to review by international tribunals. Recognizing this, within a few years Nordic domestic courts embraced the concept of judicial review themselves. In a very real sense constitutionalism, implying both limited government and judicial review, were imposed from the outside, as a condition of signing international treaties. Though deeply controversial in the Nordic states, largely this new constitutionalism has been embraced, though with varying degrees of enthusiasm, throughout the Nordic region (see Section 5, below).

Constitutional government in Sweden can be traced back to the adoption of the Instrument of Government of 1719, which established the Riksdag (Parliament) of the Estates, and in so doing formalized and expanded the authority of the Four Estates that had for centuries advised and slowly circumscribed the powers of the king. Modern Sweden has had two great constitutional moments. In 1809–10, following Sweden's disastrous war with Russia, the "Revolutionary Riksdag" representing the Four Estates—the nobility, the clergy, the merchants, and the peasants—deposed the king, drafted a new constitution, and selected a pliable monarch from abroad. Then, in the 1840s until the 1860s liberals in parliament mobilized to initiate a series of reforms that "transformed the corrupt and authoritarian state into a liberal Rechtsstaat, along with a free economy, a lively civil society, and a free press" (Schaffer, Chapter 3, Section 2.3, this volume). In exercising this control, parliament rejected the idea of an absolute monarch, assumed greater oversight of the powerful ministries, which had long been the prerogative of the monarch, and in effect transformed itself from a consultative body from the Estates into a modern elected parliament (Schaffer, Chapter 3, Section

2.1 and 2.3, this volume). These and subsequent developments were achieved through robust political contestation, but little violence. Like the authors of the other case studies, Schaffer emphasizes that those trained in the law were active in these political battles, but in their capacities as members of the traditional estates, parliament, and the ministries rather than as collective spokespeople for an autonomous legal profession. Later, lawyers would also distinguish themselves on state-sponsored law commissions and committees, and later in political parties, but there is no evidence that segments of the bar mobilized separately to press for reform. Party and corporatist practices dominated (Schaffer, Chapter 3, Section 2.4, this volume).

In Denmark, beginning with the "theologians' constitution" of 1849, a series of successive constitutions marked a steady expansion of political liberalism (Madsen, Chapter 4, Section 2, this volume). The one exception is the Constitution of 1866, which was part of the conservative backlash to the military defeat that led to Denmark's loss of the German-speaking Duchies of Schleswig and Holstein in 1864. Although significant, this setback was overcome in a series of basic laws that transformed the Danish constitution over the next half-century (Madsen, Chapter 4, Section 2).

Together the authors identify five potential factors that limited role of those trained in Nordic law in the evolution of the region's constitutional politics until the early 1970s. First, as we have seen, the bar remained tiny and unorganized until the late nineteenth century. Second, well into the twentieth century, most if not all of the judiciary in the Nordic countries was integrated into the civil service, and sometimes functionally divided and located within individual ministries rather than established as a separate branch of government. In cases involving public law, until 1903, ministry staff not independent judges handled administrative appeals, and the right of the king to chair the Supreme Court (see e.g. Schaffer, Chapter 3, Section 3.1, this volume). Third, the Estates were robust and relatively egalitarian in the eighteenth and early nineteenth centuries. Unlike their counterparts in much of Europe, they included land owning, literate, and often wealthy peasants who could clearly articulate their views even if lawyers dominated drafting. In addition, the powerful but nonhierarchical Lutheran Church promoted literacy, individual responsibility, and local self-governance in ways that encouraged widespread civic participation. Fourth, some of the early seemingly liberal constitutional movements in, for example, Finland, Iceland, and partly Norway, were animated more by nationalist sentiments than strong commitments to liberalism and limited government. Finally, as several authors in this volume point out, (see e.g., Madsen, Chapter 4, Section 3), there is a long, widespread, and continuing history of relying on informal processes and publically appointed ombudsman to resolve disputes between citizens and public bureaucracies, which has impeded the development of "rights talk," lawyers, legalism, and constitutionalism in the Nordic countries, even during the height of the rights revolution.

4.3 The Welfare State: Establishment and Dark Side

The Nordic welfare states are often described as distinctive among Western European countries and indeed the world with respect to both the rapidity with which they were constructed and their expansive scope (Esping-Andersen 1999). This dramatic transformation occurred first in Sweden, Denmark, and Norway, and later in Iceland and Finland. As farms consolidated and industrial plants opened, populations shifted from the countryside and villages to the larger towns and cities, and vast numbers emigrated to North America. Everywhere, there was significant upheaval as traditional ways of life gave way to new forms. The church as a social institution and a partly liberal political force, while strong well into the twentieth century, nevertheless began to lose its distinctive authority around the middle of the nineteenth century. Still, its commitment to communal welfare and a measure of individual autonomy remained strong and was reinforced by traditional associations of farmers and workers that morphed into powerful labor unions and political parties with still greater collective muscle (Seip 2002) and women's organizations that merged their growing economic power with political clout (Larsen 2013). Entrenched interests—the old nobility in Sweden, the elite in Norway—facilitated the initial economic and political reforms but did not bow out with grace; at times they were pushed through mass demonstrations, strikes, rising social movements, vigorous actions by political parties, and electoral politics. Yet, with the monumental exception of the Finnish civil war, there was no protracted violence, or upheaval that deeply rent the fabric of these societies.

Parliamentary power increased as industrialization, mechanization, and the economy expanded, and shifting coalitions of social liberals, labor parties, and farmers' parties expanded social services and economic regulations, pensions, unemployment insurance, disability insurance, free education, national health care, welfare benefits, and regulations governing working conditions. At the outset, the Nordic countries played catch-up with England and Germany, but by the 1930s, all of them but Finland had exceeded these countries and led the world in providing social welfare benefits (Esping-Andersen 1999). After World War II, expansion of the welfare state resumed. Finland, hobbled by the protracted effects of its civil war and the ensuing Cold War, nevertheless advanced rapidly. By the 1960s, its social welfare system was as comprehensive as any of the other Nordic states. In varying degrees of detail, all the case studies in this volume recount such developments, with Finland and Iceland lagging at the outset, but then catching up.

All the case studies reveal that lawyers and at times judges contributed to the construction of the welfare state. They were active in parliaments, the ministries, the civil service, government commissions, social service agencies, political parties, the electoral arena, labor unions, churches, and other civil society institutions. However, in their different accounts, the authors of the case studies *all* emphasize that lawyers rarely coalesced into a legal complex to advance these interests and to articulate them as "rights" in contrast to policies.

This is not to say that there were no bitterly fought claims over "rights." The welfare state embraces resource and income redistribution. Established interests fought vigorously to protect their prerogatives, and especially over legislation involving regulation of working conditions, imposition of higher taxes, expanded expropriation powers, and intrusive regulations. Similarly established interests resisted proposals to expand the franchise and liberalize representation. These claims were voiced eloquently and often by representatives of "vested interests," including lawyers, parliamentarians, and some segments of the press. But there is no indication in any of the case studies that the organized bar or some segment of it mobilized to support—or oppose—such rights claims. Nor did the civil service-anchored judiciary stand as a bulwark against such actions; it bent to the will of the parliament. The battles over property rights were widely aired in the press, but were conducted almost exclusively by political parties in the electoral process, in parliament, and at times in the streets. Members of the legal community were active engaged in these battles, but not in their capacity as lawyers.

Only occasionally did contestation of property rights emerge in the courts. In the early 1900s, a major case arose in Norway concerning an expropriation of a hydro operation (Langford, Chapter X, Section 4, this volume). Fearing that it might fall into the hands of a foreign owner, Parliament adopted a law expropriating the power plant. Opponents, including many lawyers across the country, denounced the law, and organized to challenge its constitutionality in the courts. The matter ended eight years later, when a narrow majority of justices on the Supreme Court (thanks to court-packing in the interim) held that the law did not amount to expropriation, and thus did not violate the constitution. This decision set the stage for more than a half-century of deferential judicial review of legislation.

Similarly, in a celebrated case in Denmark in the early twentieth century (Madsen, Chapter 4, Section 2, this volume), landowners turned to the courts in an effort to preserve their prerogatives after losing a bitter battle in parliament. They lost. Madsen portrays this as the proverbial straw that broke the camel's back; after this, Danish courts never again tried to constrain the parliament. Parliamentary supremacy was triumphant, and the freight train carrying the welfare state rolled on, unimpeded by objections about property rights.

Elsewhere, courts were almost absent from the contest over the new social transformation, and did not invoke judicial review to try to limit parliaments. Helgadóttir (Chapter 8, Section 3.3, this volume) does report that in 1943 the Iceland's Supreme Court overturned a conviction because the law was invalid, but notes that lower courts had been doing this for years without fuss. And, as Langford reports, in the early nineteenth century the Norwegian high court exercised judicial review in some rulings, but did not use this power vigorously.

The failure of judicial review to take root no doubt reflects a deferential judicial tradition, but it was strengthened by the Scandinavian legal realism, an influential academic theory that advocated judicial deference to parliament (Schaffer, Chapter 3, Section 2.4,and 3.3, this volume). Just to be sure, parliaments in Norway, Sweden, and Denmark occasionally sent shots across the bow of the courts. In Norway, leftist parties in parliament sought multiple times to obtain a constitutional majority in order to remove the power of judicial review from the constitution (Kierulf 2018), and at one time to assure the outcome of a high profile case, it packed the Supreme Court (Langford, Chapter X, Section 4, this volume). In Denmark, landowners turned to the conservative courts to challenge their loss of property rights, but the courts upheld parliamentary power (Madsen, Chapter 4, Section 2, this volume). In Sweden in 1979, after an election that saw the Social Democrats lose power after nearly half a century in office, Parliament took the opportunity to institutionalize an even more limited role for the Supreme Court (Schaffer, Chapter 3, Section 4, this volume).

While the authors of the case studies give varying attention to the rise of the welfare state, and to the role of lawyers and judges in the process, their accounts are remarkably similar. Unlike courts in England and the United States in the late nineteenth and early twentieth centuries, Nordic courts were not major battlegrounds in the war between the old guard and the new order. The judges were so deferential to parliaments that appeals to the courts were rarely even considered. To be sure, battles were fierce and protracted. But they occurred in the press, in the streets, in the union halls, in political parties, and in parliaments, where lawyers were active on all sides. Not even the strongest of rights—property rights—gained a foothold against parliament-authorized appropriations.

Indeed, the role of lawyers in statecraft appeared to decline during the rise of the welfare state in first half of the twentieth century. The nineteenth century was the age of lawyer-civil servants, who constructed and then operated the Rechtsstaat. The rise of the welfare state was the age of expert-civil servants, who sought to design, build, and administer policies advanced by powerful unions, strong political parties, and robust parliamentary majorities. Lawyers in the civil service were replaced by economists, psychologists, social workers, engineers, public administrators, and the like. Indeed, Langford shows that the long-term proportional growth in the numbers of law students in Norway in the nineteenth century was reversed in the twentieth, as faculties in engineering and the social sciences rapidly expanded (Langford, Chapter X, Section 4, this volume). They, not lawyers, were the architects and administrators of the welfare state. What Langford reveals for Norway holds for the other Nordic states as well. Of course, as all the authors note, lawyers did not disappear in the civil service or in society. But they came to occupy a less influential role in the civil service of the welfare state.

In this new state, parliaments authorized policies, but increasingly those policies were designed by social workers, psychologists, health care specialists, economists, educators, and public administrators. The new programs were framed in terms of social services, not individual rights, and neither the courts nor the legal profession were called upon in any deep sense to assure the nature or the administration of them, other than perhaps drafting regulations governing their administration.

Even when anticipating that disputes that would inevitably flow from the new social policies, planners by-passed legal redress, and imported the Swedish ombudsman model (Denmark in 1955, Norway in 1965), in which individual complaints were handled ombudsman's offices, not administrative hearing officers or judges, without lawyers' involvement. With this combination of responsible democratic government, mostly benign policies, and competent and attentive experts, Nordic welfare states thrived.

Still, as the authors of the case studies report, the Nordic "paradise" had its dark side. Beginning in the 1920s, the Nordic states, as did many other countries, enthusiastically embraced policies based on eugenics. Medical professionals and social welfare agencies imposed policies of forced or semi-forced sterilization, the use of abortion for social policy ends, and the removal of children from their homes for adoption elsewhere. Educators relied heavily on psychometric tests to track young people into occupational paths; psychiatrists ordered aggressive treatment for mental disorders, including shock treatment and widespread use of involuntary confinement to mental institution; and in Sweden, Norway, and Sweden, Sami were treated effectively as children in need of state supervision (Schaffer, Chapter 3, Section 3.4, this volume).

Viewed as socially progressive on both sides of the Atlantic through the 1930s, these policies were seen in a new light following World War II (Whitman 2017). However, revelations about Nazi practices did not bring eugenics-based policies to a halt; they led less visibility. Well into the 1970s, Schaffer (Section 3.4, this volume) reports, there were uncomfortable discussions about eugenics practices, but no fundamental changes in policy. More restrictive regulations were imposed, but they depended on self-enforcement within the social service agencies themselves. Experts and institutions engaged in eugenics did not abandon their policies; they only lowered their profiles.

The post-war period also saw the rise of other abuses. Vast discretion granted to government experts in the name of security permitted widespread surveillance of "enemies," both foreign and domestic. As the Cold War hardened, wiretapping and surveillance expanded proportionately. Vast numbers of communists and suspected communists were carefully monitored and found their lives interrupted. Such practices were expanded from enemies of the state to enemies of the Party. The SDP in Sweden lost its high ground and much popular support due to revelations about its aggressive and widespread use of surveillance for partisan gain. In Norway, a group of lawyers organized to defend a left-leaning newspaper that published evidence of such surveillance in 1977, but remarkably were outgunned by another group of lawyers ten times its size that supported the state's action prosecuting journalists, a rare instance of a clear legal complex for political illiberalism.

With the rise of rights consciousness in the 1970s that all the chapters (save Graver's, which does not cover the period) have reported, changed the way these and other assaults on dignity have been addressed by lawyers' organizations, parliaments, and the courts since the 1970s. Since then, the dark sides of the welfare and security state have been challenged not simply as bad professional judgments, but violations of basic human rights. (These developments are explored in Section 6, below.)

4.4 Freedom of Expression and Association

In transitional economies, one of the fiercest battles involves the struggle of labor to organize and be recognized as a stakeholder in the political process. Invariably this struggle involves massive numbers of people in protracted and at times violent conflict. Differences over the role of labor was one of the precipitating causes of the bloody civil war in Finland in the early twentieth century, and led to protracted and at times violent struggles elsewhere. Eventually, labor prevailed throughout the Nordic region. The several case studies recount these struggles, but reveal no evidence that lawyers or some segment of them mobilized either by themselves or in coalition with other civil society institutions to stand with or even defend labor's right to organize. Nor is there any evidence that judges or even some tiny portion of them took a stance for freedom of expression that would have facilitated these activities. Individual lawyers, for instance, were active in both supporting and opposing the rights of organized labor, but freedom of association was not a distinct lawyer's cause. Langford does however, mention one isolated lawyer in Norway in the 1850s, who defended labor against a particularly repressive government, but his action was one-off and did not lead to a rights-conscious movement.

The case studies show that although Nordic societies have traditions of tolerance and somewhat egalitarian traditions fostered by the church and broad-based political participation, there were clear limits. The Nordic countries are almost uniformly Lutheran, which well into the twentieth century was the established state church. Tolerance often ended at the church door. Langford notes that Jews were banned from Norway in 1647, a policy that was reaffirmed in the 1814 Norwegian Constitution, and formally remained intact until 1851. Moreover, while Jews and also Catholics (except Jesuits), Baptists, and other non-Lutheran denominations were permitted to dwell in Norway, they were prevented from constructing houses of worship or obtaining tax support (Langford, Chapter X, Section 3.1, this volume). Such restrictions remained in force well into the twentieth century; it was not until 1951 that the Swedish parliament changed the law to allow citizens the option of leaving the Church of Sweden without simultaneously designating themselves a member of another faith. That same law allowed, for the first time, Catholics to build and operate monasteries. Schaffer emphasizes that these changes came about after a forty-year debate in parliament, and without any involvement by the organized bar or challenges in court. Indeed, he points out that the change was forced upon the Parliament in light of Sweden's ratification of the European Convention on Human Rights in 1950, which outlawed such restrictions (Schaffer, Chapter 3, Section 3.5, this volume). The same pressure forced Norway to change its discriminatory practices. As a condition for joining the European Convention on Human Rights, rescinded a provision in its 1814 constitution that prohibited entry of Jesuits into the kingdom. Thus, pressure for rights was important in expanding freedom of religion in the Nordic states, but these rights were imposed externally, as a by-product of joining in international treaties.

In theory, the press throughout the Nordic region has a long history of legal protection. The Swedish Press Acts of 1809 and 1815, guaranteed freedom of the press, but they did not specify the scope of this freedom, and in fact provided broad language allowing for confiscation of sensitive materials for a great variety of reasons. Lawyers did not mobilize to challenge these restrictions when they were invoked during World War II, nor did courts attempt to limit them. However, the post-war Press Freedom Act of 1949 did strengthen and constitutionalize press freedom in Sweden (Schaffer, Chapter 3, Section 3.5, this volume). In the late eighteenth and early nineteenth centuries, Denmark swung wildly between radical and conservative laws on freedom of expression, which partly prompted Norway to seek a more liberal dispensation in its 1814 constitution. It incorporated elements of the Swedish 1809 instrument as well as the First Amendment to the American Constitution. During the course of the nineteenth century, freedom of expression and increasingly freedom of association in Norway were guaranteed. But, as in Sweden, they were qualified by broad catch-all exceptions, or at times simply ignored by officials. In the mid-nineteenth century emerging workers' movements were prosecuted for treason without consideration of freedom of expression, and the more progressive arts and literature were treated with suspicion and sometimes prosecuted—e.g., the Norwegian censorship of the 1885 novel of *Fra Kristiania-Bohêmen* of Hans Jæger, which included prostitution and suicide. There is no indication that lawyers—with some exceptions—mobilized to defend freedom of expression.

Several contributors to this volume address still other shifts in the scope of the press restrictions during the nineteenth century. Konttinen describes parliament imposing new restrictions on the press as clamor for greater Finnish autonomy increased following Russia's defeat by Japan in 1905. Madsen describes increased restrictions in Denmark during the Red Scares both before and following World War II. While legal challenges were mounted against some of these restrictions, none of the authors identifies any concerted efforts by groups of lawyers to defend free expression—with the exception of one Danish lawyer.

Restrictions on expression worsened significantly during World War II. In Norway, the Quisling Government deported Jews to the death camps, limited freedom of movement, and curbed the press (Graver, Chapter 6, Section 2, this volume). In Occupied Denmark, there were significant restrictions on free expression (Madsen, Chapter 4, Section 4.1, this volume; Graver, Chapter 6, Section, 4, this volume). In Sweden during the run-up to World War II and throughout the war, Swedish authorities imposed restrictions on the press and confiscated publications in order to prevent "misunderstandings with a foreign [German] power" (Schaffer, Chapter 3, Section 3.5, this volume). Here too, the authors of the case studies note that lawyers only occasionally challenged such restrictions. But their actions were usually limited to a single lawyer mounting a traditional defense in a single case, involving for instance, a prominent publisher. Occasionally individual lawyers took on a cause. Madsen identifies a few lawyers who mounted vigorous defenses on behalf of accused communists during the Red Scare of the 1920s and 1930s, and again after the war, but the effort did not turn into a cause or lead to the mobilization of a segment of the bar. Langford identifies a well-known conservative lawyer in Norway in the 1850s who, angered at the preemptory practices of the police, mounted a vigorous and sustained defense of labor unions to organize. At times, these actions garnered support from other groups in civil society, but none of them appears to have led to the mobilization of coalitions of lawyers or civil society groups on a sustained basis. They remained isolated if not lonely efforts.

Schaffer also reports that during the Cold War, the Swedish Government made frequent use of wire taps and other invasive violations of privacy in order to maintain a massive system of domestic surveillance of leftists and other suspect groups, practices that continued well into the 1970s (Schaffer, Chapter 3, Section 4, this volume). Despite repeated revelations and scandals, lawyers did not form a legal complex to challenge these practices. What battles there were, were framed in terms of "policies" and not "rights," and took place in parliament, which for a long period was dominated by the Social Democrats, the party responsible for the wrongdoings. It was not until scandals within the SDP itself and the upheavals of the rights revolution of the 1970s that organized legal redress was pursed, and such practices were curbed.

The authors of the all the case studies maintain that up until the 1970s, no legal complexes emerged to challenge illiberal practices. Occasionally, and it appears somewhat more frequently in Norway, iconoclastic lawyers took on individual cases and battled in the courts, but the bar did not rally around them and their efforts did not lead to expansive new legal doctrines. Freedom of expression was slowly expanded over the course of the nineteenth and twentieth centuries, but it rarely was a result of lawyers mobilizing, successful litigation, or judges handing down landmark rulings. Rather, change was achieved in discussions in the ministries and debates in the media and in parliaments, where as often as not lawyers were found on all sides of the issues. What Schaffer explains for Sweden applies to the other Nordic states as well: " Even as they had as their primary occupation law professor or judge, some of these elite jurists also occupied political offices as parliamentarians and ministers of government and served on government commissions. The legal sphere seems to have been characterized by close, overlapping personal networks." (Schaffer, Chapter 3, Section 3.3, this volume).

In reflecting on lawyers' seeming lack of concern with basic civil and political rights, several of the authors in this volume suggest an insight that lies just below the surface. Mikael Madsen makes it explicit. For the first two thirds of the twentieth century, normal public life was focused on securing social services, not promoting individual rights. Liberal social democrats pressed for expanding the power of organized labor, taming the market, and increasing health care, education, housing, employment, insurance, and the like, while conservatives mounted a rearguard action. The pursuit of collectivist objectives led left-liberals, in the words of one lawyer quoted by Mikael Madsen, to eschew "bourgeois rights." As we saw above, the one partial exception dealt with property rights. Powerful conservative forces in some Nordic states tried to protect their interests in the courts, but at the outset, they lost decisively. Social welfare took precedence over individual rights, although as part of the broader Nordic political grand bargain in which capitalism and private ownership still maintained a significant, if not dominant, place in the economy.

It was not until the 1970s that a robust jurisprudence of rights accompanied by efforts of various legal complexes, emerged in Nordic countries. In addition, this new development was partly imposed from the outside by the new post-war treaties, after the work of the European Court of Human Rights and the European Court of Justice began in earnest. Suddenly, the Nordic countries were subject to the robust judicial review of international courts. In contrast to domestic Nordic courts, these new international courts developed a strong jurisprudence of rights. Since their rulings trumped domestic law and court rulings, the Nordic countries were forced to confront a new regime of rights affecting a wide range of issues well beyond freedom of expression. This development is examined in Section 6, below.

5. War

War formed the backdrop of many of the momentous events recounted in the case studies. Sweden's decisive step towards parliamentary government and liberalism followed on the heels of its defeat by Russia in 1804. Norway's transfer from Denmark to Sweden, and Finland's transfer from Sweden to Russia were the direct result of the same war. Finland's independence one hundred years later was a consequence of the Japanese-Russian war and the chaos of the Russian Revolution. Iceland's declaration of full independence took place in the midst of World War II. The rights revolution of the 1960s was initiated in part by the reaction to illiberal policies occasioned by the Cold War, and a reaction to the war in Vietnam. Salient issues arising from some of these momentous events were examined in Section 1, and still more were addressed in the sections immediately above.

However, three case studies focus directly on war and its immediate aftermath. Hans Petter Graver's account of the judiciary following the Nazi coup is Norway. Mikael Madsen's study examines the response of Danish lawyers and judges to the treatment of suspected collaborators and others deemed enemies of the state in the immediate aftermath of World War II; while Ranghildur Helgadóttir examines the Allies' occupation.

Graver's study recounts how following the coup Norwegian judges agreed on a strategy to counter the Quisling regime. Trial court judges would remain in office and continue to perform their duties as best they could, since their work involved ordinary civil and criminal matters not implicated in political activities, and they could work largely unimpeded by the policies of the new regime. In contrast, justices on the Supreme Court recognized that much of their work would involve issues involving the legitimacy of the Quisling regime and the German war effort. Accordingly, they resigned en masse and joined the resistance in order to signal the illegitimacy of the regime.

Throughout the war, trial court judges and especially the new Quisling appointees to the Supreme Court were under pressure to bend to the will of the Nazis. At times they did so, but when they could, they relied on formalism and proceduralism to resist or at least slow down processes. Graver notes that even the Nazi-appointed justices and other judges who had joined the Norwegian Nazi party relied on these techniques in order to try to obtain some modicum of community respect. Juridical resistance was also reinforced by periodic declarations by the Association of Judges and the Bar Association underscoring the importance of judicial independence, and condemning extra-legal efforts to Nazify Norwegian institutions (Graver, Chapter 6, Section 3.4, this volume). Judges in Norway were successful to some extent because the German "visitors" established their own limited judicial system that handled the more serious political cases, and because the Norwegian judiciary had established a special court, "the People's Court" in Oslo, to consolidate political cases from around the country. This later action shielded most judges from Nazi pressures. Furthermore, the Germans were loath to use these special tribunals because they lacked legitimacy among Norwegians (Graver, Chapter 6, Section 3.4. this volume).

In contrast to Norway, Denmark was occupied. There was no coup, and Danish governmental institutions were left intact. The collective stance of the Danish Government was to accommodate German interests in virtually all areas of public administration, except for turning over Danish Jews for deportation (Graver, Chapter 6, Sections 1.4, this volume). This policy led the Danish parliament to enact a great many new laws addressing German concerns about anti-German activities, and imposing limits on the freedom of expression, the power of lay juries, and other laws strengthening prosecutorial powers and weakening the role of defense counsel (Madsen, Chapter 4, Section 4.1, this volume; Graver, Chapter 6, Section 4, this volume). In contrast to Norway, Danish judges vigorously enforced the draconian new measures. Indeed, both Graver and Madsen report that Danish officials, including courts, often worked in concert with German occupiers, at times enthusiastically, to round up and imprison members of the Danish Communist Party, and to impose harsh sentences on offenders convicted of politically sensitive offenses (Graver, Chapter 6, Section 4, this volume; Madsen, Chapter 4, Section 4.1, this volume). At times, the President of the Supreme Court seemed eager to please the occupiers by volunteering to draft harsh new legislation and then, in subsequent cases, interpreting it expansively.

Graver acknowledges that it is impossible to carefully compare the two judicial systems that were operating under such different forms of stress. Nevertheless, he shows that collective resistance of the Norwegian judiciary had considerable effect. Ironically, the Nazi coups followed by judicial resistance empowered the courts. In contrast, by keeping the law and law making in their own hands, Danish officials ended up cooperating more with the Germans, though Graver acknowledges the occasional successes in moderating the harshness of German demands. Proportionately, Norwegian courts handled fewer political cases, convicted fewer people of anti-regime activities, and sentenced those convicted less severely (Graver, Chapter 6, Section 4, this volume).

In his comparison with Denmark, Graver also emphasizes the significance of the Norwegian judges' association and the national bar association. These organizations regularly registered objections to the regime's legal actions, reaffirmed the principle of the rule of law, and at times successfully resisted government efforts to Nazify the Norwegian judiciary and bar. In contrast, Danish judges were compliant. They registered only one formal complaint during the entire period of occupation—when a Jewish colleague was removed from office, deported to Theresienstadt and later murdered. After the war judges in Norway emerged virtually unscathed and with their integrity and reputations intact. In contrast, judges in post-war Denmark received a mixed reaction. Some were subsequently removed from office, and many more lived under a continuing cloud of suspicion (Graver, Chapter 6, Section 4, this volume).

Madsen's account of the Danish courts during and after the war extends Graver's analysis. He notes that during the war Danish officials enthusiastically rounded up Communists at the request of the German occupiers, seeing it as an extension of Denmark's prewar anti-Communist policy (Madsen, Chapter 4, Section 4.1, this volume). He informs us that this policy was even intensified after the war, and remained in place throughout the 1950s. Furthermore, he continues, there is no indication—before, during, or after the war—that a legal complex mobilized to defend members of the Communist party or others suspected of membership in the name of freedom of expression and association. In his account of post-war developments, he identifies at most only lawyers acting on their own, who vigorously but largely unsuccessfully defended such people in court (Madsen, Chapter 4, Section 4.1, this volume). To Madsen, this singular effort underscores just how complicit Danish authorities and the Danish bar were in failing to protect basic rights during the war.

In a brief discussion of Icelandic policies during the war, Helgadóttir recounts the British invasion of Iceland in 1940. The British subsequently jailed some socialist members of parliament, limited speech and press, and confiscated opposition publications. The parliament vigorously protested these policies, and in particular the jailing of members of parliament. The British also announced that the 1941 elections would be postponed, a decision that was vigorously debated among Icelanders themselves, but in the end most agreed that postponement was a good idea. Here too, she finds no evidence that lawyers mobilized to resist any of these decisions (Helgadóttir, Chapter 8, Section 3.2, this volume).

6. The Rights Revolution: Access to Justice and International Human Rights

All the authors emphasize that the worldwide rights revolution eventually arrived in the Nordic region.[14] Observers have identified a vast variety of factors that account for this development: A reaction to Cold War conservatism, decolonization, reaction to modernity, opposition to American involvement in Vietnam, increased expectations of the "have nots," a belated appreciation of liberal legalism in the face of the failures of communism, the American Civil Right Movement, the abuses of socialism, the rise of youth culture, and the globalization of human rights in ways that had widespread reach and appeal (Kennedy 2006: see also Moyn 2010). Whatever the causes, there is no doubt that worldwide legal and political systems were thrown into turmoil in the 1960s by a relatively sudden and intense demand for rights and access to justice. What occurred in the streets was paralleled by developments in the language of legal liberalism. Politicians, lawyers, and judges in a great many countries mobilized around liberal legal values, to generate new sources of authority and to challenge long-standing state practices (Kennedy 2006: 59–61). Newly enfranchised citizens demanded more justice and more access to justice. New constitutions and international agreements reinforced these demands; they contained enumerated rights and embraced the power of judicial review, which gave lawyers and courts vast new powers.

In the United States and England, the rights revolution certainly had a major impact on the legal landscape, but in many respects, it was a process with a long trajectory since both countries had long histories of rights consciousness and activist

[14] For individual country accounts of developments in legal services for the poor in the Nordic countries since the 1970s, see Ronning and Hammerslev (2018).

lawyers and courts. In Europe, the post-fascist constitutions of Germany, Italy, and Austria, the post-occupation constitutions of the Netherlands and Belgium and the later post-authoritarian constitutions of Portugal, Greece, and Spain provided bills of rights, but active judicial enforcement only emerged initially in some of these states (particularly Germany and Italy and later Portugal).

In Europe, the groundwork for much of this was laid in 1949 with the founding of the Council of Europe and in 1952 with the creation of the European Coal and Steel Community, which eventually grew into the European Union, and the establishment of their respective courts, ECtHR (1953) and the ECJ (1952) (Scheingold 2013). Schaffer (Chapter 3, Section 5.2, this volume) reports the first impact of these international agreements in Sweden occurred in 1951. The impact reverberated through all the other Nordic countries as well. All the authors in this volume emphasize that these international agreements were slow in taking root, but once they did they had enormous impact on law and politics in all the Nordic states, and in so doing radically transformed the legal profession and the courts show the significant explosion in the application of human rights law occurred in the 1980s.

The international agreements embraced by Nordic governments in the 1950s, and their progeny, obligated unwitting signatories to align domestic law to international law. This provided new and unanticipated opportunities to challenge the political consensus, and energized a new generation of lawyers who not only found a new set of professional activities and sources of income, but also a new set of courts willing to rethink and overturn long-standing domestic policies and practices in favor of newly articulated international norms. In turn, this inspired domestic lawyers and judges to innovate on their own, and not wait for international court rulings to challenge and dispose of domestic laws out of sync with emerging international norms.

Spurred on by these developments, constitutional jurisprudence, which had always had a dull edge and deferential quality in the Nordic countries, was sharpened to a degree, and used successfully to challenge a wide variety of long-standing practices of the welfare state, and a host of new issues raised by European integration. Madsen's chapter (Chapter 4, Section 5, this volume) on Denmark is particularly evocative of the ethos of the early days of the rights revolution in the Nordic region, that began first in Denmark—youth questioning of the project of modernity, exposes of widespread surveillance of Communists and domestic political opponents, experiments with alternative lifestyles, penetration into the darker corners of the welfare state, the quest for access to justice for hitherto unnoticed inequalities, recognition of long-standing discrimination against indigenous minorities (Roma and Travelers), as well as an expanding number of immigrants and guest workers. Madsen reports that in the late 1960s the quest for access to justice took off, first in Denmark, but then quickly spread across the Nordic region. The other case studies describe this sudden development and explore its many implications. Duncan

Kennedy notes its appeal: "The dominant critique was civil libertarian, and permitted a de facto of alliance of left and right" (Kennedy 2006: 59).

This revolution, or at least reformulation, led to young people in Denmark and later elsewhere in the Nordic region to flock to law schools. Legal collectives, law school clinics, and public interest law firms were established in the wake of the 1968 protests and movements. Young rights-oriented lawyers led social movements, established new publications, and pressed for change in law school curricula. Soon enough they were joined by younger reform-oriented law faculties, who established legal clinics for the poor and guest workers, and challenged a variety of vestigates of privileges. Soon thereafter judges joined were swayed by the momentum (see Madsen; Schaffer; Langford, this volume; Rønning and Hamersley 2018). Ultimately, both local and national governments supported public interest law to provide enhanced access to justice. Rights discourse began to compete with the language of social planning. Langford (Chapter X, Section 5.2, this volume) reports that in 1979, the long dormant "right to property" was resuscitated and successfully asserted politically to stave off plans for construction of a hydroelectric power plant on Sami land. Schaffer describes victories by Swedish human rights lawyers who successfully challenged long-standing practices dealing with forced sterilization, civil commitments, removal of children from their families, and widespread wiretapping and surveillance. He also notes successful court cases requiring further separation of the prosecutorial and judicial functions, as well as successful challenges of government surveillance policies, and governmental violations of privacy (Schaffer, Chapter 3, Section 5, this volume). Other authors identify point to successes in challenging restrictions on Roma and growing numbers of guest workers and immigrants. In any number of ways, the language of liberal legalism began to challenge the conventions of social planners.

As noted above, the fulcrum on which this shift turned was international courts in applying international law to the Nordic governments. New treaties and new international courts all but invited lawyers to become activists. International human rights law allowed long-standing taken-for-granted practices in the welfare state to be seen in a new, less-than-flattering light. And international law provided a means by which to challenge them. As Langford (Chapter 9, Section 3.2, this volume) argues in the concluding reflection of this volume, there was a double movement: as a political opportunity structure closed (partly through SDP dominance, but also because of the backlash to the human rights amongst some sections of conservative parties and emerging populist parties), and a legal opportunity structure opened. Lawyers were quick to seize upon the opportunity to serve new clients (including many businesses, it should be said), and were empowered by the rulings of international courts and international law that overturned long-standing domestic policies. People who lacked sufficient political support and had long suffered grievances and indignities in silence, now suddenly had new hope and new opportunities. The process fed on itself, as domestic courts joined in the process, often not waiting for the international courts to rule before they exercised their own judicial review.

Four lasting (or at least long-term) developments for the Nordic states: Parliamentary supremacy was reconsidered and limited in light of judicial review imposed by international law. Social services were re-examined through the lens of individual rights, and abuses and paternalistic practices curbed. The criminal process was subjected to heightened concerns of due process and separation of powers between prosecutor and judge. Property rights emerged as a protection against a powerful state. And as if to safeguard these developments, at least since the 2010s, all the Nordic states rank at the top eleven countries in per capita expenditures for legal services for the poor (Johnsen 2018: 252).

None of this led to the collapse of strong parliamentary government or a major retreat from the welfare state. But it did lead to a recalibration of the social contract. Officials now act with greater sensitivity to more concerns, a great many policies were rethought and curtailed or abandoned, some of those who had fallen through the welfare net are now included. Social service programs are now filtered through a lens of individual autonomy and rights. Lawyers and courts are a more important player now in shaping public policy.

These lawyers asserting these claims are certainly not the equivalents of Enlightenment figures fighting for the rights of man against autocracies. Indeed, they operate in societies with long traditions of egalitarian and democratic institutions. Nevertheless, their actions challenge cracks in the foundation of the welfare states in ways that redefine citizen-state relations. Much of the rights work of this new cadre of lawyers is "negative," in that it seeks to prohibit or restrict the scope of government action by protecting individual civil rights and liberties. This constitutes a major transformation in Nordic societies, whose sustaining ideology has been social solidarity and expansive social policies, both provided by the state. Many fear that the new rights orientation will undermine the social democratic tradition on which the welfare state was erected, foster atomized individualism, and heighten inequalities.

What began in Denmark in the 1960s as an effort by a cadre of young lawyers (Madsen, Chapter 4, Section 4,2, this volume), had within thirty years spread throughout the Nordic region. It has been transformational, generating social movements that involve high-end international lawyers practicing in Europe's most highly regarded international courts, and solo practitioners serving the needs in marginalized communities. As of this writing, expansive constitutionalism, with its commitment to limited government, enumerated rights, and judicial review is now firmly ensconced in all the Nordic states in ways unimaginable in the 1960s.

The Nordic states are small, and change can often be identified in terms of the actions of a few individuals, or at times even a single crucial individual. However, deeper political changes are anchored in historical currents, and the authors have identified some of them. In Finland, for instance, the collapse of the Soviet

Union created a climate for a more robust and critical liberal activism (Konttinen, Chapter 7, Section 10, this volume). In Sweden, a series of revelations and scandals undermined support for the long-ruling SDP, and paved the way for rights-oriented parties and politics (Schaffer, Chapter 3, Section 4, this volume). In Norway, the movement expanded longstanding interest with constitutional developments in England and the United States. These actions in the 1970s prepared a large cadre of lawyers to "jump on the human rights band-wagon when it started gaining more momentum" in Denmark and elsewhere (Madsen, Chapter 4, Section 5.3, this volume). In his summary of developments in Sweden between 1970 and 2020, Schaffer calls the Nordic states the "final frontier" for judicial review. He writes, "[In the late 2010s] ... all key elements of constitutionalism—a written constitutional document, rule of law, fundamental rights, acknowledging international conventions, and so on—now exist within the five Nordic states" (Schaffer, Chapter 3, Section 5, this volume). He emphasizes that the judiciary has embraced this newfound power with enthusiasm, and that it has helped establish a number of civil rights groups that operate outside the normal corporatist arrangements, which take individual rights claims directly to the courts rather than first working through the administrative process

The Nordic countries now have increasingly what Charles Epp (1998) calls "civil society support structures" for liberal lawyers—links to other groups in civil society—university-based lawyers, activist groups, and emerging legal aid clinics and national human rights institutions.

Such developments have encountered resistance. A significant group of politicians and intellectuals across the political spectrum have decried the loss of parliamentary sovereignty. Social democrats in many Nordic countries continue to resist the expanded regime of rights, and fear that it will foster atomized individualism, undermine the quest for a cohesive social democracy, and frustrate parliamentary-based reform—although the newer liberal leftist parties tend to be more embracing of robust political liberalism. Parties on the right, have welcomed the increased protections for property rights, but do not express the same enthusiasm for human rights claims—with the new populist parties hostile to some aspects of the rule of law. Law and politics in the entire Nordic region have been significantly transformed. Many, for different reasons, worry about globalization and its impact on the Nordic states.

Still, there is considerable variation in the Nordic states in their responses to the globalization of human rights, and the expansion of political liberalism. Norway and Sweden embraced the project with enthusiasm. Finland and Iceland, after a delayed entry, eventually jumped in with enthusiasm. Although the Nordic rights revolution started in Denmark, its development there has been more muted. As Madsen reports, Denmark has acceded to a moderate form of political liberalism, an expanded role for courts, and diminished parliamentary sovereignty. But, he emphasizes, it has little choice because so many changes have been imposed by international law and courts, and because the legal arena is the only one in which to raise some types of concern in a post-2001 counter-terrorism environment in which security concerns—such as international asylum security concerns—are paramount.

Even though lawyers and judges have been empowered, and human rights is now fully incorporated into Danish law, the development has taken a distinctive Nordic twist. It is distinguished less by dynamic courts and robust judicial review, than it is by a reinvigorated system of ombudsmen and more detailed, rights-sensitive legislation (Madsen, Chapter 4, Section 5.2, this volume). What holds for Demark is also the case elsewhere when one peers more closely behind the surface of the rights revolution. Much of the Nordic rights orientation occurs within the framework of strong corporatist governance. One difference is that insurgent groups—new groups of human rights lawyers—are now stakeholders with seats at the table. New issues may be introduced through lawyers' campaigns, rights' organizations, and judicial rulings, but once they gain traction, their supporters join other stakeholders—commissions established by the government, working groups established by parliament, and the like—where they advance their concerns from within rather than from without, through deliberation and negotiation, and only occasionally with litigation. While rights-based litigation has increased, it is a last, not a first, resort. Indeed, as Madsen notes, by the mid-2010s, many radical litigators of the 1970s and 1980s now hold senior positions in the government (Madsen, Chapter 4, Section 5.2, this volume), and administer the very organizations they used to challenge. His observation, though probably to a lesser degree, holds true for the other Nordic states as well.

7. Conclusion

Collectively, the studies in this volume provide an account of the development of the modern welfare state and its major institutions. They show that men trained in the law were everywhere in the nineteenth century, but that they were almost exclusively employed by the state, in the civil service and related positions, and their actions were defined by their roles in these positions. Indeed, until well into the twentieth century, there was no organized independent bar to speak of and, with only minor exceptions, it—nor any committees of subsets of its members—did not organize as a political force. This abruptly changed in the last third of the twentieth century.

This does not say that in the nineteenth century lawyers were unimportant in public life. As all the case studies emphasize that once legal education took off, law-trained university graduates were everywhere; they staffed the Rechtsstaat. They were the backbone of an effective and efficient civil service, and they exercised power elsewhere as parliamentarians, political activists, publishers, businesspersons, and the like. At times they did act, but they did not act as lawyers in concert or in the name of the law. Furthermore, as the authors of the case studies take pains to emphasize, lawyers were always found on all sides of issues. They occupied no distinct legal sphere, nor did any distinct group of them unite around any core set of principles, liberal or otherwise.

Some of the most momentous liberal developments in the Nordic region were imposed top down, brought about by autocrats, war, the transfer of sovereignty, and the Rechtsstaat. This latter development went some considerable distance toward providing rights and due process, two essential ingredients for the rule of law. But, it was not embraced after a struggle led by lawyers; it was imposed by autocrats who feared the revolutionary spirit unleashed by the French Revolution, and who also wanted to bolster their own authority through a powerful rational-legal bureaucracy. The Nordic Rechtsstaat was not initiated by lawyers, but it was staffed by law-trained civil servants, who used their skills and training to expand it. At one and the same time, it accorded subjects an important modicum of rights, while it also strengthened the state by creating a more efficient and effective bureaucracy. No doubt, one of the reasons that the Nordic countries were able to create such successful and complete welfare states in such short order was due to this pre-existing bureaucracy. So, in this sense, law-trained administrators played a crucial role in constructing the modern welfare state, but it was rights-lawyer-bureaucrats who sought to extend state power through rational-legal administration. This underlines that fact that "lawyers" are historical constructions whose roles and tasks can vary considerably across space and time—prohibiting simple comparisons.

Political development followed a generally liberal course owing to Nordic tradition and social structure (For addition work in this vein, see Ervo, Letto-Vanamo, and Nylund 2021). Class divisions were not as sharp in the Nordic region as in many places in Europe. Many peasants were literate, owned land, and possessed a modicum of wealth. The powerful Lutheran church helped foster individual autonomy, personal responsibility, literacy, and thrift and hard work. There were few great Estates, which depended on landless tenants. A rural and dispersed population led to local autonomy and relatively egalitarian institutions of governance. Representative democracy evolved as the Estates transformed themselves into parliaments and political parties. As workers emerged to displace traditional elites, transformation was gradual. Protracted struggles took place, but violence and class conflict was minimal compared to other regions in Europe. Disciplined political parties and well-functioning parliaments managed to contain most conflict to the confines of their chambers and the ballot box. In corporatist societies such as Sweden), distinct groups are organized and have some voice in public affairs. One consequence of this is that as industrialization expanded so to did organized labor. In turn organized labor sought its place at the table of government. Indeed, it is responsible for developing the modern political parties in Sweden and throughout the Nordic societies. Once the labor parties gained electoral and parliamentary majorities, they were able to harness the competence of the existing state bureaucracy to their purposes and construct a version of the workers state.

In all this, lawyers as a profession were on the sidelines. Dominant political parties and their allies had little use for bills or charters of rights, or for litigation. When occasional voices were heard advocating for individual rights, they were challenged for espousing "bourgeois rights," and met with the retort, "parliamentary sovereignty." This issue had been fought once over traditional protections of "property rights," and the dominant parties did not want to refight the battle. However, parliamentary majorities were responsive *enough* to liberal concerns and the value of political moderation that they were not seriously challenged until the latter part of the twentieth century.

The authors of the case studies acknowledge the momentous turn of events that erupted in the 1960s and the changes that have followed. None of them provides the definitive account of this development. They associate it with anti-war protests, a worldwide youth rebellion against materialism, and emerging globalism. Whatever the causes, it sparked a new-found sensitivity to concerns that had long been just below the surface of public debate, such as limits on the Sami, religious discrimination, lack of rights for the Roma and foreign residents, eugenics practices, concerns about widespread surveillance, and the like. These inchoate concerns gained institutional purchase with the expansion of international law, and the establishment of the ECJ[15] and the ECtHR.

Rather than resisting these incursions on national sovereignty, a critical mass of both lawyers and judges in the Nordic countries felt empowered, and in Mikael Madsen's phrase "jumped on the bandwagon of human rights," and embraced the new constitutional order with enthusiasm.[16]

It is not clear where this development will lead. However, it has jolted the historically conservative judiciary in the Nordic countries, and it has transformed the historically passive and unorganized bar. Now, both the Nordic bench and bar may be counted among the most well-organized advocates of liberal principles in Europe. At present, Legal Complexes in the Nordic region are aggressive and organized in fighting for political liberalism as they are in any country in the world. Still, the Nordic miracle, the development of the modern welfare states in the region, occurred prior to and without the active involvement of a cadre of political lawyers. Indeed, it remains unclear whether these developments were facilitated by their absence. Furthermore, as several of the authors in this volume have pointed out, the Nordic countries are somewhat removed from the rest of Europe, remain small and fairly homogeneous societies, and political changes can occur in short

[15] In the case of Norway and Iceland, it is the EFTA Court that monitors compliance with EU directives that these countries have accepted as part of their non-membership arrangement with the EU.

[16] For extended treatments of how the EU and international treaties have energized the law, the legal profession, and the courts, see the several chapters in Ervo, Letto-Vanamo, and Nyland (2021).

order as a result of the concerted efforts a handful of powerful institutions. This in part accounts for the radical transformation of law and legal discourse since the 1970s. But it may also account for a rapid and far-reaching redirection in the future.

References

Abel, Richard. 1988. *The Legal Profession in England and Wales*. Oxford: Blackwell.

Abel, Richard. 1991. *American Lawyers*. Oxford: Oxford University Press.

Ancker, Dag. 1987. "Political Science in the Nordic Countries," *International Political Science Review* 8: 73–84.

Esping-Andersen, Gøsta. 1999. *The Social Foundations of Postindustrial Economies*. Oxford: Oxford University Press.

De Bengy Puyvallée, Antoine and Kristian Bjørkdahl (eds.). 2021. *Do-Gooders at the End of Aid: Scandinavian Humanitarianism in the Twenty-First Century*. Cambridge: Cambridge University Press.

Dezalay, Yves, and Bryant Garth. 1996. *Dealing in Virtue: International Commercial Arbitration and the Construction of a Transnational Legal Order*. Chicago: Chicago University Press.

Epp, Charles. 1998. *The Rights Revolution: Lawyers, Activists and Supreme Courts in Comparative Perspective*. Chicago: University of Chicago Press.

Ervo, Laura, Pia Letto-Vanamo, and Anna Nyland (eds.). 2021. *Rethinking Nordic Courts*. Cham, Switzerland: Springer Verlag.

Feeley, Malcolm and Setsuo Miyazawa. 2007. "The State, Civil Society, and the Legal Complex in Modern Japan," in Terence Halliday and Lucien Karpik (eds.), *Fighting for Political Freedom: Comparative Studies of the Legal Complex and Political Liberalism*. Oxford: Hart Publishing.

Ginsburg, Tom. 2011. "Constitutional Endurance," in Tom Ginsburg and Rosalind Dixon (eds.), *Comparative Constitutional Law*, 112. Northampton, MA, USA: Edward Elgar Publishing, Available at SSRN: https://ssrn.com/abstract=1899636

Gobe, Eric, and Lena Salaymeh. 2016. "Tunisia's 'Revolutionary' Lawyers: From Professional Autonomy to Political Mobilization," *Law and Social Inquiry* 41: 311–345.

Graver, Hans Petter. 2014. *Judges Against Justice: On Judges When the Rule of Law is Under Attack*. Berlin: Springer.

Halliday, Terence C. 1987. *Beyond Monopoly: Lawyers, State Crises, and Professional Empowerment*. Chicago: University of Chicago Press.

Halliday, Terence, and Lucien Karpik (eds.). 1998. *Lawyers and the Rise of Western Political Liberalism: Europe and North America from the Eighteenth to Twentieth Centuries*. Oxford: Oxford University Press.

Halliday, Terence, and Lucien Karpik. 2012. "Political Liberalism in the British Post Colony: A Theme with Three Variations," in Terence Halliday, Lucien Karpik, and Malcolm Feeley (eds.), *Fates of Political Liberalism in the British Post-Colony: The Politics of the Legal Complex*. Cambridge: Cambridge University Press, 227–262.

Halliday, Terence, Lucien Karpik, and Malcolm Feeley (eds.). 2007a. *Fighting for Political Freedom: Comparative Studies of the Legal Complex and Political Change*. Cambridge: Cambridge University Press.

Halliday, Terence, Lucien Karpik, and Malcolm Feeley (eds.). 2007b. "Introduction: The Legal Complex in Struggles for Political Liberalism," in Terence Halliday, Lucien Karpik, and Malcolm Feeley (eds.), *Fighting for Political Freedom: Comparative Studies of the Legal Complex and Political Change*, 1–42. Cambridge: Cambridge University Press.

Halliday, Terence, Lucien Karpik, and Malcolm Feeley (eds.). 2012. *Fates of Political Liberalism in the British Post-Colony: The Politics of the Legal Complex*. Cambridge: Cambridge University Press.

Helgadóttir, Ragnildur. 2006. *The Influence of American Theories of Judicial Review on Nordic Constitutional Law*. Leiden: Martinus Nijhoff Publishers.

Hirschl, Ran. 2011. "The Nordic Counternarrative: Democracy, Human Development, and Judicial Review," *International Journal of Constitutional Law* 9: 449–469.

Husa, Jaakko. 2011. "Nordic Constitutionalism and European Human Rights: Mixing Oil and Water?" *Scandinavian Studies in Law*, 55: 101–124.

Jensen, Steven. 2017. "Putting To Rest the Three Generations Theory of Human Rights," *Open Democracy*.

Johnsen, Jon T. 2018. "Nordic Legal Aid and 'Access to Justice,' in Human Rights: A European Perspective," in Olaf Halvorsen and Ole Hammerslev (eds.), *Outsourcing Legal Aid in the Nordic Welfare State*. Cham, Switzerland: Palgrave Macmillan, 21–39.

Karpik, Lucien. 1998. "Builders of Liberal Society: French Lawyers and Politics," in Terence Halliday and Lucien Karpik (eds.), *Lawyers and the Rise of Western Political Liberalism: Europe and North America from the Eighteenth to Twentieth Centuries*, 101–132. Oxford: Oxford University Press.

Karpik, Lucien. 1999. *French Lawyers: A Study in Collective Action, 1274–1994*. New York: Oxford University Press.

Karpik, Lucien, and Terence Halliday. 2011. "The Legal Complex," *Annual Review of Law and Social Science* 7: 217–236.

Kennedy, Duncan. 2006. "Three Globalizations of Law and Legal Thought," in David Trubek and Alvaro Santos (eds.), *The New Law and Economic Development*, 56–89. Cambridge: Cambridge University Press.

Kierulf, Anine. 2018. *Judicial Review in Norway: A Bicentennial Debate*. Cambridge: Cambridge University Press.

Langford, Malcolm and Karianne Saevereide. 2018. *Jurister og offentlig utvlag*. Mimeo: University of Oslo.

Langford, Malcolm, and Johan Karlsson Schaffer. 2014. "The Nordic Human Rights Paradox," University of Oslo Faculty of Law Research Paper No. 2013-25.

Langford, Malcolm and Eirinn Larsen. 2018. *Branding the Nordics: The politics of exceptionalism*. UiO: Norden Working Paper.

Larsen, Eirinn. 2013. "Næringsfrihet som likestilling 1850–1880," in Hilde Danielsen, Eirinn Larsen, and Ingeborg W. Owesen (eds.), *Norsk likestillingshistorie 1814–2013*, 40–65. Bergen: Fagbokforlaget.

Larsen, Eirinn. 2021. "The Gender-progressive Nordics: A Matter of History," in Eirinn Larsen, Sigrun Moss, and Inger Skjelsbæk (eds.), *Gender Equality and Nation Branding in the Nordic Region*, 13–38. London: Routledge.

Larsen, Eirinn, Sigrun Moss, and Inger Skjelsbæk (eds.). 2012. *Gender Equality and Nation Branding in the Nordic Region*. London: Routledge.

Letto-Vanamo, Pia. 2014. "Nordic Democracy Facing the EU: Traditions, Myths, and Challenges," in M. Fichera, K. Tuori, and S. Hänninen (eds.), *Polity and Crisis. Reflections on the European Odyssey*, 217–234. Farnham: Ashgate.

Letto-Vanamo, Pia, Ditlev Tamm, and Bent Ole Gram Mortensen (eds.). 2019. *Nordic Law in European Context*. Cham, Switzerland: Springer Verlag.

Letto-Vanamo, Pia, and Ditlev Tamm. 2019. "Nordic Legal Mind," in Pia Letto-Vanamo, Ditlev Tamm, and Bent Ole Gram Mortensen (eds.), *Nordic Law in European Context*, 1–19. Cham, Switzerland: Springer Verlag.

Letto-Vanamo, Pia. 2021. "Courts and Proceedings: Some Nordic Characteristics," in Laura Ervo, Pia Letto-Vanamo, and Anna Nylund (eds.). 2021. *Rethinking Nordic Courts*, 21–36. Cham, Switzerland, Springer Verlag.

Liu, Sida, and Terence C. Haliday. 2016. *Criminal Defense in China: The Politics of Lawyers at Work*. New York: Cambridge University Press.

Massoud, Mark. 2013. *Law's Fragile State: Colonial, Authoritarian, and Humanitarian Legacies in Sudan*. New York: Cambridge University Press.

Michalsen, Dag. 2014. *Nordic Legal Profession*. Mimeo. University of Oslo.

Modeer, Kjell and Helle Vogt (eds.). 2021. *Law and the Christian Tradition in Scandinavia: The Writings of Great Nordic Jurists*. London: Routledge.

Moyn, Samuel. 2010. *The Last Utopia: Human Rights in History*. Cambridge, MA: Belknap Press of Harvard University Press.

Myhre, Jan Eivind. 2008. "Academics as the Ruling Elite in 19th Century Norway," *Historical Social Research* 33: 21–41.

Pálsson, Páll S. 1981. "Lögmannafélag Íslands 70 ára," *Tímarit lögfræðinga* 31(4): 178–183.

Parsons, Talcott. 1951. *The Social System*. Glencoe, IL: The Free Press.

Pihlajamäki, Heikki. 2009. *Kansan ja esivallan välissä. Suomalaisen asianajajakunnan historia*. Helsinki: Edita.

Rajah, Jothie. 2012. *Authoritarian Rule of Law: Legislation, Discourse and Legitimacy in Singapore*. New York: Cambridge University Press.

Reuschemeyer, Deterich. 1997. 'State, Capitalism, and the Organization of Legal Counsel: Examining an Extreme Case—the Prussian Bar, 1700–1934', in Terence Halliday and Lucien Karpik (eds.), *Lawyers and the Rise of Western Political Liberalism: Europe and North America from the Eighteenth to the Twentieth Centuries*, 207–228. Oxford: Oxford University Press.

Reuschemeyer, Deterich. 2014. *Lawyers and their Society: A Comparative Study of the Legal Profession in Germany and the United States.* Cambridge: Harvard University Press.

Rytter, Jens Elo and Marlene Wind. 2011. "In need of juristocracy? The silence of Denmark in the development of European legal norms." *International Journal of Constitutional Law*, 9(2): 470–504.

Rønning, Olaf Halvorsen and Ole Hammerslev (eds.). 2018. *Outsourcing Legal Aid in the Nordic Welfare States.* London: Palgrave MacMillan.

Sarfatti-Larson, Magli. 1977. *The Rise of Professionalism: A Sociological Analysis.* Berkeley: University of California Press.

Scheingold, Stuart. 2013. *The Rule of Law in European Integration*. New Orleans: Quid Pro Press.

Seip, Jens Arup. 2002. *Utsikt over Norges historie: Tidsrommet ca. 1850–1884.* Oslo: Gyldendal.

Shamir, Ronen. 1995. *Managing Legal Uncertainty: Elite Lawyers in the New Deal.* Durham, NC: Duke University Press.

Silkenat, James, James Rickley Jr., and Peter Barenboim (eds.). 2014. *The Legal Doctrines of the Rule of Law and the Legal State (Rechtsstaat)*. New York: Springer.

Slagstad, Rune. 1995. "The Breakthrough of Judicial Review in the Norwegian System," in Eivind Smith (ed.), *Constitutional Justice Under Old Constitutions*, 81–112. The Hague: Kluwer Law International.

Slagstad, Rune. 1998. *De Nasjonale Strateger.* Oslo: Pax Forlag.

Smith, Merete. 2015. "Advokatenes samsfunnansvar," in Sigurd Knudtzon (ed.), *Å Være Advokat*. Oslo: Universitetsforlaget.

Strath, Bo. 2004. "Nordic Modernity: Origins, Trajectories and Prospects." *Thesis Eleven*, 77(1): 1–23.

Strang, Johan. 2009. "Two Generations of Scandinavian Legal Realists. Retfærd." 24(1): 62–82.

Weber, Max. 1946. *From Max Weber* (translated and edited by Hans Gerth and C.W. Mills). Glencoe, IL: The Free Press.

Wessel-Aas, Jon. 2011. "Når selv jurister svikter rettsstaten," *Bergens Tidende (Online)*: 1.

Whitman, James. 2017. *Hitler's American Model: The United States and the Making of Nazi Race Law*. Princeton, NJ: Princeton University Press.

3

The Legal Complex in Struggles for Political Liberalism in Sweden

Johan Karlsson Schaffer[*]

1. Introduction

What role have judges and lawyers played in the expansion of political liberalism in Sweden? The research program on the legal complex has sought to capture how lawyers and judges, and the broader legal profession, sometimes emerge as a key collective actor in struggles for political liberalism, defined in terms of a constrained government, basic civil liberties, and an independent civil society (Karpik and Halliday 2011). The causal role of lawyers and judges, acting as self-appointed defenders of liberal rights and the rule of law, has been documented in comparative case studies of political lawyering in Europe and North America (Halliday and Karpik 1998), Latin America, Asia, and the Middle East (Halliday, Karpik, and Feeley 2007) and the British post-colonial states (Halliday, Karpik, and Feeley 2012).

Within this research program, Sweden, like the other Nordic states, may seem to pose an anomaly, since legal professions have rarely taken that public role of using law to defend liberty. Traditionally, jurists have played a different role in the Swedish legal-constitutional order than in the continental civil law systems or the Anglo-Saxon common law systems that offered the starting point for the legal complex research program. Swedish jurists have been seen as, first and foremost, civil servants in the service of the state or as social engineers operating the facts of law, rather than as an autonomous profession with an interest in constraining governmental power or defending justice. However, as I shall argue in this chapter, at some formative moments in Swedish political and legal history of the past two

[*] Associate Professor, University of Gothenburg. I presented an early draft of this chapter at the Centre for the Study of Professions, Oslo and Akershus University College of Applied Sciences in April 2015, and a revised version at the School of Public Administration, University of Gothenburg in November 2015. I thank Fredrik Thue, Anders Molander, Gregg Bucken-Knapp, and other participants at these events for their generous comments on my emerging argument. I am also very grateful to the editors of this volume, Malcolm Feeley and Malcolm Langford, for challenging me to dig deeper, and to the other contributors for their friendly engagement over the course of this project. Finally, I thank Anna Andersson for getting me on the right track at some formative moments.

Johan Karlsson Schaffer, *The Legal Complex in Struggles for Political Liberalism in Sweden* In: *The Limits of the Legal Complex*. Edited by: Malcolm Feeley and Malcolm Langford, Oxford University Press.
DOI: 10.1093/oso/9780192848413.003.0003

centuries, legal professionals acting in concert have played important political roles—sometimes expanding political liberalism, sometimes contracting it.

My focus will be on both *événements*, i.e., key historical moments when particular actors have mobilized on a circumscribed issue, and the longue durée. Specifically, I focus on (1) the constitutional revolution in 1809, where liberals ended Gustavian autocracy; (2) the Law Commission and the emergence of the liberal Rechtsstaat in the nineteenth century; (3) the fate of political liberalism after the breakthrough of democracy and the welfare state; (4) the protracted struggle over rights in the constitutional reforms of the 1970s; and (5) the slow return to political liberalism since the 1980s.

The legal complex research program has shown legal professions to use two distinct repertoires of action in mobilizing for political liberalism: To use courts to get issues on the agenda; or to rise as spokespersons for publics. However, in the Swedish case, a different action repertoire has been, I shall argue, more central. Jurists have played an important role in the numerous governmental committees preparing new legislation (Modéer 2011; Zetterberg 2011) and serving in the ministry of justice as a legal expert has been an integral career step for judges. Moreover, certain institutionalized legal actors—e.g., courts, prosecutorial offices, ombudsmen, law faculties, or professional organizations—are regular consultative bodies submitting statements of opinion in public hearing rounds on proposed legislation. Early on, the governmental committee apparatus (*kommittéväsendet*) also provided a public sphere, since proposals and hearing responses were printed, publicly available, and often debated in the press and parliament. The output of the committee procedure also forms part of the *travaux préparatoires* that are an important source of law in Sweden. On the other hand, the participation of judges in the committee apparatus may also serve to compromise their independence, since, complicit in the law-making process, they become reluctant "to criticise relevant legislation in the process of a judicial review" (Nergelius and Zimmermann 2012: 217).

2. From Constitutional Revolution to a Liberal Rechtsstaat

Throughout the nineteenth century, a series of struggles and successive reforms, occasionally pushed back by conservative forces, expanded political liberalism, establishing constraints on government in the form of a new constitution introducing separation of powers between the king and the parliament, a cabinet government, an increasingly independent judiciary, and a bicameral parliament; basic civil liberties, including press freedom, religious freedom, economic freedom, and the emancipation of women; and, as both cause and effect of these other reforms, a flourishing civil society. This section discusses, first, the constitutional revolution of 1809 and, second, the Law Commission and the breakthrough of liberalism in the mid-1800s.

2.1 The Constitutional Revolution of 1809

The revolution of 1809, replacing absolutism with a constitutional framework based on separation of powers and power-sharing, established the institutional framework that set the terms for subsequent struggles over political liberalism and the conflicts between king and parliament and between conservatives and progressives that would dominate much of the ensuing century.

After a devastating defeat in the Finnish War, Sweden lost Finland, which had been a fully integrated part of the kingdom for five hundred years, to Russia. In March 1809, Count Georg Adlersparre, a major-general commanding the western army, sent his troops marching on Stockholm. As a publicist, Adlersparre had previously propagated enlightenment ideas, and in his revolutionary proclamation, he now declared that war and autocracy had brought the country to ruins (Brusewitz 1918; Norberg 1998). Concurrently, co-conspiring officers in Stockholm arrested King Gustav IV Adolf to prevent him from escaping to regain control through the southern army. The revolutionaries formed a provisional government under the ousted king's elderly uncle, Duke Karl, who failed to halt Adlersparre. Entering the capital as a hero, Adlersparre managed to outmaneuver conservative ministers, took a seat in the government himself and maintained control of his forces and the capital as a de facto dictator.

However, Adlersparre soon split with other leading coup plotters on how to carry forth the revolution and was eventually marginalized (Brusewitz 1918). Adlersparre wished to see the Duke-Regent Karl proclaimed as king, but other leading revolutionaries insisted, successfully, that parliament first had to adopt a new constitution. The provisional government appointed two short-lived committees to draft a new constitution (Carlsson 1990: 15ff), in which Anders af Håkansson came to play a central role. Håkansson had a background as a judge and a politician and, back in 1789, he had helped to strengthen the king's autocratic powers vis-à-vis the nobility (Jägerskiöld 1971), so many revolutionaries rejected his draft as out of tune with the liberal spirit of the revolution. Yet Sweden desperately needed a new constitution and a new monarch, if nothing else because Russia refused to negotiate a peace treaty until Sweden again had a legitimate government. Thus, the provisional government assembled the Four Estates to a riksdag (parliament) for the first time since 1800.

Settling the procedural issue at the 1809 riksdag, liberal reformists insisted, against the provisional government, that parliament must adopt a constitution before electing a new monarch, rather than the other way around. A few days later, parliament appointed a constitutional committee, the first of its kind in Swedish history, with six representatives from the nobility and three from each of the other Estates, to draft a new constitution—a task it completed in only two weeks. Little is known about the committee's internal work, as it did not keep a protocol, but it seems to have been based on Håkansson's draft and two critical commentaries on it (Carlsson 1990: 17f). After debate and adoption by the four Estates, the new Instrument of Government (*Regeringsformen*, RF) entered into force on June 6, 1809.

The process of drafting, adopting, and implementing a new constitution intensified the struggle between, on the one hand, reformers and, on the other, reactionaries, who sought to restore the Gustavian lineage and constitution, and radical groups inspired by the French revolution. However, on the constitutional committee the so-called liberal party held a majority. The resulting Instrument of Government was, in many respects, a victory for the liberal constitutionalists (although its liberalism has been subject of some academic debate). It introduced a mixture of separation of powers and power-sharing between the king and the Four Estates. The RF stipulated that "the King alone is entitled to rule the Kingdom" and to appoint a council of nine ministers (Carlsson 1990: 20). The king was to make law together with the Riksdag, and the Riksdag held the right to levy taxes and control the state's financial and monetary agencies, thus restricting the king's control of the state budget. Furthermore, even though the Riksdag had no say in the appointment of ministers, it could hold them to account for the advice they gave the king (Möller 2011: 27).

However, the RF gave no prominent role to the judiciary. Although the judicial branch was assured a degree of independence (courts were autonomous, and justices could only be removed through impeachment and needed a permit to occupy any other office), the RF did not mandate the judiciary to balance the legislature and executive through, for example, constitutional review. It saw courts as part of, rather than as checking and monitoring, the executive and the bureaucracy—indeed, the king would chair the Supreme Court. Furthermore, the RF had no bill of rights in a modern sense, although it contained some provisions on the king's responsibility to prevent injustice and promote justice, the rule of law, personal liberty and privacy, religious freedom, and so on (§16), provisions that citizens should enjoy equality before the law, and a ban on ad hoc courts (Wiklund 2008: 167). Moreover, the constitution also introduced the ombudsman institution (§96) as a supervisory agency under the Riksdag to monitor the legality of the exercise of governmental and judicial authority, an office to be held by "a man known for his legal knowledge and excellent probity."

The RF also re-established press freedom and freedom of information. Effected by proto-liberals such as clergyman Anders Chydenius at the 1766 Riksdag, Sweden's Press Freedom Act—the first of its kind in the world—had been suspended under Gustavian autocracy. Already in April 1809, the provisional government lifted restrictions on the press, unleashing a wave of pamphlets and articles to debate the constitutional reforms, and appointed a committee to propose a new press freedom act. The RF enshrined press freedom in the constitution (§86), prohibited proactive censorship, and recognized the principle of legality in matters of press freedom, authorizing courts, not administrative organs, to determine its limits (Hirschfeldt 2009: 399).

While on balance the new RF implied a great improvement in terms of liberal constitutionalism, the liberal reformists failed to carry through their agenda on some issues, most notably their plans to abolish the Estates' privileges, to introduce economic freedom, and to reform national representation. When the Estates were to ratify the constitution, the peasantry filed reservations against a paragraph affirming noble privilege, and only after partial concessions and hard pressure from the other higher Estates, united across party divisions, did their speaker sign the constitution (Wibling 1954: Ch. 3).

Partly, the failure seems to have resulted from a counter-offensive by the opposition, which sought to delay the new constitution and also plotted a counter-coup late in 1809. Seeking to build a broader oppositional coalition, the leaders of the Gustavian opposition, Jacob Gustaf de la Gardie and Eric Ruuth, two landed aristocrats and high-ranking military officers, proposed a complete revision of all basic laws, a representation reform to include for example rural industrialists (who were excluded from the urban bourgeoisie), and a voluntary renouncement of noble privilege (Gidlöf 1998). In 1810, the constitutional committee proposed to abolish the Four Estates and replace them with a bicameral parliament and, in order to complete the separation of powers, the king would have only a suspensive veto on legislation (Norberg 1998, 64). The Four Estates adopted the proposal, yet never implemented it, and it was rejected at the 1815 Riksdag; it would take another half-century to achieve representation reform.

Alongside the new constitution, Sweden also needed a new monarch, and parliament eventually elected Jean Baptiste Bernadotte, a French officer who had made a remarkable career in Napoleon's army, who ruled as crown prince from 1812 and was crowned as King Karl XIV Johan in 1817. Because of his immense popularity, he managed to outstep the constitutional constraints on the executive, and his authoritarian rule effectively countervailed the power-restraining intentions behind the 1809 constitution. In 1812, one of his first decrees curtailed press freedom by giving the government a prerogative to stop the publication of periodicals that were deemed to offend public order or good taste; henceforth, the publishing of newspapers required a permit from the Royal Court Chancellor (Norberg 1998; Wichman 1971). Karl Johan's reign became known as the "era of ruling alone"—an allusion to the opening paragraph of the RF, which had actually been intended to constitutionally regulate the king's executive powers, balanced by the Riksdag (Möller 2011: 27). However, the king met growing liberal opposition from the 1820s onward. Hence, with the constitution of 1809, Sweden had established the constitutional fundament for subsequent reforms toward political liberalism. It also anticipated the political conflicts that would dominate much of the ensuing century, between king and parliament, between conservative and progressive forces.

Do the agents pushing for liberal constitutional reform in 1809 represent a legal complex in action? One group of actors at the 1809 Riksdag had some form of legal training, typically having obtained a lower civil servant degree (*kansliexamen*), before embarking on a civil servant career, which could include serving as a court clerk. This group includes members of the constitutional committee such as its chair Lars August Mannerheim, Gudmund Jöran Adlerbeth, and Axel Gabriel Silverstolpe.

Some were legal professionals in a stricter sense. For instance, Hans Järta, who participated in the conspiracy against the king and then served as secretary of the constitutional committee, had been a civil servant and member of Svea Court of Appeals in the 1790s, before starting a law practice in Stockholm in 1800 (Landberg 1973). Similarly, Anders af Håkansson, whose draft constitution the liberals rejected, had obtained a law degree at the age of 17 and then served as a district judge; devoted to the kingship, he also had served as a government official and quasi minister of finance during Gustav III's reign (O. Jägerskiöld 1971). Likewise, Gabriel Poppius, who declined to serve on the constitutional committee but who wrote an essential memorandum that influenced the RF, had pursued a judicial career and, once appointed Supreme Court Justice in 1809, he helped strengthen the judicial preview function prescribed by the new constitution (Grage 2016).

Other key agents had different professional backgrounds. Some central proponents of political liberalism were militaries—notably Adlersparre, but also Jacob Cederström, whose home in Stockholm became a hub for the conspiracy against the king and who became a vital spokesperson for the liberal party at the 1809 Riksdag—while others were clerics or academics. And although few of them were on the highest rungs of aristocracy, almost all of the central actors in 1809 belonged to the nobility, which had seen its influence shrink under Gustavian autocracy, compared to the so-called Era of Liberty (1718–1772), a period of parliamentary rule that had reduced the king's constitutional role to a literal rubber stamp.

However, more than professional ethos, social rank, or personal networks, a form of liberalism seems to have been the primary motive for the reformists (Norberg 1998: 56ff). The "men of 1809," as they have later become known, were well read in political philosophy and well acquainted with the political developments in the surrounding world. They had personally experienced the increasingly arbitrary, incompetent, and oppressive rule of the king and their opposition had come at a price. Järta and Adlersparre, for instance, already led the nobility opposition at the Riksdag in 1800 (where Järta in protest renounced his nobility) but were forced to retreat from political life in the following decade (Brusewitz 1918; Landberg 1973).

In their concerted action for political liberalism, they could draw on networks that had been established long before the revolution. Many liberals had been part of the so-called Junta in the 1790s, a political and literary society in Uppsala formed around Professor Benjamin Höjer, a Kantian philosopher, and Gustaf Abraham Silverstolpe, the publisher of an influential oppositional journal, who also participated at the 1809 Riksdag (Norberg 1998: 53ff). The Junta circle also partially overlapped with the contributors to *Läsning i blandade ämnen*, a periodical published by Adlersparre from 1795 to 1801 that became a mouthpiece for Enlightenment ideas, economic reform, and social issues (Norberg 1998: 56ff).

The reformists were inspired by Enlightenment ideas, had been influenced by leading philosophers such as Voltaire, Montesquieu, Rousseau, Kant, Hume, and Adam Smith, and called for republican civism, constitutionalism and a balanced system of government, rule of law and equality before the law, economic freedom, and abolition of privilege. Many of them regarded England, rather than revolutionary France or the United States, as the model of a free society with a balanced political system. Some had first-hand experience of the political and constitutional revolutions elsewhere in Europe. For instance, Adolph Mörner, who had studied Kant and Montesquieu at Uppsala, witnessed, as a diplomat to France in 1795, the debates in the constitutional convention and was much impressed by Abbé Sieyès' ideas about a strong executive power controlled by popular representation (Jägerskiöld 1987).

Yet law, apparently, was both the means and the end for their struggle, putting an end to the era of Gustavian autocracy. Not only did they craft a constitution that placed constraints on the executive, entrenched certain basic liberal rights in the constitution, such as press freedom, and thereby also creating a potential space for public debate and civil society; they also initiated a project of using law to reform society in a liberal direction, which would unfold, in fits and starts, throughout the rest of the century.

2.2 The Law Commission

Having successfully given Sweden a new constitution, the Estates at the revolutionary Riksdag in 1809–1810 noted the deplorable state of other laws and regulations, and decided to appoint a commission tasked with simplifying and improving legislation (Wieselgren 1895: 334; Warburg 1905: 37) with a view to replacing the Civil Code of 1734. They also mandated the commission to publish its proposals in order to allow the public to comment, and to take those comments into account when drafting legislation. Originally, the commission was supposed to deliver a proposal at the next ordinary Riksdag, yet the comprehensive law revision would turn out to take more than a century without ever being completed.

In 1811, the mandate of the commission was defined by a preparatory committee, which included leading revolutionaries from 1809 such as Gabriel Poppius, who participated in the ousting of the king in 1809 and was later appointed justice on the Supreme Court; Hans Järta, now secretary of state in the trade and finance ministry, and Mannerheim, Justice Ombudsman (Warburg 1905: 38). The committee suggested the commission focused on reviewing the general civil and criminal code, finding the criminal and penal code in particular need of revision in order to achieve humane forms of punishment serving the improvement of the criminal (Wieselgren 1895: 335). The committee assumed that the proposal, after a hearing round, could be adopted at the 1815 Riksdag. Based on the preparatory committee's proposal, the government appointed a Law Commission, composed of twelve unsalaried supervisory members (including senior judges, the justice chancellor, and the justice ombudsman) and five working members: Uppsala professor of law Lars Georg Rabenius, judges Magnus Flinck, Carl Petter Thörneblad, and Olof Zenius, and lawyer Pehr Staaff.

The Commission started by revising the penal code. In 1814, Rabenius presented a proposal, based on a deterrence theory, which preserved most forms of corporal punishment. Although it did not promote the rehabilitation of the criminal, Rabenius argued, corporal punishment was of a transient nature and also economical (Wieselgren 1895: 335). However, as the proposal so flagrantly contradicted the enlightenment spirit in which the commission had been formed, the majority rejected it and Rabenius resigned, along with Flinck and Thörneblad. Olof Zenius, the key opponent of Rabenius' proposal, persuaded the young judge Johan Gabriel Richert to fill one of their seats, and legal scholar Anders Erik Afzelius filled the other (Warburg 1905: 43–63).

The reformist troika of Zenius, Staaff, and Richert would come to have a decisive impact on the work of the commission, and by extension on political liberalism in Sweden. All three were profiled legal professionals: Zenius had studied law at Uppsala, served on the Svea Court of Appeals and the Board of Commerce; he declined an offer to serve on the Supreme Court, instead devoting his work to the Law Commission. Inspired by Kant, Zenius had a philosophical approach to law and corresponded with leading foreign law scholars, such as P.J.A. Feuerbach (Warburg 1905: 41ff). Staaff had obtained a civil servant degree at Uppsala and served in the administration and the judicial system, but he was also a well-reputed, skillful practicing lawyer (Tjerneld 2007). While Zenius was the leading force in the early years, Richert later assumed that role—and expanded it greatly. Having obtained a law degree in Lund at the age of 17 and subsequently a court apprenticeship at Göta Court of Appeal, Richert served as a junior judge at a district court in Västergötland, led by his father, where he made a name for himself as a spokesperson of the common people, using his judicial authority to challenge bureaucratic abuse. Authorities reacted by fining Richert for unwarranted appeals and defamation. Adlersparre, the despotic revolutionary leader, had been appointed governor of Västergötland in 1810 and used his contacts with the Justice Chancellor in Stockholm to pressure the president of the Göta Court of Appeal to reprimand Richert (Grimberg 1923: 187). However, Richert appealed to the Royal Majesty, which eventually decided to promote him to district judge. The affair only seemed to enhance Richert's reputation as a fearless, righteous judge, and brought him to the attention of Zenius, who consulted him on the penal code and subsequently advocated his appointment to the Law Commission.

The Law Commission set to work on both the penal and civil law code. In 1815, it delivered proposals on reforms to the procedural code and on new penal facilities in order to replace corporal punishment with custodial detention. The Commission advocated correctional facilities where each prisoner's regimen could be graded according to the severity of the crime, and where prisoners as far as possible should work in order to contribute to their support, but also to facilitate their reintegration in society (Wieselgren 1895: 337). The commission also delivered a first draft for a simplified and streamlined judicial organization in order to increase the expedience and access to justice (Warburg 1905: 72ff).

In the following years, the Commission published proposals for a new marriage code (1815), inheritance code and land code (1818), and procedural code and enforcement code (1822). The partial proposals were already causing friction with the increasingly authoritarian king Karl XIV Johan and, in 1823, Richert resigned from the commission and resumed his judgeship (Warburg 1905: 145ff). Reformists unsuccessfully sought to persuade him to return to Stockholm, nominating him for Justice Ombudsman and Supreme Court justice. Only after Zenius had declared that he too would resign from the Commission did the Prime Minister for Justice persuade Richert that the king wished him to reconsider, which Richert did (Modéer 1998).

Revising its proposals based on the commentaries received, the Commission published a *Proposal for a general civil law code* in 1826. Inspired by the French *Code civil*, the proposal was a manifesto in the spirit of Enlightenment liberalism. The Commission aimed to create a civil code oriented toward the individual citizen, abolishing intermediary corporations and their privileges, and thereby enacting equality before the law (Peterson 2001: 226). As a consequence of this liberal individualism, the commission's proposals were radical, for instance granting men and women equal inheritance and marriage rights and granting unmarried women the right to gain their majority by the age of 25. It also suggested abolishing special courts for nobles, arguing that a "all are equal before the law [and a] court that is good enough for one, is good enough for all" (Peterson 2001: 227). However, the Royal Majesty failed to present a bill based on the proposal at the 1828 Riksdag, and conservative mobilization ensured that liberal motions to adopt it were rejected (Jacobson 1925).

Having thus completed its review of the civil law code, the Law Commission proceeded to revise the penal code. As the Royal Majesty wished to ensure maximal coherence of the laws of the two kingdoms, the Commission's working members convened with a sibling committee in Norway. Published in 1832, the Commission's proposal consisted of a penal code and a procedural code for criminal trials. Inspired by French and Bavarian penal codes, the commission authored its proposal in a radical liberal spirit, suggesting the abolition of corporal and shaming punishment and expatriation (Inger 2011: 297). While the commission failed to reach an agreement on also suggesting the abolition of the death penalty and using juries in criminal trials, it presented such alternative proposals in appendices (Modéer 1998). The proposal also suggested certain legal-technical innovations and to entrench the principle of legality.

Having taken into account commentaries received in the hearing round, the Law Commission presented its civil code proposal to the Estates at the 1834 Riksdag. The proposals had already been sharply criticized in the hearing rounds, and at the Riksdag the nobility and clergy, who saw the civil code proposal as a threat to their privileges, blocked the reforms (Peterson 2001). In order to thwart the proposals, Johan Ludvig Boije, an ultraconservative politician who had opposed reforming the cabinet, the Riksdag, and the legal code since the 1820s, gained support for requiring a summary of the proposals, their basic principles, and how they differed from existing law to be published before the next ordinary Riksdag (Jacobson 1925). The task was given to a so-called tableaux committee, on which Boije, however, failed to agree with the other members on the procedure, and so by 1837, it had only completed its tableau of the civil code; the tableau of the criminal code was not published until four years later, and both were sharply criticized in the liberal press for failing to consider the proposals as a whole. The conservative strategy was successful, but although the proposed codes as a whole were never enacted as law, their principles of individualism and equality before the law, and their view of the role of legislation in a modern market society, would make their mark on future major revisions of Swedish legislation (Peterson 2001: 227).

At the 1840 Riksdag, the Royal Majesty declared that the civil and criminal code proposals would only be reviewed by the next ordinary Riksdag. However, the Estates proposed a new committee to further review the proposals at a later Riksdag. Appointed in 1841, the Legal Advisory Committee (*Lagberedningen*) consisted of five working members: two Supreme Court justices, the Chancellor of Justice, and the Justice Ombudsman. Asked to sit on the new committee, Richert conditioned his participation on the exclusion of Johan Ludvig Boije (Jacobson 1925). The king responded by appointing Boije and not Richert, against the unanimous will of the cabinet (von Koch 1966), a decision which caused such intense opposition in the liberal press that all committee members chose to resign, much to the king's chagrin (Jacobson 1925). However, Boije died later the same year and, in 1844, the conservative King Karl XIV Johan passed away too and was succeeded by his more liberally inclined son Oscar I, who had been tutored by Richert and had taken interest in, for example, reforming the penal system.

In 1844, the Royal Majesty appointed three new members to the Legal Advisory Committee: law professor Carl Schlyter, judge and law professor Pehr Bergfalk, and Richert. Staaff also shortly participated in the committee after 1845. The committee started by reviewing the Law Commission's proposals for a new criminal code, presenting a proposal for a new penal code at the 1844 Riksdag. Approving of the basic principles of the proposal yet lacking time to evaluate it in total, the Estates only adopted it partially, yet rejected bills for its adoption at the following two Riksdags. After this failure to adopt a complete penal code, the government and the Estates agreed that further legislative reform had to proceed step by step, adopting statutes addressing specific parts of the criminal code at the 1853, 1856, and 1860 Riksdags. Partial reforms had already abolished corporal and shaming punishments such as the breaking wheel (1835) and brutal forms of the death penalty and stocks penalty (1841); the 1850s also saw the abolition of caning, the stool of shame (1855) and hanging (1858) (Inger 2011: 298). These gradual reforms paved the way for a bill, drafted in the ministry of justice but based on decades of work by the Law Commission and the Legal Advisory Committee, and presented to the Riksdag in 1862. Richert, by then long retired, commented on the bill in correspondence with Nils von Koch, who had also served on the Committee (von Koch 1966), but he did not live to see the new penal code come into force in 1864. Yet the many rounds of committee work, political tug-of-war and gradual reforms had made the new penal code a compromise between conservative views and the radical proposals of 1832 and 1844; in some respects, such as the extensive use of bread-and-water punishments, it actually implied harsher penalties (Inger 2011: 299).

Having reviewed the criminal code, the Legal Advisory Committee proceeded to revise the civil code. In 1847, it presented proposals for new marriage, inheritance, land, and construction codes. After some conservative members of the committee left their positions, it proceeded in 1849 to propose revised procedural, commercial, and enforcement codes, and in 1851 a bills of exchange law. After that, its work was done, though the complete overhaul of the civil code was never adopted as law.

2.3 The Liberal Breakthrough in the Mid-nineteenth Century

The reform frenzy of the mid-nineteenth century was not limited to revising the legal code. The 1840s initiated a massive wave of liberal reforms that peaked in the 1860s, and which effectively transformed the corrupt and authoritarian state into a liberal Rechtsstaat, along with a free economy, a lively civil society, and a free press.

In terms of constraints on government, parliament modified the governmental structure in 1840, organizing it into departments, headed by ministers, and a cabinet council. As a result, the government became more independent vis-à-vis the king, but also in relation to parliament, which held ministers legally, if not politically, accountable, while the state bureaucracy's autonomy from the government ministries was preserved (Möller 2011: 29). The self-rule of local municipalities was successively improved. In 1862, Prime Minister for Justice Louis De Geer initiated a municipality reform, which replaced the old parish councils with local municipalities and introduced county councils responsible for health care. These reforms strengthened local self-government, but also introduced limited censitarian suffrage (i.e., based on wealth rather than membership of the Estates) at local and regional levels.

A series of reforms helped professionalize the judiciary. In 1817, the king appointed a committee to examine the comprehensive jurisdiction that Uppsala University held over professors, their servants, and students in criminal law and more general matters of discipline and decency. In 1818, Richert joined the committee, which in its report two years later proposed the abolition of academic jurisdiction, arguing that it rested on an outdated principle of corporatism, that it was unnecessary for academic freedom and that the boundaries between academic and general courts were nearly impossible to determine (Warburg 1905: 107ff). The proposal led to a debate in the press between Richert and Erik Gustaf Geijer, professor of history at Uppsala, who through this debate established himself as a leading conservative intellectual (in 1844, he would infamously "defect" to liberalism). Mobilizing an individualist conception of the state, Richert (1822) argued that everyone who lived in the same geographical area should be subject to the same jurisdiction, whereas Geijer, for whom academic freedom also entailed jurisdiction, maintained that everyone should be judged by their peers, preserving the independent jurisdiction of each corporation (Fryxell 1861: 6:88ff; Lindberg 2014, 55f). While Richert's proposal was not directly enacted, the university's jurisdiction was eventually reduced and abolished in 1852.

Following this debate, a number of other special or corporative courts were abolished, such as tariff courts (1831), postal courts (1836), castle courts with jurisdiction over servants and courtiers at royal castles (1844), port courts with jurisdiction over fisheries (1852), and mining courts with comprehensive jurisdiction in the mining industry (1852). Their jurisdiction was transferred to public courts as part of the effort to modernize and simplify the judicial system. Moreover, the 1840 Riksdag changed the RF so that the Prime Minister for Justice was no longer to be a member of the Supreme Court (Inger 2011: 285), while the 1844 Riksdag abolished the requirement reserving half of the Supreme Court justice offices for nobles (Ställvik 2009: 99f), which conflicted with other provisions in the RF disregarding pedigree in appointing public officials and which had anyway been circumvented by knighting prominent jurists to make them appointable. Furthermore, in order to increase the expedience of justice, the Law Commission had long suggested simplifying the court system (Warburg 1905: 72ff), a proposal the Riksdag heeded in 1849 by abolishing one level of the court structure (the lower-level *kämnärsrätt* in the cities and the appellate *lagmansrätt* in rural areas) (Inger 2011: 283).

Finally, in 1865, De Geer managed to resolve a constitutional controversy over popular representation that had dominated more than three decades. Already during the revolution in 1809, reformists had argued that the Four Estates were an antiquated, inefficient anachronism, but the proposal for representation reform had never been enacted. In order to revitalize the reformist spirit of 1809, Richert co-authored a proposal for representation reform together with Carl Henrik Anckarsvärd in 1830 (Anckarswärd and Richert 1830). Anckarsvärd was an aristocratic officer who had served as Adlersparre's aide-de-camp during the 1809 coup; in the 1820s, he became a reputed oppositional orator at the Riksdag debates, and his reputation only increased when the government had him charged with lese-majesty in 1823 (Grade 1918). Anckarsvärd and Richert based their proposal on the 1809 constitution and proposed a semi-bicameral system strategically modeled on the Norwegian constitution of 1814, which Karl XIV Johan, ruling over both kingdoms, had accepted, even as he resisted abolishing the Four Estates in Sweden. Their proposal did not lead to constitutional change, but it inspired several attempts at representation reform in the 1840s and sparked a political controversy that would span more than three decades. The Estates became ever less representative of the population as industrialization increased the number of people who did not belong to any of the old Estates (Möller 2011: 30). Reformists met significant resistance, however, chiefly from conservatives in the nobility appealing to tradition and cautioning against radical change. During the four days in 1864 when the nobility debated the proposal, masses gathered outside the House of Nobility, and, fearing that a veto from the nobility would spark riots, the government kept the military on guard (Möller 2011: 23).

The representation reform paved the way for further democratization, by, for example, introducing unitary elections, and the modernized parliament (now to assemble annually, rather than just every five or three years) successively strengthened its influence vis-à-vis the government (Möller 2011: 23). Parliamentarians also became more active and profiled, and began forming the first political parties. However, in the Second Chamber elections, only men aged 21 or older with an annual income of at least 800 *riksdaler* and who owned property of a tax value of at least 1,000 *riksdaler* were entitled to vote, which meant that only about 10 percent of the adult population (aged 20 or older) was enfranchised, and for the indirectly elected first chamber, graded voting rights followed even more demanding censitarian criteria. Tax-paying corporations also had voting rights.

In terms of liberal rights, the mid-nineteenth century also saw a series of struggles to abolish feudal privileges and restrictions on civic freedom, including press freedom, religious freedom, economic freedom, and emancipation of women. In 1845, parliament finally abolished the king's prerogative to confiscate publications deemed defamatory or harmful to public safety. In 1830, Lars Johan Hierta founded *Aftonbladet*, an evening newspaper that both revolutionized mass media, by its quick, witty news reporting and its innovative advertisement-based business model, and relentlessly advocated liberal reform, challenged privileges, and exposed bureaucratic abuse. Soon, it became the leading national newspaper. Provoked by its defiant attitude toward the government, the Royal Court Chancellor withdrew *Aftonbladet*'s publishing permit for the first time in 1835. However, helped by a frontman, Hierta could obtain another permit, publishing his newspaper under a slightly different title: *Det nya Aftonbladet*—a way of bypassing censorship he would use a dozen times, publishing his newspaper under twenty-six different titles and generously remunerating his frontmen for their willingness to risk prosecution (Norberg 1998: 106f). The state's attempts to stop *Aftonbladet* only boosted its popularity, and eventually the Royal Court Chancellor, realizing the futility of retroactive censorship, slowly ceased using his prerogative to withdraw publishing permits even before press freedom was enacted by parliament in 1844.

Another struggle concerned religious freedom. The 1726 Conventicle Statute (*Konventikelplakatet*) prohibited religious gatherings outside the Church of Sweden. However, from the early nineteenth century, often inspired by emigrants returning home from America, various revivalist movements gained hold, arranging independent prayer meetings led by lay preachers. Authorities met revivalism with harsh repression. For instance, when Baptists in the 1850s refused to have their children christened—a criminal offense—the state responded by coercively baptizing children and exiling Baptist leaders. Such repressive measures, however, attracted much international criticism (Harvard 2006, 79ff) and anyway did little to reassert the Church's monopoly of faith. After several attempts, liberals in parliament succeeded in repealing *Konventikelplakatet* in 1858 and, two years later, citizens were granted the right to leave the Church, but only if they joined another Christian community of faith approved by the state. Some remaining restrictions on religious gatherings were removed in 1868 and non-Lutherans were allowed to occupy most public offices (1870). Even after the new regulations, however, the authorities continued to prosecute and harass illegal preachers, and by the 1873 so-called Dissenter Act, citizens who left the Church of Sweden lost some of their civic rights (Werner 2002).

Similar struggles propelled the expansion of other liberal rights. The guild system, which made it obligatory for craftsmen to belong to a guild in order to practice a craft or trade, was partially abolished by parliament in 1846. Following the abolition of the Four Estates and most of their privileges, De Geer introduced full economic freedom in 1864, meaning that anyone could establish a shop or industry without a craftsman's certificate issued by a guild. In the spirit of the Law Commission's emphasis on individualism and equality before the law, liberals also managed to abolish laws discriminating against women and securing an expanding array of rights for women to, for instance, pursue academic degrees and professional careers (1870, 1873), inherit on equal terms with men and administer their own property, income, and inheritance (1841, 1874, 1884). In 1858, parliament approved a motion, repeatedly filed by Lars Johan Hierta, to abolish the husband's right to chastise his wife and servants (however, the right to chastise under-age servants remained until 1920). Through such reforms, women successively gained citizen rights on equal terms with men.

One can hardly exaggerate the importance of these liberal reforms, and their radical pace, for the advent of a modern, Weberian, uncorrupt state bureaucracy (Rothstein 2011), for the ensuing breakthrough of democracy, and for the remarkable industrialization that would make Sweden one of the wealthiest nations over the next hundred years (Bergh 2009). They were also facilitated by other reforms, such as the introduction of four-year primary school education for all children (1842), which promoted literacy in the population, and unitary postage (1855), which facilitated the circulation of newspapers, as did the construction of the state main railway system and a national telegraphy network (1856–1866). And as both cause and effect of these struggles and reforms, a vibrant civil society had formed, including trade unions, free churches, temperance societies, suffrage lodges, emerging political parties, and a free press.

2.4 The Legal Professions in the Push for Liberalism in the Nineteenth Century

During the eighteenth century, political liberalism was successively expanded in Sweden. As we have seen, legal professionals played an important role in these struggles, but to the extent that they mobilized collectively for political liberalism, their dominant repertoire of action was not to litigate in courts or to act as spokespersons for publics or the legal profession. Rather, they pursued a less visible strategy of mobilizing through committees, tasked with revising the laws.

The Law Commission and its successor committees are an important example of legal professionals mobilizing law in order to expand and defend political liberalism. It included persons from various legal occupations: Richert and Zenius were judges, Staaff a practicing lawyer, others civil servants. Some were law professors, although academics seem chiefly to have been conservative or moderate forces on the various legal commissions. As there were no sharp boundaries between different legal careers and since offices sometimes had to be combined because they were insufficiently salaried, some worked in more than one legal profession over their career. Moreover, even as they disagreed in substantive matters, they seem often to have appreciated each other as legal professionals. For instance, Carl Schlyter, who often held a minority view on the Legal Advisory Committee, as he found the radical liberal proposals insufficiently anchored in Swedish legal tradition (Modéer 1979), still acknowledged that "from a scientific point of view ..., these proposals, with the therewith enclosed motives, belong to the best that our juridical literature can demonstrate" (cited in Modéer 2000), and he and Richert, who had advocated Schlyter's appointment to the Committee, developed a deep respect for one another, in spite of their disagreements (von Koch 1966).

Outside the committee apparatus, many other key agents also had a legal background. Lars Johan Hierta, for instance, started his career as a jurist and civil servant, before he turned to politics, serving in parliament from 1828 to 1872 (Wichman 1971). His *Aftonbladet* provided a new, liberal public sphere, but he also started a number of successful industries. He became a central figure, coalescing the different forces pushing for liberalization, but his achievements for liberalism were brought about by means other than legal activism. Similarly, Louis de Geer, who, together with Minister of Finance Johan August Gripenstedt, unleashed a wave of liberal reforms in the 1860s, had pursued a judicial career and served as president of the Göta Court of Appeal, before King Karl XV appointed him Prime Minister for Justice in 1858 (Thermenius 1931).

But were they primarily driven by their legal profession or by their liberalism? As the chief architect behind many of the liberal reforms of the nineteenth century, Richert has been dubbed the father of liberalism in Sweden. A son of the enlightenment, he advocated an individualist political liberalism inspired by, among others, Jeremy Bentham (Norberg 1998: 81ff). He was frequently consulted by the liberal opposition in the Riksdag, but his role was chiefly that of an *éminence gris*, who influenced through his committee work and correspondence rather than through political action, and he declined prestigious offices. A rural commoner, he was also excluded from the Estates. Zenius, likewise, was an emancipatory liberal rooted in the French Enlightenment and Kant's philosophy. He had already published in 1809 a pamphlet on economic freedom, in which he argued against the patriarchal conservatism of the privilege system (Peterson 2001). Nils Samuel von Koch, a senior civil servant who served on the Legal Advisory Committee and several other reform committees, had attended lectures by Tocqueville in France and cited Bentham and Mill in debates. He was also much influenced by his wife Frances Lewin, who had been born in an English whig family, and their Stockholm home became a meeting place for liberal politicians and writers such as Fredrika Bremer, Erik Gustaf Geijer, and Lars Johan Hierta (Jägerskiöld 1975). Generally, liberal reformers in the committee apparatus collaborated with like-minded groups in parliament. Thus, mobilizing law through collective action among legal professionals was only a part, if a crucial and central part, of a broader emancipatory, individualist project.

Why did the struggle for political liberalism, to the extent it involved legal professionals, take place in legislative committee work rather than in the judicial arena? A key reason seems to be that the immaturity of the judicial apparatus and the legal professions, and their dependency on the state bureaucracy, made other arenas and strategies more effective. At the start of the nineteenth century, corporatism still governed the judicial system, with numerous special courts for every corporation, and just as in the civil service, nobles had precedence in judicial appointments; thus, simplifying the court structure and abolishing special courts was an important target of liberal reformers.

Moreover, in spite of numerous attempts, legal reformers failed to reform the rules of procedure. The Law Commission had already presented a radical proposal for procedure reform in 1815, which it further specified in its proposed procedural laws for civil and criminal cases. The commission recommended replacing the inquisitorial procedure and legal sifting of evidence with an accusatorial procedure based on the principles of oral proceedings, public attendance, and free production of evidence (Warburg 1905: 221ff). Later repeated by the Legal Advisory Committee in 1839 and 1849, the proposals became stranded at the Riksdag. In the 1850s, however, courts started disregarding the procedural code to allow free sifting, a practice which the Supreme Court later surprisingly confirmed (Inger 2011: 286).

Liberal lawyers continued to demand an overhaul of the procedural code, yet faced resistance chiefly from conservatives, judges, and legal academics. In the 1880s, the New Legal Advisory Committee (*Nya lagberedningen*) presented a proposal for reforming the judicial system and procedure, yet parliament enacted only minor, partial revisions. Many liberal lawyers—among them Karl Staaff, who was to become parliamentarian and prime minister (and whose grandfather had served on the Law Commission)—passionately argued for more substantial reforms, inspired by the Norwegian system, and demanded that the state should provide the defendant with an attorney (Brandberg and Knutson 2006). Even lawyers at the time disagreed on whether defending criminals was an honorable job, but for Staaff, public legal aid was a matter of social justice and providing the poor with the same rights as the rich.

Likewise, law education at the universities was in "a veritable intellectual as well as organizational morass that lasted into the first decades of the nineteenth century" (Rothstein 2011, 241): Obtaining a law degree was close to a mere formality and aristocratic families enrolled their children at the universities in their early teens, hoping to hasten their entrance into a lucrative civil service career. Moreover, while university law degrees had been regulated since the mid-eighteenth century, legal education was primarily aimed at producing civil servants for the state bureaucracy, rather than legal professionals to pursue careers in an independent judiciary or private practice. In a querulous overview of legal education and research in Sweden, law professors Hans Collin and Carl Schlyter (1829) complained that the poor quality of legal research and education produced civil servants with "contempt of eruditeness and thorough cultivation" and judicial decisions that completely lacked "any deeper legal insight other than that which results from routine."

However, reforming legal education became a contentious issue in the mid-nineteenth century. Echoing Richert's proposals in the debate about the universities' jurisdiction, Hierta motioned the Riksdag in 1823 to move practice-oriented faculties, including law, to Stockholm (Sandström 1998). In the coming decades, liberals would continually motion for making legal education more practically relevant and tailored to the needs of the state by moving it to the capital. In a critical response to an anonymous pamphlet calling for a reduction in the number of professorships, the abolition of lectures, and moving legal education to Stockholm, Uppsala law professor Knut Olivecrona argued in 1859 that the critics had missed that legal education had already changed: Ever since Schlyter had been appointed professor at Uppsala in 1835, the so-called historical school had superseded the stagnant natural law tradition (Sandström 1998), and, emphasizing law as a system that had evolved historically, it also offered a more scientific approach to the study of positive law (incidentally, Schlyter had built his reputation as an innovative legal historian after having been commissioned by Richert to compile overviews of medieval Swedish laws for the Law Commission [Modéer 2000]). Moreover, in Olivecrona's view, the theoretically anchored method of legal science taught at universities was also a guarantee for the coherent, predictable application of the law, which might be endangered by replacing them with practice-oriented law schools (Sandström 1998). However, both those who proposed a practice-oriented law school in Stockholm and those who wished to preserve law education at universities seem to have agreed that the key purpose of legal education was to produce civil servants for the state bureaucracy, including the judiciary.

New regulations on legal education did little to improve its sorry state, as long as a career as judge or civil servant depended more on aristocratic pedigree and personal relationships than on merit, years of service, or academic qualifications. Only with the rapid reforms of the 1860s did the state bureaucracy turn toward a meritocratic, Weberian civil service (Rothstein 2011), and "legal education and legal science developed under strong influence from Germany" (Modéer 2003). However, nobles continued to dominate the civil service, the judiciary, and other elite professions long into the twentieth century: Where previously nobles had been privileged by formal regulations and informal connections, they now were advantaged by their better access to education (Sundell 2015: 43).

An organized bar was also non-existent for much of the nineteenth century and legal counsels often lacked legal education. While the legal code of 1734 had allowed parties to use attorneys, without any requirement for legal training, defendants in criminal cases had to conduct their own case; not until 1866 were persons prosecuted for lesser crimes allowed to use a counsel in court (Inger 2011: 287). Throughout the nineteenth century, civil servants and court clerks commonly moonlighted as legal counsels—even Richert, Staaf, and Zenius practiced law on the side while serving on the Law Commission, as did a justice ombudsman (Bomgren 1937: 166). The abolition of the guild system in the 1840s gave rise to new free professionals standing outside the old class and estates system, who, although they lacked legal training, often acted as legal counsels. By the 1870s, the situation improved somewhat, as increasing numbers of jurists opted for a career as a lawyer rather than as civil servant or judge.

Throughout the century, the underdevelopment of the lawyer profession prompted debates among policymakers on whether and how to create and regulate a professional bar (Bomgren 1937). On the one hand, reformers criticized existing restrictions on the right of the parties' to choose freely their counsel and certain restrictions officially prohibiting higher court clerks from practicing law. Free competition, some argued, would eventually weed out apparently incompetent legal practitioners. On the other hand, reformers also sought to regulate existing legal practitioners in order to improve the judicial process. In its proposal for a new criminal code in 1832, the Law Commission radically suggested not only to grant the defendant a right to use a legal counsel, but also that the authorities should provide detainees with an attorney if they could not afford one on their own. Every court should furthermore accredit two unsalaried public attorneys. Recognizing the lack of competent lawyers, motions in parliament called for competence criteria, court accreditation, or attorneys salaried by the state in order to put pettifoggers out of business and improve the access to legal counsels in all parts of the realm.

In 1867, Olof Beckman, a district deputy judge, complained in a pamphlet addressed to the justice ombudsman about the predicament of the bar in Sweden. Beckman saw the establishment of an independent bar as essential for defending liberty, providing legal expertise to the common people, reducing the number of trials, and checking the authority of judges and the state bureaucracy:

> In the whole country, one can hardly find fifty persons who deserve even the denomination of lawyer, and even fewer are those who possess the knowledge and probity to fulfil in a dignified way such an essential vocation.
>
> (Beckman 1867: 10, author's translation)

Yet repeated motions in parliament to enact the Law Commission's proposals failed, chiefly because the Supreme Court opposed it, arguing that it would be difficult for every district court to ordain two competent lawyers, but also because of fears in parliament that the proposal would create a new and expensive class of civil servants (Bomgren 1937: 155ff). As part of renewed attempts to reform the procedural code, the New Legal Advisory Committee presented a report in 1884 that also proposed reforming the bar. While discussing the option to preserve the free choice of counsel, the Committee leaned toward making it mandatory for parties to use officially authorized lawyers, at least in higher courts and especially if oral proceedings were to be introduced, which required the testing of skills and knowledge and a corporation exercising professional control. The Committee argued these reforms would benefit the lawyer profession, facilitate international commerce, reduce the use of moonlighting civil servants and court clerks as counsels, and, most importantly, improve the administration of justice (Bomgren 1937: 162ff). Reviewing the proposal, the Enhanced Legal Advisory

Committee (*Förstärkta lagberedningen*) sought to further improve the position of public lawyers by extending the monopoly of the bar in higher courts and prohibiting civil servants from acting as counsels, aiming to create an independent profession. However, these reforms had been framed as an integral part of the major overhaul of the procedural code, a project that stalled again in the final decades of the nineteenth century.

Yet while the reform proposal failed, it provided an important impetus for the creation of an organized bar. In 1885, a group of university-educated lawyers met in Stockholm to write a commentary to the New Legal Advisory Committee's proposal (which eventually the Enhanced Committee by and large heeded). The meeting also appointed an interim board to draft the statutes of a Swedish Bar Association (*Sveriges advokatsamfund*), which held its constitutive meeting in March 1887 (Bomgren 1937: 169). Aiming to prohibit legal counsels that lacked legal education and to obtain a lawyer monopoly for the Bar Association, it only partially succeeded, however: Only with the new Procedural Code in 1948 did the Bar Association gain legal recognition so that only its members were allowed to use the title of attorney (*advokat*), but failed to obtain a monopoly (Inger 2011: 287). For several decades, the Bar Association's membership remained small and concentrated in the major cities (Modéer 1999).

In sum, to the extent that we see legal complexes mobilizing for political liberalism in Sweden in the nineteenth century, they were striving to create the fundamental prerequisites for a rule of law state: A constitutional monarchy, a modern legal code, an independent judicial system, and professionalized legal occupations. That required concerted action in other arenas than the legal-judicial institutions they sought to create.

3. Legal Reformers in the Democratic Welfare State

For all the liberal reform efforts of the nineteenth century, Sweden remained by its end one of the least democratic and most authoritarian states in Western Europe, and also a highly unequal society. The first two decades of the twentieth century saw an escalating political conflict between, on the one hand, the king and the conservative establishment, and, on the other hand, liberals and social democrats, who demanded general and equal voting rights for both men and women. Rallies, protests, strikes, and riots, sometimes met with harsh repression by the police or military, intensified the social tensions and the suffrage issue became a predominant, overarching, and uniting cause for progressive forces. Conservatives opposed suffrage reform, but sensationally conceded by extending suffrage to all men in 1907, thereby doubling the franchise. In 1917, with a war raging in Europe, food being rationed, and a series of riots and mass protests across the country causing fears of revolution, the conservative government appointed by the king was forced to resign, and Liberals and Social Democrats, who combined held a majority of seats in parliament, formed a coalition government. In 1919, finally, parliament extended the franchise to all women, who could exercise their right to vote in the 1921 election.

Hence, by 1917 democrats had finally established parliamentarism, yet the 1809 constitution, which emphasized separation of powers and that "the King alone rules the Kingdom," was never amended to reflect this new practice, where the King had lost his key political role and the executive ruled at the mercy of the legislative branch. The Instrument of Government remained unchanged, but significant parts of it were ignored in practice. While the triumph of parliamentarism paved the way for democracy, it also served to undermine the status of the constitution in Swedish politics and society.

Sweden's late but rapid transition to democracy (Rustow 1971) also had broader implications for political liberalism. While the movement toward expanding individual rights continued in some areas, for instance removing laws discriminating against women and introducing freedom of religion, the democratic era also saw the state extending its authority, especially through the corporatist welfare state. As the state expanded, so did the law. The dominant doctrine of Scandinavian legal realism, which served the social democratic reform project well, also cast legal professionals in new roles, as engineers operating the law as a technical fact. By the 1960s, this project of rationalist modernization and social engineering reached the constitution, with a new Instrument of Government (1974) affirming the principles of popular sovereignty and parliamentarism, while absorbing the judiciary as but a cog in the state bureaucracy.

Beyond enfranchisement, women's groups struggled for broader emancipation. In the early decades of the century, parliament introduced new laws discriminating against women, for instance prohibiting their work in mines (1900) and at night (1909, in order to comply with a 1906 International Labour Organization convention) and prohibiting contraception (1910). On the other hand, after decades of struggle to repeal laws that barred women from academic education, certain professional careers, and offices in public administration, the so-called Competence Act of 1923 granted women equal access with men to all positions in public administration, except clerical and military positions. In the following decades, other laws were abolished that discriminated against women, enacting their status as full citizens with equal civil rights.

3.1 Judicial and Procedural Reform

Reforms in the early twentieth century increased the independence of the courts. In 1909, the Supreme Administrative Court (*Regeringsrätten*) was created to further separate judicial and public administration (Ställvik 2009: 99). The issue had been on the agenda several times, not least after the departmental reform of the 1840s, yet parliamentarians—mostly liberal lawyers—had failed to win support for the proposed reform. However, in 1903, parliament endorsed a proposal by the constitutional committee, chaired by Hugo Blomberg, a professor of public law at Uppsala University and a key advocate of the reform, to ask the Royal Majesty to investigate the creation of a supreme administrative court, in order to relieve the ministries of the time-consuming task of hearing and deciding on administrative appeals, but also to improve predictability and legal certainty for individuals (Kuylenstierna 1959). Furthermore, the king's right to chair the Supreme Court was abolished. Both highest courts continued to deliver their judgments in the name of the king, but were in practice more independent from the executive branch. Justices from the two supreme courts formed the Council on Legislation, taking over the judicial preview function previously served by the Supreme Court. By the 1920s, Social Democrats had already motioned to restrict the Council's purview to purely juridical matters and the conflict would resurface in the 1940s to 1960s (Algotsson 2009). In the early twentieth century, courts also developed a practice of judicial review. By the late 1920s, the Supreme Court had established the authority to review the constitutionality of statutes and administrative ordinances, a practice which developed over the next fifty years, although it lacked support in the 1809 constitution (cf. Bindreiter 2009).

However, while liberals in the nineteenth century had sought to abolish special courts with jurisdiction over specific corporations, the rise of the democratic welfare state saw corporatism return in a different guise, and with it also specialized courts. The 1918 Water Act had already created six regional water courts. However, it was the new Labor Court, created in 1929, that would serve as model for several other courts established for special purposes, such as consumer courts, tenant courts, the Market Court (1970), and the Court of Patent Appeals (1978). In the decision-making of these courts, special interest representatives typically outnumbered professional judges.

One area of the law where the successive reform attempts of the nineteenth century had failed was the judicial procedure. In 1906, after heated debate (and a bill blocked by the first chamber two years earlier), parliament introduced the defendant's right to a publicly financed counsel, but only for severe crimes, a restriction that was removed in 1919 (Brandberg and Knutson 2006). In 1911, the government appointed the Procedure Commission (*Processkommittén*), tasked with reforming the procedural code. Apart from the substantial issues, both policymakers and legal professionals would continue to disagree on whether to proceed through stepwise reforms or a major overhaul of the procedural system, and this reform attempt, too, would be marked by adversities (Mellqvist 2016: n. 1). While the Commission was chaired by a succession of three senior judges, its secretary Karl Schlyter, by then a young junior judge, would become a key agent in seeing through its proposed reforms. Schlyter, namesake of his grandfather who had served with Richert on the Legal Advisory Committee, had joined the Social Democratic Party (SDP) when he was studying law at Lund in 1906—a radical move for a young career judge (Sundell 2000). As a chief district judge in Askim 1923–1929, Schlyter would also experimentally introduce oral and concentrated proceedings and other desired reforms, arguing that he was really just resurrecting procedural regulations from the old Code of 1734 (Modéer 1999). The Commission proceeded thoroughly and conducted study visits to France, Germany, and Austria. Only in 1926 would it deliver its report suggesting the basic principles of a reformed trial procedure, but no specific legislation (Mellqvist 2016). After a hearing round and consultation of the Council on Legislation, the government presented in 1931 a bill on the basic principles for procedural reform, but no legislation, which parliament adopted. Having parliament thus agreeing on the basic principles, Karl Schlyter—who now headed the ministry of justice in the first Social Democratic government—appointed a new commission, the Procedural Law Commission (*Processlagberedningen*), chaired by Natanael Gärde, an experienced judge and former minister of justice, to finalize the reform. The commission presented a draft procedural act in 1938. After another review of a revised proposal by the Council on Legislation in 1941, parliament adopted the bill in the spring of 1942. Entering into force in 1948 and completing a reform project first attempted by Richert's Law Commission in the early 1800s, the procedural reform has been called the most significant legislative project of the twentieth century. The procedural reform also necessitated reforms to the judicial organization, in part because the oral, concentrated procedure required a more decentralized system of appellate courts.

3.2 Penal Reform

The egalitarian spirit of the democratic era also inspired reforms in criminal law. A key agent behind these reforms was Johan Thyrén, professor of criminal law at Lund University (and, like his cousin Karl Schlyter, grandson of law professor Carl Johan Schlyter). Commissioned by the government, Thyrén published *Principles for a Criminal Law Reform* (1910–1914), introducing a pragmatic, sociological perspective on criminal law aimed at individual prevention. Fines and imprisonment would be the normal penalties, but Thyrén also suggested a type of protective measure for criminals that posed "atypical dangers to society," such as juvenile delinquents, chronic criminals, and alcoholics (Inger 2011: 306). Thyrén's reformist ideas would become highly influential. He helped bring about the abolition of the death penalty in 1921 and introduced the day-fines system to Sweden, as a form of penalty that would punish rich and poor equally. Thyrén served in parliament as an independent and as minister of justice in a liberal government from 1926 to 1928. When Karl Schlyter became justice minister in the first Social Democratic government in 1932, the two cousins initiated a broad reform program, which Schlyter later radically revised. Many of the reforms would be implemented by his successor from 1936, K. G. Westman, another law professor politician (Sundell 2000).

In 1935, Schlyter introduced a law on juvenile prison, aiming to rehabilitate juvenile delinquents through professional education, with sentences without fixed terms. Realizing the ethical problems with non-fixed sentences, Schlyter nevertheless argued that the social rehabilitation of criminals required radical, unconventional methods. Under the slogan "Depopulate the prisons!" Schlyter further abolished the law on conversion of pecuniary penalties, under which persons who failed to pay their fines instead had to serve prison sentences. The law primarily affected poor people, and its abolition in 1937 helped reduce the number of fine prisoners from 11,000 in 1930 to 650 in 1940 (Sundell 2000). From 1937 to 1953, Schlyter also chaired the penal law section of the Criminal Law Commission. Together with justice minister Thorwald Bergquist, a liberal and equally passionate criminal law reformer, Schlyter was the key force behind a partial penal law reform in 1945 that abolished cell confinement, although a lack of resources would delay the implementation.

Inspired by his long-time friend, law professor, and parliamentarian Vilhelm Lundstedt, justice minister Schlyter criminalized blackmail in 1934—a reform intended to improve the situation of homosexuals, the chief target of extortionists, and ten years later, as chair of the parliamentary law committee, decriminalized homosexual acts (Sundell 2000). Schlyter also sought to reform abortion and contraception policies, and contributed to the decriminalization of fornication and adultery. An energetic reformer, Schlyter was chiefly inspired by the sociological school of criminal law and, like Thyrén, pragmatically sought to combine individual and general prevention by designing the system of sanctions with an aim of resocializing criminals into good citizens (Sundell 2000). Criminal law reform, in his view, was also a matter of broader social reform.

3.3 Scandinavian Legal Realism

After the democratic breakthrough, the SDP became increasingly dominant, forming the government between 1932 and 1976 without interruption (except for the summer of 1936). While the social democratic project of expanding the welfare state has sometimes been described as based on a collectivist, corporatist ideology, it also expressed a particular Swedish ideology of "state individualism": social democratic welfare state reform programs aimed at promoting individual autonomy (Rothstein 1998a) and liberating individuals from their dependency on any powerful body other than the state (Berggren and Trägårdh 2009). The era of the democratic welfare state also saw the emergence of a new cadre of radical legal professionals mobilizing law for political reform, but their progressive agenda was not necessarily politically liberal, even as it sometimes overlapped with liberal causes.

In the interwar years, the legal philosophy of Scandinavian legal realism (SLR) began shaping both Swedish political culture and the legal professions. Influenced by the value nihilism of Uppsala philosopher Axel Hägerström, the legal realists rejected all talk of natural rights as metaphysical nonsense, sought to restrict legal science to positive law, and viewed international law as superstition because of its lack of enforcement. Law, on this view, was "technical facts operated by jurists" (Modéer 2003: 163; on SLR, see Pihlajamaki 2004; Bjarup 2005; Strang 2009). Scandinavian legal realism also served the social democratic welfare state project: If the development of the Rechtsstaat in the late nineteenth century assigned lawyers the role of protectors of the individual against the state, the expansion of the welfare state instead saw lawyers as social engineers, supportive of the state's expansion, and the emphasis shifted form civil, private law to public law (Modéer 2003). This also resonated with a new ideal of the civil servant as an engaged, benevolent bureaucrat, who, as a representative of the strong state, served to improve the conditions of society's weak and poor (Ställvik 2009: 100).

Key proponents of SLR were to become prominent public figures in the mid-twentieth century. Östen Undén, who had studied law under Thyrén, became professor of civil law and international private law at Uppsala University in 1917, its rector from 1929 to 1932 and university chancellor from 1937 to 1951. He also served in government, most influentially as foreign minister (1924–1926, 1945–1962). Another key proponent of legal realism, Vilhelm Lundstedt, professor of civil law at Uppsala, had experienced a revelatory conversion in his legal philosophy during his conversations with Hägerström and came to revitalize legal philosophy in Sweden. He had joined the SDP in 1910 and represented the party in the second chamber from 1929 to 1948. A strident academic and politician, Lundstedt unsuccessfully motioned the SDP and parliament to reject international law and the League of Nations (Molin 1982) and later argued that Sweden ought to abandon neutrality and join the Western alliance.

Even as they had as their primary occupation law professor or judge, some of these elite jurists also occupied political offices as parliamentarians and ministers of government and served on government commissions. As a result, the legal sphere seems to have been characterized by close, overlapping personal networks. The jurists also featured in a new public sphere for legal debate, for instance in *Svensk Juristtidning*, a law journal founded in 1916 that would become a central forum for a younger generation of jurists, connecting academics, practitioners, and policymakers (Modéer 2016). Karl Schlyter served as its editor for thirty-six years, in addition to his work as a judge, lawmaker, and minister. Apparently, the leading jurists did not form a monolithic block; they interacted across political cleavages and had substantial disagreements in matters of practical policy and legal philosophy. The pragmatic reformers Thyrén and Schlyter, for instance, disputed the legal realists' view that general prevention was paramount in criminal law (Molin 1982; Sundell 2000), while fellow social democrats and legal realists Undén and Lundstedt diverged in their views on many policy matters, such as the war-time curtailment of press freedom and Sweden's post-war foreign policy orientation.

3.4 Sterilization Laws

Increasing worries over the degeneration of the Swedish race led the ministry of social affairs to appoint a commission in 1927 to investigate "sterilization in certain cases of imbeciles, the mentally ill and epileptics." Led by judge Gustaf Lindstedt, the commission delivered its report and proposed legislation in 1929 (Socialdepartementet 1929). Noting the lack of scientific knowledge about hereditary diseases, the commission proposed to allow sterilization only on informed and consenting individuals suffering from genetic diseases that made them dependent on social care or incapable of caring for their children. The National Board of Medicine would grant permits for sterilization. Emphasizing the individual's right to bodily integrity vis-à-vis the societal interest of preventing imbeciles from reproducing, the commission also noted the juridical difficulties in allowing sterilization. Lindstedt argued that a doctor performing sterilization for purely social reasons would risk facing criminal charges even if the patient had consented to the operation.

In the hearing round, the medical profession harshly criticized the commission's limited proposal (women's organizations were not invited to comment). Informed consent, several consultive bodies argued, was a criterion impossible to fulfil and the exaggerated juridical caution and insistence on certain medical knowledge would unduly restrict the scope of action of the medical profession (Runcis 1998: 73ff). In the legal profession, the proposal stirred debate, as radical jurists charged Lindstedt with having a conservative agenda. Ragnar Bergendal, professor of criminal law at Lund, argued that modern medicine had made sterilization a safe, minor operation. Some, like law professors Nils Stjernberg and Johan Thyrén, argued that consent would be illusory in practice and argued that the law ought to allow explicitly for forcible sterilization. Karl Schlyter, by then newly appointed president of the Court of Appeal for southern Sweden, claimed that the proposal mismatched the public conception of justice and questioned the need for regulations since, in his view, sterilization of imbecile or uneducable girls, giving their informed consent, could hardly be considered a form of bodily harm; instead, he wished to grant doctors full freedom of action (Schlyter 1930; Runcis 1998: 78; Zaremba 1999: 222ff). Responding to their criticism, Lindstedt argued that it was legally and constitutionally impossible to allow sterilization for purely social reasons in the name of public interest and advocated instead social measures to prevent undesirable reproduction (Runcis 1998: 76, 79). In the end, the proposed law was never presented to parliament and Lindstedt, the lone defender of individual rights in this debate, would, in a strange twist, become a co-founder of the National Socialist Bloc later in the 1930s (Zaremba 1999: 220 n. 5).

The discourse of racial hygiene had proved insufficient to justify a flexible sterilization law, but in the early 1930s the issue would return, now framed in terms of rational public interest, but also merging with feminist demands for policies on abortion, contraception, and sex education. In 1932, the Social Democrats formed a government. Schlyter, now heading the ministry of justice, appointed law professor Bergendal to re-investigate the issue of sterilization. The law he drafted permitted sterilization of persons permanently incapable of giving their consent (Justitiedepartementet 1933). Compared to the 1929 proposal, the proposal expanded the grounds for sterilization (Runcis 1998: 85): As valid reasons for sterilization, Bergendal included both "social indication," that is, on persons incapable of caring for their children due to mental illness, and "eugenic indication," based on the risk of transferring hereditary mental illness to the children. The National Board of Medicine would make decisions on sterilization of the insane (*sinnessjuka*), whereas for "imbeciles" (*sinnesslöa*) it sufficed with a consensus decision by two doctors. In the hearing round, no legal objections were raised, but the medical profession still requested more comprehensive regulation. Specifically, several consultative bodies also wished to see regulation of sterilization of legally capable persons to restrict the discretion of doctors and prevent the risk that doctors would sterilize genetically valuable persons or prescribe it as a permanent method of contraception (Runcis 1998: 87). The Second Chamber adopted the bill without much debate, while in the First Chamber, a few conservative jurists criticized the proposal, among them Hjalmar Hammarskjöld, a judge, law professor, and former prime minister, who called for stricter control of sterilization operations in order to prevent rights violations. Adopting the bill in 1934, parliament also requested a new inquiry commission on sterilization.

Two years later, the new commission, consisting of a zoologist, a botanist, a chief physician, and an associate judge, proposed to allow for sterilization of persons capable of consenting to it, to widen the grounds for sterilization, and to place the decision-making authority with a central board. The commission considered the legal aspects to have been settled by the previous commissions. While the medical profession was largely positive about the new proposal, it also raised some concerns on how to implement the law in practice. In 1940, the government presented a bill that softened restrictions on sterilization of the legally incapable, introduced a "medical indication," whereby women could be sterilized because of physical defects, and expanded the "eugenic indication" to include hereditary physical defects and the "social indication" to include asocial lifestyles, thus enlarging grounds for sterilization far beyond the medical sphere (Runcis 1998: 159). The bill triggered a debate in parliament, where a group of social democrats, arguing in terms of pragmatism, rationality, and public interest, were concerned that the centralized decision-making procedure would harm the effectiveness of the sterilization law, and some wished to expand forcible sterilization. Explicit racism was voiced by Minister of Justice K. G. Westman of the Agrarian Party, greeting the law as a step toward "sanitizing the Swedish race" (Runcis 1998: 167).

Liberals and conservatives rather emphasized hereditary hygiene, which implied an evidence-based limitation on the practice of sterilization, and individual rights. The sharpest critique, however, came from Georg Branting, a lawyer and social democrat, who argued that the consent required for sterilization required extra precaution since the persons subject to the law were in a position of dependency vis-à-vis the authorities. Furthermore, he found the expanded social indication to be based on a reactionary idea, and argued that instead of advocating sterilization of vulnerable persons, social democrats ought to improve the social circumstances for parents and children (Runcis 1998: 165f). After this debate, parliament adopted the bill with an expanded social indication.

The 1941 law gave doctors considerable discretion in recommending sterilization and the indications proved quite arbitrary in practice, for instance sterilizing women because of promiscuity. While the law formally required consent (except for those incapable of giving it), the requirement turned out to be illusory in practice: Authorities could obtain consent by conditioning social support, custody of children, or permission to marry (for those under the age of 25) on agreeing to undergo sterilization, and sometimes medical staff did not inform patients prior to the operation. The practice of sterilization culminated in the 1940s, yet continued until 1975.[1] From 1935 to 1975, a total of 62,888 persons were sterilized, of whom 93 percent were women. In the region of 27,000 persons were subject to direct or indirect coercion (Socialdepartementet 2000). The sterilization debate indicates, on the one hand, a divide between certain liberal-conservative jurists, who insisted on the rule of law and individual rights, and radical jurists, who saw public interest as paramount. On the other hand, it also shows how the radical reformers actively sought to bypass a conservative state bureaucracy dominated by jurists, to instead rely on other professions in expanding the welfare state (Rothstein 1998b).

3.5 Curtailment of Press Freedom During the War

During World War II, the inclination to prioritize public interest over individual rights would also lead some leading jurists to support restrictions on press freedom and political freedoms. Hitler's *Machtübernahme* in 1933 had already put Swedish

[1] According to a 1972 law on gender identity, however, sterilization was made mandatory for sex reassignment surgery—a requirement abolished by an administrative court of appeal only in 2013.

press freedom to the test. Initially, government—the first all-social democratic cabinet, led by Per Albin Hansson, himself a former journalist—dismissed demands by German authorities to act against critical press coverage, and acting foreign minister Östen Undén explained in an interview that his ministry gave a standard response to such complaints: Swedish newspapers were independent of the government. However, later in 1933, justice minister Karl Schlyter ordered the Chancellor of Justice to prosecute leftist newspapers for having insulted Hermann Göring, which led to prison sentences for the editors (Vallinder 2000: 223). Government took no further legal action until 1939, but informally appealed to some editors to soften their criticism of foreign powers.

However, the national unity government formed after the outbreak of the war, which included all political parties except the Communists, increasingly curtailed press freedom, through legislation, confiscation without trial of periodicals, and prosecution under the Press Freedom Act. The 1809 constitution gave little guidance, as it included no regulations for a state of exception. In December 1939, justice minister Karl Gustaf Westman—a professor of legal history and a leading figure in the Agrarian party—appointed a committee led by Ragnar Bergendal to propose changes to the Press Freedom Act, chiefly to introduce various forms of censorship (Justitiedepartementet 1940). In 1940, parliament adopted the resulting bill and also an ordinance granting authorities the right to prohibit the circulation by post or public transport of a periodical if a jury had found it to violate the Press Freedom Act (e.g., by endangering national security). Although parliament adopted the bill in 1940 and confirmed the constitutional changes in 1941, it never implemented the Censorship Act. However, the government would use the so-called prohibition of transportation ordinance in order to stop the circulation of six periodicals, three of which were Communist and one a Nazi magazine (Vallinder 2000: 245).

Besides these legislative measures, government used prosecution and confiscation as a two-pronged strategy for curtailing press freedom. In November 1939, the Swedish minister to Berlin Arvid Richert (incidentally, great-great-grandson of the liberal reformer) urged Westman to order the prosecution of *Trots allt*, an anti-Nazi weekly, for an editorial titled 'Hitler's hell machine'. This was the start and the pattern of a campaign that would continue until May 1943; initially, it targeted chiefly democratic or Communist publications but eventually achieved some balance by increasingly prosecuting pro-Nazi publications. However, prosecution was a risky strategy since the Press Freedom Act of 1815 stipulated trial by jury, and government could never be sure to win the case. While eight out of ten trials against periodicals in 1939 led to conviction, the conviction rate dropped to 50 percent in the thirty-eight trials conducted between 1940 and 1943; consequently, the government became less inclined to order prosecutions after 1940 (Vallinder 2000: 248, 303). Moreover, the procedure was biased against the state, and not only because conviction required a qualified majority in the jury: While prosecutors were often unenthusiastic about carrying out orders from the justice ministry, defense attorneys were both competent and passionate for their cause and sometimes managed to recruit prominent public intellectuals to the jury (Vallinder 2000: 307).

Instead, justice minister Westman turned to confiscation. The Press Freedom Act of 1815 contained a paragraph (3:9) allowing government to confiscate without trial publications that, although not libelous, could cause "misunderstandings with foreign powers" (Hirschfeldt 2009, 408). The paragraph had never been used without a trial and by the interwar years an authoritative constitutional lawyer considered it to contradict the fundamental principles of the Press Freedom Act. Yet Westman innovatively resuscitated the paragraph and thereby gained an effective means for stopping publications, yet bypassing, as he put it, "the unpredictable and in foreign policy matters injudicious jury" (Vallinder 2000: 237f). From 1939 to 1943, the government would confiscate a total of thirty-seven books or pamphlets and 280 periodicals, including both extremist (Communist or, to lesser extent, pro-Nazi) and democratic publications. In March 1942, Westman ordered the confiscation of nearly twenty newspapers, which, in a coordinated effort, had published reports about atrocities in prisons and concentration camps in Norway (Vallinder 2000: 246).

Although the wartime cabinet represented all democratic political parties, its repressive press policies met harsh criticism in parliament (Hirschfeldt 2009: 409) and also in the media. Leading jurists seem to have been split on the issue. While Östen Undén—by this time university chancellor and member of the second chamber—criticized the restrictions on press freedom in a radio debate with Westman (Vallinder 2000: 227), his fellow legal realist Vilhelm Lundstedt, who sat on parliament's legal committee, defended the transportation prohibition, which was primarily aimed at Communist newspapers: A regulation that served to save the nation from ruin, he claimed, could never violate the constitution (Molin 1982).

By 1943, however, the situation had shifted. After Stalingrad, Germany's pressure on Sweden eased, and Thorwald Bergquist, a Liberal, succeeded Westman as justice minister. A second chamber election was coming up in 1944; nearly everyone agreed that press freedom should be restored after the war, which required parliament to adopt constitutional changes both before and after the election (Vallinder 2000: 312f). But the unity government was split: Liberals and most Social Democrats wished to abolish the press freedom restrictions quickly, but were outnumbered by Conservatives and Agrarians. In order to resolve the deadlock, Minister of Justice Bergquist proposed a parliamentary commission to comprehensively revise the Press Freedom Act (Vallinder 2000: 314). The resulting Press Freedom Act of 1949 abolished the wartime restrictions, preserved the special procedure for press freedom trials, including the jury, and introduced constitutional protection of rights for persons providing information to journalists.

Aside from press freedom, the post-war era saw a significant improvement in freedom of religion. In 1951, parliament granted citizens the right to leave the

Church of Sweden without entering another community of faith and abolished the prohibition against Catholic monasteries (Werner 2002). Since the 1880s, several parliamentary motions had demanded liberalization of the dissenter law. After the democratic breakthrough, two subsequent committees, appointed by Liberal and Social Democratic governments, suggested liberalization, but their proposals did not result in any bills, partly because the Social Democrats shifted from radical anti-clericalism to regarding the state church as an important guarantor of a democratic system. Moreover, many liberals and progressives considered the Catholic Church a transnational organization seeking political power and saw monastic orders as violating individual freedom of religion (Werner 2002). However, ratification of the European Convention on Human Rights (ECHR) provided a decisive reason to remove restrictions on freedom of religion.

3.6 The Relative Decline of the Jurists

If the legal profession had earlier provided the state with unique expertise on how to govern a modern, impersonal mass society, facilitating capitalist industrial transformation, the expansion of the welfare state diminished its relative importance for the state machinery. Up until 1964, however, a law degree was a formal requirement for employment in ministries and higher echelons of the state bureaucracy, and still by the 1970s, a majority of director-generals were law graduates (Holmström 1995: 346f). Moreover, senior civil servants and judges formed a substantial part of the legislature: 40 percent of first chamber deputies and 10–15 percent of second chamber deputies held law degrees, while 10 and 6–8 percent, respectively, were judges, but private lawyers were unusual (Holmström 1995: 347).

From 1950 to 1987, the number of legal professionals increased by a factor of 2.5, but other academic professions grew much faster, for example, engineers (x 10), social workers (x 7), and psychologists (x 23) (Bertilsson 1989). While the proportion of the legal profession employed in private enterprise increased from 13 to 21 percent in the same period, the majority—61 percent—remained employed in the public sector. Compared to Norway and Denmark, Sweden had (and perhaps still has) a different balance between the bar and the bench: 17 percent of Swedish jurists were practicing lawyers (1987), compared to 34 percent in Denmark (1986) and 30 percent in Norway (1970), while 16 percent of jurists in Sweden were employed in the judicial or prosecutorial system, but only 5 percent in Denmark (1986) and 8 percent in Norway (1970). This difference might be due to the fact that Denmark and Norway had more small businesses, which consult private law firms, whereas state-led industrial rationalization in Sweden favored major corporations, which have internal legal departments, thereby reducing the demand for private law firms (Bertilsson 1989).

Court and procedural reforms undermined the autonomy of the bench, by, for example, strengthening the role of lay judges (Ställvik 2009: 102). Jurists also lost ground to other professions in the numerous committees preparing law reforms, especially in a series of committees on constitutional reform from 1941 onward, where instead political scientists assumed the expertise role (Modéer 2011: 748). On the other hand, the expansion of other professions in the welfare state and the relative decline of jurists may have helped define the domains of the legal professions: Rather than a generalist bureaucrat in the state administration, the jurist became a specialist on the interpretation, implementation, and application of the law.

4. Mobilization on Rights in the 1970s Constitutional Reforms

After the democratic breakthrough, political life had turned to consolidating democracy and to substantive political issues (Möller 2011: 103). Eventually, however, and increasingly after World War II, calls for reform pointed to the glaring discrepancies between the 1809 Instrument of Government and the way in which Sweden was actually governed. The RF still proscribed separation of powers between king and parliament, which had in practice been superseded by parliamentarism, now a core principle of Swedish democracy, which lacked constitutional regulation. Opponents of constitutional reform, however, argued that the flexibility of the 1809 RF had contributed to political stability in the turbulent inter-war era, and that it could be pragmatically amended through piecemeal reforms. An inquiry commission headed by political science professor Herbert Tingsten suggested expanding rights protection, but this never led to a bill (Justitiedepartementet 1941).

In 1954, the government appointed a constitutional inquiry commission (*Författningsutredningen*) with a wide mandate to conduct a complete oversight of the constitution, which presented its final report in 1963. It failed, however, to agree on whether parliament should have one or two chambers, and so presented proposals for both models. In 1966, the four major political parties agreed to appoint a new constitutional commission (*Grundlagsberedningen*, GLB). Having reached agreement on the parliamentary and electoral system, the commission could proceed with a total constitutional overhaul. In 1971, parties agreed to preserve the monarchy, yet stripping the monarch of all but a ceremonial constitutional function (Möller 2011: 185ff; Ohlsson 2014: 407ff).

While they reached compromises on most elements of the new constitutional architecture, parties failed to find a workable agreement on civil rights and liberties, a struggle that continued throughout the 1970s. In the GLB commission, Liberals and Conservatives wished to strengthen the protection for individual rights, in particular rights that were central to political participation, such as freedom of expression. By contrast, Social Democrats were skeptical of both the means of protection, that is, a suggested qualified majority requirement and judicial review, and the substance of the rights provided: The RF would give the wrong impression if it focused only on rights protecting citizens against abuses of power; it should also declare the ambitious egalitarian purposes of the welfare state (Algotsson 1987: 44). The commission reached a compromise, by which the Social Democrats ceded their demands for manifesto provisions and a prohibition against judicial review, while Liberals and Conservatives backed away from their insistence on a qualified majority requirement for rights restrictions.

Compared to the monarchy issue, rights and liberties initially did not stir much debate when the commission presented its proposal. In the hearing round, some key consultative bodies, including the Supreme Administrative Court, Svea Court of Appeals, the Justice Chancellor and the Swedish Bar Association, rejected the proposal in its entirety on both substantive and formal grounds, and specifically addressed the lack of protection of basic rights and liberties (Justitiedepartementet 1973: suppl. 2). In public debate, however, the only person to challenge the GLB's proposal was Gustaf Petrén, Justice of the Supreme Administrative Court, who warned against the dangers of allowing a parliamentary majority to restrict basic rights and freedoms by ordinary statute (Algotsson 1987: 47ff). However, in January 1973, FiB-juristerna, a group of lawyers associated with the leftist freedom of expression organization FiB/Kulturfront, sharply criticized the lack of rights protections in the GLB in an op-ed in the leading daily newspaper *Dagens Nyheter*. Their article was followed by editorials and op-eds in major liberal newspapers (Algotsson 1987: 51).

By coincidence, the so-called IB Affair further fueled the debate on civil rights (Lampers 2002): In a series of articles in the magazine *FiB/Kulturfront* in May 1973, two reporters had exposed IB, a secret intelligence agency collaborating not only with the SDP and trade unions, but also with foreign intelligence services, which monitored and registered left-leaning Swedish citizens. In October 1973, the two journalists were arrested and eventually sentenced to prison for espionage.

Influenced by this public debate, the compromise agreement from the GLB had been lost as the ministry of justice prepared its bill (Algotsson 1987: Ch. 3). All four opposition parties filed separate motions where they criticized the constitutional bill's lack of protection of rights. While the Communists and the non-socialist parties diverged in their views on substantive rights, they partially mobilized similar arguments against the bill. In the ensuing debate, Conservatives focused on the need for protecting individual citizens against everyday governmental reform zest, whereas Liberals demanded stronger constitutional rights provisions as vital protection in possible future political emergencies. The Social Democrats, on the other hand, regarded the right of a parliamentary majority to carry out political reforms as an essential expression of the people's democratic rights, which should be curtailed neither by parliamentary minorities nor by unelected judges.

A divided parliamentary majority now opposed the constitutional bill. However, the parliamentary Constitutional Committee solved the problem by appointing a new commission, mandated to consider expanding constitutional rights protection, and by meeting some concerns of both the Communists and the non-socialist parties (Algotsson 1987: s. 3.9). Hence, on June 6, 1973, parliament adopted the new RF and its provisional rights catalogue, containing a set of core rights to freedoms of opinion (e.g., expression, information, assembly, association, and religion), but which could be curtailed by a simple majority decision in parliament, and a set of non-derogable rights provisions, such as prohibitions against retroactive penal legislation, capital punishment, and exilement.

The run-up to the second vote after the 1973 election, required for the new RF to enter into force, saw intensified mobilization: "numerous gatherings and demonstrations were held; resolutions were adopted; petitions were in circulation; the constitutional proposal was debated in editorial and cultural sections in the press" (Algotsson 1987: 114; cf. Svanberg 2013: 38ff). Seemingly strange bedfellows campaigned against the bill: On the non-socialist side, critical voices included Petrén, law professors Stig Strömholm and Håkan Strömberg, and liberal intellectuals; on the left, FiB-juristerna, but also radical intellectuals and various Marxist groups (Algotsson 1987: 115f). Parliament, however, did not heed the calls for a referendum on or a complete rejection of the proposal. In the debate preceding the second decision, all four major parties stood by the proposal, and portrayed the critics as an unholy alliance of the extreme left and right (Algotsson 1987: 119ff). The new Instrument of Government (RF1974) entered into force on January 1, 1975.

However, the constitutional rights dispute continued, now delegated to another commission, the Liberties and Rights Commission (*Fri- och rättighetsutredningen*, FRU), which, delivering its final report in October 1975 (Justitiedepartementet 1975), failed to resolve the controversy (Algotsson 1987: Ch. 4). On the majority view, represented by the Social Democrats and the Centre Party, rights should be secured by a material method, detailing their substance along with permissible and impermissible derogations, complemented by judicial review, permitting courts to set aside laws that "obviously" violate a constitutional law. Conservatives and Liberals repeated their demand for a qualified majority requirement for legislation constraining civil liberties. The Commission also proposed expanding the rights catalog with additional negative opinion liberties, prohibition against torture, corporal punishment, and registration of the political views of citizens, and expanded prohibition against discrimination. It also specified a set of economic and social rights, necessary for the fulfilment of democracy as objectives of the constitution, of lesser juridical weight than the negative civil liberties.

The FRU report received mixed responses during the hearing round (Algotsson 1987: 168). Both of the supreme courts endorsed the suggested judicial review model, whereas other consultative bodies in the legal sphere criticized it for being either too modest or too ambitious. The Confederation of Trade Unions sharply criticized the judicial review mechanism. In the resulting bill, the ministry of justice mainly followed the commission's recommendations, but saw no need to regulate the practice of cautious judicial review in the constitution. In any event, the ministry suggested, yet another inquiry commission would investigate judicial review and related issues.

The rights protection issues continued to draw public interest, and the non-socialist press sharply criticized the proposal, but activism outside parliament had faded, particularly on the left. As the Constitutional Committee and parliament processed the bill, the opposition continued to insist that rights restricting legislation should require a qualified majority vote. In part, the failure to resolve the conflict may have been due to the peculiar parliamentary situation: Not only was an election coming up in the fall of 1976, where some parties feared and others prepared for mobilization on the issue of civil rights and liberties (Algotsson 1987: 233f); in the 1973 election, the two blocs had gained exactly 175 each of the new single-chamber parliament's 350 seats, meaning that parliament had to draw a lot on issues where it failed to build a majority across the bloc divide (subsequently, the number of seats was reduced to 349). Presumably, most parties wished to avoid having contentious constitutional matters decided by chance.

In the 1976 election, the Social Democrats found themselves having to leave government for the first time in forty years, and the Centre Party formed a government together with Conservatives and Liberals. In 1977, minister of justice Sven Romanus appointed Gunnar Heckscher, former leader of the Conservatives, to head a new inquiry commission, the Rights Protection Commission (*Rättig-hets-skydds-ut-red-ning-en*), instructed to specify constitutional safeguards for civil liberties (Algotsson 1987: 238). When it presented its report (Justitiedepartementet 1978), all parties except the Communists had finally agreed to write judicial review into the RF, but with an important restriction: Courts could review a law only if it "obviously" violated the constitution. Moreover, for those rights that could be derogated by statutory law, two separate decisions by parliament would be required to allow time for reflection and debate. Finally, a parliamentary minority could demand a referendum on proposed changes to the constitution. The bill was confirmed by parliament after the 1979 election, which again gave the non-socialist bloc a majority.

After a quarter-century of constitutional reform, what did this settlement mean in terms of political liberalism, on balance? On the one hand, the new constitution improved on the 1809 Instrument of Government insofar as it sought to reflect actual constitutional practice and made the procedural rules for changing the constitution more rigid (Algotsson 1987: 284). Codifying civil liberties, every new constitutional commission also added rights provisions to the constitution. The reform process, long and contentious as it was, probably contributed to raising public awareness of civil liberties and rights. On the other hand, the new constitution also removed the last remnants of separation of powers, by scrapping the first chamber, strengthening the link between parliament and government, and regulating courts and public administration in one common chapter. The previously mandatory judicial preview by the Council on Legislation was made facultative in 1970–1, putting an end to recurring disagreements between the judiciary and policymakers (Modéer 2003: 165; Algotsson 2009). And the compromise on allowing judicial review only if statutory law "obviously" violated the constitution codified but effectively curbed a practice that had evolved, without support in the constitution, since the 1920s.

The closest we get to legal professionals emerging as a collective agent for political liberalism appears to be in 1973–1974, when some judicial consultative bodies, the Bar Association, justice Petrén, FiB-juristerna, and certain law professors sharply criticized the 1973 bill, accompanied by debates in the mass media and broader mobilization in civil society. However, consultative bodies in the legal sphere seem not to have mobilized in unison. The critics did not speak for the legal profession as a whole—the political parties targeted them as an unholy alliance of political extremists (Algotsson 1987). After that phase, the non-parliamentary critics, particularly on the left, moved on to other forms of activism and partly rights issues other than constitutional reform, while Petrén founded the Civil Rights Movement (*Medborgarrättsrörelsen*), a group whose commitment to natural rights and separation of powers placed it on the far side of the Conservative Party.

The 1970s were a period of protracted economic crisis, increasing radicalization, and political confrontation, yet the Social Democrats did not halt their ambitious reform agenda. Some other reform projects also had a bearing on political liberalism. First, in a series of reforms of the municipal structure from 1952 to 1974, more than two thousand towns, boroughs, and rural municipalities were merged into 278 municipalities. In 1969, the socialist majority in parliament decided to speed up the process by enforcing amalgamations (Erlingsson, Wångmar, and Ödalen 2010). While the new RF accorded municipalities local self-government and fiscal autonomy, parliament retained unlimited discretion in determining their tasks. Both the involuntary process and the resulting radical restructuring of local government weakened the municipal level as a balance to the central government. Second, the judicial system was the target of a similar rationalization program. Paralleling the municipality reform, urban and rural district courts were harmonized and brought together under state jurisdiction and regulation in 1971. In 1975, district courts were further centralized under a new National Court Administration (*Domstolsverket*, DV) in Stockholm—criticized by some as a government tool to control the judiciary (Nergelius and Zimmermann 2012: 192). The administrative court system was reformed by the creation of new administrative appellate courts (*kammarrätt*, 1972) and primary courts (*länsrätt*, 1979). By separating the judicial function from public administration, these reforms contributed to extending 'the scope for judicial review of administrative and governmental action' (Holmström 1995: 353), especially after the 1988 law enhancing the right to appeal administrative decisions.

5. The Return to Political Liberalism

While the 1970s may represent the peak of the social democratic project, they also represent the start of its demise, not only because the Social Democrats lost power for the first time since the 1930s. In the following decades, the pendulum turned again toward individual rights, constitutionalism, and judicial review, not least under the influence of European law. These trends may indicate more profound changes in the link between the legal complex and political liberalism in Sweden, and in their different ways they are all related to Sweden's integration into the European community.

First, Sweden ratified the ECHR in 1952, including individual petition without restrictions, and in 1966, only after the retirement of foreign minister Östen Undén, Sweden accepted (non-permanently) the compulsory jurisdiction of the European Court of Human Rights (ECtHR) (Schaffer 2017; 2020). The Convention system had little impact on Swedish political and legal realities during the first thirty years (Sundberg 1986; Wiklund 2008). However, by the mid-1970s, the Strasbourg court was up to speed, since most states in Western Europe had accepted its jurisdiction, and it began to reinterpret its mandate: Rather than serving as an inter-state pact against totalitarianism, the Convention provided a bill of rights for European democracies (Bates 2010). In this new, empowered role, the Court delivered its first judgment against Sweden in the landmark case *Sporrong and Lönnroth v. Sweden* (1982).[2] The case concerned two property owners in Stockholm, whose buildings the city had put under an unlimited expropriation permit. The Court found that since the property owners could neither have the permits time-limited nor demand compensation for their economic damage, and since, moreover, they were denied a right to appeal the city's decision, the state had violated both the right to protection of property and the right to a fair trial. The defiant attitude of the Swedish government—at a press conference, Prime Minister Olof Palme denigrated the Strasbourg court as a "playhouse for Supreme Administrative Court Justice Gustaf Petrén"—spurred the court to take up a series of cases that also resulted in judgments against Sweden. Slowly, it dawned not only on Swedish judges but on policymakers too that the Convention had profound implications for domestic legal and administrative practices.

In 1992, the government (a non-socialist coalition since the 1991 election) appointed a commission to investigate, again, constitutional rights protection

[2] European Court of Human Rights. 1982. *Case of Sporrong and Lönnroth v. Sweden*. App. no. 7151/75; 7152/75.

and incorporation of the ECHR into national law (Justitiedepartementet 1993). The commission concurred with the government's proposal to incorporate the Convention and permanently accept the jurisdiction of the Court, recognizing that the Convention was considered part of the legal order of the European Community, to which Sweden was preparing to accede. Furthermore, it noted, the Swedish system was becoming an anomaly, as other dualist states had already incorporated the ECHR or planned to do so. Finally, incorporating the ECHR into national law would signal its importance as a guarantee for individual rights, but also improve the authority of Swedish courts on ECHR rights. Consequently, Sweden incorporated the ECHR in 1995. It would take some time, however, before courts and the legislator began developing legal remedies (Bernitz 2011). In a series of precedent judgments, the Supreme Court successively expanded public authorities' tort law liabilities for violations of the Convention (Schultz 2009).

Moreover, in 1995 Sweden joined the European Union, which not only introduced another supranational legal-judicial layer, with the Court of Justice's doctrines of supremacy and direct effect, but also an additional source of rights and anti-discrimination law. As an effect, Swedish citizens overnight came to have stronger rights protection under European law than in the national constitution. More generally, EU membership also introduced a novel form of dualism into the Swedish constitutional order, incorporating a vertical separation of powers (Algotsson 2001)—a major transformation of the constitutional system which, however, left few direct marks on the Instrument of Government.

Second, the paradigm shift brought about by Sweden's integration into a European legal order also provides an important background to recent constitutional changes, which have enhanced rights protection, judicial review, and judicial independence. By the 1980s, the practice of judicial and administrative review had already departed from the compromise of the 1970s, not least influenced by the ECHR (Holmström 1994). Following more than a decade of public debate and a parliamentary inquiry commission on constitutional reform (*Grundlagsutredningen* 2004–2008), the Instrument of Government was revised in 2011. These revisions served to strengthen the protection of fundamental rights and liberties, remove the much-criticized restriction on judicial review, and make the constitutional preview by the Council on Legislation mandatory again. Moreover, the revisions also enhanced judicial independence by affording courts a new, separate chapter of the Instrument of Government and by moving the authority to appoint judges from the government to an independent board (*Domarnämnden*).

What these constitutional changes imply in terms of political liberalism and legal activism may still be too early to tell. A conservative member of the constitutional commission enthusiastically proclaimed that these changes turned "every district court into a constitutional court" (von Sydow 2011). Other commentators have more cautiously pointed out that the revisions may have strengthened the constitutional role of courts, but they are still not strong and independent enough, from the point of view of constitutionalism, rule of law, and legal security (Nergelius 2011). Legal scholars and lawyers have debated whether a series of recent prominent cases indicate that the Supreme Court has become more activist, appropriating a law-making function, and whether this new role is in line with the constitution (Wiklund 2014; Wersäll 2014).

However, with a slightly longer perspective, it seems evident that Sweden has been moving, steadily if incrementally, toward a more continental style of constitutionalism since the early 1990s. As in other Nordic states, a paradigm shift has occurred, "where it is now understood that courts have the competence and even the duty to apply a catalogue of fundamental rights, even of a 'foreign' origin, as a normative basis for reviewing decisions or other measures taken in the application of domestic law" (Scheinin 2008: 139f). Among consolidated democracies, the Nordic states may be a "final frontier" for judicial review, yet all key elements of constitutionalism—a written constitutional document, rule of law, fundamental rights, acknowledging international conventions, and so on—now exist within the five Nordic states (Nergelius 2008).

As an illustration of courts acting collectively in their new, more self-confident role, the so-called Haparanda uprising deserves mentioning. In 2010, the Supreme Court passed a judgment that approved of a common practice whereby the state could both levy a tax surcharge on persons who had given incorrect information in their tax declaration and prosecute them for fiscal offense. Finding this system to violate the *ne bis in idem* principle in both the ECHR and the EU Charter on Fundamental Rights, the district court in far northern Haparanda rejected the Supreme Court's reasoning and requested a preliminary ruling from the European Court of Justice (Kindbom 2011). Other district courts across the country soon followed suit and, faced with this extraordinary uprising of lower-level courts armed with European rights law, the Supreme Court eventually reversed its judgment, prohibited prosecution for tax offense after a tax surcharge, and started allowing retrial in double jeopardy cases. The government also responded by proposing new legislation whereby a court would decide on both penalties in a single procedure.

Third, since the early 2000s, if not earlier, a support structure for rights litigation has emerged in Sweden. In the 1980s, interest organizations that previously had been well integrated into the corporatist state had already started using strategic litigation, rather than working within the corporatist system, in order to pursue their interests (Holmström 1994). For instance, the landmark case *Sporrong and Lönnroth v. Sweden* was initiated and financed by the Swedish Property Federation, rather than by the plaintiffs their lawyers represented. Whereas organized interest groups that felt frustrated with established political channels brought these earlier cases, the emerging support structure today is composed of a variety of disparate organizations that have individual rights litigation as their main purpose. It includes a groups such as *Centrum för rättvisa* (Centre for Justice), a non-profit founded in 2002 that has taken on numerous cases, such as representing prospective students against discriminatory university admission criteria; Civil Rights Defenders (founded in 1982 as the Swedish Helsinki Committee), which has taken on notable rights cases against Swedish authorities, for example the "extraordinary rendition" of Agiza and Alzery to Egypt; and Sveriges Antidiskrimineringsbyråer (Anti-Discrimination Bureaus of Sweden), a network of fourteen local organizations financially supported by the state, which offer legal support and represent individuals, sometimes in much publicized cases, for example overturning mandatory sterilization prior to sex reassignment surgery.

These organizations have utilized the opportunities provided by national, European, and even international law to take rights cases to court (or other relevant forums), offering individuals legal expertise and financial support for litigation, but they also contribute to broader publicity and mobilization around individual rights. Lacking systematic data on cases and success rates, however, it is difficult to judge whether this budding support structure may lead to a broader rights revolution (Epp 1998)—or if it already has.

6. Conclusion

What role have lawyers and judges played for political liberalism in Sweden? This chapter has covered struggles for political liberalism in Sweden from the constitutional revolution in 1809 to the impact of European rights law—a revolution in a quite different sense—in the late twentieth century. What broader conclusions can we draw from this historical exposé? First, previous research on the legal complex has chiefly focused on legal professionals acting through courts or arising as public spokespersons for political liberalism. There are examples of such political lawyering in the Swedish case, for instance during the wartime press freedom trials. However, to the extent that legal professionals have shaped the expansion or contraction of political liberalism in Sweden, their most notable achievements have occurred through the slow and less theatrical work in governmental committees. Ever since the Law Commission was created in 1811, the committee apparatus not only suggests an arena for enacting political liberalism; the notion that government should make public policy by commissioning experts to draft new legislation and exposing their proposals to public scrutiny by official consultative bodies and the broader public also represents a potential constraint on government per se. However, sometimes committees have also been used as a means to defuse political conflict, as in the 1970s struggle over constitutional rights and liberties, or to obstruct important reform, as in the 1840s tableaux committees.

Second, the Swedish case also suggests that legal professionals acting as defenders of liberal rights may be a product of just as much as a causal force for political liberalism. For instance, in the nineteenth century, liberal reformers confronted authoritarian rule on multiple fronts, but their weapon of choice was rarely to mobilize law in courts, simply because the existing legal-judicial system was part of the problem rather than of the solution. Reformers first had to create an independent judiciary, a professional legal education, a competent bar, and, most importantly, a Rechtsstaat based on equality before the law. Likewise, the expansion of individual rights since the 1980s was in part caused by the changing nature of European human rights law, but also by domestic interest groups, dissatisfied with the corporatist system, turning to strategic litigation. Legal occupations have successively moved into the space provided by European rights law, both driven by and driving an expansion of political liberalism.

Finally, the Swedish case also raises questions about whether legal professionalism or liberalism is the primary cause behind legal action for political liberalism. Throughout two hundred years of political history, liberals have, at times, mobilized to enact individual rights and constrain government and civil society, using whatever strategies, arenas, and alliances they thought would help them achieve their goals. Some of these liberal reformers have been jurists using their legal competence collectively to promote political liberalism, such as Richert and his fellows on the law commissions of the nineteenth century. However, at other times legal professionals have been acting in concert to promote illiberal causes, such as Karl Schlyter and other radical jurists who contributed to the enactment of the sterilization laws in the 1930s. The professional role alone seems insufficient to account for why some groups of jurists promote liberalism whereas others oppose it. What does seem necessary, however, is to have a critical mass of people who believe individual rights and constrained government offer a solution to the grievances and difficulties they experience, who are determined to act on those beliefs and who are able to overcome their collective action problems.

References

Algotsson, Karl-Göran. 1987. *Medborgarrätten och regeringsformen: debatten om grundläggande fri- och rättigheter i regeringsformen under 1970-talet*. Stockholm: Norstedt.

Algotsson, Karl-Göran. 2001. "From Majoritarian Democracy to Vertical Separation of Powers: Sweden and the European Union," *Scandinavian Political Studies* 24(1): 51–65. doi:10.1111/1467-9477.00046.

Algotsson, Karl-Göran. 2009. "Lagrådets politiska betydelse," *Svensk Juristtidning* 94(2): 165–176.

Anckarswärd, Carl Henric, and Johan Gabriel Richert. 1830. *Förslag till national-representation*. Stockholm: Johan Hörberg.

Bates, Ed. 2010. *The Evolution of the European Convention on Human Rights: From Its Inception to the Creation of a Permanent Court of Human Rights*. Oxford: Oxford University Press.

Beckman, O. A. 1867. *Framställning om nödvändigheten att införa ett advokatstånd i Sverige*. Stockholm: Alb. Bonniers Boktryckeri.

Berggren, Henrik, and Lars Trägårdh. 2009. *Är svensken människa? Gemenskap och oberoende i det moderna Sverige*. Stockholm: Norstedt.

Bergh, Andreas. 2009. *Den kapitalistiska välfärdsstaten*. Stockholm: Norstedts akademiska förlag.

Bernitz, Ulf. 2011. "Rättighetsskyddets genomslag i svensk rätt – konventionsrättsligt och unionsrättsligt," *Juridisk Tidskrift*. 22(3): 821–846.

Bertilsson, Margareta. 1989. "Juristerna i välfärdsstaten," in Staffan Selander (ed.), *Kampen om yrkesutövning, status och kunskap: Professionaliseringens sociala grund*, 147–166. Lund: Studentlitteratur.

Bindreiter, Uta. 2009. *Lagprövningsdebatten 1955-1966: i skärningsfältet mellan juridik och politik*. Lund: Juristförlaget.

Bjarup, Jes. 2005. "The Philosophy of Scandinavian Legal Realism," *Ratio Juris* 18(1): 1–15.

Bomgren, Gunnar. 1937. *Det svenska advokatväsendet före bildandet av Sveriges advokatsamfund: en historisk överblick*. Stockholm: Norstedt.

Brandberg, Ulrika, and Tom Knutson. 2006. "En politisk reform som engagerade juristerna," *Advokaten* 72(9). https://www.advokaten.se/Tidningsnummer/2006/Nr-9-2006-Argang-72/En-politisk-reform-som-engagerade-juristerna/.

Brusewitz, Axel. 1918. "Georg Adlersparre." *Svenskt biografiskt lexikon*. https://sok.riksarkivet.se/sbl/artikel/5563.

Carlsson, Sten. 1990. "Departementalreformens förhistoria," in *Att styra riket: Regeringskansliet 1840–1990*, 11–42. Stockholm: Allmänna förlaget.

Collin, Hans Samuel, and Carl Johan Schlyter. 1829. "Kurze Uebersicht über den gegenwärtigen Zustand der Gesetzgebung und Rechtswissenschaft in Schweden," *Kritische Zeitschrift für Rechtswissenschaft und Gesetzgebung des Auslandes* 1: 423–433.

Epp, Charles R. 1998. *The Rights Revolution: Lawyers, Activists, and Supreme Courts in Comparative Perspective*. Chicago, IL: University of Chicago Press.

Erlingsson, Gissur Ó, Erik Wångmar, and Jörgen Ödalen. 2010. "Kommunsammanläggningarna 1952–1974. Hur blev de politiskt möjliga?" *Scandinavian Journal of Public Administration* 14(3/4): 3–36.

Fryxell, Anders. 1861. *Bidrag till Sverges Litteratur-Historia / Sjette häftet: Geijer. Uppsala-ultraismen*. 6. Stockholm: Joh. Beckman. http://runeberg.org/afbtsvlihi/6/0097.html

Gidlöf, Leif. 1998. "Eric Ruuth." *Svenskt biografiskt lexikon*. https://sok.riksarkivet.se/sbl/artikel/7059

Grade, A. 1918. "Carl H Anckarsvärd." *Svenskt biografiskt lexikon*. https://sok.riksarkivet.se/sbl/artikel/5765

Grage, Elsa-Britta. 2016. "Gabriel Poppius." *Svenskt biografiskt lexikon*. https://sok.riksarkivet.se/sbl/artikel/7345

Grimberg, Carl. 1923. *1809 års män, Karl Johans och Oskar I:s tid samt vårt näringsliv och kommunikationsväsen under teknikens tidevarv*. Svenska folkets underbara öden, VIII. Stockholm: Norstedt.

Halliday, Terence C., and Lucien Karpik (eds.). 1998. *Lawyers and the Rise of Western Political Liberalism: Europe and North America from the Eighteenth to Twentieth Centuries*. Oxford: Clarendon Press.

Halliday, Terence C., Lucien Karpik, and Malcolm Feeley. 2007. "The Legal Complex in Struggles for Political Liberalism," in Terence C. Halliday, Lucien Karpik, and Malcolm Feeley (eds.), *Fighting for Political Freedom: Comparative Studies of the Legal Complex and Political Liberalism*, 1–42. Oxford: Hart.

Halliday, Terence C., Lucien Karpik, and Malcolm M. Feeley. 2012. *Fates of Political Liberalism in the British Post-Colony: The Politics of the Legal Complex*. Cambridge: Cambridge University Press.

Harvard, Jonas. 2006. *En helig allmännelig opinion: Föreställningar om offentlighet och legitimitet i svensk riksdagsdebatt 1848–1919*. Umeå: Umeå universitet.

Hirschfeldt, Johan. 2009. "Den återerövrade tryckfriheten 1809," in Margareta Brundin and Magnus Isberg (eds.). *Maktbalans och kontrollmakt: 1809 års händelser, idéer och författningsverk i ett tvåhundraårigt perspektiv*, 373–414. Stockholm: Sveriges riksdag.

Holmström, Barry. 1994. "The Judicialization of Politics in Sweden," *International Political Science Review/Revue Internationale de Science Politique* 15(2): 153–164.

Holmström, Barry. 1995. "Sweden," in Torbjörn Vallinder and C. Neal Tate (eds.), *The Global Expansion of Judicial Power*, New York: New York University Press.

Inger, Göran. 2011. *Svensk rättshistoria*. 5th edition. Malmö: Liber.

Jacobson, G. 1925. "Johan Ludvig Johansson Boye (Boije)." *Svenskt biografiskt lexikon*. https://sok.riksarkivet.se/sbl/artikel/18027

Jägerskiöld, Olof. 1971. "Anders af Håkansson." *Svenskt biografiskt lexikon*. https://sok.riksarkivet.se/sbl/artikel/13953

Jägerskiöld, Stig. 1975. "Nils S von Koch." *Svenskt biografiskt lexikon*. https://sok.riksarkivet.se/sbl/artikel/11689

Jägerskiöld, Stig. 1987. "Adolph G Mörner." *Svenskt biografiskt lexikon*. https://sok.riksarkivet.se/sbl/artikel/8699

Justitiedepartementet. 1933. "Förslag till lag om sterilisering av vissa sinnessjuka, sinnesslöa eller av annan rubbning av själsverksamheten lidande personer." SOU 1933:22. http://weburn.kb.se/metadata/013/SOU_1280013.htm

Justitiedepartementet. 1940. "Promemoria med förslag till vissa åtgärder mot missbruk av tryckfriheten." SOU 1940:5 http://weburn.kb.se/metadata/336/SOU_8219336.htm

Justitiedepartementet. 1941. "Betänkande med förslag till ändrad lydelse av § 16 regeringsformen." SOU 1941:20. Stockholm.

Justitiedepartementet. 1973. "Kungl. Majts proposition med förslag till ny regeringsform och ny riksdagsordning m.m." Prop. 1973:90 Stockholm http://www.riksdagen.se/sv/dokument-lagar/dokument/proposition/kungl-majts-proposition-med-forslag-till-ny_FW0390

Justitiedepartementet. 1975. "Medborgerliga fri- och rättigheter i regeringsformen." SOU 1975:75. Stockholm.

Justitiedepartementet. 1978. "Förstärkt skydd för fri- och rättigheter." SOU 1978:34. Stockholm. http://weburn.kb.se/metadata/977/SOU_7258977.htm

Justitiedepartementet. 1993. "Inkorporering av Europakonventionen och andra fri- och rättighetsfrågor." Prop. 1993/94:117 http://www.riksdagen.se/sv/dokument-lagar/dokument/proposition/inkorporering-av-europakonventionen-och-andra_GH03117

Karpik, Lucien, and Terence C. Halliday. 2011. "The Legal Complex," *Annual Review of Law and Social Science* 7(1): 217–236. doi:10.1146/annurev-lawsocsci-102510-105512

Kindbom, Mikael. 2011. "Bernitz med i upproret mot HD," *InfoTorg Juridik*, January 18. http://infotorgjuridik.se/premium/mittijuridiken/article158199.ece

Koch, Mikael von. 1966. "Johan Gabriel Richert och 1864 års strafflag," *Svensk Juristtidning* 51: 413–418. https://svjt.se/svjt/1966/413

Kuylenstierna, Carl W. U. 1959. "Regeringsrätten 50 år," *Svensk Juristtidning* 44: 374–405. http://svjt.se/svjt/1959/393

Lampers, Lars Olof. 2002. *Det grå brödraskapet: En berättelse om IB*. Forskarrapport till Säke rhetstjänstkommissionen. SOU 2002:92. Stockholm: Fritzes.

Landberg, Georg. 1973. "Hans Järta." *Svenskt biografiskt lexikon*. https://sok.riksarkivet.se/sbl/artikel/12286
Lindberg, Bo. 2014. "Akademisk frihet före moderniteten." *Lychnos* 79: 39–62.
Mellqvist, Mikael. 2016. "Rättens gång—vad är meningen?" *Svensk Juristtidning* 101: 253–290. http://svjt.se/svjt/3016/253
Modéer, Kjell Å. 1979. "Carl Johan Schlyter i ett hundraårigt perspektiv," *Svensk Juristtidning* 64(1): 1–13. http://svjt.se/svjt/1979/1
Modéer, Kjell Å. 1998. "Johan Gabriel Richert." *Svenskt biografiskt lexikon*. https://sok.riksarkivet.se/sbl/artikel/6730.
Modéer, Kjell Å. 1999. "Den stora reformen: Rättegångsbalkens förebilder och förverkligande." *Svensk Juristtidning* 84(4): 400–427. http://www.svjt.org/svjt/1999/406.
Modéer, Kjell Å. 2000. "Carl Johan Schlyter." *Svenskt biografiskt lexikon*. https://sok.riksarkivet.se/sbl/artikel/6386.
Modéer, Kjell Å. 2003. "From 'Rechtsstaat' to 'Welfare-State': Swedish Judicial Culture in Transition 1870–1970," in W. Wesley Pue and David Sugarman (eds.), *Lawyers and Vampires: Cultural Histories of Legal Professions*, 151–167. Oxford: Hart Publishing.
Modéer, Kjell Å. 2011. "Jurister På Politikernas Arenor." *Svensk Juristtidning* 96(8): 735–751. http://svjt.se/svjt/2011/739
Modéer, Kjell Å. 2016. "Katalysator för rättsliga diskurser." *Svensk Juristtidning* 101(10): 881–904. http://svjt.se/svjt/2016/881
Molin, Karl. 1982. "A Vilhelm Lundstedt." *Svenskt biografiskt lexikon*. https://sok.riksarkivet.se/sbl/artikel/9892
Möller, Tommy. 2011. *Svensk politisk historia: Strid och samverkan under tvåhundra år*. Lund: Studentlitteratur.
Nergelius, Joakim. 2008. "Between Collectivism and Constitutionalism: The Nordic Countries and Constitutionalism – a 'Final Frontier' or a Period of Transition?" in Joakim Nergelius (ed.), *Constitutionalism: New Challenges. European Law Form a Nordic Perspective*, 119–134. Leiden: Martinus Nijhoff Publishers.
Nergelius, Joakim. 2011. *Stärkta – men inte starka: Om svenska domstolars svaga konstitutionella ställning*. Stockholm: Timbro.
Nergelius, Joakim, and Dominik Zimmermann. 2012. "Judicial Independence in Sweden," in Anja Seibert-Fohr (ed.), *Judicial Independence in Transition*, 185–229. Beiträge zum ausländischen öffentlichen Recht und Völkerrecht 233. Berlin; Heidelberg: Springer http://link.springer.com/chapter/10.1007/978-3-642-28299-7_6
Norberg, Johan. 1998. *Den svenska liberalismens historia*. Stockholm: Timbro.
Ohlsson, Per T. 2014. *Svensk politik*. Lund: Historiska Media.
Peterson, Claes. 2001. "Lagstiftning eller självreglering i ett rättshistoriskt perspektiv," *Svensk Juristtidning* 86(3) 219–233. http://svjt.se/svjt/2001/219
Pihlajamaki, Heikki. 2004. "Against Metaphysics in Law: The Historical Background of American and Scandinavian Legal Realism Compared," *American Journal of Comparative Law* 52(2): 469–488.
Richert, Johan Gabriel. 1822. *Ett och annat om Corporationer, Privilegier, Nämnd i Domstolar etc. i anledning af Consistorii Academici i Upsala Betänkande om den Academiska Jurisdictionen*. Stockholm: Fr. B. Nestius. http://urn.kb.se/resolve?urn=urn:nbn:se:umu:eod-105
Rothstein, Bo. 1998a. *Just Institutions Matter: The Moral and Political Logic of the Universal Welfare State*. Cambridge: Cambridge University Press.
Rothstein, Bo. 1998b. *The Social Democratic State: The Swedish Model and the Bureaucratic Problem of Social Reforms*. Pittsburgh, PA: University of Pittsburgh Press.

Rothstein, Bo. 2011. "Anti-Corruption: The Indirect 'Big Bang' Approach," *Review of International Political Economy* 18(2): 228–250. doi:10.1080/09692291003607834

Runcis, Maija. 1998. *Steriliseringar i folkhemmet*. Stockholm: Ordfront.

Rustow, Dankwart. 1971. "Sweden's Transition to Democracy: Some Notes Toward a Genetic Theory," *Scandinavian Political Studies* 6(6): 9–26.

Sandström, Marie. 1998. "Slaget om juristutbildningen," *Juridisk Tidskrift* 9(3): 584–595.

Schaffer, Johan Karlsson. 2017. "Mellan aktivism och ambivalens: Norden och de mänskliga rättigheterna," *Retfærd: Nordic Journal of Law and Justice* 40(1): 55–72.

Schaffer, Johan Karlsson. 2020. "The Self-Exempting Activist: Sweden and the International Human Rights Regime," *Nordic Journal of Human Rights* 38(1): 40–60.

Scheinin, Martin. 2008. "Constitutionalism and Approaches to Rights in the Nordic Countries," in Joakim Nergelius (ed.), *Constitutionalism: New Challenges. European Law Form a Nordic Perspective*, 135–153. Leiden: Martinus Nijhoff Publishers.

Schlyter, Karl. 1930. "En diskussion i steriliseringsfrågan." Svensk Juristtidning. 15(1):139–144. https://svjt.se/svjt/1930/139

Schultz, Mårten. 2009. "Rights Through Torts: The Rise of a Rights Discourse in Swedish Tort Law." *European Review of Private Law* 17(3): 305–333.

Socialdepartementet. 1929. "Betänkande med förslag till steriliseringslag." SOU 1929:14. http://weburn.kb.se/metadata/017/SOU_1280017.htm

Socialdepartementet. 2000. "Steriliseringsfrågan i Sverige 1935–1975: Historisk belysning, kartläggning, intervjuer." SOU 2000:20. http://www.regeringen.se/rattsdokument/statens-offentliga-utredningar/2000/03/sou-200020/

Ställvik, Olof. 2009. *Domarrollen: Rättsregler, yrkeskultur och ideal*. Uppsala: Uppsala universitet.

Strang, Johan. 2009. "Two Generations of Scandinavian Legal Realists," *Retfærd* 32(1): 62–82.

Sundberg, Jacob W. F. 1986. "Human Rights in Sweden: The Breakthrough of an Idea," *Ohio State Law Journal* 47(4): 951–983.

Sundell, Anders. 2015. "Public Administration and Corruption: How To Get the Institutions That Work." Gothenburg: University of Gothenburg. https://gupea.ub.gu.se/handle/2077/38877

Sundell, Jan-Olof. 2000. "Karl J D Schlyter." *Svenskt biografiskt lexikon*. https://sok.riksarkivet.se/sbl/artikel/6387

Svanberg, Mikael. 2013. "Demokratisyner på kollisionskurs: Debatten inför författningsreformen 1974." Karlstad: Karlstads universitet. http://www.diva-portal.org/smash/record.jsf?pid=diva2:675481

Sydow, Henrik von. 2011. "Varje tingsrätt en författningsdomstol." *Dagens Juridik*, August 22. http://www.dagensjuridik.se/2011/08/varje-tingsratt-en-forfattningsdomstol

Thermenius. 1931. "Louis G De Geer." *Svenskt biografiskt lexikon*. https://sok.riksarkivet.se/sbl/artikel/17356

Tjerneld, Anders. 2007. "Staaff, Släkt." *Svenskt biografiskt lexikon*. https://sok.riksarkivet.se/sbl/artikel/20021

Vallinder, Torbjörn. 2000. *Nio edsvurna män: Jury och tryckfrihet i Sverige 1815–2000*. Oskarshamn: Carlssons.

Warburg, Karl. 1905. *Johan Gabriel Richert: Hans lefnad och uttalanden*. Stockholm: P. A. Nordstedt & söners förlag.

Werner, Yvonne Maria. 2002. "Katolicism och religionsfrihet. Den svenska religionsfrihetslagen 50 år." *Signum*, no. 9. http://www.signum.se/archive/read.php?id=935

Wersäll, Fredrik. 2014. "En offensiv Högsta domstol. Några reflektioner kring HD:s rättsbildning." *Svensk Juristtidning* 99(1): 1–8. http://svjt.se/svjt/2014/1

Wibling, Jöran. 1954. *Opinioner och stämningar i Sverige 1809–1810*. Uppsala: Almqvist & Wiksells boktryckeri AB.

Wichman, Knut. 1971. "Lars Johan Hierta." *Svenskt biografiskt lexikon*. https://sok.riksarkivet.se/sbl/artikel/13575

Wieselgren, Sigfrid. 1895. *Sveriges fängelser och fångvård från äldre tider till våra dagar. Ett bidrag till svensk kulturhistoria*. Stockholm: P. A. Nordstedt. http://runeberg.org/wsfangelse/

Wiklund, Ola. 2008. "The Reception Process in Sweden and Norway," in Helen Keller and Alec Stone (eds.), Sweet *A Europe of Rights: The Impact of the ECHR on National Legal Systems*, Oxford: Oxford University Press. http://www.oxfordscholarship.com/view/10.1093/acprof:oso/9780199535262.001.0001/acprof-9780199535262.

Wiklund, Ola. 2014. "Om Högsta domstolens rättsskapande verksamhet — löper domstolen amok?" *Svensk Juristtidning* 99(4): 335–347. http://svjt.se/svjt/2014/335

Zaremba, Maciej. 1999. *De rena och de andra: Om tvångssteriliseringar, rashygien och arvsynd*. Stockholm: Bokförlaget Forum.

Zetterberg, Kent. 2011. "Det statliga kommittéväsendet — En del av den svenska modellen." *Svensk Juristtidning* 96(8): 753–763 http://svjt.se/svjt/2011/753

4

Denmark

Between the Law State and the Welfare State

Mikael Rask Madsen[*]

1. Introduction

The key argument put forward by the trio of Malcolm Feeley, Terrence Halliday, and Lucien Karpik (FHK) is that what they term the *legal complex*, that is, broadly speaking, the legal profession and its institutions, tends to further political liberalism. They understand the legal complex as "the system of relations among legally-trained occupations which mobilise on a particular issue as the 'legal complex'" (Halliday, Karpik, and Feeley 2007: 6–7). The analytical core interest is thus to explore *how* this complex of legal professionals mobilizes and *when* it seeks to further political liberalism (ibid: 7). The interest of this chapter is to test this thesis against the case of Denmark, a country that—as many other Nordic countries—has transformed into a complex welfare state society that is governed by law but with a clear objective of attaining social justice. The latter is characterized by a strong notion of redistributive economic justice. This configuration of legal and economic rationalities is of key importance for understanding the both limited and extensive role the legal complex has played in Danish political history and culture. In the nineteenth century, a host of actors entered the political arena, seeking to challenge the status quo by pursuing forms of political liberalism. Legal professionals generally gained from these changes and consolidated themselves as the core administrative elite. They played a double role with regard to politics, and they were found in both the progressive and reactionary movements. Although legal rationality became a cornerstone of the welfare society, and thereby has made jurists highly central to the administration of the modern state, political liberalism in a more narrow sense has never dominated the debate in the twentieth century, particularly as it was seen as lacking substantive solutions to real-life social issues.

The *legal complex* is a multifaceted and elastic notion: First, the relationships between key positions in the legal field—professors, prosecutors, judges, private

[*] Mikael Rask Madsen is Professor of Law and Director of iCourts, The Danish National Research Foundation's Center of Excellence for International Courts. His research is funded by the Danish National Research Foundation Grant no. DNRF105 and conducted under the auspices of iCourts.

Mikael Rask Madsen, *Denmark* In: *The Limits of the Legal Complex*. Edited by: Malcolm Feeley and Malcolm Langford, Oxford University Press. DOI: 10.1093/oso/9780192848413.003.0004 practitioners, in-house counsel, etc.—vary greatly from one legal cultural location to another; and second, the actual mobilizations for political liberalism also vary within cultural locations over time.[1] As it is well known, lawyers have fought both for and against revolutions (Karpik 1995; Dezalay and Garth 2010; Dezalay and Madsen 2012). The only way to possibly answer these questions is by comparative empirical studies as FHK also readily admit.

The other key notion is *political liberalism*, which equally is conceptualized for the purpose of comparative empirical studies. Like the legal complex, FHK define this as a somewhat dynamic ideal-type concerning the "contingent relationship between basic legal freedoms, on the one hand, and the moderate state and civil society, on the other. Basic legal freedoms, arguably, are achieved through moderation of state power and mobilization of civil society as a realm of power" (Halliday, Karpik, and Feeley 2007: 11). Conceptually, the notion of political liberalism, however, differs from that of the legal complex as it has a substantial, even normative, component. It is in other words a particular kind of politics that is in focus, that of fighting for basic liberal rights. This excludes from the analysis the mobilization of the legal complex for illiberal causes. Moreover, the conceptualization particularly raises analytical problems when only smaller parts of the profession or even individual lawyers mobilize for political liberalism. I will return to this in the conclusion as this is very much an issue in the empirical case study presented here.

Overall, both notions of the legal complex and political liberalism are interesting and difficult to apply to the Danish case, where particularly the post-World War II society sought an extensive state structure legitimized in redistributive social justice but moderated by legal rationality, especially via administrative law as evidenced in the success of the institution of the parliamentary ombudsman. It was an extensive state in sharp contrast to the moderate state FHK have in mind. The obvious sites for the kind of legal political mobilizations identified by the legal complex project are therefore in some ways less likely to be found during the golden age of the Danish welfare state. That is, however, not to claim that legal mobilizations for fundamental rights were absent; they were just less so at the center of public policy debates—or they were mobilized in sync with conventional politics and processes. To meet this challenge, my research strategy has been to focus on the one area of politics in which the kind of liberal legal politics on which the legal complex

[1] The idea of rethinking the legal system in terms of the space of relations was pioneered by scholars using Bourdieusian sociology to study the field of law as a set of objective relations. See most explicitly Dezalay and Madsen (2012). Although also approaching law as a structure of relations, the idea of legal complex is different. Comparatively, the notion of legal complex is based on a more functionalist notion of the connected system of legal professionals and their normative potential in the formation of state and society where political liberalism is that normative potential. In the approaches of reflexive sociology of law, it is argued that law does not have such an in-built script or potential but is always formed vis-à-vis other fields, notably the administrative field. Because of this key difference regarding the in-built political potential of law, these two approaches also differ on their understanding of the power of legal professionals in society.

project is focused are most likely to occur, namely human rights. I will, however, contextualize this by also examining both the period marked by the breakthrough of political liberalism, that is the last half of the nineteenth century, and the fundamental societal transformation triggered by the construction of the social welfare state.

In what follows, I seek a structural sociological analysis of the mobilization of various segments of the legal field for the cause of human rights, constitutionalism, and political liberalism. Emphasis will be on the post-World War II period in which the internationalization of human rights provided a new stimulus for this core area of the liberal political project, eventually also in Denmark and Scandinavia more generally. As I have argued elsewhere the main arena for Danish and Scandinavian engagements in human rights has been abroad, notably in the Scandinavian "moral superpower" politics which took form in the 1960s by combining the virtues of social justice of the social welfare state with small-state strategies (Madsen 2010; Christoffersen and Madsen 2011). In this analysis, I will focus on the domestic side of Danish politics and society alone and only make reference to the external dimensions when necessary for explaining the specific object of inquiry. I will also, when relevant, generalize my analysis to other Scandinavian countries. Following a section on the historical evolution of the constitutional state in Denmark and the role played by the legal complex in this process, the analysis turns to the rise of the welfare state and the ambiguous role of jurists within it. I then address human rights more specifically, first during the postwar period and then in the critical law movement starting in the 1970s and in the nascent field of human rights.

2. Toward a Liberal State: Early Constitutional Politics

If constitutional history provides a prism for understanding the relative power of law and lawyers in history, the Danish case is somewhat puzzling. While the democratic constitutional state emerged in the mid-nineteenth century as we will discuss below, the administrative elite had already incrementally imported liberal ideas into the Danish state prior to that. During the absolute monarchy—established in 1665 by the *Lex Regia*—the new *Lex Fundamentalis* of the state was for instance introduced. The background for the centralization and monopolization of power at the royal court was a disastrous war against Sweden, which had put the country in a dire financial situation and delegitimized the aristocratic elite of the state council. It is from the starting point of the absolute monarchy that the bureaucratization of the state occurs in many steps throughout the seventeenth and eighteenth centuries. A novelty was the Supreme Court, which opened in 1661, but the separation of executive and judicial powers was far from a fait accompli (Tamm 1990: 115–125). In fact, Danish history reveals the king's interference with the court as late as the mid-eighteenth century. Legal diplomas were only a requirement for holding office in the court from 1771—for the lower court that did not happen until the introduction of the exam for legal officials in 1821 (*candidatus juris*). It was a court society—to use Norbert Elias's term (Elias 2006)—where the power of the state was exercised at the royal court. Meanwhile state power itself was gradually differentiated into departments.

One actor often highlighted with regard to the importation of new liberal ideas in the making of the modern state is Henrik Stampe (1713–1789), a top civil servant for decades. He contributed significantly to the introduction of the idea of the separation of powers, which in the context of the absolute monarchy implied that the courts should rule based on the law and be independent. Moreover, as a consequence of the introduction of these new ideas the monarchy became increasingly enlightened (*oplyst*) and, as argued by Norwegian historian J. A. Seip, this enlightenment of the power meant that public opinion started having some influence on the direction of new legislation (as cited in Tamm 1990: 184). It was by no means yet a democratic or even liberal state, but it demonstrated an ability to adapt to changing societal and political demands that most likely had an impact on the transition to democracy. In 1814, the state Council was established, as were forms of consultative assemblies in the provinces in 1831 and 1834. Denmark did not experience a bloody revolution, not even a revolution. But, the country nevertheless transitioned to democracy, stating in the early nineteenth century.

The standard narrative of the emergence of the democratic constitutional state, that is, to be precise, the Danish Constitutional Monarchy, in 1849 highlights the roles played by a relatively small group of statesmen. This included lawyer-politicians, for example Orla Lehmann (1810–1870) and learned lawyers, for example Anders Sandøe Ørsted (1778–1860). But also theologians and pastors have—justifiably or not—come to be associated with the first constitution. The pastor N. F. S. Grundtvig (1783–1872) is often mentioned in this regard. Strictly speaking, he was not particularly liberal in his outlook and likely preferred the absolute monarchy over the new arrangement. But as a leading advocate of the enlightenment of the peasantry through popular education and a reform of the Evangelical Lutheran Church, he joined the Constitutional Assembly.[2] More consequential was Grundtvig's role in reforming the Evangelical Lutheran Church away from a highly institutionalized and compulsory regime toward a more personal engagement. This had an impact on the 1849 Constitution, which allowed for religious freedom with the exception of the Royal Family whose members were obliged to follow Lutherans beliefs. The Evangelical Lutheran Church was, moreover, the only recognized church receiving aid from the state. Freedom of religion was thus institutionalized in the 1849 Constitution, but not the equality of religion.

[2] The most famous example of this educational role is his part in the creation of folk high schools (*Folkehøjskoler*), a concept which spread to all of Scandinavia, and subsequently Germany and even the United States.

Another theologian, the later bishop and Prime Minister D. G. Monrad (1811–1887) was also undoubtedly a key person with regard to the first constitution. Together with a group of co-drafters, he contributed to the first draft of the 1849 Constitution and represented the national liberal movement of the time. The latter was the Danish variant of the similar revolutionary movements in other European countries, centered on establishing a free constitution and a democratic government of qualified men—more than actual democracy per se. In practice, however, national liberalism in Denmark was largely determined by finding solutions to the place of Schleswig and Holstein in the new constitutional order. Monrad's less than glorious place in Danish history is in fact a direct result of his dismal leadership during the Second Schleswig War (1864), which led to the break-up of the Danish unitary state (*Helstaten*). The war was linked to new constitutional reforms, where the national liberalists sought by the means of a common constitution to integrate the Duchy of Schleswig into the ordinary Danish state/Kingdom, regardless of mounting ethnic frictions with the German-speaking parts of Schleswig and Holstein. The war was on the one hand detrimental for the Danish state, losing both (mainly) German-speaking areas and a significant part of Southern Jutland. It also resulted in an almost complete reorientation in world affairs. On the other hand, it enabled the process of forming the current, much smaller, Danish nation-state which as its main foreign policy objective had to reintegrate the Danish-speaking parts of Schleswig.

The fact that Monrad had a background in theology should not be overstated, however. Many lawyers played key roles in the drafting of the 1849 Constitution, and the national-liberal camp in particular counted numerous jurists—typically from the state administration and academia. One of them was the aforementioned Orla Lehmann (1810–1870). Although not a formal member of the Constitutional Assembly, he has been credited with rewriting the draft by Monrad and twisting the wording to reflect a modern society founded in the will of the people. But like other national liberals, the question of the Danish unitary state, in part sparked by a deep Scandinavism in his case, also led to his fall. Although Lehmann had been among the first to demand an end to absolute monarchy and had become a celebrated spokesman for a more democratic and liberal society among peasants, his speeches also revealed unease with popular democracy. In 1860 he infamously noted that the state was never meant to be transferred to the unenlightened peasantry but was for "De begavede, de dannede og de formuende" [the educated, the men of property, and the intelligent] (Hall, Korsgaard, and Pedersen 2014: 206). Needless to say, the members of the national-liberal camp, which was made up of such an economic-academic intelligentsia, were the ones he deemed particularly fit.

Another key lawyer of the day, and particularly in the period leading towards the first constitution, Anders Sandøe Ørsted (1778–1860), equally exhibited an ambiguity toward the new legal and democratic order. Unlike many lawyers of the period, he was not a national-liberal but he rather represented the old regime. Known as the most eminent legal scholar of his time, Ørsted had held all key positions in the legal and political administration of the late monarchy and he became part of the Constitutional Assembly of which he was a highly active member. He is known for having intervened numerous times and at length but only in a few cases influencing the actual outcome. In fact, his position was pro the unitary state and contra the new constitution, notably its civil and political rights. One of his rare victories in this regard concerned whether courts should be given the power of constitutional review, a measure favored by many national-liberals, but Ørsted argued forcefully that this would put the courts above the parliament. The power of the courts was therefore limited to trying the decisions of the administration (Bagge 1980: 144–145)—in fact thereby constitutionalizing the status quo since 1795. At the end of the day, Ørsted voted against the new constitution, yet ended up as Prime Minister in 1853. In this position he attempted to introduce a new constitution for the entire realm, a move rightly seen by opponents as circumventing the 1849 Constitution, which only applied to Denmark. He was eventually impeached and accused of high treason over undocumented expenses related to the Crimean War, an investigation undoubtedly triggered by his constitutional maneuverings. The Supreme Court (of which he had formerly been a member [1810–1813]) eventually acquitted him and other members of his cabinet, which then led to accusations of the legal establishment protecting one of their own.

Generally, the first Danish Constitution (1849) constitutionalized a number of rights already being practiced such as habeas corpus (1796), as well as importing a catalogue of rights from the constitutions of fellow European countries, notably Belgium and its new constitution. It was a conforming process rather than a revolutionary event and, as noted by the legal historian Ditlev Tamm, not even all members of the Constitutional Assembly found it necessary to include a catalog of rights (Tamm 1990: 219). Moreover, not all voted in favor of the Constitution, as we have seen. In the bigger picture, however, the liberalization and democratization of the monarchy in Denmark was a gradual process which even prior to the constitutional moment had seen a growing bureaucratization of the king's power and the emergence of a corps of administrators, virtually all with a legal background.[3] Consolidating the juristic monopoly of the state administration, law degrees had been made compulsory in 1821 for holding office in the central administration in Denmark and when this act was abolished jurists continued to enjoy a de facto monopoly by recruiting each other. However, bureaucratizing, legalizing, and constitutionalizing the state apparatus and providing the legal technology of the Rechtsstaat did not equal a pursuit of political liberalism in all cases. Turning to law and constitutionalism undoubtedly cemented the importance of law (and lawyers)

[3] In Denmark, for example, the democratization of state decision-making processes started with the consultative regional assemblies (*stænderforsamlinger*) of the 1830s.

to the state, but it did not per se secure a particularly liberal agenda. The kind of legal formalism that was cherished by the legal administrative elite lacked a normative component, and in some cases even a democratic one.

The original constitution-making process also reveals significant rifts over the future of the Danish state, notably with regard to the governance and status of the remoter parts of the realm. But as exemplified by the cases of the elite lawyer-politicians such as Lehmann and Ørsted, it also reveals deep divides among the constituent legal members, representing both the before and after of the liberal state. Adding to the difficulties, the changes in the aftermath of the 1864 war also saw the rise of new forces to be reckoned with in the legal-political game, namely the various socialist and communist movements and the free farmers' movement (split between the Liberals (*Venstre)* and the Social Liberals (*Radikale Venstre*). The Constitution of 1866 was, however, a victory for the landed elite (the later Conservatives) as it tightened election rules and gave them dominance. In 1866, the first bar association was also formed with clear inspiration from the larger European countries and with the goal of enhancing the respect for the profession and its independence from the state. However, the timing was not good. The 1866 Constitution led to a severe constitutional crisis over the proposal from the Liberals that the government should reflect the majority in Parliament. The result was that the legislative process was paralyzed for long periods, notably between 1885–1894, and the country was ruled by provisional laws. The long rift over the 1866 Constitution and its related questions of parliamentarianism made constitutional lawyers re-enter the political scene. But they did so on both sides of the conflict, that is, fighting for both democratic liberalism and illiberalism. The legal complex, if it makes sense to speak in those terms at the time, continued to remain deeply divided along the lines of the dominant political questions of the time. Legal academics from the University of Copenhagen certainly stand out in this regard as some of the most ardent supporters of the government and its semi-legal practices (Tamm 2005).

The new constitution of 1915 eventually reversed the changes of the 1866 Constitution and introduced a very robust procedure for constitutional change—in fact it almost made constitutional change impossible. Moreover, the 1915 Constitution provided for women's access to the vote. In 1920 the constitution was once again changed, this time to reunify Upper Schleswig following a referendum held after the German defeat in World War I. What ultimately shifted the power were demographic changes in society, and in particular the rise of the workers' movement and the liberals.[4] In both cases, legal professionals were not the key spokesmen. The legal complex, however, got its day in court—and a decisive one with critical importance to Danish society and its future organization. A key

[4] There is an extensive literature on these questions. The most recent work is found in Friisberg (2007).

question in the transition to a democratic society was the future of the landed elites and the many privileges they had acquired over the centuries, notably with regard to their control of vast possessions of land through special laws of succession. The 1849 Constitution had already included a promissory declaration of the liberalization of the privileges with regard to large entails (Erichsen and Tamm 2014). But because of the long constitutional crisis of the last decades of the nineteenth century, the landed elite had been protected against any action being taken on the "promise." Instead it was to occur in the aftermath of World War I and in a very different social context marked by both the fear of a peasant uprising and a fundamentally transformed state as a backdrop. While the October Revolution of 1917 had made revolutionary change a real option, World War I, of which Denmark had generally steered clear and from which it had even benefitted in some ways, had transformed the country from one of the least regulated in Europe to one of the most regulated as a result of state interventions to ration food and supplies.

In charge was the Social-Liberal Prime Minister C. Th. Zahle who politically went all out against his historical enemy, the old landed elite (Erichsen and Tamm 2014). Described as the legal case of the century in the press at the time, the landed elite first won against the government at the High Court where the expropriation was found unconstitutional and a violation of property rights. Yet they eventually lost in the Supreme Court, which found that the state had acted within the margin of the constitution. It was game over for the old landed elite—and the beginning of a new, presumably more egalitarian, society that was spearheaded by an interventionist state, even in questions of property rights. Another effect of the case of key importance to this analysis was the broader legal-political consequences of its conclusions. It was clear that the highest Danish court was not ready to overrule the direction given by a majority of the Danish Parliament (*Folketing*). Among legal professionals it therefore became clear that even the best case and the best lawyers did not stand a real chance in matters of state policy introduced by a majority in parliament. In particular social policy would always trump legal-political liberalism in the new society in the making. It was the supremacy of parliament combined with the supremacy of a new social orthodoxy. Consequentially, as noted by Danish legal historian Ditlev Tamm, claiming constitutional rights before Danish Courts was regarded as "slightly ridiculous" (Tamm 1997). This was hardly the ideal context for the pursuit of political liberalism by the legal complex.

The last constitutional change occurred in 1953. The 1953 Constitution made further changes to the procedure for constitutional change but most notably abolished the Upper Chamber, which had been the stronghold of the Conservatives and landed elites since its establishment in 1849. The 1953 Constitution also introduced the institution of the Parliamentary Ombudsman, made changes to the law of succession allowing for a possible future Queen, integrated Greenland into the Danish state, and explicated and qualified the procedure for engaging in international organizations. The resulting election for approval of the constitution saw the emergence of what for decades would be a common landscape in Danish politics: a large but non-majoritarian Social Democratic Party, a Liberal Party coming in second, followed by the Conservatives, the Social Liberals and a set of smaller parties, including the Communists. However, with none of these parties ever winning a majority, governments were to be either minority governments or coalition governments who had to act within the boundaries of negative parliamentarianism. Consequently, political results had to be negotiated in Parliament, often in close consultation with the various interest organizations underpinning the different political parties.

The voice of the legal complex rarely spoke a unison in the negotiations of day-to-day politics that this model prescribed. Generally, the profession was divided between the majority working within the central state administration, followed by the courts and prosecution, the organized bar, and legal academia. Yet, even though a unified voice was practically impossible to muster on more politicized questions, the continuous key role of lawyers in the administration of the state made lawyers have a rather large imprint on the drafting and execution of law. Their influence should not be exaggerated, however. At the heart of the welfare state project, which had already been molded in the 1930s, other experts, particularly economists, started challenging the jurists' hegemony as providers of the rationality of the state. As suggested by FHK, lawyers have overall been more active in promoting more classic civil and political rights than second- or third-generation rights (Halliday, Karpik, and Feeley 2007: 4). In the context of the extensive welfare state, which was rolled out in Denmark from the 1960s onward, the guardians of the rule of law had likewise little to offer in terms of the core idea of redistributive social justice on which the new society was effectively based. The battle between a legal rationality of public administration and an economization of public administration was to mark the evolution of the state. The next section examines the structural implications for the legal complex of the rise of the Danish welfare state.

3. A Real Challenge to Political Liberalism: Liberty as Solidarity and Social Justice

The ascendancy of the welfare state was to more generally challenge the position of the legal complex and its relative commitment to a political liberal agenda. The welfare project, which was initiated in the 1930s, coincided with the consolidation of the social democratic parties into a carefully crafted position as workers' parties but distanced from Marxist orthodoxy. Further, the so-called "red–green alliances" between the Socialist/Social Democratic parties and the Agrarian parties were instrumental in the initial political genesis of the welfare state in the 1930s as it effectively minimized the power of the traditional societal elite organized around the conservative parties and an administrative elite of jurists.[5] Helped by this new political "deal," the development of the postwar Scandinavian welfare states went along with a dominance of the social democratic parties: Most strikingly in Sweden from 1945 to 1976 and in Norway from 1945 to 1963; in Denmark, however, the social democratic parties were more often challenged by other constellations—the Social Democrats were in government from 1947 to 1950 and again from 1953 to 1968 in Denmark (Arter 1999: 201–208). Importantly, the parliamentary power of these parties, combined with their vast networks into broad parts of society, made them generally capable of defining the overriding visions of postwar Scandinavian society, and to such an extent that the competing parties practically felt compelled to develop quasi-social democratic programs. The double impact of these parties—both as hegemonic in Parliament and as the producer of the hegemonic ideology—in some ways made all the major political parties subscribe to the overall agenda of the social welfare state. It was not until the 1970s and 1980s that dissatisfaction with the Social Democratic welfare orthodoxies was turned into new government constellations.

The building of the welfare state and the support it gained across the political middle was also partly due to the fear of the potential impact of the Communist Parties, particularly in the aftermath of World War II. Capitalizing on the heroic wartime role of the communist branches of the resistance movements, the Communist Parties in particularly Norway and Denmark increased their parliamentary shares during the postwar elections. Facilitated by an express anti-communist stance, the success and expansion of the social democratic parties virtually thwarted the communists' position in Scandinavian politics. A "non-Soviet pro extreme Left" eventually emerged, but these new parties in fact only helped to occasionally secure the parliamentary majority of Social Democratic governments. There were some differences in the three countries in this respect, most notably the non-socialist parties were historically fragmented in Sweden facilitating the social democratic dominance, whilst in Denmark and Norway the political right could muster cooperation to periodically challenge the otherwise hegemonic status of the Social Democrats.

Significant economic growth and the special relationship between the Social Democratic Parties and the marketplace and industries made these parties and their vast network virtually "states in the state," particularly in Sweden and Norway. From 1870 to 1970, Sweden's economy grew faster than any other Western country, partly due to its dual profile as both the home to large multinationals—Volvo, Ericsson, Electrolux, ABB etc.—and to the new social deal of the comprehensive

[5] In Denmark it was the so-called "Kanslergadeforlig" of 1933 between the Social Democrats, Liberals, and Social Liberals that formed the political support for developing social protection of both workers and farmers. In Sweden, similar "deals" between the Workers Party (Social Democrats) and the Agrarian Party were put together in 1936, the same year as the Popular Front was formed in France.

welfare state. Providing a new chapter to the Weberian story of Protestant ethics and the marketplace, it was the anticipation of Keynesian economics by such figures as Gunnar Myrdal promoting the general economic framework of the welfare laboratory but also allowing private business to progress alongside the expansion of the state apparatus.[6] While the Swedish case is the extreme, both Norway and Denmark followed similar patterns, although the public–private relationship was more complicated as the private sector tended to rely on protégées of conservative or liberal political observance. Across the region, these characteristics meant that, in principle, a kind of parallel system (with important overlaps) between the administration of private business and the administration the welfare state developed. In regard to law and lawyers, a small elite became consultants to the international businesses, providing expertise on commercial law and conflict resolution, while the majority of the profession remained entangled in the day-to-day running of the welfare state. And the solidarity between the elite business lawyers and the jurists of the welfare state was limited. Among practitioners a common bar association was maintained, but solidarity was mainly preserved for the instrumental interest of securing the monopoly (Madsen 2000). The politics of the bar was therefore above all the politics of the monopoly. That, obviously, occasionally included a collective defense of basic legal guarantees of due process, what locally was referred to as *retssikkerhed* ("legal security") which often had a procedural law orientation. In light of the inclusive approach to the democratic process, such "activism" has been recurrent and the bar has become an almost institutionalized voice in favor of *retssikkerhed* in the development of new legislation.

The Danish and more generally Scandinavian welfare state can best be characterized by its core idea of a comprehensive protection of social rights. The key innovation of the Scandinavian welfare state in regard to *rights* was more precisely the state's strong and unrivalled position as sole provider of *basic services* to every citizen, thereby monopolizing social policy as a state enterprise. The consolidation of this position came through the development of a wide-ranging socioeconomic service catalog closely linked to the explicit objective of *equality*, both a social and economic notion in the Scandinavian context. While private business was allowed a degree of freedom of movement, the backbone of the state's expansion was the equally expanding taxation of the citizens that allowed for a comprehensive income redistribution to take place as an integral part of the social and economic policies (Arter 1999: 177–181). Thereby the Scandinavian "interventionist state" was placed as the very guarantor of (social) democracy and (social) justice, and it grew to become virtually synonymous with democracy by the internalization of its objectives in the population at large (Premfors 1991: 84). In the same way, human rights became largely a state business: The Scandinavian welfare state was

[6] One scholar, David Arter, argues that the Scandinavian states were characterized by greater non-intervention in the marketplace than the other continental welfare states. See Arter (1999).

somehow the "state of human rights" by a different name, reflecting how state and civil society in the social democratic vision had a clear overlap.

As a result of the welfare state's monopolization of social and economic rights, human rights claims were generally to be framed within the umbrella of civil and political rights. This indirect attachment to the pre-welfare law-state made such claims come across as, if not bourgeois, then slightly out of line with the collective ethos of the "state of solidarity." It should be underlined here that the connotations of the term *human rights* were mainly international at this point: as either intrinsic to the new United Nations system's overall objective of seeking international peace or, but to a far lesser extent, as part of the international advocacy of the rights to form trade unions and other labor rights.[7] Nationally, Scandinavian perceptions of human rights, both linguistically and legally, mainly consisted of a mélange of constitutional freedoms and liberties. In addition, there was only a limited legal or political "*rights* culture" in these countries, making the recourse to "human rights" anything but a strong claim against new postwar orthodoxies on the definition of the relationship between the state, individuals, and society.

In many ways, civil and political liberties, and thereby indirectly human rights, were the claims of the extreme voices—Communists or radicals on the one hand, various far-right or liberalistic voices on the other—but it was neither politically nor legally a particularly powerful strategy. The first postwar human rights organizations that gained a foothold was, for example, the International Commission of Jurists (ICJ), which set up local Scandinavian branches in the 1950s, but it pursued an almost exclusively international agenda. This did not mean that lawyers—often with very clear political affiliations—sought to argue agendas resembling those of the Human Rights League in France or the National Council for Civil Liberties in the United Kingdom (Madsen 2004), but their engagement was typically either part of a broader sociopolitical project than a simple question of rights, or they were entangled in legal specificities related only to the microcosm of law such as procedural law. The problem was that claiming individual rights somehow clashed with the new orthodoxies of social justice which implicitly assumed an individual and a collective justice that was far more advanced than these ideas deriving from the ancien régime.[8]

One might consider the innovation of the Parliamentary Ombudsman symptomatic of the new order, as it was, for example, included in the Danish Constitution of 1953. It was in many ways the most important new institution for strengthening and policing the relationship between citizens and the expanding state.[9] Although

[7] For example, legal textbooks did not use the term until the late 1980s and continued to regard "human rights" as a mixture of constitutional liberties, *libertés publiques*, and "civil rights."

[8] There was, for example, a general democracy debate immediately following World War II in Denmark. Instigated by the law professor Alf Ross, and the social debater Hal Koch, these debates, however, only marginally concerned the role of human rights. See Rasmussen and Nielsen (2003).

[9] The Norwegian *Sivilombudsmannen* was set up in 1962 to operate in a way similar to the Danish model. Created in 1809, the Swedish *Justitieombudsmannen* was in principle the first institution of this

the later success of the institution was hardly foreseen and indeed many were opposed to its creation, retrospectively it comes across very much as an institution of the new postwar society. Corresponding with the new sociopolitical context, human rights thereby, to a large extent, went "public." They became a matter of administrative law and procedural justice, moved away from the courtroom and the legal intimacy of a lawyer-judge-controlled interaction to become a free service to all citizens, provided by the state. Further underscoring the place of the ombudsman institution as a key exponent of the new Danish welfare state's politics of law, the decisions of the ombudsman were in principle not legally binding but based on the friendly cooperation of the implied state agencies. Importantly, the institution of the ombudsman quite effectively anticipated many of the human rights standards eventually defined under the European Convention on Human Rights (ECHR). Thereby they did not simply foresee potential human rights claims; they also contributed to an implosion of human rights law as an area of state critical legal practice in the region.

Generally, the Scandinavian welfare states were not initiated by revolutionary constitutional reform, but were instead the outcome of the political compromises of the 1930s and rolled out fully after World War II. As part of this development, the new state model increasingly altered the position of law and lawyers by the transformation of some of the key "state logics." These developments essentially implied a double challenge to the previous legal hegemony, reflecting both the new political leaders' deep skepticism and even contempt of the elite of the pre-welfare state, that being the jurists par excellence, and their redefinition of state expertise (Dalberg-Larsen 1994: 114). On the *political level* the legal profession was greatly challenged due to the fact that the Socialist and Agrarian Parties relied little on legal candidates as parliamentarians. In fact the proportion of parliamentarians with a legal background was as low 2–4 percent (Dalberg-Larsen 1994: 103). Simultaneously, on the *administrative level*, the administration of the new visions began transcending the state departments. This greatly altered the recruitment patterns of the state administration, seeing economists rather than jurists becoming the natural state experts.

This produced a relative decline in the position of jurists: the number of jurists was rising but the monopoly was crumbling (Hammerslev and Madsen 2014). However, this development was exacerbated by the simultaneous legislative innovations, making law increasingly the subject of an economic logic: For example, the social and economic approach to the planning of the welfare program through a "legislative framework" approach left a great deal of discretion to local bureaucrats and blurred the boundaries between law production and legal application. Equally, the growth in the number of administrative boards, relying as much on non-jurists

kind. Subsequently, the role and powers of the institution have been altered on several occasions, and the institution has been transplanted to also function in specialized fields (Banakar 2003).

as jurists, challenged the jurists' traditional control of the adjudication of law (Dalberg-Larsen 1994: 189). Whereas the Scandinavian welfare states initiated a phenomenal legalization process, they also instrumentalized legal knowledge and know-how to become more of a functional auxiliary to the state and not the *raison d'état* as previously.[10] The growing acceptance of legal formalism at the legal academies helped educate jurists as mere civil servants allegedly freed from the burden of politics. Because of the impact of these new anti-political orthodoxies of law on the general habitus of jurists, the legal profession was generally rather weak in its interface with the new experts of the welfare state, all having a specialization in both the academic theories and politics of the new state, a double profile ironically resembling that of the jurists during the nineteenth century.[11]

4. Episodes of Legal Mobilization during the Postwar Period (1945–1970)

Besides the overall structural challenge the legal complex faced with the rise of the comprehensive social welfare state, in Norway and Denmark law and lawyers also faced additional challenges related to restoring law and order, as well as professional prestige, after both collaboration and the ad hoc justice at liberation.[12] As in other European countries facing similar issues, this was to have a significant influence on who became the leaders among lawyers with regard to the mobilization of human rights. Generally, the leading actors were former resistance fighters, who used their experiences and prestige to access the new postwar politics of justice. Moreover, although representing both liberal and communist political agendas, they had a shared outlook of perceiving human rights as the means of continuing the unfinished business of seeking justice against fascists and collaborators. This legal engagement was soon to be subject to the dominant international orthodoxies of the time, in particular Cold War politics, and thereby be inscribed in the framework of opposing forces generally characterizing the Cold War of human rights (Madsen 2012). In the remainder of this section, I trace first the legal politics of the purge and then turn toward the Cold War politics of human rights in Denmark.

[10] In regard to the transformation of law and lawyers under the Scandinavian welfare states, it should be noted that among the Scandinavian countries there are some differences in the composition of the legal profession. Most notably, whereas lawyers in private practice in the period was some 35 percent of the total profession in Norway and Denmark, the number in Sweden was considerable lower at a mere 21 percent in 1951 and 16 percent in 1971 (Bertilsson and Carleheden 1995).

[11] See Bertilsson (1995).

[12] See also the chapters by Graver and Langford in this volume.

4.1 The Purge: Restoring the Legal System

As in France and the Netherlands, both Denmark and Norway undertook a legal confrontation with the collaborators of the occupying Nazi regime. In this regard, the three Scandinavian countries provide three considerable different variations of the post-Nazi challenge to law and the legal system: While Sweden generally avoided this problem by having remained neutral and outside the Nazi occupation, the political patterns of occupation in Norway and Denmark were very different. Norway was ruled by an express but illegitimate pro-Nazi regime while having, simultaneously, a legitimate exiled government in London, whilst in Denmark the legitimate government initially cooperated with the Nazi occupants, leaving fewer politicians to seek exile. Legally, the differences between the Norwegian and Danish situations influenced the conduct of the legal as well as political processes at liberation. Similar to the situation in the Netherlands, the Norwegian case was marked by the fact that there had been open war between Nazi Germany and Norway, clearly recognizable in the conduct of the Norwegian Resistance and the firm course taken by the exiled government (Tamm 1984: 704). The purge took as its starting point the biggest and most symbolic case, the case against the Norwegian Nazi leader Vidkun Quisling, who had illegitimately proclaimed himself governor of Norway, as well as having actively participated in the deportation of Jews and executions of members of the Resistance, and supported the Nazi war machine (Andenæs 1979). After only two weeks of legal proceedings, he was found guilty and executed. It was on this firm background that the subsequent trials took place using an extended version of the Norwegian Criminal Code to convict some forty-six thousand persons, of which some thirty received capital punishments and six hundred were sent to prison for more than eight years (Tamm 1984: 705–706). Although this hard-line legal course momentarily made a group of Swedish jurists intervene and criticize the legal process, the Norwegian purge generally took place in a comparatively controlled manner avoiding excessive revenge liquidations; according to one observer, it was "almost like a fairy-tale" (Andenæs 1979: 263).

Resembling more the situation in France, the Danish case was far less straightforward because of the initial cooperation between the Danish government and the local German representatives from April 9, 1940 to August 29, 1943. In practice, this particular political course implied that the Danish government increasingly had to bend to German demands. And, importantly, these compromises were implemented by using the legitimate officials of the Danish state, whereby law and the legal system became deeply implicated in a number of Acts that curbed constitutional freedoms.[13] The most notorious example was the internment of all Danish

[13] Moreover, the general policy of securing Danish jurisdiction over Danish citizens made lawyers and judges, as well as the Danish police, charged with carrying out the increasingly draconian measures (Tamm 1984).

Communists by German decree, legalized first by the Danish government and subsequently approved by the Supreme Court.[14] Indeed the President of the Supreme Court, Troels G. Jørgensen, helped prepare the legislation and subsequently publicly defended it, greatly weakening the position of the Supreme Court in society (Tamm 1984: 58). The applicability of the Act was tried by several of the interned Communists. One of their leaders, the lawyer Carl Marius Madsen, even sought to challenge its constitutionality. But the Supreme Court, relying on the legal convention of limited access to judicial review under the Danish constitution, failed to see good reasons for overturning what appeared to be crystal-clear political will. The human consequences of the banning and internment were probably more brutal than anticipated by the government or the Court. When the politics of cooperation was terminated in August 1943, a significant number of the interned Communists, some 150, were sent to concentration camps, where many were persecuted and killed. Because of the role of the courts, the Supreme Court President in particular, in the internment cases, there were claims at liberation that the courts should not play any role in the purge, and the Supreme Court judges should be discharged and even tried (Tamm 1984: 58).[15] The outcome of the controversy was to use the normal court system but to specially recruit a corps of judges who could be approved of by the resistance, in particular its Communist branch (Tamm 1984: 133).

Suffering from the fact that it was questionable whether war had actually ever been declared between Denmark and Germany, this confrontation with the immediate past was carried out with a set of penal laws with retroactive effect. This was a measure that in respect to penal law posed serious problems as it was generally assumed, but not codified in the constitution, that the principle of *nulla poena sine lege* applied and excluded retroactive effect, *vis retroactive*, in respect to penal law. The carrying out of this legal trick was helped by law professor Stepan Hurwitz, later first Danish Ombudsman and a member of the War Crimes Commission in London in 1944–1945, as he provided an authoritative interpretation of the question of retroactivity of penal laws justifying such measures in the specific context, as well as providing academic justification for applying capital punishment and other harsh punishments to the collaborators.[16] The subsequent trials sentenced some 13,500 persons for Nazi collaboration, of whom the vast majority had served in various kinds of armed entity of the occupant. While the trials, thus, went for a

[14] It should be underlined that the Danish Communist Party at this point was not enjoying great popularity, partly because of the Soviet aggression in Finland, partly because of the Nazi–Soviet Pact of Non-Aggression. See for example Hertel (2002).

[15] The Supreme Court President Jørgensen had, however, retired in 1944.

[16] First Danish Ombudsman (1955–1971), Hurwitz was professor of procedural law at the University of Copenhagen (1935–1955). During World War II, he fled to Sweden and was in London in late 1944 to help prepare the war crimes tribunals and the laws related to the purge in Denmark. In this context it is interesting to remark how his works in criminology generally sought to bring a human or individual focus to administrative law. This particular approach influenced the initial jurisprudence of the institution in a way that could be described as pro-human rights, albeit in a very vague sense.

solution fitting the general sentiment of revenge-justice at liberation, the legal system, ironically by using these flexible standards, helped regain some of its prestige and resurrect its role as the guardian of justice. It was, however, a short-lived normalization. As suggested above, the terrain of law was to change considerably by the progressive development of the welfare state stripping law and lawyers of their traditional central role as both legal administrators and legal politicians.

These trials also saw the mobilization of lawyers from both the communist and liberal camps of the resistance movement. It was particularly among these actors that the pioneers of human rights were to be found. One example, the aforementioned communist lawyer, Carl Madsen, was appointed special prosecutor, a position he rapidly exploited to focus on the economic collaborators, an area little scrutinized by his more moderate legal colleagues less inclined to question their equals of the business world. Madsen's crusade, however, came to a sudden halt as he, in the middle of his case against the contractors Wright, Thomsen & Kier (WTK), was caught drink driving and therefore discharged as prosecutor by the Attorney General. The same Attorney General subsequently dismissed the WTK case, and thereby quashed the prospects of getting justice in what supposedly was the biggest of all the Danish collaborator cases.[17] Another resistance fighter, a key contact between the British security service and the Danish resistance movement, as well as a member of the Liberal Party, Per Federspiel (1905–1994), was appointed Minister of Special Affairs (*Særlige anliggender*) in charge of the war crimes prosecution against the Nazis and the highly sensitive cases concerning resistance fighters and their killings of collaborators and informers during the occupation and at liberation. Helped by Professor Hurwitz, he unsuccessfully sought to convince the War Crimes Commission to prosecute the Nazis under the auspices of the Nuremberg Tribunal. At the same time, Federspiel sought a collegiate solution to the question of the legal consequences of the killing of collaborators and informers. He emphasized that the resistance movement was at war with the Nazis, as well as generally making it clear that it would be disrespectful to the Resistance to pursue these issues. Besides being a popular solution in respect of public sentiment of the time, this solution was supported by the legal authority of Hurwitz.[18]

[17] The Communist daily, *Land og Folk*, further pursued the allegations against Wright, Thomsen & Kier in a number of articles that eventually led the editor to be found guilty of defamation and sent to prison for ninety days and fined DKK 40,000, a considerable sum at the time.

[18] But, as the degree, or even existence, of actual collaboration in certain cases was questioned by relatives, the course changed, in particular when the Ministry of Justice took over the caseload in 1947. The issue was to remain unfinished as well as highly controversial and was to be reopened in the subsequent periods in the discussion of the purge.

4.2 The Legal Cultural Cold War

There is a direct link between these immediate postwar legal processes and the subsequent investment in human rights made by a number of lawyers. Hurwitz was notably to embody the Danish ombudsman institution and helped bring about an important development of administrative practices considering citizens' rights. While Hurwitz thereby was to hold a key human rights position, the practices of the two other emblematic Danish "lawyers-résistants," Carl Madsen and Per Federspiel, generally fit into the grand scheme of Cold War and human rights, which in the field of law was marked by the two competing organizations of the International Association of Democratic Lawyers (IADJ), eventually dominated by French Communist lawyers, and the ICJ, in part sponsored by the CIA (Madsen 2012).

Besides his anti-communist beliefs, Federspiel's reputational capital as a "politician-lawyer-résistant" made him the perfect recruit to the ICJ to pursue their strategy of challenging the IADJ and their colonization of the concept of human rights. Whereas Federspiel's role at the ICJ was in many ways an international and European one, a number of more national anti-communist organizations were launched in Denmark as local chapters of the Congress for Cultural Freedom (CCF), the organization which had been launched to counterattack the emerging cultural dominance of the Soviet pro-intellectuals and their institutions.[19] However, attempts to develop an organization called "Intellectual Freedom and Human Rights" (*Intellektuel Frihed og menneskerettigheder*) failed in the early 1950s, despite the fact that funding had already been promised through CCF contacts (Philipsen 2002: 41). In many ways, law did not become the terrain of choice for these practices, and lawyers only played a marginal role in the more general Cold War politics in Denmark and Scandinavia.[20] Conversely, helped by contacts in the British branch of the CCF, another organization, "The Society for Freedom and Culture" (*Selskab for Frihed og Kultur*) (SFK), was, for example, set up in 1953 in Denmark. It was launched by deeply anti-communist members of the Danish resistance movement with close ties to Danish and US intelligence circles, and who had been involved in the tapping of Danish communists in the postwar period. The organization also recruited several jurists, including Jens Buhl, son of Wilhelm Buhl, Prime Minister during the cooperation and in the interim government at liberation, as well as the law professor Dr. Jur. W. E. von Eyben (Philipsen 2002).

[19] It is worth noting that leading Social Democrats such as Trygve Lie or the German Willy Brandt all took an active part in the setting up of the CCF. A recent report on Cold War intelligence operations in Norway has shown that the Cold War fears instigated a considerable number of intelligence activities in particularly Left-wing milieus.

[20] Comparatively, it is interesting to note that "Intellectual Freedom and Human Rights" was supposed to be modelled in the same image as, for example, the ICJ: A presidency made up of "cultural persons," a secretariat, and a broader network of "confidential agents inside various cultural and intellectual circles all over the country" (Philipsen 2002).

Initially the idea had been to create a pan-Scandinavian branch of the CCF, but the idea failed, mostly because the Swedish activists involved did not appreciate the strategies of the Danish hard liners (Philipsen 2001). Initially the Danish branch only marginally used the cultural framework of the CCF and was instead very focused on, indeed almost possessed with the idea of, a strategy of "psychological warfare," a tactic of which one of the founders, Arne Sejr, had acquired knowledge during the war as a member of the Students' Intelligence Service and subsequently on ad hoc jobs for the Danish secret service. This slightly paranoid and very national orientation was, however, reversed soon after by the arrival of the liberal journalist, Jørgen Schleiman, who had been on a NATO scholarship in Paris to study "intellectuals and Communism," as well as working briefly at the CCF headquarters in Paris (Philipsen 2002: 45).[21] With his arrival, the organization moved more in line with the overall CCF objectives, and increasingly became an intellectual barrier against Communism through cultural and intellectual means. Basically, contrary to his predecessors, Schleiman sought to attract moderate left-wing intellectuals and cultural personalities, rather than battling them with "psychological warfare." At this time, human rights and broader issues of democracy were notions included in the cultural artillery, but because of the composition of the local Cold War cultural battle lines, human rights never directly became the key strategic subject.

There is something striking about the early days of the Danish branch of the CCF that encapsulates the extreme polarity of the Cold War on the cultural terrain. The bottom line was that a very considerable number of writers, artists, and intellectuals were more convinced by the other "pole," that is Communism, making a cultural takeover in the "name of freedom" highly problematic and even illusory for the local Danish CCF leaders. The battles between writers and cultural personalities in and around the great events of Prague 1948, the Berlin Crisis 1948, and the Danish entrance into NATO 1949, did not alter the convictions of many "true believers" in social justice and peaceful cooperation. Having roots in the Communist resistance movements, many of them simply concluded that the West did not offer the solution and, therefore also that the grand discourse on human rights was fundamentally empty in those hands (Hertel 2002). On the contrary, many Communists saw themselves as holding the torch. One of them was the mentioned lawyer, Carl Madsen, who remained faithful to the Communist Party even after Khrustjov's revelations and Hungary 1956—the latter he in fact openly supported. Notwithstanding their common links to the resistance movements and the postwar purge, Carl Madsen in many ways was the absolute counterpart to the emblematic ICJ internationalist Per Federspiel. An outspoken Communist from

[21] At the same time, Arne Sejr launched yet another organization *Frihed og folkestyre*, Freedom and Peoples' Democracy, as a platform for continuing his "psychological warfare." On Jørgen Schleimann, see Aagaard (2003).

a modest social background, Madsen had even before the war established himself in the inner circles of the Danish Communist Party. Also, he had proven to be an extraordinary well-spoken legal orator before the courts, giving him the name "Brain-Madsen" when in Court defending the powerless and, at the same time, denouncing the allegedly "true" character of capitalism.[22]

After the war, Madsen resumed his legal practice, and started publishing critical essays and short stories on the nature of the Danish legal system, repeating the stance he had developed in the late 1920s. For Madsen, the purge and the confrontation with the traitors did not stop in the immediate postwar period. Above all influencing the positioning of the one-man army that was Madsen in the legal field was his ambition to vindicate himself and his confreres of the Resistance against the irresponsible state elite and continue the denunciation of Danish businesses' dubious standards, actions he was deprived of during the purge.[23] Madsen found his clientele in the gutter of the welfare state, pickpockets and prostitutes, as well as among the supposedly politically persecuted. It was hardly a coincidence that one of his most celebrated moments became his defense of anti-US demonstrators arrested at the increasingly heated demonstrations against US conduct in Vietnam in the late 1960s.[24] This occasion crystallized his engagement and his defense proceedings became as much a criticism of the police and the formal support of the United States as an actual legal defense of his clients. It was this role as political defense attorney blended with an almost complete disrespect for the guardians of the legal system—he allegedly named his pigs after leading Danish judges—which made him specialize in challenging police practices.[25] But it was largely a one-man army of a particularly driven individual: A lawyer with a cause driven by strong personal convictions and operating on the outskirts of the welfare state, as well as in more or less complete opposition to the legal establishment.

Generally, the two examples of Carl Madsen and Per Federspiel underline how early postwar human rights practices were highly fragmented and identified with individual actors rather than the legal complex more generally. The exception to this trend was the processes related to the purge. But here the role of the state should not be underestimated. It was not personal vendettas or projects that controlled these proceedings but rather state policies. The attempt by single individuals such as Madsen to use the occasion for a broader challenge of the state ultimately failed. This is not a unique Danish case but also representative of Scandinavia more

[22] On the occasion of his defense of Danish volunteers in the civil war in Spain in 1938, he had already gained a crowd of followers, comprising young Communists. His defense was deemed worthy of being published in full in the Communist daily, *Arbejderbladet*. See, for example, Thing (1993).

[23] The engagement of, for example, the founder of the IADJ in France, Joë Nordmann, equally dedicated his life-long work to pursuing the oppressors of Vichy, in particular Pétain.

[24] Another noteworthy case was his defense of the Free Town of Christiania in Copenhagen in the 1970s, his last case before his death in 1978.

[25] For the anecdote about the pigs see Carlsen (2001). For his critique of the police, see Madsen (1969).

generally. One of the problems for politically motivated lawyers was that the terrain of the struggle was dominated by other actors, above all a cultural elite, comprising leading writers, artists, and academics, clearly siding with Communism and seeing it as one of their basic objectives to denounce the political networks of the welfare state establishment. Regardless of the overall decline of lawyers during the period with respect to politics and the administration of the state, law and lawyers were perceivably deeply entangled in these networks and practices and, therefore, if not the enemies of this cultural elite, then hardly the obvious allies.

5. From Critical Law to Human Rights Lawyering (1970–2000)

Because of the ways in which human rights had been launched as an international project in the postwar period, as well as the subsequent Cold War polarization of the subject, the subject area remained largely in the hands of a small elite of international law professors and diplomats. This gradually changed throughout the 1970s when certain segments of the legal profession, notably academics and left-wing private practitioners, sought to use rights approaches as part of a general critique of the Danish state and society. The legal critics of the welfarist Danish society, many of which were originally Marxist inspired, turned over the course of the 1980s increasingly toward human rights. In what follows, I will trace a number of key mobilizations during both periods, first the critical law movement and then the rise of human rights as a critique of domestic state practices in Denmark.

5.1 The Radical Critique of Law in Society

This new legal activism in Denmark and Scandinavia more generally was closely linked to the social upheavals of the late 1960s. As it was also the case in other European countries, these practices were centered on public law and overall sought to popularize justice. Partly because of the considerable political and cultural gap between these aspiring "legal radicals" and the diplomatic circles formally in charge of international human rights, human rights were not initially perceived as a key measure for social change and popularization of justice. In these self-described critical environments the legal system was paradoxically conceived as a hindrance for the broader semi-revolutionary goals: a system built up and around the paradigms of constitutionality and the rule of law inherently favoring the bourgeoisie, following the text-book Marxist definition. At this moment, fifteen years after the publication of thoughts and strategies of the French lawyer and anti-colonialist Marcel Willard on "la défense accusatoire" (1955), the translation of Jacques Vergès' *De la stratégie judiciaire* (1968) into Scandinavian languages in the 1970s became a key intellectual input into these environments. It helped bring about a heated debate in the nascent legal environments on the prospects of applying such legal strategies (*legalstrategier*) in the Scandinavian context. It raised the fundamental dilemma faced by Marxist lawyers, namely whether adhering to such methods was indirectly accepting the hegemony of the legal system and its processes (Dalberg-Larsen 1994: 278–284).

The writings and debates in this movement's in-house journal, the pan-Scandinavian *Retfærd*, generally confirmed the emergence of a critical socio-legal milieu counting a number of highly industrious and skilled socio-legal academics, including, for example, the Norwegians Thomas Mathiesen and Nils Christie. This specific segment of socially aware lawyers helped initiate a number of access to justice projects, such as the law bus (*jussbus*), providing mobile legal aid to the people, or the creation of *Gellerupparkens Retshjælp*, a legal aid shop in the suburbs of Århus, Denmark. Focusing on legal questions related to public law, criminology, and sociology of law, both the innovations and the agents of these critical environments had many common pan-Scandinavian traits (see generally Hammerslev and Madsen 2014). It was mainly an academic movement but it did also count among its activists defense attorneys and, later, refugee, human rights, and labor law lawyers. From a more or less well-defined Marxist position, the basic objective was to exercise a critique of the different disciplines and subjects of law. Implicitly, it was the role of the jurist in society and the relationship between law and society that was on the agenda and the visions of, for example, Nils Christie, the Norwegian criminologist, and Carl Madsen, the Danish postwar lawyer described above, were debated in study groups.

One of the first critical legal groups in Denmark was the Legal Front (*Jura-Fronten*), a student political organization formed at the Legal Institute of the University of Århus in the early 1970s. Although the Front was abolished around 1977, the Legal Political Society (*Retspolitisk Forening*) was formed soon after but with a toned down Marxist tone. The association became a center for critical jurists, and in the journal *Retfærd* they found the alternative platform for expressing their positions on law. It was very much in this environment that many of the later key human rights academics and practitioners first encountered each other and developed their common interests. Closely related, another core site for this activism in Denmark was Institute B [originally *Studiestræde*] of the Faculty of Law, University of Copenhagen. It was part of the Law Faculty, but housed in a separate building and clearly marked apart by Marxist beliefs.

One of the key spokesmen of the movement, the Copenhagen law professor Ole Krarup, exemplifies this convergence between the radical Marxist left and instances of broader legal mobilization. In 1976, acting as counsel together with Carl Madsen, one of Ole Krarup's first public cases, he was fighting against the closure of Christiania, the self-proclaimed independent community within the city of Copenhagen. Using the imported French strategies known as *défense de rupture*, they were well aware that the case inevitably would be lost, but because of the havoc created in the media via the legal proceedings Christiania ultimately survived due to popular sentiment. Similar strategies were deployed in a series of later cases, notably a highly publicized case on the constitutionality of the Danish ratification of the Maastricht Treaty and even later, together with an all-star team of the critical legal community, a similar case in which Krarup et al. argued that the Danish ratification of the Amsterdam Treaty was unconstitutional. None of the cases was won, but counter-images were created which greatly impacted society. It was a strategy of winning by losing and the latter by exhibiting the state's unwillingness to protect certain rights or entitlements. This activism, although having a significant impact on society and politics, was never a broader movement, however. It remained into the mid-1980s a small community of like-minded activist lawyers who were not part of the mainstream of the legal field. They were "cause lawyers" (Sarat and Scheingold 1997), to use a contemporary term, but their cause reached beyond the individual cases. Deep down many of them imagined an entirely different state. Regardless of their utopian tendencies, many of them were well placed to jump on the human rights bandwagon when it started gaining more momentum in Danish law and society beginning in the early 1990s.

5.2. Human Rights as Critique of the Danish State

It is very telling of the problems in using human rights to criticize the state that in Denmark the financiers of what eventually was to become an internationally acclaimed human rights institute was the Danish Parliament. The Danish Center for Human Rights, set up in 1987, was created with a broad consensus in the Danish parliament agreeing to further prioritize human rights and democracy in development aid. Although focus was on the large international engagements in the area, the mandate also provided that the Center should conduct research and take action with regard to human rights in the domestic national setting. The impetus had come from both the need for professionalizing growing international engagements in development projects involving human rights and from legal academics—most from the critical milieus described above—who anticipated the new importance of human rights in national law. The Center quickly attracted a striking blend of the traditionally more diplomatically inclined international lawyers who had so far dominated the international dimension of the subject and a group of slightly converted activist lawyers. The outcome was the well-known combination of international rule of law ideas and universalist idealism that overall has become characteristic of human rights discourses more generally (Madsen 2011b). The Center also rapidly became by far the largest employer in the area of human rights in Denmark, a situation greatly facilitated by the solid public funding for its activities. The latter also triggered criticism, arguing that the Center was not at all independent of the state, at best a "state NGO" (Madsen 2005). Also researchers at the Copenhagen Law Faculty questioned the seriousness of the so-called research coming out of the Center where policy recommendations went hand in hand with research.

At the domestic level, the Center was almost immediately involved in lobbying efforts for the incorporation of the ECHR into Danish law. This was done in 1992 after extensive preparation by a committee which took notice of the fact that since the mid-1980s the Danish Supreme Court was already conducting an intense review of the conformity of Danish law with the standards of the ECHR (Justitsministeriet 1991: 80). It was therefore much in line with the overall picture of Danish legal politics, seen as a reaction to a development already under way. The committee, however, underlined that the Danish courts were to exercise restraint in adopting interpretations that would have wide-ranging consequences for society and the contents of Danish law, and in general to simply hold back (Justitsministeriet 1991: 197, 149, and 146). The political ambition was clearly to make sure that Danish courts would not consider themselves in a position to imitate the dynamic interpretive style of the European Court of Human Rights (ECtHR). Most importantly, the goal was that the existing separation of power between law and politics should not be altered because of the incorporation of the ECHR. As in many other instances of Danish human rights politics, the state sought to integrate the new, potentially critical legal subject into its pre-existing modes of production.

There had, however, been a number of signs that human rights were perhaps not simply goods for export in terms of Scandinavian moral superpower politics but also questions that were not that easy to control at the domestic level. In particular the emergence of immigration as a heated national political subject was linked to a set of broader processes that in practice meant that the social backsides of immigration were increasingly revealed to the middle classes from their cover in the ghettos. A new extreme right was emerging which sought to make the most of the uncertainty related to the integration of waves of Iranian refugees. Similar to the original reactions to le Pen in France at about the same time, a broad coalition including academics and artists as well as the mainstream political parties sought to thwart the voices of the extreme right. It was altogether a different situation than in the late 1990s, when the mainstream parties increasingly adhered to a more critical political line toward immigration and the integration of refugees.

Importantly, these controversies also became linked to the general showdown with the comprehensive welfare state, a process gradually undertaken by both non-socialist governments and the social democrats themselves. In general, these processes related to liberalization of the state coincided with the orientation toward the new national political discourse on human rights as a possible means of finding new rationality of the transformed welfare state. It was also in this context that segments of the legal community made an attempt at using human rights as a way of recovering the profession's traditional role as both the representative of the state and the progressive voice against it. Using human rights to criticize the state, however, collided with deep-held views of Danish and Scandinavian exceptionalism in this regard. Illustratively, when Amnesty International for the first time ever criticized Denmark in its annual report in 1992, the critique was considered by many an absurd accusation. In fact, Amnesty rapidly lost about a fourth of its members. Two factors, however, contributed to keeping this line of liberal politics alive: the continuous pressure from the Danish Center for Human Rights, particularly in the area of immigration broadly speaking, and the growing effects of the ECtHR in combination with the incorporation of the ECHR into national law.

The Danish Center was to become the key actor in an increasingly expanding national human rights lobby seeking to challenge Danish practices in the area of asylum and refugee law. The impact of this mobilization is probably best illustrated by the fact that less than ten years after the first Amnesty report on Denmark, it became commonplace to accuse the Danish state of violating human rights, and even to accuse certain parties of flirting with fascism. This had the effect that the formerly sacred notion of human rights was eventually to be directly written off by a growing right-wing force as simply the political project of a left wing mafia having its leaders at the Danish Center of Human Rights. The Center had indeed successfully introduced Danish obligations under international conventions in a number of quarrels over particularly the rights of asylum seekers and refugees. It found its allies in a complex movement of both critical lawyers, NGOs, and some politicians. However, it was also countered by segments of the legal profession, notably from legal academia, noting publicly that the relevant international obligations and principles were first and foremost far less clear-cut than suggested by the Center and their allies, and the latter was tentative in its more political than legal interpretations. Also, it was argued that Denmark in principle could withdraw from these obligations if needed as it was after all a sovereign state in regard to international law, as well as in regard to the human rights lobby. The underlying argument was, however, that politics should be left to politicians and not to the self- or state-appointed guardians of morality (Jyllandsposten 2001).

This onslaught had a real effect on the Center. In the process of establishing a new liberal minority government in early 2002, reform of the Center became more or less the "sacrifice" for allowing the new minority government parliamentary support with back-up from the far-right-wing Danish People's Party (*Dansk Folkeparti*). The Danish People's Party had effectively become Enemy No. 1 of the milieu around the Center in general and its Director in particular.[26] Yet, because of the Center's very high international profile, the incident raised eyebrows in the international human rights environment and media—a "tornado of international

[26] Danish newspapers covered the case extensively at the time. See for example Jyllandsposten (March 6, 2002) and Politiken (March 1, 2002).

criticism," to quote a Danish newspaper—and even the UN Commissioner of Human Rights, Mary Robinson, wrote a letter to the new Danish Prime Minister on these regrettable developments.[27] The government nevertheless went ahead and restructured the Center and made it part of a larger foreign policy institute acting under the name of the Danish Human Rights Institute. For the post of Chair, they secured the services of a former liberal foreign minister who had ironically helped launch the Center in 1987. This was, however, the least paradoxical outcome of the situation. A veteran of refugee law with vague links to the critical legal milieus of the late 1970s and early 1980s, the former head of the closed Center, Morten Kjærum, was not only reappointed Director of the new Institute, the Institute was to expand its repertoire and also house a complaints board for racial discrimination.

These battles underscored with all possible visibility the growing force of human rights, as well as the curious boomerang effect of globalization: If measured by Danish procedures of "human rights and democratization conditionality" when allocating development aid, closing down a human rights center would clearly have implied a disqualification for receiving development aid as the measure was not advancing democratization; The Danish Center and the foreign policy establishment had, moreover, helped lobby the international notion of human rights institutes as a new institutional framework in international human rights politics as a form of new ombudsman. Having not only presented its own jewel in the crown, the Human Rights Center, as an example in these proceedings, the government was also bound by the United Nations' so-called Paris Principles of 1993 for the institutional and independent structures of such institutions, which were the outcome of this lobbying. In fact, the Prime Minster felt the necessity to respond to the UN High Commissioner's letter, using the occasion to underline that these changes in fact would only enhance the Danish commitment to human rights and that the criticism was based on misunderstandings in the international media.[28] No matter what the original intentions of the government were, in light of these episodes, the process underlined that human rights offered a way of criticizing the state on legal-political grounds far exceeding the legal activism of the previous generation of activist lawyers. It was, as suggested, however, not a clear-cut victory for the human rights advocates. Through their aggressive pursuit of international human rights norms as a political framework for domestic political actions, they opened up a critique of international law as merely another form of politics. Put differently, the almost sacred status international law had hitherto held in Danish society—when it was used only for criticizing and changing other states—was lost (Christoffersen and Madsen 2011).

[27] Quote from Politiken (February 26, 2002). Mary Robinson's letter is available in Politiken (January 16, 2002).
[28] Letter from the Prime Minster to Mary Robinson of January 16, 2002. On file with author.

It was also in this context of a deep politicization of international and European law that the ECHR had been implemented into Danish law. In Denmark the incorporation proceedings had been controlled by mainly conservative political and legal forces. The underlying rationale was that vague international provisions should not alter the far more effective domestic approach of a dense regulation of relevant matters. Denmark had been among the very first states to accept the ECHR and its optional clauses on the jurisdiction of the ECtHR and the right to individual petition, thus lending important legal and political legitimacy to these nascent institutions (Madsen 2011a). Historically, Denmark had also faced very little trouble in Strasbourg. The country did not experience a single declared violation in Strasbourg for some thirty-six years; from 1953 to 1989, and European human rights law played practically no role in domestic Danish law and politics (Christoffersen and Madsen 2011). Cases brought against Denmark were summarily dismissed, with only limited exceptions, for which no violations were found. Equally important, the Danish government concluded that very few legislative revisions were required to conform Danish and European human rights standards—with the exception of securing a minimum level of protection of the (negative) freedom of association with respect to "closed- shop" unions due to the Court's ruling in *Young, James and Webster v. United Kingdom* (1981). Not until 1989, in the *Hauschildt* case concerning impartiality of single-judge provincial courts in criminal proceedings, was Denmark found in breach of the Convention.[29] Illustratively, Denmark was instead among the most active countries using the provision on interstate complaints filing suits against other member states for their human rights record.[30]

In this light, expectations were not too high in terms of the possible impact of the incorporation of the ECHR. But one surprise actor came out of hiding and made a stance for the importance of the ECHR in Danish law. In 1996, the then president of the Supreme Court gave an interview to a weekly newspaper—in itself a novelty. In the interview he embraced European human rights and strongly emphasized the need for a dynamic understanding of law. In the Danish context, this meant considering, at the time, the growing interest in classical civil rights, according to the judge (Eiby 1996). He further went on to argue that as a remedy of the lack of a modern human rights protection in the Danish Constitution of 1953, the Supreme Court had turned to the European Convention for an up-to-date catalogue of rights and a substantial jurisprudence on human rights (Eiby 1996). This openly constitutional blessing and support for dynamic interpretation regardless of the incorporation committee's insistence on self-restraint took place

[29] *Hauschildt v. Denmark*, App. No. 10486/83 Eur. Ct. H.R. (ser. A) (1989).

[30] *The Greek Case*, App. No. 3321/67, 3322/67, 3323/67, and 3344/67, 1969 Eur. Conv. On H.R. 1 (1970). App. No. 9940/82 to 9944/82 (Turkey) and in 1997 *Denmark v. Turkey*, App. No. 34382/97 (2000).

without noteworthy critique—academics were instead concerned with more legalistic aspects of the incorporation of the law, for instance whether it implied that all of the *acquis* of the ECtHR could be used before Danish courts or only cases against Denmark. It was probably the traditionally very limited practices in respect of judicial review that made this potential enhancement of the courts' quasi-constitutional repertoire less than frightening to the Parliament. In fact, the intervention of the president of the Supreme Court was generally perceived as mainly an attempt to tease the legal public and to get lawyers to use the ECHR.

It is of course somewhat paradoxical that the call for taking the new opportunity seriously came from an insider of the system, a judge not known for any form of activism but rather for being a traditional Scandinavian pragmatist with a background in the central state administration, indeed at the heart of it: the Ministry of Justice. Generally, the incorporation had an effect, but it was not by any means revolutionary. The usual suspects from the critical environments described above added European human rights to their existing repertoire and so did other lawyers. The ECHR was integrated into the fabric of domestic law but no one expected it to cause radical changes. European human rights, in other words, became a supplement rather than a specific or autonomous new area of legal practice. In fact, scrutinizing Danish lawyers' usage of the ECHR reveals than only one single lawyer managed to make a career out of using the ECHR as well as the ECtHR. A collaborator with the first director of the Center for Human Rights, as well as an external legal consultant to the Ministry of Foreign Affairs, Tyge Trier managed to carve out a position as the leading human rights attorney in Denmark and Scandinavia more generally. But as indicated by his position vis-à-vis the state, he is by no means a radical or someone in pursuit of a particular legal-political agenda. Human rights are instead more simply his line of business. More generally, it is probably fair to say that the mode of producing human rights in the Danish state—notably via the ombudsman and detailed legislation—triumphed over more specific rights-based approaches. The heated debates on immigrants probably also helped implode the subject before the courts, as Danish courts were not particularly interested in being drawn into these highly politicized debates. That said, the legal system has in recent years stepped up on these matters and pushed back on government initiatives related to immigration (Christoffersen and Madsen 2011).

6. Conclusion

This final analysis of episodes of legal-political mobilization in Denmark in the area of human rights over the past half-century might at first glance suggest that the framework put forward by FHK does not yield significant results when studying highly developed democracies such as Denmark. One easy, and in my view too easy, explanation is that in highly developed democracies, the kind of political liberalism based on civil and political rights that FHK argue is a trademark of the mobilization of the legal complex is not really called for. The state is simply too reactive to leave massive gaps in its legal-political armor to be exploited by civil society organizations or the legal complex. Put differently, the state is in itself an advocate of liberal political causes, including civil and political rights. Because of the well-established political-democratic pathways, critique is anticipated or channeled into ordinary politics. This seems to broadly explain why the critique in the first three decades after World War II seems to predominantly (but not only) come from legal actors who have rejected the ordinary means of inclusive democracy, in some cases rejecting the welfare state model altogether. The potential of a liberal-political critique based on European human rights is also initially countered by the Danish state sponsoring a large human rights center with a mandate to also monitor domestic practices in this regard. The Danish welfare state appears as the great pacifier—and not on fully legitimate grounds. The state both absorbed and marginalized liberal-political critique, from the legal complex or other agents, when the European Convention was first domesticated.

In light of the early history of the Danish state addressed at the start of this chapter, one could even observe this as an evolutionary process in which the state gradually turns toward political liberal ideas and absorbs them. Ironically, this process starts with the establishment of absolute monarchy because it helps to centralize and monopolize state power. Ideas about the separation of powers are turned into practice by elite state administrators who also push the process of differentiation jurists as a legal profession. The defining characteristic of these processes is that the role of lawyers—even their exam—is that of an official position in the state. The *candidatus juris* is what in Danish used to be termed an *embedseksamen*, that is, an exam allowing access to certain positions as officials in the state. The bar association only emerged later and the power of private practitioners within the state remains limited, at least until recently (Madsen 2008). The key figure thus becomes that of the jurist—not the American lawyer or English barrister. Law. These jurists become not only the operators of the state; their vision of legal rationality becomes the operative code of the state.

This line of argument, however, requires more sociological finesse to be used as an explanation. In more sociological terms, human rights—and notably civil and political rights—have arguably been central to the expansion of the state rather than to its moderation; that is, contrary to popular belief, human rights have been key to the massive build-up of modern welfare states (Madsen and Verschraegen 2013; Thornhill 2013). This is partly due to the ways in which human rights have helped to justify and legitimize state power vis-á-vis individuals. Conversely, without individual rights it would have been close to impossible to construct the extensive Scandinavian welfare state and needless to say its redistributive mechanism. The place of the ombudsman is emblematic in this regard. This, the most archetypical of Scandinavian institutions, providing citizens the protection of individual rights free of charge, has in large part enabled the kind of self-critique of the extensive state which in the long run has legitimized it. This is, of course, also precisely what distinguishes the Scandinavian model of the social democratic welfare state from the equally egalitarian but repressive socialist states that were established in Eastern Europe during the Cold War. The latter lacked what in systems theoretical terms would be called self-reflection and, thereby, was subject to intense political-liberal critique the very moment it did not repress critique entirely.

Another answer to the puzzle of the Danish case is arguably at the more theoretical level. Basically, why is it that the theoretical coupling between political liberalism and the legal complex does not entirely work when tested against what arguably is one of the most advanced welfare states and democracies in the world? I would argue this is due to two features of the framework. First, it leaves out the kind of smaller or more individualistic mobilizations that generally characterize the Danish case. Likewise, and more importantly, by its focus on broader mobilization it is not particularly adept at analyzing the fine-grained politics of lawyers in and around the state that is the trademark of advanced democracies. It is almost impossible to identify an instance where the larger legal complex has mobilized across its sub-sections in Danish history. We need only look at the reactions to the highly questionable laws issued by the Danish government during the Nazi occupation. As described above, the courts simply followed political directives, even made extra efforts to legitimize them, and only individual maverick lawyers dared stand up. On the contrary, one could highlight plenty of examples of discreet lobbying by legal professionals on legislation and practices. Second, the framework leaves out legal mobilizations for causes other than political liberalism. This tends to exclude key mobilizations in the Danish case which were triggered by, for example, Marxist motivations—in many cases against the political liberalism of the Danish welfare state and its alleged failure to produce a genuine social(ist) state because of social democratic double standards.

At the general theoretical level, these limitations of the coupling of the two notions of legal complex and political liberalism delineate the analysis to only a specific kind of legal mobilization. The framework seems to have a particular kind of lawyering in mind, perhaps the great legal profession encountered by Tocqueville in his voyage to the nascent United States, namely the lawyer statesmen who acted as both guarantors and entrepreneurs of the new free state (Tocqueville 1842). However, Tocqueville, and Weber after him, were acutely aware that these spokesmen of the new more meritocractic and democratic society might well speak with two tongues. The *ancien régime* collided with *la révolution* in Tocqueville's analysis; legal rationalization was an ideal-type and not an empirically exhaustive depiction of modern society in Weber's analysis. The coupling of legal complex and political liberalism seems to suggest mainly one avenue. It is undoubtedly true that lawyers, at least in the western world, had many of the traits described by FHK, notably in the period between the late nineteenth century and the construction of the welfare state in the second half of the twentieth century. But it is equally true that jurists since the genesis of the Italian city state have also played on both being insiders and outsiders to the formation of the state. The proposed framework seems to work best when jurists are the outsiders and opposing state practices. The problem in the Danish case, and arguably in a number of other European cases, is that the majority of jurists are working for the central state administration. They certainly exercise a certain legal-political liberalism in that function in their daily work but rarely are mobilized on a larger scale in coalition with other segments of the profession.

In conclusion, and in defense of FHK's framework, it can be argued that it is intended mainly—or only—as a scope theory, that is, the goal is to study *how* and *when* such specific mobilizations occur. It is probably fair to say that the form of mobilizations identified by the theory do not occur very often in the Danish case. That moves the inquiry into *why* this is the case, which I have attempted to answer. At first glance, this generally makes Denmark a less singular case with respect to the framework. However, in the broader comparative perspective of the project on the legal complex and political liberalism these findings might well be of significant interest. To speak within the theoretical framing of the project, it basically suggests a different societal function of the legal complex than legal-political liberal activism. Or, to be more precise, it suggests that the inherent liberalism of the profession has been supplemented with other political rationalities. The Danish legal complex has adapted to the logics of the welfare state and gradually situated itself at the crossroads of the law state and the welfare state. It is from this mixed position that it exercises its impact on society. But to fully make this power of legal professionals intelligible, the theory will have to be adapted in order to test for more variations of political commitments and allow for more complex and often downplayed forms of legal activism.

References

Aagaard, Sune. 2003. *For tidligt ude: Jørgen Schleimann – en biografi*. Copenhagen: Lindhardt & Ringhof.

Andenæs, Johannes. 1979. *Det vanskelige oppgjøret: rettsoppgjøret etter okkupasjonen*. Oslo: Tano Aschehoug.

Arter, David. 1999. *Scandinavian Politics Today*. Manchester: Manchester University Press.

Bagge, Poul. 1980. "Ørsted som politiker," in Ditlev Tamm (ed.), *Anders Sandøe Ørsted 1778–1978: Foredrag i anledning af 200-året for Anders Sandøe Ørsteds fødsel*, 139–148. Copenhagen: DJØF.

Banakar, Reza. 2003. *Merging Law and Sociology: Beyond the Dichotomies in Socio-Legal Research*. Berlin: Galda + Wilch Verlag.

Bertilsson, Margareta (ed.). 1995. *Rätten i Förvandling. Jurister mellan stat och marknad*. Stockholm: Nerenius & Santerus Förlag.

Bertilsson, Margareta, and Mikael Carleheden. 1995. "Juristerna i välfärdsstaten" in Margareta Bertilsson (ed.), *Rätten I Förvandling*, 155–177. Stockholm: Nerenius.
Carlsen, Rasmus. 2001. "Den nådeløse forsvarsadvokat." Article available through Danish Radio at http://www.dr.dk/P1/montage_old/madsen.htm
Christoffersen, Jonas, and Mikael Rask Madsen. 2011. "The End of Virtue? Denmark and the Internationalisation of Human Rights," *Nordic Journal of International Law* 80(3): 257–277.
Cordsen, Christine. 2002. "Krigerisk tavshed fra finansministeren", Politiken. March 1, 2002.
Dalberg-Larsen, Jørgen. 1994. *Lovene og livet: En retssociologisk grundbog*. Copenhagen: Akademisk Forlag.
Dezalay, Yves, and Bryant G. Garth. 2010. *Asian Legal Revivals: Lawyers in the Shadow of Empire*. Chicago, IL: University of Chicago Press.
Dezalay, Yves, and Mikael R. Madsen. 2012. "The Force of Law and Lawyers: Pierre Bourdieu and the Reflexive Sociology of Law," *Annual Review of Law and Social Science* 8: 433–452.
Eiby, Tine. 1996. "Domstolene vil få mere magt," in *Weekendavisen*. Copenhagen.
Elias, Norbert. 2006. *The Court Society*. Dublin: University College Dublin Press.
Erichsen, John, and Ditlev Tamm. 2014. *Grever, baroner og husmænd – opgøret med de store danske godser 1919*. Copenhagen: Gyldendal.
Friisberg, Claus. 2007. *Ingen over og ingen ved siden af Folketinget: partiernes kamp om forfatningen 1848–1920*. Odense: Odense University Press.
Hall, John A., Ove Korsgaard, and Ove K. Pedersen. 2014. *Building the Nation: NFS Grundtvig and Danish National Identity*. Montreal: McGill-Queen's Press.
Halliday, Terence C., Lucien Karpik, and Malcolm Feeley. 2007. "The Legal Complex in Struggles for Political Liberalism," in Terence C. Halliday, Lucien Karpik, and Malcolm Feeley (eds.), *Fighting for Political Freedom: Comparative Studies of the Legal Complex and Political Liberalism*, 1–41. Oxford: Hart.
Hammerslev, Ole, and Mikael Rask Madsen. 2014. "The Return of Sociology in Danish Socio-Legal Studies: A Survey of Recent Trends," *International Journal of Law in Context* 10(3): 397–415.
Hertel, Hans. 2002. "Kulturens kolde krig," *Kritik* 158: 9–23.
Jepsen, Signe Damgaard. 2002. "FN-kommissær kritiserer Fogh", Politiken. January 16, 2002.
Josevski, Aleksandar. 2002. "Center for Menneskerettigheder til Sverige", Polititken, February 26, 2002.
Justitsministeriet. 1991. *Betænkning 1220*. Copenhagen.
Karpik, Lucien. 1995. *Les avocats: Entre l'état, le public et le marché XIIIè–XXè siècle*. Paris: Gallimard.
Madsen, Carl. 1969. *Proces mod politiet*. Copenhagen: Stig Vendelkærs Forlag.
Madsen, Mikael Rask. 2000. "Fra sagførerkontorer til store advokatfirmaer: En retssociologisk analyse af ændringerne af den danske advokatbranche." *Juristen* 3:127–141.
Madsen, Mikael Rask. 2004. "France, the UK and 'Boomerang' of the Internationalization of Human Rights (1945–2000)," in Simon Halliday and Patrick Schmidt (eds.), *Human Rights Brought Home: Socio-Legal Perspectives on Human Rights in the National Context*, 57–86. Oxford: Hart Publishing.
Madsen, Mikael Rask. 2005. *L'Emergence d'un champ des droits de l'homme dans les pays européens: enjeux professionnels et stratégies d'Etat au carrefour du droit et de la politique (France, Grande-Bretagne et pays scandinaves, 1945–2000)*. Paris: l'École des hautes études en sciences sociales.

Madsen, Mikael Rask. 2008. "Return to the Copenhagen 'Magic Circle': First Elements of a Longitudinal Study of Large Law Firms in Denmark," *Scandinavian Studies in Law* 53: 303–319.

Madsen, Mikael Rask. 2010. *La genèse de l'Europe des droits de l'homme: Enjeux juridiques et stratégies d'Etat (France, Grande-Bretagne et pays scandinaves, 1945–1970)*. Strasbourg: Presses universitaires de Strasbourg.

Madsen, Mikael Rask. 2011a. "Legal Diplomacy: Law, Politics and the Genesis of Postwar European Human Rights," in Stefan Ludwig Hoffmann (ed.), *Human Rights in the Twentieth Century: A Critical History*, 62–81. Cambridge: Cambridge University Press.

Madsen, Mikael Rask. 2011b. "Reflexivity and the Construction of the International Object: The Case of Human Rights," *International Political Sociology* 5(3): 259–275.

Madsen, Mikael Rask. 2012. "Human Rights and the Hegemony of Ideology: European Lawyers and the Cold War Battle over International Human Rights," in Yves Dezalay and Bryant Garth (eds.), *Lawyers and the Construction of Transnational Justice*, 258–276. Milton Park: Routledge.

Madsen, Mikael Rask, and Gert Verschraegen. 2013. "Making Human Rights Intelligible: An Introduction to Sociology of Human Rights," in Mikael R. Madsen and Gert Verschraegen (eds.), *Making Human Rights Intelligible: Towards a Sociology of Human Rights*, 1–22. Oxford: Hart.

Pedersen, Lars Nørgaard. "Konventioner kvæler debat", Jyllandspostens, December 18, 2001

Pedersen, Lars Nørgaard. "Nævnet for Etnisk Ligestilling nedlægges", Jyllandspostens, March 6, 2002.

Philipsen, Ingeborg. 2001. "Antikommunismens många ansikten: motståndsmannen Arne Sejr och Selskabet for frihed og kultur," *Arbejderhistoria* 4(100): 48–51.

Philipsen, Ingeborg. 2002. "Selskabet for frihed og kultur. Congress for Cultural Freedom i Danmark 1953–1960," *Kritik* 158: 38–51.

Premfors, Rune. 1991. "The 'Swedish model'and public sector reform," *West European Politics* 14(3): 83–95.

Rasmussen, Søren Hein, and Niels Kayser Nielsen. 2003. *Strid om demokratiet*. Aarhus: Aarhus Universitetsforlag.

Sarat, Austin, and Stuart Scheingold. 1997. *Cause Lawyering: Political Commitments and Professional Responsibilities*. Oxford: Oxford University Press.

Tamm, Ditlev. 1984. *Retsopgøret efter besættelsen*. Copenhagen: DJØF.

Tamm, Ditlev. 1990. *Retshistorie: Bind 1: Dansk retshistorie*. Copenhagen: DJØFs forlag.

Tamm, Ditlev. 1997. "Domstolene som statsmagt-set med en retshistorikers øjne," *Ugeskrift for Retsvæsen* 131(9): 87–95.

Tamm, Ditlev. 2005. *Juraens på Københavns Universitet 1479–2005*. Copenhagen: Copenhagen University.

Thing, Morten. 1993. *Kommunismens kultur. DKP og de intellektuelle 1918–1960*. Copenhagen: Tiderne Skifter.

Thornhill, Chris. 2013. "State Building, Constitutional Rights and the Social Construction of Norms: Outline for a Sociology of Constitutions.," in Mikael R. Madsen and Gert Verschraegen (eds.), *Making Human Rights Intelligible: Towards a Sociology of Human Rights*, 25–59. Oxford: Hart.

Tocqueville, Alexis de. 1842. *De la démocratie en Amérique*: Ch. Gosselin.

Vergès, Jacques. 1968. *De la stratégie judiciaire*. Paris: Minuit.

Willard, Marcel. 1955. *La défense accuse*. Paris: Éditions Sociales.

5

Norwegian Lawyers and Political Mobilization 1623–2015

Malcolm Langford[*]

1. Introduction

Nordic states present a strong challenge to legal complex theory and particularly to claims that it is of "universal application" (Halliday, Karpik, and Feeley 2008). Sitting atop most global indexes on core civil rights, the Nordic states seem curiously devoid of visible mobilization by the legal community (Kagan 2001; Hirschl 2011). Yet is the trajectory of political liberalism in the Nordic countries a story to be told without lawyers? It might certainly be in the case of Sweden and Denmark up until the 1970s (see the previous two chapters). However, a common error in accounts of Nordic exceptionalism is the presumption of regional homogeneity. From studies of social policy through to the role of courts or lawyers, the idea that these two countries are representative of their state siblings is not infrequent. While this assumption resonates in the field of early private law or later social welfare policy, it is problematic when applied to the most dynamic period of political liberalism in nineteenth century.

The young Norwegian nation and proto-state followed the American and French revolutions in 1814 by adopting the most liberal constitution of its time, replete with core civil rights and the separation of powers. This constitutional moment ushered in both a long-standing practice of judicial review and an initially lawyer-dominated parliament and state apparatus, in which liberal politics found a generally warm reception. The result is that the pioneering study by Aubert (1960) provides a picture of "lawyers" playing a prominent role in the construction of the rule of law, civil rights, and the conditions for liberal capitalism even if they were anxious to preserve as much as reform.[1] Many of the leading lawyers would pass

* Professor, Faculty of Law, University of Oslo and Co-Director, Centre on Law and Social Transformation. He led the project *Nordic Branding: The Politics of Exceptionalism* 2017–2020 and this chapter draws on work conducted at the Norwegian Centre on Human Rights and Pluricourts Centre of Excellence, University of Oslo. I am grateful for comments on an earlier version by Ragnhildur Helgadóttir, Mikael Madsen, Johan Karlsson Schaffer, Hans Petter Graver, Malcolm Feeley, Adam Hill, and Terry Halliday. Frida Pareus also collated the *Advokatforeningen* documents.

[1] Aubert (1960: 5). See also Slagstad's (2014: 16–17) rendering of Aubert as well as his broader history of national strategists and bureaucrats (Slagstad 1998: see particularly 26–54).

Malcolm Langford, *Norwegian Lawyers and Political Mobilization 1623–2015* In: *The Limits of the Legal Complex*. Edited by: Malcolm Feeley and Malcolm Langford, Oxford University Press.
DOI: 10.1093/oso/9780192848413.003.0005

the Feeley "statue" test for the legal complex—they sit proudly as statues in central Oslo or their home towns. To this picture, we might add the contemporary period, in which Norwegian lawyers are remarkably visible in domestic struggles and debates on human rights[2]—a phenomenon also apparent in other Nordic countries.

Yet it is equally possible to find a counter-narrative in the Norwegian literature. Espeli, Næss, and Rinde (2008) paint a more materialist picture of the legal profession. Beginning in the 1600s, with a focus on *practicing* lawyers, the dominant narrative is one of a collective dominated by self-interest. Lawyers struggled for survival in the face of state and public skepticism, monopolized steadily new branches of commercial practice, defended tenaciously their professional privileges, and were disproportionately represented amongst collaborators with the German occupiers in the period 1940 to 1945.[3] This account of Espeli, Næss, and Rinde (2008) is certainly interpolated with sunnier accounts of lawyers struggling for political liberalism and other public goods. Nonetheless, their primary depiction is of a profession dominated by self-interest—a point not lost in the book's reception (see, e.g., Blandhol and Mahler 2015: 27).[4] Such a narrative of lawyers' potential not only undergirds the idea of Nordic exceptionalism but suggests a legal profession consumed by the concerns of profit and prestige rather than politics and public goods. This is precisely the materialist and realist sociology of the legal profession of the 1970s and 1980s that legal complex researchers were seeking to debunk.

In my view, neither of the above two narratives gives a sufficiently nuanced sense of the role of Norwegian lawyers in the development and defense of political liberalism over the longue durée. Instead, this chapter makes two primary arguments. The first is empirical. Norwegian lawyers have been a *regular* though not constant feature in the arc of political liberalism. Although, with some notable exceptions, Norwegian lawyers have mobilized in smaller groups or wings—and in lightening-rod struggles, the profession almost always finds itself on both sides of the barricades. The second is theoretical. The variance in the Norwegian experience suggests that the legal complex theory needs rethinking, which is expanded upon in a concluding essay in this book. That chapter argues that we need to move beyond the theory's origins in historical sociology and embrace contemporary thinking in political science, political sociology, and constitutional theory. It proposes an alternative legal complex theory that is constructed along two axes, which foreground the *individual agency* and motivations of lawyers and their relative

[2] See further Section 6.
[3] See also Graver in this volume.
[4] The materialist depiction is even stronger in a chapter elsewhere summarizing the book's finding (see Espeli and Rinde 2014).

opportunity structures. Moreover, it suggests that the idea of political liberalism needs to be viewed as a fluid social norm rather than an abstract transcendental idea. Some of these ideas will be touched upon in this chapter.

The chapter is structured according to four broad historical periods: Mercantilism and monarchism 1623–1814; liberal nationalism 1814–1884; social liberalism and welfarism 1885–1980; and globalization and legalization 1977–2015. A relatively early starting point was chosen because the role of Norwegian lawyers in the nineteenth century can only be understood in historical perspective; and the period itself sheds interesting light on the question at hand. The primary focus across the chapter is on lawyers in their capacity as *practicing advocates*. Judges, academics, civil servants, and prosecutors are included in the broad historical sweep but their full and proper treatment requires a separate study.

Methodologically, the chapter mostly follows a common approach in legal complex research. It sketches the longue durée of political liberalism and contemporaneous professional activity while also examining in depth particular *événements* or episodes (Karpik and Halliday 2011: 226–227). The overview of historical periods is punctuated by case studies (ten in total), which mostly draw on secondary literature and interviews. These vignettes represent primarily flashpoints in political liberalism—a particular threat to the *liberal rettsstat*. Some cases were partly "selected on the dependent variable"—it was known in advance that lawyers were central in those particular struggles. These include the *Litlasund* witch-drowning case (1723), the *Fra Kristiania-Bohêmen* censorship case (1887), and the *Liste-saken* case concerning publication of state security activities (1977). However, the remaining studies were chosen in a more detached fashion. In any event, selection on the dependent variable should not be lightly dismissed as this method can provide deeper insight into causal processes. Indeed, these episodes strengthen the two central arguments of the chapter rather than offering a Panglossian view of a noble and united legal profession.

The chapter seeks to expand the methodological remit by including a quantitative content analysis of lawyerly discourse (only initial results reported here) and interviews with some key actors. Discursive methods help avoid one particular risk in using high-profile cases. Such moments may be so politicized that cross-professional mobilization is unrealistic—political loyalties or national security concerns trump professional sensibilities. A focus on flashpoints may paper over the possibility of less visible but broader legal complexes that operate on second-order or more technical questions of political liberalism. To check this phenomenon, the parliamentary submissions and press releases of the Norwegian Bar Association were analyzed. Interviews also provide a deeper exploration of explanatory hypotheses. Hopefully, in the future, the research agenda could also move toward using experimental studies (as is common in other collective action research).

2. Mercantilism and Monarchism 1623–1814

We now turn to the Norwegian case. The early development of the legal profession in Norway can be characterized as a peculiar dialectic between the demands and opportunities of emerging strong state mercantilism under the Danish crown.[5] In 1623, in the city of Stavanger, the legal profession was first formalized and defined by an order of the provincial court (Espeli, Næess, and Rinde 2008: 31–33). It was proclaimed that only a municipality could grant the title of procurator despite a royal letter in 1609 allowing any citizen to use the designation.

This local model was extended across the Kingdom in 1638 by a Danish Royal Decree and followed by a wave of regulation over the next two centuries. After 1666, a lawyer required royal assent to operate in major population centers and, from 1736, needed a formal legal education. Regulation accelerated dramatically in the late eighteenth century. In 1779, royal assent or permission from provincial authorities was required for a lawyer to appear in a higher court; in 1784 only lawyers remunerated by the state could appear in higher courts; and from 1797, an additional assent was required to appeared in the highest two courts. By 1814, lawyers required formal appointment as a civil servant before they could practice and had to accept posting by the state to anywhere in the country, even if their practice was for private clients.

The initial objective of regulation was to control if not eliminate the rapid rise of lawyering. While formal rights to represent others in legal and other proceedings can be dated to the 1200s in Norway (as an ombudsman), the rise of a complex and hierarchical bureaucratic state together with a trading-based economy provided numerous opportunities for remunerative legal practice. The reforms of Christian IV in the 1500s were pivotal. They introduced a paper-based bureaucracy and a raft of new legislation, generating demands from citizens for specialized assistance. Opportunities for legal services also expanded rapidly in the commercial areas of debt recovery, delivery of goods and services, and shipping construction. And courts began to proliferate (church, military, mining, and eventually debt tribunals) with a shift to document-based proceedings, creating numerous opportunities for the development and deployment of legal expertise.

The initial reaction of both the authorities and the public to the rise of lawyers was one of alarm. The many regulatory decrees and orders were often accompanied by a paternalistic reminder that self-representation was the most appropriate form of representation. The first reported paid lawyer, Matz Rytter, was accused in 1618 of pursuing needless litigation and inflicting on "innocent people" enormous "damage and destruction."[6] The uproar led to the king issuing a letter calling for his prosecution and imprisonment. A century later, Hans Villumsen Hoff was

[5] This first part of this section draws heavily on Espeli, Næss, and Rinde (2008: 18–61).
[6] Sundt (1929: 438) cited in Espeli, Næss, and Rinde (2008: 31).

prosecuted for similar practices after a mass citizen protest. In 1723, he achieved the rare feat of appearing 123 times in court over 11 months for a few very simple cases. His strategy of perpetual requests for deferral of proceedings in order to enhance his fees was characterized by Norwegian historian Hilde Sandvik as the "rhetorical ballet" of many early procurators.[7] As with their English brethren at the time (Wesley Pue and Sugarman 2003:2), Norwegian lawyers were the source of public consternation for their self-serving activity.

However, this extensive regulation of lawyers had unintended consequences. It created a new and powerful monopoly of legal professionals. Economically, the procurators profited greatly from their control of the market for legal services. By the end of the 1700s, the demand for genuine legal services far outstripped supply, particularly in rural areas, allowing this new legal class to considerably expand its wealth. Politically, lawyers joined doctors and priests as a new powerful elite: the "thousand academic families" (see generally Seip 1974; Myhre 2008; Neumann 2010). In the absence of an aristocracy in Norway, lawyers emerged as a core component of the bureaucratic, social, and cultural elite. This was to have significant consequences in the breakthrough of full-bodied political liberalism in the nineteenth century.

While the poor professional reputation of the early Norwegian lawyers was of Shakespearean proportions, some important observations should be made on their social role. Many procurators were not full-time advocates and some gained respect for their conscientious work. Moreover, the combination of the right to represent and the growing number of courts also provided a space to further develop the fledgling liberalism of Christian IV's reforms.

For example, in 1680, Tyri Litlasund was prosecuted for witchcraft with a demand that she face the drowning test.[8] The task of legal representation was given eventually to a historian, Tormod Torfæus, who approached the role like a modern criminal defense lawyer. Operating in accordance with legal process theory (Fuller 1978), Torfæus proceeded through stepwise rational arguments and submitted a range of concrete evidence. He argued that the charges were either based on vague testimonies and town gossip or given under the influence of alcohol (Titlestad 2001: 11). Torfæus demanded a full acquittal, which, unusually for the time, was ordered by the provincial court (Espeli, Næess, and Rinde 2008: 37). As Næss (1982: 238–239) wrote on the trial: "At that moment, suspected witches obtained for the first time a professional defender who was capable of demonstrating inconsistencies and uncovering legal holes in prosecutorial evidence."[9]

[7] Cited in Espeli, Næess, and Rinde (2008: 39).

[8] As was the case elsewhere in Europe, if a bound and accused woman floated it was evidence of guilt and she would be later executed by sword.

[9] Cited in Titlestad (2001: 11).

Such a case study provides an early illustration of the potent structural power of courts to provide a space for liberal politics. Criminal trials provide a very particular space for a legal complex to emerge even if limited. Not only are they one of the few opportunity structures for politics that often exist in authoritarian regimes, but they provide a legitimate space for lawyers and by their very nature raise questions of political liberalism such as due process and different freedoms.[10]

However, it is not clear how widespread such actions were. Future research could examine the reactions of Norwegian lawyers to the bouts of Danish state illiberalism in the late eighteenth and early nineteenth centuries in the wake of the brief liberal Struensee period. In 1771 the King's personal doctor, Johan Freidrich Struensee from Germany, assumed full royal powers as Prime Minister and issued a stunning 1,800 decrees in sixteen months, many of them of a radically liberal character. Serfs were freed, torture and capital punishment abolished, and Denmark became "the first country to declare unlimited freedom of the press as official public policy" (Laursen 2000: 191). The conservative backlash was swift and brutal. Struensee, compromised by his intimate relationship with the queen, was executed and his reforms rapidly reversed.

When Frederik VI assumed power as regent in 1784 a gradual liberal reformism emerged but it soon gave way to new waves of illiberalism. Fears of the spread of the French Revolution reawakened the Danish censorship regime and critical voices were soon deported or punished (Alnæs 2013: 80). These cases could be closely scrutinized. Later in 1799, censorship rules were tightened, criminal penalties raised, and the monitoring of oppositional figures heightened—a pattern that only intensified during the Napoleonic wars in the light of foreign policy sensitivities (Holmøyvik and Michalsen 2015: 153). Thus, despite the signs of change, "Denmark-Norway was an illiberal society" at the beginning of the nineteenth century (Alnæs 2013: 81). Yet, taking a departure point in legal complex theory, we might also expect that lawyers joined in the critical response to this authoritarianism. We know that many Norwegian jurists were taught in Copenhagen by the leading law professor and relatively liberal J. F. W. Schlegel (Mestad 2015) and the Danish turn to illiberalism strengthened the resolve of the Norwegian founding fathers in their constitutional convention to recognize civil rights and limited government (Alnæs 2013: 222).

[10] For an in-depth discussion on this in Norway, especially after the Alta trials, see Mathisen (1997).

3. Liberal Nationalism 1814–1884

3.1 The Constitutional Moment

It was in 1814, in a brief intermezzo of geopolitics, that Norway declared independence from Denmark, adopted a markedly liberal constitution, and created an elected parliament. While Sweden had gained Norway from Denmark under the January 1814 Treaty of Kiel, on account of Swedish participation in the anti-Napoleonic forces, an alliance of elite Norwegian civil servants, businessmen, free peasants, writers, and the Crown Prince of Denmark sought to thwart the transfer in the spring of 1814. In early summer, Swedish troops largely overpowered the undermanned Norwegian forces but a series of negotiations led to a compromise: Norway would maintain its constitution and parliament as part of a United Kingdom with Sweden and the latter would control defense and foreign policy.

This partial rebirth of the Norwegian state after four centuries under Danish rule was constitutional and proto-liberal. As Seip (1974: 70) states:

> [T]wo independent powers of state were juxtaposed: the parliament and the king. It was a basic principle that both powers would have to agree in order something to be decided. The arrangement was a split one. It was a state with two heads and two wills.[11]

The constitution thus created the structure for a *moderate state*. The king was physically separated from his cabinet, a parliament was introduced, the right to vote was partly expanded, and hermeneutic space was carved out for the recognition of judicial review. A partial form of bicameralism was introduced whereby a quarter of elected parliamentarians would sit as an upper house (*Lagting*) together with Supreme Court judges.[12] However, as Holmøyvik and Michalsen (2015: 225) point out, Montesquieu's theory of balanced powers bears only a partial imprint—notions of popular sovereignty were also deeply embedded in the structure.

The constitution was also replete with a set of *core civil rights*, partly inspired by the US Declaration (Mestad 2014; Michalsen 2015). Inspired also by the French Declaration, the 1812 Spanish Constitution, the writings of Kant, Rousseau, Voltaire, and Adam Smith, and experiences with English liberalism, it included habeas corpus, protection against torture, freedom of expression, and the right to property. However, some of these rights were qualified. Incitement to illegal

[11] Cited in (Neumann 2010: 241).

[12] This was effectively abolished in 1884 with the introduction of parliamentarism and formally abolished in 2009.

behavior, blasphemy, lèse majesty, and defamation were not constitutionally protected.

Lawyers were at the center of the constitutional convention, which met in Eidsvoll in April and May 1814. Of the 112 men elected from around the country, twenty-seven were advocates and judges (Alnæs 2013: 212). Lawyers were also the dominant "profession" amongst the powerful civil servant class (which totaled fifty-seven), with the rest of this group rounded out by priests, military officers, and provincial governors. Finally, lawyers were the most prominent and influential force in shaping the constitution. Advocate and judge Christian Magnus Falsen chaired the drafting committee, produced the first version of the constitution, and represented the dominant wing that wanted to appoint the Danish Crown Prince as an independent Norwegian king. The legally trained Herman Wedel-Jarlsberg represented the "Swedish wing" that pragmatically saw a peaceful union with the Swedish Union as the only realistic way to develop Norwegian freedom and sovereignty. Whether lawyers evinced more liberal tendencies than other groups is certainly difficult to say. On the one hand, some of the most radical proposals emanated from lawyers. Seventy years before the principle of parliamentarism was instituted in Norway, Judge Wulfsberg from Moss was the only Eidsvoll delegate to propose and vote for the motion that the cabinet be elected by the parliament rather than the king (Bolin 2009). On the other hand, lawyers were amongst those who proposed adding a constitutional provision banning Jews from entering the Kingdom of Norway—flying in the face of European trends to recognize the civil rights of Jews. Some lawyers such as Wedel rallied against the proposal as "illiberal" (Fure and Mykland 1989: 51) but he was also joined by some equally indignant priests such as Ulrik Midelfart (Alnæs 2013: 226). When it came to the general civil rights provisions, these all sailed through the convention with little dissent and peasants were more vocal champions of some civil freedoms than lawyers.

Moreover, caution is needed in designating certain delegates a "lawyer." Some might be better labeled as politicians or polymath renaissance men. The 36-year-old Wedel was legally trained but he was also one of the richest men and leading business figures in the country; served as the private secretary to the Danish finance minister (1801–1805); was a provincial governor (1806–1813); led a militia in the war against Sweden (1808); re-established and cofounded Norway's ambitious Norwegian Society to promote Norwegian economic and intellectual development (1809); and was a member of the Government Commission (1809). It is not the customary curriculum vitae of an advocate or judge.

Thus, overall, it is difficult to conclude that lawyers as a group at Eidsvoll were particularly more liberal than other representatives. However, the constitution does partly owe its character to a certain conjunction: the leading lawyerly figures and draftsmen could be counted amongst the most liberal delegates at Eidsvoll. It is this conditional and historical intertwining of agency and structure (demand and supply) that allows the claim that a peculiar legal complex mobilized for political liberalism at Eidsvoll. It is this conjunction of biography and place that partly explains later moments in history when a Norwegian legal complex emerged *for* political liberalism.

3.2 The Lawyer's State

Lawyers were certainly dominant at the center of the wave of subsequent economic and political reforms that gave life to these constitutional guarantees (Slagstad 1998; Mestad 2008; Larsen 2013). In a short period of time, Norway moved from a mercantilist economy dominated by royal privileges to a liberal market economy, although one partly guided by the state and one with a heavy emphasis on the rule of law and other basic freedoms (Slagstad 1998). It was driven by the powerful elite of civil servants (*embetsmenn*): the "thousand academic families" or the "authorities" (*øvrigheten*). Often foreign-born and always university educated, this elite dominated the running of government until the late nineteenth century as well as parliament until the mid-nineteenth century (even when they constituted a minority) (see generally Seip 1974; Myhre 2008; Neumann 2010).

Three particular circumstances permitted this elite to exercise such extraordinary power: (1) the absence of an aristocracy in Norway (and its constitutional banning in 1821); (2) the collapse of the commercial sector in the wake of the Napoleonic wars; and (3) the vacuum of power created by the new constitutional arrangements. To this we might add the high level of literacy of the Norwegian population, particularly amongst peasants, which permitted this university-educated elite to wield, initially, a significant degree of discursive power.

This caste was principally constituted by three professions—lawyer, priests, and doctors—and to a certain extent military officers. Of these, the former was perhaps the most powerful: "The jurists dominated the government totally" (Myhre 2008: 27).

This dominance was partly a function of education. Figure 5.1 shows the annual number of graduates for different disciplines in the nineteenth century and the overwhelming proportion of law graduates amongst academic disciplines.

However, legal power was also a result of the exercise of political and social capital. Two examples are telling. First, throughout the mid-nineteenth century, civil engineers complained bitterly that transport was allocated to the Ministry of Justice (Slagstad 1998: 39). To rub salt into the wound, lawyers dominated the entire planning and management of roads despite their evident lack of qualification. Second, at this moment lawyers also dominated parliament—both the pro-government and oppositional wings. In 1851, Johan Sverdrup, a practicing advocate and politician, went as far as to propose the establishment of an Advocates Party, which would unite the many advocates in the parliamentary opposition and form a united front with the oppositional peasants in parliament (Libell 2008: 44). Like

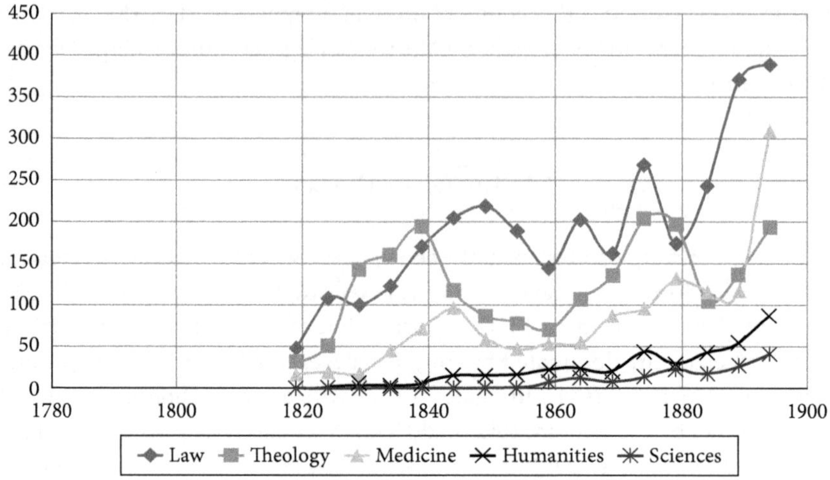

Figure 5.1 Graduates—By Faculty: 1814–1895
Source: Raw data extracted from Aubert (1960: 15).

all attempts at party formation at the time (Seip 2002b: 74), the proposal faltered. Nonetheless, the idea of a political party composed only of advocates is possibly a historical first.

This dominance of lawyers in the civil service and in parliament was complemented by "professor politicians," often drawn from the University of Oslo law school. Of the four most powerful and influential political figures of the nineteenth century, two were life-long law professors (Anton Martin Scheweigaard and Francis Hagerup) and a third was a professor and also advocate before entering politics full-time (Frederik Sverdrup). It was only the advocate Johan Sverdrup who did not study at University of Oslo's Domus Academica. Two of these academic figures functioned as a formidable political partnership: Scheweigaard (the dominant government-aligned figure in parliament from 1842 to 1869) and Stang (who served as First/Prime Minister from 1861 to 1880 but exerted considerable power from the moment he entered the civil service in 1846).

This elite was deeply committed to a project of political liberalism:

> [While] some of them participated in businesses, as partners, investors or experts, ... Their major involvement in the economy in the 19th Century was of another kind. As the effective political rules in the early and middle decades of the century, they saw it as their task to prepare the ground for economic modernization. As economic liberalists, they did away with old economic privileges to encourage economic enterprise.
>
> (Myhre 2008: 28)

The elite commitment to political and economic liberalism was partly based in self-interest. It would constrain the power of the Swedish monarch and build legitimacy with the governed, which were even more seduced by ideas of romantic and popular nationalism. It was also driven by a European-shaped enlightenment perspective, partly idealistic but also deeply culturally embedded. Neumann (2010: 242, 53) highlights both these instrumental and norms-based drivers: As the "civil servant state was a state of law" when "dissenting voices quickly surfaced they had to be met by discursive moves, not force." And, in discussing the later challenge of romantic and popular nationalism to the civil servant state, he notes:

> What the bearers of the statist representation feared above all was isolation – that Norway in its hankering after what specifically national should instead end up as a province cut off from the rest of European civilization.

Importantly, law had a double-edged role in this process of state-building as represented in the philosophy of Scheweigaard and Stang (Slagstad 1998: 26–36). Law was partly viewed as an intrinsic good—the rule of law and associated rights served a constitutional function in sharing and limiting power.[13] Yet, law was also viewed instrumentally. Along with technical and educational competence, legal knowledge and techniques were to help modernize one of the poorest and underdeveloped states in Europe—foreshadowing a vision to later emerge in the social welfare state.

However, this lawyer-dominated state cannot really be described as a manifestation of a legal complex. While many lawyers did *practice* law they exercised their political power through *other positions*, as government ministers, parliamentarians, and civil servants. In other words, elite lawyers used the political opportunity structure which was very favorably disposed toward their participation.[14] There was no need to use legal opportunity structures when lawyers could simply advance their liberal politics directly. Norwegian lawyers formed, so to speak, *the* political complex.

3.3 The Judiciary and Advocates

Thus, a more theoretical coherent approach would be to examine the politics of judges and practicing advocates. As Figure 5.2 shows, the number of permanent

[13] Both conceptions of law were underscored by an early legal positivism, particularly in the writings of Scheweigaard (Slagstad 1998). While Hagerup defended German idealism and natural law a half-century later (Blandhol and Michalsen 2007: especially 46–64), this modern approach to rights may explain some of the freedom and pragmatism in legal thinking in the nineteenth century but also the reluctance to use the full range of judicial review powers.

[14] See Chapter 9 for a discussion of legal and political opportunity structures.

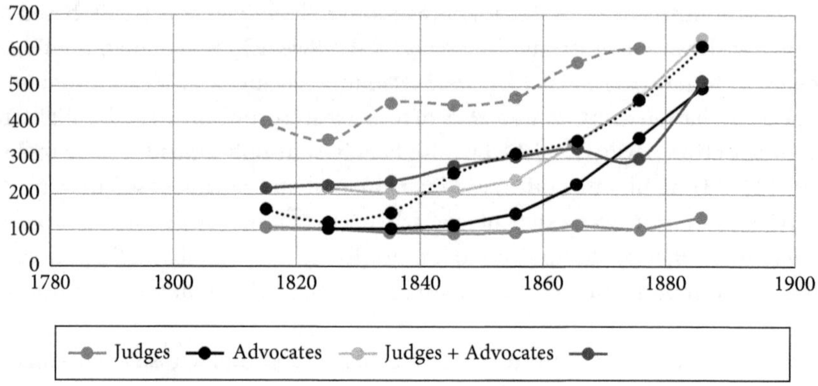

Figure 5.2 Occupations: 1815–1885
Source: Raw data extracted from Aubert (1960: 16).

judges was relatively stable throughout the nineteenth century—approximately a hundred at any one time. The number of advocates increased rapidly during the century for reasons to be discussed below—from a mere hundred in 1825 to five hundred by 1885. By the end of the century the bar and bench outnumbered priests and almost military officers (the latter is not shown).

Judges

In the post-1814 period, the judiciary was comparatively active. Like its American cousin, the newly minted Norwegian constitution was ambiguous on the powers of judicial review but this did not halt the Norwegian Supreme Court in assigning to itself the power to invalidate legislation contravening the constitution (Smith 2010: 1–2). A mere nineteen years after the 1803 judgment of *Marbury v. Madison*,[15] the Norwegian Supreme Court first exercised its power of judicial review. The cancellation with retroactive effect of the rights of certain civil servants in Trondheim to auction copper was found to violate constitutional rights on property expropriation and non-retroactivity (Hølmoyvik and Michalsen 2015: 334–335). To avoid a formal conflict with parliament, the relevant constitutional provisions were read into the law.

This judgment and its successors were undoubtedly influenced by the American experience but they were equally a product of indigenous factors in Norwegian political and judicial development (for the background, see Slagstad 1995: 82–84).[16] Initially, the Norwegian court largely issued brief formal conclusions, although

[15] *Marbury v. Madison*, 5 U.S. 137 (1803) (U.S. Supreme Court). However, state courts in the United States had exercised this power much earlier: see Friedman (2009).
[16] See also Kierulf and Slagstad (2012) and Hølmoyvik and Michalsen (2015: 339–346).

these were the subject of public and legal debate (Slagstad 1995) and in 1866, in the *Wedel Jarlsberg* judgment, the Chief Justice formally articulated the grounds and method for exercising judicial review.[17] However, this willingness to exercise judicial review was not necessarily oriented to limiting state power. The Supreme Court increasingly aligned itself with parliamentary conservatives and, as the next section shows, they were not always unable to defend core civil rights in controversial cases. One might speculate that the court's motivation was dampened by their closeness and identification with the ruling elite.

Advocates

As the century drew on, advocates began to grow in number and influence. In the period between 1814 and 1829, only 14 percent of law graduates worked as advocates—a proportion that rose to 35 percent by the end of the century (Aubert 1960: 23). Their general influence is reflected in Aubert (1960) crediting them with creating conditions of trust between the new institutions and citizens and within commercial and social life.

As to political liberalism, it is possible to find again high-profile criminal defense cases in which a concern for due process and civil rights trumped political considerations. The most notable illustration was the engagement of the high-profile, sharp-tongued, and deeply conservative lawyer, Bernhard Dunker. In 1845, he had written the provocative tract, *On the Norwegian Constitution*, calling for an increase in monarchial power and an absolute royal veto over all law in the absence of any express constitution exception (Lorenz 2009). Yet Dunker was also Norway's leading criminal defense lawyer, undertaking eight hundred cases before being appointed crown attorney. Most notably he defended the nascent labor movement, which was accused of treason.

Under Marcus Thrane's leadership, a local union of 160 rural and urban workers in 1848 grew rapidly into a national organization by 1850 with a critical and satirical magazine, *Arbeiderforeningernes Blad* (Seip 2002a: 183–206). In that year, the national union delivered a petition with 13,000 member signatures to the king and parliament. It demanded universal voting, mandatory military service for all classes of society, equality before the law, better schools, the reduction or elimination of customs taxes on staple crops, and cheap loans to poor farmers for land grants. The petition was dismissed and in the following year the union's national conference sought a revolution. While Thrane halted these insurrectionary plans, the authorities seized the opportunity to arrest him and 132 members.

Bernhard Dunker engaged himself deeply and publicly in the case, which eventually came before the Supreme Court in 1855. Dunker's final submission lasted nine days and amounted almost to a prosecution of the authorities themselves

[17] *Wedel Jarlsberg* case, Ufl 1866, p. 165 (Supreme Court of Norway). See further Slagstad (1995: 96–98); Smith (2009: 43, 311–312); and Hølmoyvik and Michalsen (2015: 334–335).

rather than the reverse (Espeli, Næss, and Rinde 2008: 97). Despite the imprisonment of Thrane for another four years, the case captured the entire nation: "The courtroom, court hallways and stairs were full of workers, their wives, children and relatives and in the *Christiania Daily*, Ludwig Kristensen Daa claimed that the whole nation followed every moment" (Østvedt 1940: 50).

Dunker's unrelenting legal defense of his political enemies not only strengthened the rule of law materially but contributed to a deeper public understanding of its meaning according to some authors. In his biography of Dunker, Østvedt (1940: 50) makes the following "psychological" observation:

> In education, experience and sympathy, he stood on the side of the privileged, but his fanatical sense of justice was outraged by the arbitrary treatment meted out to the defenseless workers and their case.

This sense of justice was clearly part of Dunker's individual psyche but it is notable that he was also a student and fervent admirer of Stang (Østvedt 1940: 17, 27–29). Stang's modernization of legal theory may have found fertile ground. However, the case is also an illustration of the effect on lawyers of encountering concrete and state arbitrariness and their greater motivation to struggle for political liberalism. Østvedt (1940: 50) notes that the arch-conservative Dunker moderated his political views in the wake of the case.

This engagement of criminal defense lawyers in the nineteenth century for political liberalism cannot be isolated to a single case or lawyer. Legislation to establish child welfare boards (passed in 1900) was driven by two professional groups: teachers and lawyers. According to Aubert (1989: 73):

> Many criminal lawyers disliked the practice of putting wayward children in prison. They were troubled by the plight of these children and were concerned about the kind of influences they were exposed to in prison. They wanted children removed from prisons and responsibility for them transferred to other agencies.

This drive by lawyers to narrow the use of the criminal justice system to solve problems of juvenile delinquency is notably liberal. However, it is also colored by a broader sense of justice. As Aubert (1989: 72) reflects, it represented again the instrumentalization or positivization of law—where law was to be used for the "optimal pursuit of goals with the most effective means."

Nuancing the account

This positive narrative of the bipartisan contribution of advocates to political liberalism in the nineteenth century requires nuance and contingency. First, other political actors must be named. The liberal ruling elite was supported and superseded by a distinctive Nordic group, the free peasants. For reasons of pragmatism and principle, this group represented a peculiarly powerful force for political liberalism in Norway and other Nordic states. As Bo Strath (2004: 9) has argued:

> The figure of the peasant, constructed by intellectuals and clergy with a view to defusing the conflict between freedom and equality, was not just a romantic fiction with no relation to the real world, but an increasingly active participant in economic and political processes. In most other parts of Europe, the peasant was a more utopian figure, eliminated from political processes and revitalized on the level of rhetoric. In more specific terms, the Nordic peasant was too conservative to be radical but too radical to be conservative.

Steeped in Lutheran traditions and schooled in the democratic protestant politics of local parish meetings, the farmers "expressed specific educational ideals" and "individual-oriented Protestant notions like responsibility and ethics, rather than holistic collectivism" (Bo Strath 2004: 9). In the absence of an aristocracy in Norway, these attributes made peasants partners with the civil servant elite in struggling for political liberalism but eventually the key actors in an oppositional movement that would displace this ruling elite and drive political liberalism further in the second half of the nineteenth century. Indeed, the literature is not unanimous on the extent of the initial power of the civil servant state. Some argue that power was shared with economic elites or that civil servants were absent from some spaces such as employer–employee, producer–consumers, and farmer–crofter relations.

The second wrinkle is that in major battles for political liberalism, the legal profession was divided rather than united—as foreshadowed in the discussion of theory. Lawyers formed an important part of the emerging oppositional movement to the civil servant state as much as they constituted it. As Myhre (2008: 28, 34) notes in passing:

> [A]n open public sphere flourished from the 1830s on. Civil servants and other academics (University-educated) founded nearly all the contemporary newspapers and journals in the first few decades. Many of the founders were oppositional academics, who were sometimes joined by men from lower echelons of society, eager to point out how civil servants abused their position in society.

Many of these "oppositional townsmen" included "artisans," and "barristers" (Myhre 2008). The former, mostly novelists, gained the most public attention but the latter provided editorial capacity and regional breadth. One remarkable feature of this oppositionalism was the role of lawyers in newspapers, which blossomed from the 1850s. In the period 1850–1940, sixty newspaper editors were practicing advocates (Espeli, Næss, and Rinde 2008: 133–136). Considering that Norwegians were and remain voracious readers of newspapers, the influence wielded in this role cannot be discounted. Again, however, structural reasons seem important in explaining this peculiar role of lawyers in creating new spaces for political liberalism. In the civil servant state, lawyers were forcibly posted throughout the country. With their superior education and independent role, they were intellectually and institutionally able to fulfill a demand for a free press.

This oppositionalism and the divided nature of the legal profession also expressed itself in some of the flashpoints in the second half of the nineteenth century. Sometimes the legal profession split down clearly political lines. In the Marcus Thrane case for example, the lawyer-dominated parliamentary opposition was frightened by the radical rhetoric of the workers' movement. While it might be true that Thrane had tactically erred in petitioning the government instead of building alliances with the opposition (with whom he shared some common causes) (Seip 2002a: 201–205), the silence of many lawyers in the face of repressive state behavior is startling.

Across the mainstream political axes, this division amongst lawyers was also manifest. In Norway's second constitutional moment in 1884, the conservative civil servant alliance suffered its most significant political setback, full parliamentarism. The parliamentary majority was to appoint the cabinet rather than the king and bicameralism was effectively abolished. Despite always possessing a minority of parliamentary positions, elite civil servants had dominated the cabinet and were aided in the "upper house" by non-elected members.

In this constitutional dispute, lawyers were divided. The political parties that formed around this split, with the civil servants forming the now conservative *Høyre* (Right) and the oppositional liberal nationalists *Venstre* (Left), reflected the politics of the preceding few decades. This "left" alliance included not only teachers, farmers, and small businessmen, but also oppositional lawyers with its main figure, as earlier discussed, the advocate Johan Sverdrup. Its emergence was supported by social and economic forces. Teachers and peasants gained increasing access to university education and political and social capital; commerce recovered and a new business elite reasserted its earlier power; and most lawyers could not secure civil servant positions.

Shortly, the new Venstre-led government was able to finally implement reforms to the criminal justice system which had been demanded since the 1840s. The so called "jury reform" of 1887 moved criminal proceedings from an inquisitorial mode of proceedings to an adversarial one, created a separate prosecutor's office, introduced a full jury system, and shifted the burden of proof. The reform was largely opposed by the lawyers in Høyre, who defended the old system. While an inquisitorial system is not necessarily less liberal, the package of reforms was more liberal in its orientation as state power was diffused and the trial system partly democratized.

Likewise, these forces were split over the legal profession's monopoly, which had significant consequences for access to justice and by extension the rule of law. As early as 1815, proposals were made to the newly instituted parliament to remove the mandatory requirements of royal assent and civil servant status. Instead it was argued that lawyers with the requisite training should be able to compete on the open market for legal services on the basis of their merit. The frustration with the monopoly was two-fold: Farmers and rural areas lacked access to lawyers, physically and financially; and the number of unemployed law graduates was steadily rising. Despite the ideological commitment of the civil servant elite to the dismantling of mercantilist entitlements, the removal of their own legal privileges was a bridge too far. After oppositional forces gained a majority in parliament in 1855, the civil servant-led cabinet was force to concede; although it took another twelve years before the right to appear before the Supreme Court was granted. The law was groundbreaking with its new title of *sakfører*, superseded by *advokat* (advocate), and has been hardly amended in the last century and a half.

In other instances, the liberals and conservative wings of politics were strongly united in resisting political liberalism, particularly on civil rights. It was left to very small collectives of lawyers to defend radical positions against the establishment. A good illustration is the censorship of the 1885 novel of *Fra Kristiania-Bohêmen* of Hans Jæger. The leading character not only freely philosophizes but ends his days with prostitution and suicide. The book was banned immediately and Jæger was fined and imprisoned for sixty days for infringing modesty and public morals and engaging in blasphemy. Both the conservative and liberal parties condemned the book and the emerging advocates society made no public comment.

The oppositional voices in this instance were intellectuals (which emerged as the Bohemian movement) but also some lawyers. Ludwig Meyer, a lawyer and leading political figure in Venstre, was already an active participant in political debates (Terjesen 2009). He vigorously defended the case in the Supreme Court and, although the case was lost, the group of lawyers around Meyer were actively involved in the debate and went on to establish the Society for Free Legal Services a year later. Meyer also broke with Venstre and joined the social democratic movement, published a workers' magazine, and became the first Chairman of the Labor Party in 1897.

4. Social Liberalism and Welfarism 1884–1980

In the century following the introduction of parliamentarism, it is notable that the visibility of lawyers declined dramatically even if their numbers increased dramatically. Lawyers' participation in parliament and cabinet dropped, their role as newspaper editors steadily decreased, and the vast majority of lawyers were consumed by remunerative opportunities. Commercial lawyers profited from their leading role in debt recovery, real estate, bankruptcy, and eventually administrative law, while the emerging social welfare state provided employment for numerous law graduates even if it was to be dominated by economists and engineers post-World War II (Espeli, Næess, and Rinde 2008).

On the one hand this waning political influence of lawyers might not be viewed as problematic for the legal complex theory. Norway had entrenched political liberalism and could move in a Marshallian direction through to the advancement of expansive political and social rights. Such progression involves a widening cast of actors, which not only struggle for rights but partially displace each other in the process. Along such a trajectory, we might expect *lawyers as a collective* to gradually disappear from the narrative, only to emerge when political liberalism was under threat. To put it another way, the very success of lawyers in struggling for civil rights paved the way for their political demise as the expansion of the franchise (political rights) and then the welfare state (social rights) required lawyers to partly relinquish power and influence and/or become servants of the newly configured state.

This underlying strength of political liberalism and the new role of lawyers may be evident in the approach of the Norwegian Supreme Court to the Nazi occupation and Quisling collaborationist government (see generally Graver 2015; Graver, Chapter 6 in this volume). The Court would not bow to fascism in 1940 and many Supreme Court justices joined the resistance and its leadership, which was dominated by the Labor Party. The statement of one of the former justices, Berg, captures best this dialectical understanding on the role of law and lawyers in the Marshallian transition: "We shall build up again an old rule-of-law state, but our times demand that the State does not only have the task of protecting life and property. The State shall and will be a welfare state that has its task to make life worth living for us all." And, while many advocates and judges collaborated with the Nazis, their respective associations resisted the ever-expanding Nazification of Norwegian law and legal institutions. The Bar Association was particularly active in its protests, which led to the arrest of its leader and eventually it was dissolved by the authorities in July 1941 along with many other associations (Graver, Chapter 6 in this volume). However, the association continued its activities underground, communicating with its members (with news and commentary, and urging resistance) and cooperating with other underground resistance movements.

On the other hand , the risk of this view is that it overlooks the many challenges and conflicts over the ongoing development and defense of political liberalism in the twentieth century. The transition to social democracy meant that some dimensions of political liberalism would have to bend. The most notable and obvious was the right to property. Norwegian jurists were well aware of the American judiciary's attempt to hold back social reforms (Helgadóttir 2006). They were deeply divided over whether law should serve as an instrument of the emerging social state or a firewall. One view of the development of Scandinavian legal realism was that it was an attempt to rein in conservative lawyers and naturalistic and formalistic ideas of rights. Removing the metaphysical and rights dimensions would ensure that lawyers became implementers rather than interpreters of the law.

The rupture came to a head in the *Waterfall* case concerning expropriation of hydro operations after the expiry of a concession. The law was passed by a Venstre-led government but drafted by the Minister of Justice, Castberg, a prominent lawyer from a more left-leaning party. The law was particularly targeted at foreigners who were beginning to invest in Norwegian hydroelectric power. However, Castberg defended the law on a general basis: the right of all Norwegians to benefit. Indeed, it was opposed by the right wing on principled grounds—as a threat to the market economy. Not only was Høyre deeply opposed but many lawyers across the country were particularly prominent in denouncing the law. The matter ended in the Supreme Court eight years later in Rt. 1918 s. 403, and a narrow majority (thanks to some branch-stacking by the social liberals) finding that the law did not amount to expropriation. While the general principle of judicial review was retained, the case was representative of a number in which the Supreme Court moved to a distinctively deferential model of judicial review (Holmøvik and Michalsen 2015: 348–359).

The faultline was raised again in 1952 when the Labor-led government moved to give itself full price- and ration-setting powers (Espeli, Næss, and Rinde 2008: 347). Høyre's leadership raised the prospect of invoking constitutional rights before the Supreme Court while commercial-oriented lawyers strongly agitated against this move to "full powers." However, the matter was resolved after the Labor Party withdrew many of the controversial proposals. Of interest, the historian Francis Sejerstad has suggested that academic lawyers and a judge associated with the Labor party had worked behind the scenes to convince the party to scale back some of the absolute powers granted in the law.

Moreover, the idea that political liberalism was otherwise deeply rooted or did not require development is deeply problematic. Throughout the twentieth century, it is possible to find numerous instances of abuses of the rule of law and core civil rights. Travelers and Roma minorities and the Sami indigenous people were the target of a broad range of coercive assimilation social policies; children placed in foster care and orphanages were subject to systemic abuse; and Social Democratic Party cadres and trade unions engaged in extensive illegal surveillance of citizens on the political left wing (Minde 2003a; Langford and Karlsson Schaffer 2014).

Even when these issues gained national attention, lawyers were slow or reluctant to mobilize. In 1950, the Labor government proposed a new security law that included detention for three months for suspicion of certain crimes, censorship during armed conflict, and speedy implementation of the death penalty when ordered by the special court for treason offenses. The Bar Association and some academics confined themselves to protesting against only a few provisions (with very procedural solutions). However, it was a public opinion backlash that helped motivate or support leading lawyers in the conservative Høyre party to work for a compromise in the parliament's justice committee. Once again, the specter of rights interfering with national security concerns seemed to dampen lawyer's enthusiasm for political liberalism and/or raise the reputational costs of struggle.

In the *Liste-saken* case of 1977, the close connections between lawyers and the dominant parties on national security questions was even more evident (Espeli, Næss, and Rinde 2008: 352–355). In July 1977, the Socialist Left's party newspaper disclosed details of secret Norwegian surveillance in the 1950s. This was followed by an announcement on August 1, 1977 that the newspaper would disclose the names of six hundred Norwegian secret service agents and staff. On August 9, their offices were raided by police and one of the journalists, Teigene, who was later convicted, was interrogated extensively without a lawyer present. The elderly leader of the parliamentary justice committee, Unneberg, a lawyer and member of the centrist farmers party, criticized the police for "fascist tendencies"—to which the Crown Prosecutor, Dorenfeldt, responded by asking a local prosecutor to charge Unneberg with defamation.

The legal fraternity rallied largely behind the police *not* Teigene. The leaks and threatened leaks were viewed by the vast majority of lawyers as an unacceptable attack on the general political consensus on security policy and membership of NATO. Only a small group of lawyers were willing to name the issues of liberalism and due process at stake. Teigene's defense lawyer called the arrest politically motivated—an attempt to destroy the emerging Socialist Left party. A meeting of sixteen lawyers on August 23, 1977 resolved that the rule of law had been undermined and called in sharp language for the resignation of Dorenfeldt. Two days later they also created a rival law association: the Free Defenders' Society.

On the August 24, a competing meeting of 111 lawyers was called to draft a statement expressing full confidence in the actions of the prosecutors. Despite the requests of some present for a mention of the importance of due process, it was not included in the counter-statement. The Bar Association was paralyzed by this division but was captured by the conservative grouping. The association did not mobilize for the counter-statement, but its leader and secretary-general were amongst the remarkable 1,100 lawyers who signed it and there are questions over how the membership list was obtained. This vignette leaves us with perhaps the most visible indication of the absence of any clear or full legal complex in the period. Not only were lawyers deeply divided across various political fault lines, but a petition signed en masse by lawyers was dismissive of due process. The eventual judgment of the Supreme Court on the four journalists was very mild, raising questions about the ferocity of support for the prosecutor authorities.

5. Globalization and Legalization 1977–2015

5.1 Structures and Legitimation

While the Norwegian legal profession was relatively divided and invisible in the social welfare period it has undergone a significant change since the late 1970s. The background ideational and structural conditions resemble the nineteenth century with the return of Europeanized frames and legal frameworks together with concerns over minority protection. Dense legalization within a complex global economy has led to a vast expansion of the commercial legal enterprise while the return of constitutionalism (including a new bill of rights in 2014) and the rise of international human rights law has provided a new superstructure for advancing and defending political liberalism—the boomerang effect of new state commitments (Christoffersen and Madsen 2011). These changing conditions have simultaneously legitimated deeper and broader forms of political liberalism as a lawyerly goal and widened legal opportunity structures.

In 1976, the Supreme Court in the *Kløfta* case signaled, by a narrow majority, a return to a more robust form of judicial review, especially in cases concerning core civil rights.[18] The court moved slowly over the next few decades in enforcing this new approach, but it has made landmark decisions such as on the rights of asylum seekers and the retroactive application of the law. While there remains a divide in the Court over its appropriate role, there is a significant openness to questions of rights.

The Court was partly pushed in this direction by the European Court of Human Rights (ECtHR). In 1952, the first and rather solitary case from Norway, on military service objection, was dismissed by the Strasbourg Court on admissibility grounds—the case was manifestly ungrounded. However, the ECtHR underwent a decisive shift in its jurisprudence in the mid-1970s and Norwegian lawyers gradually noticed. Between 1980 and 1992, they cited Strasbourg jurisprudence in forty-seven cases before the Norwegian Supreme Court and sent approximately one hundred cases to the European Commission on Human Rights (Espeli, Næss, and Rinde 2008: 349), even if both strategies initially had little impact. In 1992, Knut Rognlien became the first Norwegian lawyer to win a case in the European Court. This signaled the beginning of a rise of cases from Norway (with different law firms and sometimes NGOs specializing in different sorts of case) and the more active application of the European Convention by the Norwegian Supreme Court.

[18] *Kløfta* case, 41 Rt. 1976 s. 1 (Supreme Court of Norway).

5.2 Mobilizing Lawyers

There is one crucial difference from earlier periods. It is that the lawyers most committed to political liberalism (the agents) have enhanced their mobilizing power in *non*-political spaces and institutions (structures). It is partly represented in the balance of power of new legal advocacy networks or a "civil society support structure," in the words of Epp (1998). These new approaches and relationships superseded the very ad hoc spaces through which lawyers previously mobilized—such as high-profile criminal trials and serendipitous parliamentary processes debates and media debates. By the early 1970s a new form of legal mobilization and consciousness was already emerging. The "1968 generation" drove the establishment of the first student legal center, Juss Buss (1971) at the University of Oslo. Three years later came JURK (legal aid for women, 1974), the Rettspolitisk forening (Law & Politics Society, 1974) and a new journal, *Kritisk Juss* (*Critical Law*). While the latter was partly in sync with the emergent American critical legal studies movement, many of its participants were much more open to the use of litigation—whether to advance political ends or reveal, even through failure, the flaws of democratic capitalism.

This university-centered wave of activity was followed by specialized law firms and individual lawyers taking up particular types of rights case and engaging as public spokespersons on those issues, whether it was solitary confinement, freedom of expression, or the rights of asylum seekers. The extent of this new underlying structure should not be overstated but it is now possible to identify a diverse group of organizations and individuals that mobilized directly, broadly, and quickly on issues of political liberalism and beyond.

The *Alta Dam* controversy of the late 1970s and early 1980s reflected this greater capacity for bipartisan lawyerly mobilization but also provided the seeds for future networking and advocacy (Dalland 1994; Semb 2001; Minde 2003b). A plan of a government directorate called for the construction of a dam and hydroelectric power plant that would create an artificial lake and flood the Sami village of Máze in northern Norway. This initial plan was partly modified due to political resistance but it catalyzed a broad popular movement of Sami indigenous people and environmentalists against development of the Alta-Kautokeino waterway. As construction started in 1979, civil disobedience began with the blocking of machinery, and hunger strikes outside the Norwegian parliament, which included two prominent criminology professors (Johansen 2014). When work recommenced two years later, more than one thousand protesters chained themselves to the site and were forcibly removed and charged by the police. The mass arrests by police (10 percent of the Norwegian police force was stationed at the dam site) led to the first charges of violating laws against rioting. Lawyers mobilized in Oslo and Alta to represent protestors but also acted as mediators between the groups and parliament and the police, moving continuously between the two locations.

5.3 The Advocates Society—A Legal Complex

The transformation of the Bar Association in recent times is perhaps the most dramatic manifestation of the emergence of new legal complexes for political liberalism. In 1952, the association created twenty sub-committees in order to engage in political lobbying, particularly through submissions on public consultations on new law and policy proposals. Due to concerns of members over politicization it adopted a clear policy in 1972 that it should only engage on issues concerning *rettssikkerhet* (the core of political liberalism) and technical aspects of law and regulation. However, the association was only partially active and its leadership was often close to the major political parties. Critique was infrequent. The passivity of the association's president, Christian Mellbye, during the 1960s onward was the subject of critique by the Lund Commission's report in 1996 on illegal surveillance of citizens.

The situation has changed quite dramatically since then. The shift was clear in the early 1990s when the Bar Association proposed that the government incorporate international human rights conventions domestically, a policy that was adopted a decade later in the Human Rights Act. By 2004, the Law Society had thirty-one sub-committees, which made seventy-six submissions in that year (Espeli, Næess, and Rinde 2008: 350). By 2014, the number of submissions was eighty-seven, accompanied by a growing stream of press releases on different topics.

A brief document content analysis was undertaken. A total of 272 submissions to government authorities were collated for the period 2011–2016. In almost all submissions, the association indicates that it is acting as expert organ rather than speaking in its own self-interest. The Bar Association is clearly dedicated to the concept of *rettsikkerheten*—it is used 1,046 times in the substantive sections of the 272 submissions. As to concrete civil rights, the freedom of expression is referenced, for example, in forty submissions.

Interestingly, the Bar Association is not confined by a narrow construction of political liberalism—commenting often, for example, on the right to privacy and also supporting social rights. When questioned, the Secretary-General of the Bar Association indicated that there had been no internal division in speaking out positively on social rights in the context of government policy or constitutional reform. The only tensions that seemed to arise were statements that contained occasionally a strong policy content where there might be different policy choices (particularly on asylum questions). She also noted that the key conflicts tended to be with some lawyers elsewhere in the government where the question of judicial review remained a polarizing theme.

Moreover, the Bar Association has engaged in coordinated strategic litigation in the past five years. Their committee for migration law studied 1,755 rejections of asylum applications and selected seventy-four cases for judicial review applications under administrative law (Humlen and Myhre 2015). The appeals were handled by various members of the association, with great willingness, and 70 percent of them were successful. The aim of the action was not only to rectify individual injustice but also to reveal the systematic problems in adjudication—with poor legal representation for some asylum seekers, questionable assessment of evidence, and problematic interpretations and applications of the law.[19] This strategic litigation was followed in a single and successful case concerning solitary confinement in 2015. Norway has been the subject of repeated critique by UN bodies and the European Committee on the Prevention of Torture for the overuse of solitary confinement and, notably, the Norwegian Advocate-General declined to appeal the case.[20]

How has the Bar Association emerged as such a unified and active actor with a broad conception of political liberalism? Three explanations might be offered. The first is that its Secretary-General possesses a clear commitment to political liberalism but appears also equipped with the leadership skills to facilitate and drive a common agenda and orient sufficient resources toward committees wishing to take action. The second is that the Free Defenders' Society rejoined the Bar Association in June 2012, which provided a united front. The third is that the political opportunity structure on a range of questions (such as asylum processes, detention) has been closing as mainstream parties tilted to the right or were deferential to other organized groups such as the police trade unions. Strategic litigation on particular topics offered a much greater chance of success.[21]

6. Conclusion

This brief distillation of the engagement of Norwegian lawyers with political liberalism over four centuries presents a series of mixed results. Norwegian lawyers are clearly a social, intellectual, and political elite (Olaussen 2015) and mobilize without doubt for their own material interests (Espeli and Rinde 2014). However, legal complexes for political liberalism have also emerged, often intermittently and sometimes spectacularly. This chapter has argued that the presence and absence of Norwegian legal complexes across time is not necessarily explained by a theory of Nordic exceptionalism. As expanded upon in Chapter 9, one should also take as a departure point the choices of lawyers in context, understanding that the motivations of individuals to suffer costs in the struggle for political liberalism varies greatly (a question of agency) and that lawyers are often rational in choosing whether to engage on the legal or political terrain (a question of structure).

19 Interview with Merete Smith, January 6, 2016—on file with the author.

20 TOSLO-2013-103468, Oslo Local Court, 2 June 2014. The judgment became legally binding on 6 May 2015 after the Government withdrew its appeal. See http://www.aftenposten.no/nyheter/iriks/Staten-domt-for-ulovlig-bruk-av-glattcelle-7588564.html.

21 Interview with Merete Smith, January 6, 2016.

As to agency, the historical studies and contemporary interviews reveal that Norwegian advocates vary greatly in their individual willingness to struggle for political liberalism. The profession was often divided. With some exception, and certainly irony, predominantly left-leaning, sometimes Communist, and certainly always "oppositionalist," lawyers in Norway have constituted the key representatives for lawyerly liberal forces. After the 1850s, right-leaning lawyers were mostly only prominent in struggles over property rights. Lawyers connected with the premier twentieth-century social democratic force, the Labor Party, were relatively active before the 1930s (or 1945) but more muted afterwards—tending toward more pro-state positions or concentrating, possibly, their struggles within the party apparatus. However, lawyerly motivations appear to have been boosted across the political spectrum by concrete experiences with injustice, the self-satisfaction of engaging in some altruistic behavior, and the legitimating effect of two constitutional moments (1814 and the recent period of legalization), both of which have been partly driven by advocates and other lawyers.

At the same time, the openness of legal opportunity structures seems to help explain the nature of the mobilization of lawyers. It is not surprising that distinct legalistic forms of mobilization were generally unnecessary in the nineteenth century. Lawyers formed the political complex—in government and opposition. However, some advocates mobilized in other spaces (e.g., court trials) when the political complex turned distinctly repressive. Or they mobilized for law reform on distinct issues within distinct sub-groups (e.g., criminal lawyers for child welfare reform). In the social welfaristic period, the major challenge seems to have been the inability of lawyers to find a unified form of collective mobilization, particularly in times of polarized politics and the Cold War national security climate. Moreover, lawyers were no longer the center of political and academic debates, their political power waned as other professions gained positions and legitimacy, and the bureaucratic social welfare state and hierarchical consolidation within political parties limited the space for more individualistic lawyers and their looser structural relations.

Yet, the Bar Association has also shown itself capable of mobilizing its organizational power for political liberalism, particularly during the German occupation and in the twenty-first century. Advocates faced a closed political space and/or a more open legal space, the leadership of the Bar Association was distinctly liberal in political orientation, and internal divisions were overcome through adroit management. By creating new organizational forms and capturing existing ones, political liberalism managed to find its wayward legal defenders.

References

Alnæs, Karsten. 2013. *Miraklenes År*. Oslo: Schibsted forlag.

Aubert, Vilhelm. 1960. *Norske Jurister fra 1814 til Den Annen Verdenskrig*. Oslo: Institutt for Samfunnsforskning.

Aubert, Vilhelm. 1989. "Law and Social Change in 19th Century Norway," in June Starr and Jane Fishburne Collier (eds.), *History and Power in the Study of Law: New Directions in Legal Anthropology*. Ithaca, NY: Cornell University Press [Page range going in PDF proof].

Benford, R., and D. Snow. 2000. "Framing Processes and Social Movements: An Overview and Assessment," *Annual Review of Sociology* 26: 611–639.

Blandhol, Sverre, and Tobias Mahler. 2015. "Advokaten i fremtiden," in Sigurd Knudtzon (ed.), *Å Være Advokat*. Oslo: Universitetsforlaget, online at https://nbl.snl.no/Gregers_Winther_Wulfsberg

Blandhol, Sverre, and Dag Michalsen. 2007. *Rettsforsker, Politker, Internasjonalist: Perspektiver på Francis Hagerup*. Oslo: Unipax.

Christoffersen, Jonas, and Mikael Rask Madsen. 2011. "The End of Virtue? Denmark and the Boomerang of the Internationalization of Human Rights," *Nordic Journal of International Law* 80: 257–277.

Dalland, Øystein. 1994. *Altakrønike*. Kárásjohka: Davvi Girji.

Epp, Charles. 1998. *The Rights Revolution: Lawyers, Activists and Supreme Courts in Comparative Perspective*. Chicago, IL: University of Chicago Press.

Espeli, Harald, Hans Eyvind Næess, and Harald Rinde. 2008. *Våpendrager og Veiviser: Advokatenes Historie i Norge*. Oslo: Universitetsforlag.

Espeli, Harald, and Harald Rinde. 2014. "Advokatene," in Jan Messel and Rune Slagstad (eds.), *Profesjonshistorie*. Oslo: Pax: 46–80.

Friedman, Barry. 2009. *The Will of the People: How Public Opinion has Influenced the Supreme Court and Shaped the Meaning of the Constitution*. New York: Farrar, Straus and Giroux.

Fuller, Lon. 1978. "The Form and Limits of Adjudication," *Harvard Law Review* 92: 353–409.

Fure, Eli, and Knut Mykland. 1989. *Eidsvoll 1814: Hvordan grunnloven ble til*. Oslo: Dreyer.

Graver, Hans Petter. 2015. *Dommernes Krig*. Oslo: Pax Forlag.

Halliday, Terence, and Lucien Karpik (eds.). 1998. *Lawyers and the Rise of Western Political Liberalism: Europe and North America from the Eighteenth to Twentieth Centuries*. Oxford: Oxford University Press.

Halliday, Terence, Lucien Karpik, and Malcolm Feeley (eds.). 2008. *Fighting for Political Freedom: Comparative Studies of the Legal Complex and Political Chang*. Cambridge: Cambridge University Press.

Helgadóttir, Ragnhildur. 2006. *The Influence of American Theories on Judicial Review in Nordic Constitutional Law*. Dordrecht: Martinus Nijhoff.

Hirschl, Ran. 2011. "The Nordic Counternarrative: Democracy, Human Development, and Judicial Review," *International Journal of Constitutional Law* 9: 449–469.

Holmøyvik, Eirik, and Dag Michalsen (eds.). 2015. *Lærebok i forfatningshistorie*. Oslo: Pax Forlag.

Humlen, Arild, and Jonas Myhre. 2015. *Advokatforeningens aksjon og prosedyregruppe i utlendingsrett 2007–2014*. Oslo: Advokatforeningen.

Johansen, Jørgen. 2000. *Sosialt forsvar: ikkevoldskamp mot vår tids trusler*. Oslo: Militærnekterforlaget.

Kagan, Robert A. 2001. *Adversarial Legalism: The American Way of Law*. Cambridge, MA: Harvard University Press.

Karpik, Lucien, and Terence Halliday. 2011. "The Legal Complex," *Annual Review of Law and Social Science* 7: 217–236.

Kierulf, Anine, and Rune Slagstad. 2012. "Historikeres Fortellinger om Juss," *Tidsskrift for Rettsvitenskap* 4: 421–457.

Langford, Malcolm, and Johan Karlsson Schaffer. 2014. "The Nordic Human Rights Paradox," University of Oslo Faculty of Law Research Paper No. 2013-25.

Larsen, Eirinn. 2013. "Næringsfrihet som likestilling 1850–1880," in Hilde Danielsen, Eirinn Larsen, and Ingeborg W. Owesen (eds.), *Norsk likestillingshistorie 1814–2013*. Bergen: Fagbokforlaget: 40–65.

Laursen, John. 2000. "Spinoza in Denmark and the Fall of Struensee, 1770–1772," *Journal of the History of Ideas* 61(2): 189–202.

Libell, Henrik Pryser. 2008. "Al makt og kraft i denne sal," *Juristkontakt* 44–45.

Lorenz, Astriid. 2009. "Bernhard Dunker," *Store norske leksikon*, 13 February, online at https://nbl.snl.no/Bernhard_Dunker

Mathisen, Thomas. 1997. *Retten i samfunnet: En innføring i rettssosiologi*. Oslo: Pax.

Mestad, Ole. 2008. "Næringsfridom i 1814-grunnlova," in D. Michalsen (ed.), *Forfatningsteori møter 1814*. Oslo: Akademisk Publisering.

Mestad, Ole. 2014. "Amerikansk inspirasjon i den norske grunnlova. Frihetstreet i Nord-Amerikas jord," in Gudleiv Forr (ed.), *Rødt, hvitt og blått. Norsk grunnlov, amerikansk inspirasjon*. Drammen: ART PRO Forlag.

Mestad, Ole. 2015. "Schlegels |Alminnelig Statsrett|: Oppskrift for Grunnlovsfedre," in Eirik Holmøyvik, and Dag Michalsen (eds.), *Lærebok i forfatningshistorie*. Pax Forlag.

Michalsen, Dag. 2015. "The Many Textual Identities of Constitutions," in Karen Gammelgaard and Eirik Holmoyvik (eds.), *Writing Democracy: The Norwegian Constitution 1814–2014*. Berghahn Books.

Minde, H. 2003a. "Assimilation of the Sami: Implementation and Consequences," *Acta Borealia* 20: 121–146.

Minde, Henry. 2003b. "Urfolkoffensiv, Folkerettsfokus og Styringkrise: Kampen for en ny Samepolitikk 1960–1990," in Bjørn Bjerkli and Per Selle (eds.), *Samer, makt og demokrati: Sametinget og den nye samiske offentligheten*. Oslo: Gyldendal.

Myhre, Jan Eivind. 2008. "Academics as the Ruling Elite in 19th Century Norway," *Historical Social Research* 33: 21–41.

Næess, Hans Eyvind. 1982. *Trolldomsprosessene i Norge på 1500-1600-tallet –En retts- og sosialhistorisk undersøkelse*. Oslo: Universitetsforlaget.

Neumann, Ivar. 2010. "State and Nation in the Nineteenth Century: Recent Research on the Norwegian Case," *Scandinavian Journal of History* 25: 239–260.

Olaussen, Leif Petter. 2015. "Juristprofesjonen: en lagdelt sosial elitegruppe," *Kritisk Juss* 41: 134–160.

Østvedt, Einar. 1940. *Bernhard Dunker: juristen, politikeren og kulturmennesket*. Oslo: Gyldendal.

Seip, Jens Arup. 1974. *Utsikt over Norges historie*. Oslo: Gyldendal.

Seip, Jens Arup. 2002a. *Utsikt over Norges historie: Tidsrommet 1814– ca. 1860*. Oslo: Gyldendal.

Seip, Jens Arup. 2002b. *Utsikt over Norges historie: Tidsrommet ca. 1850–1884*. Oslo: Gyldendal.

Semb, Anne Julie. 2001. "How Norms Affect Policy: The Case of Sami Policy in Norway," *International Journal on Minority & Group Rights* 8: 177.

Slagstad, Rune. 1995. "The Breakthrough of Judicial Review in the Norwegian System," in Eivind Smith (ed.), *Constitutional Justice Under Old Constitutions*. The Hague: Kluwer Law International: 81–112.

Slagstad, Rune. 1998. *De Nasjonale Strateger*. Oslo: Pax Forlag.

Slagstad, Rune. 2014. "Profesjonene i norsk samfunnsforskning," in Rune Slagstad and Jan Messel (eds.), *Profesjonshistorie*. Oslo: Pax Forlag: 13–45.

Smith, Eivind. 2009. *Konstitusjonelt demokrati*. Bergen: Fagbokforlaget.

Smith, Eivind. 2010. "Constitutional Courts as 'Positive Legislators': Norway," in International Academy of Comparative Law, XVIII International Congress of Comparative Law. Washington, 25–31 July.

Strath, Bo. 2004. "Nordic Modernity: Origins, Trajectories and Prospects," *Thesis Eleven* 77(1): 1–23.

Sundt, Trygve. 1929. "Av saksførernes saga i Norge," *Tidsskirift for Rettsvitenskap* 409–479.

Terjesen, Einar A. 2009. "Ludwig Meyer," in *I Norsk biografisk leksikon*, 13 February, online at https://nbl.snl.no/Ludvig_Meyer.

Titlestad, Torgrim. 2001. *Tormod Torfæus: ei innføring*. Erling Hafrsfjord: Skjalgssonselselskapet.

Wesley Pue, W., and David Sugarman (eds.). 2003. *Lawyers and Vampires: Cultural Histories of Legal Professions*. Oxford: Hart Publishing.

6

The Legal Complex

Denmark and Norway under German Occupation 1940–1945

Hans Petter Graver[*]

1. Legal Aspects of the Occupation of Denmark and Norway

German forces invaded Denmark and Norway on April 9, 1940. In Denmark, the national authorities capitulated to the invaders on the same day without resistance, and the national authorities continued in their functions under German control. In Norway, Norwegian and allied forces put up resistance to the invasion for two months with heavy fighting. The king and the cabinet evaded German capture by leaving the capital. The main cities of Oslo, Bergen, and Trondheim quickly came under German occupation, but in parts of the country fighting continued until the final capitulation of the Norwegian forces on June 8.

With the German occupation, Norway and Denmark underwent an instant transformation from democracies based on the rule of law into authoritarian regimes. In both countries, judges and courts were important to the authoritarian rulers, to impose law and order in general, but also to combat all forms of resistance. In Norway, there was a legal program to transform Norwegian society into a national socialist state. The topic of this article is to examine the role of judges and courts when a foreign authoritarian ruler puts the institutions under the extreme stress of occupation.

By Decree of the Führer concerning the Exercise of Government authority in Norway, April 24, 1940, Norway was set under German civil administration under the leadership of a Reichskommissar.[1] Hitler himself gave the Reichskommissar "supreme governmental authority," including the power to issue laws in the form of orders. The laws and statutes of Norway were to remain in force "in so far as is compatible with the fact of occupation."

The cabinet and the king left the country and established an exile government in England. After a failed attempt by the leader of the National Socialist Party (Nasjonal Samling), Vidkun Quisling, to establish a revolutionary government, the

* Professor, Faculty of Law, University of Oslo.

[1] This and other decrees in English translations are reproduced in Lemkin (2008: 498–505).

Hans Petter Graver, *The Legal Complex* In: *The Limits of the Legal Complex*. Edited by: Malcolm Feeley and Malcolm Langford, Oxford University Press. © Hans Petter Graver 2021. DOI: 10.1093/oso/9780192848413.003.0006

Supreme Court established an administrative council to maintain the civil administration of the parts of the country under German occupation. After the capitulation, the Germans and leaders of the parliament and the Supreme Court negotiated to establish a state council to oversee the civil government. The negotiations broke down, and the German Reichskomissar Terboven appointed a government dominated by the Nasjonal Samling and Quisling.

The case of Norway was particular in a western European context in that an established, albeit marginal, national socialist party with German backing filled the posts left by the Norwegian Government. From these positions, the party sought to transform Norwegian society into an authoritarian state based on the principles of national socialism. Therefore, Norway was not only under foreign occupation, but also experienced a *coup d'état* by national political forces during this time.

The Nasjonal Samling revolution was, as many other fascist revolutions, portrayed as a revolution in legal form. The revolution depicted the new society as built upon a national socialist rule of law. Members of the legal profession fared better compared to other professionals, such as teachers. The relative number of lawyers who joined the party was greater than from any other profession, and persons with legal training constituted the most numerous group of people with higher education within the party. Of the approximately four thousand persons with legal education in Norway after the war, 8 percent were prosecuted for collaboration (Dahl 2004: 14, 15; Espeli, Næss and Rinde 2008: 191, 209).[2]

Overrun by German forces, the reaction of the *Danish* authorities was to cooperate with the occupying authority. The occupation did not bring about any immediate change in the Danish order of government, which remained intact (Lemkin 2008: 159). The king carried out his royal functions, and parliament remained in session. Parliamentary elections were held in 1943. The Germans did not legislate in Denmark, but brought pressure on the Danish authorities to legislate in their interest (Lemkin 2008: 163). This legislation mainly protected the military interests of Germany and, with the exception of pressure to legislate against Jews and Communists, did not amount to attempts to any nazification of Danish society. However, the Gestapo assumed control over news and information, and censorship was established. Danish authorities handled the censorship under the control of the Gestapo.

Resistance against the Germans increased in 1943, and culminated with demonstrations and strikes in August. This led to the demand from Werner Best, chief German civilian administrator of Denmark, that the government declare a state of emergency. The government refused, and resigned its positions. From then on the civilian administration was led by leading Danish civil servants, who issued regulations within their respective fields (Gamborg 1946: 652–653). The courts

[2] See Andenæs, Skodvin, and Riste (1966: 122–163) for a general overview of the Norwegian postwar proceedings against collaborators.

continued their functions, but with increasing competition from German military courts and later an SS Court with jurisdiction over civilians.

My topic in this chapter is primarily the relationship between the holders of power and the judiciary in authoritarian regimes. In particular, I am interested in the extent to which well-established legal institutions can offer resistance to measures that run contrary to basic elements of the rule of law, such as the separation of powers and the protection of fundamental individual rights. This part of our recent history has still not been fully uncovered. The Danish history has not yet been written, though some pieces are provided by Tamm (1984) and Garde and Tamm (2000). Graver (2015b) gives the first comprehensive account of Norway. The scope of a chapter does not allow for a systematic account of the legal history of the occupation. I will therefore illustrate my points by looking at selected episodes and processes that reveal the tensions and their resolution. Since many aspects of the history is still not unveiled, it is difficult to deliver parallel accounts of the two countries. Unfortunately, there is not yet much available knowledge on the actions of the Danish bar during the occupation.

In both countries, but particularly in Norway, judges and other members of the legal profession were active in the resistance against the occupiers and national usurpers of power. The president of the Supreme Court headed the resistance movement during the whole of the occupation. In the last years of the war, a young lawyer was the chief of the military resistance organization. These parts of the history of the occupation are well known. They tell of how lawyers and judges were central in the resistance against Nazi rule. Less known is the function of the judicial institutions, and the response of the judges in their capacity as judges. Most lawyers did not take an active part in the resistance, but kept to their normal jobs doing business as usual. I am going to explore the reaction of this part of the legal complex to the extreme situation of foreign occupation and authoritarian rule by looking at selected episodes and processes within the judiciary. For Norway, I also include the reaction of the bar to the national socialist policy on the courts. In conclusion, I will reflect on the issue of Nordic exceptionalism and the legal complex.

In my study of Norway, I draw upon archival sources, and to a certain extent accounts written by contemporary actors. Some accounts were given and published right after the war by the bar association and members of the bar. In addition, some of the more prominent members of the Supreme Court published their stories, but apart from that, I have found no accounts from the judiciary, published or unpublished. Most of the material on Norway is presented with further references in my book on the German occupation and the Norwegian judiciary (Graver 2015b).

The relationship between the Nazi rulers and the courts in Norway falls into four distinct categories. First, is the relationship between the occupation authorities and the Norwegian Supreme Court in the initial phase of the occupation. Second, is the relationship to the established courts in Norway. Third, is the role of the courts established during the occupation by the national socialist regime. Finally, there is the role of German courts in occupied Norway. I will not deal with the German courts other than as a contrast to the Norwegian Courts. The history of an important part of the German judiciary is presented by Robert Bohn in his seminal work on the German Reichskommissariat in Norway (Bohn 2000: 91–114).

For Denmark, I base myself on secondary sources. Here the situation was that judges wrote about their experiences right after the war. In addition to that, I have had the possibility to build on the thesis published by the legal historian Ditlev Tamm (1984). I also draw upon a growing literature on law and Nazism, and law and fascism.

2. Authoritarianism and Judicial Contribution

The states of Western Europe under German occupation form interesting cases for the study of how legal institutions react to authoritarian demands. They were all well-established democracies based on the rule of law, with legal institutions deeply set in the centuries-old Western legal tradition. Norway is of particular interest because of the domestic Nazi coup that took place under German protection. Since Denmark and Norway are so similar in their legal histories and institutions, a comparison of these two countries may reveal interesting insights. This comparison may also throw some light over the particulars of a Nordic legal complex, since Denmark and Norway are the only Nordic states that have experienced fascist rule.

Experiences from the German occupation of European states during World War II display courts that comply, protest, resign, or define the occupation regime outside the scope of their jurisdiction. The Belgian courts opposed the occupiers on vital issues throughout the occupation by regarding the occupation measures as outside their competence and refusing to apply them as law. The courts of Denmark and the Netherlands complied with the core interests of the German occupier and applied oppressive laws passed in the interest of the occupier.

The Supreme Court of the Netherlands never questioned the legality of the measures taken by the German occupying authority or the measures by the Netherlands' authorities under powers delegated by the Germans, and judges in the other courts mostly followed its line. This even led to the Nazis being able to use the Netherlands courts to implement their measures against Jews (Michielsen 2004: 125–131). The judges appointed during the occupation agreed to take an oath of allegiance to "the laws in force on the occupied Netherlands territory," which clearly included the measures of the occupying force (Michielsen 2004: 122). The Supreme Court defended its position by reference to the rights of an occupier under public international law. It held that "it was customary that judicial officials would fulfil their duties in the interest of their country, as long as sufficient independence was left to them and they were not forced to dispense justice in the name of another sovereign" (Michielsen 2004: 153).

The Norwegian Supreme Court reserved the right to review the legality of the measures of the German occupation authority, and resigned when the Reichskommissar denied them this possibility. In Belgium and Norway there were, in other words, important instances of judicial resistance; in Denmark and the Netherlands the courts complied.

Courts offer four main types of contribution in support of authoritarian rule (Graver 2015a: 53–74). The first is outright departure from the law in order to accommodate the needs of the regime. Judges distort, overlook or construe facts or rules and apply sanctions illegally to opponents of the regime. Such rulings may be the result of pressure applied to the judge by interference from the executive or other organs of the state, or of an identification of the judge with the interests of the state in oppressing political opposition. The second is the acceptance of the legality of authoritarian measures and the lack of protest against measures that are formally legal, but are nevertheless clearly in breach of basic rule of law principles, thus accepting the creation of a "dual state" (Fraenkel 1941). A major effect is that the police and security forces can terrorize the population with impunity and that victims are deprived of any access to justice. The third is the unquestioning application of any measure dressed up in legal form. We can find the most notable examples of this in the interpretation and application of anti-Jewish legislation by the French and Italian courts (Graver 2015a: 53–74). The fourth is the independent recreation of the existing body of law to accommodate the aims and interests of the authoritarian regime. The German courts' reinterpretation of the German civil code to deprive Jews of their status as legal subjects and holders of rights is illustrative of this.[3] The judges "interpreted enacted law liberally when liberal interpretation furthered Nazi ideology, and strictly when strict interpretation furthered it" (Curran 2005: 511).

The development in Norway during the German occupation shows examples of all four types of contribution. Not only the judicial institutions established by the national socialists, but also the ordinary courts were involved in this. The ordinary courts accepted the limits to their jurisdiction and did not launch effective protests against the powers allotted to the security police. After the protests by the Supreme Court, the other courts agreed to operate based on the new rules introduced by the Nasjonal Samling, and they applied subsequent legislation introduced by the regime. The creative reinterpretation of the law to transform it into national socialist law was the task of the national socialist writers. They on their part employed the same techniques and models that German legal scholars had introduced under national socialism into German law.

In Denmark, the courts cooperated with the efforts of the government to keep the administration of internal affairs in Danish hands. There was no change in the

[3] The most thorough study of this is still (Rüthers 2012) (first edition 1968), but see also Graver (2015a: 59–79).

Danish government with the German occupation and, unlike in many of the other occupied countries, the established government or the head of state did not go into exile. One of the overriding considerations of the government in the field of the administration of justice was to maintain jurisdiction over Danish citizens for the Danish police and courts. In order to achieve this, the government enacted oppressive reforms of the criminal law and the criminal procedure in order to accommodate German demands. The Danish courts followed a strict line in the application of these laws imposing strict punishment (Tamm 1984: 35–62).

3. The Norwegian Legal Complex during the Occupation

3.1 Introduction

The resistance in Norway was not only a resistance against German occupation, but also against the Nasjonal Samling and their endeavors to perform a political and social revolution.[4] Judges and lawyers took prominent positions in this resistance. The president of the Supreme Court, Paal Berg, became the leader of the Norwegian Resistance Movement. During the war, the young lawyer, Jens Christian Hauge, took the position of leader of the armed branch of the resistance, Milorg. Hauge later became a member of the social democrat government and was an important political figure in the development of the Norwegian state and society after the war. In addition, other members of the legal complex had active and important parts in the resistance movement. Several others of the Supreme Court judges held positions high up in the illegal resistance organization. Marius Coucheron, the president of the City Court of Bergen, the largest city on the west coast, was regional leader of the resistance in Western Norway.

The conduct of judges and lawyers in their professional capacity as judges and lawyers is a very different story. The Norwegian legal community has bracketed off this part of their history, and 1940–1945 has until now not been seen as part of the country's legal history. The legal establishment has not recognized the court that functioned with judges appointed by the commissarial Minister of Justice in January 1941 as the Supreme Court, and its judgments are without any value as precedents. The legal institutions after the war refused to recognize that the courts that the Quisling regime established were courts at all, regarding the judgments these courts delivered as criminal acts.

In the following, I will present four different aspects of the history of the courts in Norway during the occupation. First, I will give a short account of the unique role of the judges of the Supreme Court during the first phase of the occupation. Their

[4] For an overview over resistance in Norway see Zezza (2015).

role culminated in their collective withdrawal of their positions in December 1940, over a conflict with the German authorities concerning judicial review. I will then present the courts established by the national socialist government: The People's Court and the special courts. Finally, I will examine the role of the ordinary courts and the Norwegian bar.

3.2 The Resignation of the Supreme Court of Norway

As German forces occupied the southern part of Norway, the Government retreated north, leaving the occupied parts of Norway without a national government. Quisling tried to fill this vacuum by staging a coup, but he received no support, neither from the Germans, nor from leaders of Norwegian civil society, and was forced to step down. The obvious need for a responsible authority to coordinate the efforts of the Norwegian civil administration led the chief justice of the Supreme Court Paal Berg to take the initiative and appoint a chief administrative council to undertake the functions of government in occupied Norway.

After the occupation of the whole of the country, the Germans wanted to establish a Norwegian government. Their preference was for this government to have a formal mandate from the Norwegian parliament, and for parliament to dismiss the government in exile. Paal Berg was central in the negotiations over this during the summer of 1940. After the fall of France to the German forces, the Norwegian negotiators seemed willing to go along with such terms. The negotiations nevertheless broke down, partly because the king refused to accept any settlement with the Germans, and partly because Quisling, having traveled to Berlin, managed to convince the Reichschancellery to support him and the Nasjonal Samling over the solutions proposed under the negotiations in Oslo.

Paal Berg and the Supreme Court thus played a political role in the initial phases of the occupation. After the breakdown of the negotiations, Reichskommissar Terboven appointed a set of ministers to lead the different Norwegian ministers under his direction. Most of these were members of the Nasjonal Samling and compatriots of Quisling. At the same time, Terboven and his Norwegian co-workers issued a whole set of laws and regulations aimed at transforming Norwegian society into a national socialist state. This legislative activity continued, and in November 1940, Minister of Justice Riisnæs issued a regulation that enabled the ministry to appoint and dismiss juries and lay members of the courts in criminal and civil cases.

There were discussions among the Supreme Court justices over these developments, and they agreed that these measures were unacceptable attacks on the independence of the judiciary. They wrote a letter to the Reichskommissar that such legislation was ultra vires the rights given an occupying authority under the international law of war and occupations, and that it was for the Supreme Court to exercise judicial review over the measures enacted by the ministers.

The Supreme Court also wrote a letter to the ministry protesting this measure and argued that it was contrary to the general principles of justice of the Norwegian constitution, and that it exceeded the powers of occupying forces under public international law. The judges got two reactions to this letter. The first was a regulation lowering the retirement age for public officials from seventy to sixty-five, combined with a right for the responsible minister to prolong the judges' tenure indefinitely. The second was a letter from the Reichskommissar stating that Norwegian courts did not have the power to review the legality of laws and regulations enacted by or on behalf of the occupation authorities.

With the new retirement arrangement, the conditions under which the justices should function became unacceptable to the judges of the Supreme Court. The "unreliable" would be dismissed at sixty-five, and replaced with persons loyal to the regime. The letter from the Reichskommissar Terboven made clear that the Germans would not accept judicial review of the legality of occupation measures under public international law. Terboven claimed to be the supreme source of law in Norway. On December 9, all of the judges signed a letter where they asked Riisnæs to revoke the retirement regulation. Three days later, they sent a new letter to the minister where they all resigned, because "we cannot adhere to the view expressed by the Reichskommissar on judicial review without acting in contradiction with our duties as members of the Norwegian Supreme Court." The minister replied by dismissing the judges who were sixty-five years or older and by summoning the remaining to individual conferences in the ministry. When these conferences failed to provide submission by any of the judges, the ministry was forced to accept the resignation of the judges as a fait accompli.

There were close discussions between the Supreme Court judges and the leadership of the Bar Association and the Judges' Association during the weeks leading up to the resignations. The president of the Bar Association writes that he had meetings with the justices on a daily basis, and regular contact with the leadership of the Judges' Association.

The only other Western European country where judges also offered resistance of substance to the German occupiers was Belgium. A main difference between the approaches of the Norwegian and Belgian courts was that the Norwegian Supreme Court was willing to apply the regulations of the occupation authority if they were within the competence of the occupier under public international law. The Belgian courts refused to apply the occupying authority's regulations or the regulations by the Belgian authorities based on a delegation from the Germans, claiming that these were not Belgian, but German law. However, they were willing to apply measures by the Belgian authorities if they had a basis in Belgian law as interpreted under the emergency conditions of the occupation.

One should probably see this stance on judicial review by the Norwegian court against the background of the resistance against Quisling and his project, and the illegality under Norwegian law of the establishment of a government in substitution for the king and government in exile. The Supreme Court had been quite clear on this position in the negotiations, and had made it publicly known in a statement of June 15, 1940.[5] The same position was taken by the king after a request forwarded by the presidents of parliament asking him to resign. The position to review the legality of the measures of the administration established by the Reichskommissar was therefore directed as much against the Quisling administrators as against the Germans. When some months later it came to an open confrontation, this was also the case, as the topic of the conflict was a measure on the constitution of the courts issued by the commissarial minister of justice. The basic constitutional issue on the legality of the Quisling administration was therefore decided as an issue of the application of international law by national Norwegian courts. The resignation of the Norwegian Supreme Court judges at the beginning of the German occupation may have contributed to the general perception of illegitimacy of the Quisling regime during the occupation in Norway.

In both cases, the national courts reserved the right to review, and in both cases, the occupying authority denied this right. The Norwegian judges found it unacceptable to continue under these circumstances and resigned. Staying in office would have involved a transfer of their loyalty from the Norwegian constitution to the occupation regime. The Belgian judges, on the other hand, stayed in office. Belgian law, enacted before the war, prohibited them from abandoning their post. However, the judges attempted to refuse to try cases where regulations by the authorities were grounds for criminal sanctions, but were pressured into submission. When they tried to lay down their work in protest against repressive measures, the German occupiers threatened them with criminal proceedings with a possible death penalty.

The resignation of the Supreme Court judges became an act of great symbolic importance to the resistance both against the Germans and against the Government of Nasjonal Samling. It was a clear statement of the illegitimacy of the measures enacted by Quisling and his ministers. On the other hand, it did not have any clear effect on the question of judicial opposition. The other judges were encouraged to stay in office and "make the best of it."

3.3 The People's Court

The German occupation authority established early provisions against political activity against the regime supported by the occupiers and authorized German courts to deal with cases under these rules. The orders were Order Prohibiting Political Parties in Norway, September 25, 1940 and orders concerning the Prohibition of

5 Schjelderup (1945: 117–118).

Activities on Behalf of the Royal House of Norway and concerning the Dismissal and Transfer of Officials, October 7. This in effect made all political opposition to the occupation and to national socialism illegal.

German courts were given jurisdiction in all cases regarding activities contrary to the interests of the occupying forces and authorities. The occupation rules also provided for the establishment of Norwegian special courts to deal with cases that did not directly affect German interests. Under these provisions German army courts, The Reichskriegsgericht in Berlin and an SS- und Polizeigericht established in Norway dealt with a large number of cases against members of the Norwegian resistance.

The German occupation authorities provided for the establishment of a Norwegian special court to deal with issues of civil resistance. The order prohibiting all political parties other than the National Socialist Party stated that a Norwegian special court would try infringements of the order. This court was intended as a measure to lessen the burden on the German institutions in the curbing of resistance against the remodeling of Norwegian society toward a Nazi state. The Norwegian National Socialist authorities seized on the opportunity to establish a "People's Court" outside the existing judicial system by a decree of November 8, 1940. According to Minister of Justice Sverre Riisnæs, this court should be a permanent institution with an important role in creating the National Socialist state. The ambitions for the court, in other words, went far beyond enforcing temporary restrictive measures necessitated by the conditions of war and state of occupation. The inauguration of the court was on February 12, 1941.

The People's Court consisted of three judges, all recruited from the ranks of the party. The court dealt with 111 cases against more than 150 accused. All the cases were political in nature, ranging from harassment and violence toward members of the National Socialist Party to the distribution of illegal pamphlets and newspapers. In one case, a lecturer of the law faculty received one hundred days in prison for using the symbol 'H7' on the blackboard when explaining a legal problem, signifying support to King Haakon VII.

One of the first cases before the court was the case against sixteen members from the Labor Party on the city council of Oslo. They were accused of illegal political activity because they had formulated a proposal to the council not to follow a circular from the ministry to act in the interests of National Socialism and the regime in power. Three of the accused received prison sentences of one year and six months, one a sentence of one year and three months, and the rest a one-year suspended sentence. Some months later, the court tried a case against a father and his son and some friends of the son for producing and distributing a leaflet with news and opinions of the government in exile distributed over the BBC network. The father received four years in prison, the son and his friends around one year each.

The first year of the People's Court, dealing with a growing number of cases, was considered by the occupiers a success. The court's jurisdiction was expanded to include violations of the general criminal code in cases of political importance. The chief prosecutor decided whether to bring a case to the People's Court or to the ordinary courts. The judges soon established themselves as professional judges. This meant that they fell into the established judicial role, where loyalty to the law took precedence over loyalty to the party. The significance of this was soon to be tested.

The test case for the court as an instrument for the National Socialist regime appeared in the winter of 1942–1943. The border pilot Karsten Løvestad had shot dead a police officer who had tried to apprehend him and some Jewish refugees while they were attempting to cross the Swedish border. Both the German and Norwegian authorities demanded the execution of the border pilot. The public prosecutor approached the president of the People's Court in order to obtain a prior assurance that the court would sentence Løvestad to death. The president refused to give such an assurance because he could not see that the murder had been premeditated. As a result, the case was handed over to the German SS court where Løvestad received the death sentence.

The National Socialist Minister of Justice was furious with the court for not accommodating the demands of the regime. As a result, the court was marginalized and the political cases were dealt with either by the security police without court proceedings, and for the more serious cases by the German SS court. By 1943, the court received only a handful of cases, and its judges were offered other positions in the Supreme Court and the Ministry of Justice.

3.4 The Special Courts

The next time the need for a conviction in a serious case by a Norwegian court arose was in August 1943 when police officer Eilifsen declined to order the police to arrest young women who had refused to report for obligatory work duties. The German Reichskommissar Terboven demanded that the Norwegian authorities set an example by condemning Eilifsen to death. According to Norwegian law at the time, refusal to obey orders within the police was an offense with a jail sentence as maximum punishment. Quisling immediately enacted a law introducing capital punishment for the offense, making the military criminal code applicable with retroactive effect. At the same time, he enacted provisions for the establishment of a special court to deal with offenses within the police force. The provisions established a special court to deal with Eilifsen's case. The judges were one of the judges from the Supreme Court sitting with two chiefs of police: The head of the political department and the head of the department of public order. Initially the court returned with a two to one ruling for a prison sentence. When reporting this to the minister, the two judges were threatened and coerced into changing their ruling. They were told that if Eilifsen was not sentenced to death, they themselves would be shot. Consequently, one of the judges changed his ruling so that Eilifsen was sentenced to death by a two to one vote. The dissenting justice was the judge from the Supreme Court.

Subsequently, Quisling enacted permanent legislation for the establishment of special courts in cases against members of the police, party members, and members of the Norwegian branch of the armed SS forces. The special court for police was also given jurisdiction to deal with cases against civilians. Altogether, the special courts dealt with approximately twenty-five cases against fifty accused, presided over by at least twelve judges or prosecutors. All the cases were major cases involving murder, theft, looting, black market offenses, and armed resistance against the occupying authorities. The courts pronounced nineteen death sentences for resistance activities, making this a conviction and death sentence rate of 100 percent. Taking the other cases into account, the death sentence rate of the courts was 50 percent, making these courts harsher even than the People's Court in Berlin with its rate of capital punishment between 46 percent and 49 percent in the years 1942–1949. The SS Court in Norway had a death rate of 74 percent in its political cases, but this number must be seen in relation to the *Nacht und Nebel* order of December 12, 1941, according to which courts in occupied countries should only have jurisdiction in cases where the death sentence was demanded by the prosecution. Therefore, the rate of 74 percent indicates that the court ruled against the prosecution in 26 percent of its cases against members of the Norwegian resistance.

The files show that in political cases, the special courts functioned as mere formalizations of decisions taken by the political authorities. Quisling and Riisnæs decided, after German pressure, who to charge and convict, and whether they should receive the death penalty. They took these decisions before they appointed the persons to serve as prosecutors and judges in the special courts, and the judges were left with the task of going through the formalities of a court proceeding and sentencing. In many cases, the persons appointed protested, but to no avail. The prosecutors and judges were coerced to participate in the trials.

This use of show trials with coerced judges marks an exception in the Norwegian experience as compared to other countries under Nazi rule, in both Germany and the occupied countries. The Nazi rulers generally respected the independence of the judges in individual cases, and sought to control the judges both through more general letters from the ministry on "correct" judging and through the refusal to confirm judgments that contradicted the interests of the executive power. However, judges were not told how to decide the facts and the law in individual cases, and they were not sanctioned for judgments that went against the wishes of the party executives. Not one single judge in Germany was penalized for disloyal rulings, although some were forced to resign (Graver 2015a: 39–42).

3.5 The Regular Courts and the Bar

Due to the provisions by the occupying authorities, the regular courts in Norway were not involved in political cases during the occupation to any substantial degree. There are a few incidents that involved the regular courts from the very beginning of the occupation, before the special Nazi courts were established. These few examples show that it is hard to predict how the Norwegian judiciary would have enforced the coercive measures of the regime, had they been given the task. In an early case against sixteen members of the Labor Party in the city council of Oslo in the fall of 1940, the district court of Oslo followed the demand of the Nazi authorities to remand them pending trial for charges of political activity. The existing rules of procedure obviously did not authorize the use of custody under the circumstances. The Court of Appeals ordered their release. From this case, it is difficult to predict what the reaction of the regular Norwegian Courts would have been had the occupying authorities involved them in the enforcement of the laws made to protect their aims and interests.

We know from Denmark and the Netherlands that the courts went far in accommodating the interests of the occupying authorities, in the Netherlands even in enforcing the German measures against Jews. Even after having been approached by leading academics and civil servants the Supreme Court refused to protest against German measures against Jewish civil servants, and found that the measures were legal since the occupying authority was in its right to dismiss civil servants who lacked their confidence (Michielsen 2004: 127–128).

Following the resignation of the Supreme Court justices, there seems to have been little opposition from the Norwegian judiciary to the measures enacted by the NS. When the justices resigned, the president of the Supreme Court issued a statement that the other judges should stay in their positions and "take such measures as called for by the situation" (Nissen 1983: 174). The Judges' Association wrote a letter on January 7 to the ministry in which they voiced their concerns over the fact that it had become necessary for the judges of the Supreme Court to resign. The Bar Association wrote a similar letter. Both letters were distributed to the members of the two organizations. In February, after the appointment of new judges loyal to the regime, the association stated in another letter that the new judges did not have the support or confidence of the judiciary or of the Norwegian people (Nissen 1983: 173).

The judges resisted the efforts of the regime to have them join the NS Party and only eight complied. Following an episode where a judge claimed that a party member had threatened him into joining the party, the Judges' Association wrote a letter to the ministry in October 1940 protesting, stating that forcing a judge to become a member of the party would be a serious breach of judicial independence.[6]

[6] The correspondence is presented in Innberetning til Det Kgl. Justis- og Politidepartement fra konstituert riksadvokat Ø. Thommessen om undersøkelser foretatt i anledning O.H. Langelands

The minister replied that party membership should not be seen as contrary to the professional duties of a judge. The regime removed fourteen judges as politically "unreliable." Due to the removals and retirement of judges, the NS had the opportunity to appoint sixty-five judges, most of whom were party members. Probably as many as fifty judges and assistant judges were members of the party during the occupation, or about 20 percent of the total.

In 1941, the NS Party tried to take control of all trade unions and trade associations according to the national socialist idea of the corporate state. This was part of general measures to bring the trade unions and trade associations under NS control. These measures were directed against associations within labor, trade, farming and fishing, and culture. The measures lead to widespread protests, including from the Judges' Association. In April and May 1941, forty-three associations with a total membership of hundreds of thousands wrote letters of protest to the Reichskommissar, complaining about injustices and encroachments by the NS regime (Wyller 1953: 114). The judges participated in the protests, but did not take the same leading role as the Bar Association.

The letters led to action by the Germans, proclaimed in a speech by Terboven in parliament on June 18, 1941, where he proclaimed a new order disbanding some of the organizations that had joined the protest and placing the others under leadership appointed by the NS. He also proclaimed the arrest of the leaders of the participating organizations. The measures also included the Judges' Association and the Bar Association. In total, he dissolved eleven organizations and placed a further twenty-seven under the control of the Reichskommissar, including the teachers' organization, the organizations for medical doctors, engineers, and priests. In many of the organizations the measures led to the mass withdrawal of members, with 80 percent of doctors and dentists, 70 percent of engineers and again 80 percent of advocates leaving their organizations (Wyller 1953: 126). The NS replied by trying to impose forced membership of the organizations, but the regime had to give up its attempts to coerce professionals into Nazified organizations. Because of this struggle, the Chairman of the Judges' Association was removed from his position as a district judge. In addition, the majority of the judges left the Judges' Association, and in July 1941, it in effect ceased to exist as an active organization. This seems to have terminated any attempts at organized protests by the judges against the regime. The Judges' Association established an illegal action committee comprised of two Supreme Court justices and a justice from a probate and bankruptcy court, but I have not been able to find any reference to their activity. It is difficult to find traces of any protests by the judiciary after the first half of 1941.

bøker «Dømmer ikke» og «Forat I ikke skal dømmes» og Arne Bergsviks skrift «We are no Criminals», Attachment nr. 2 til St.meld. nr. 64/1950, ss. 24–25.

The president of the Bar Association, Henning Bødtker, was the first to be arrested as a result of the protests. The Germans held him as the responsible mind behind the letters of protest, and arrested him on June 12. Soon thereafter, his arrest was followed by arrests of other prominent leaders of the Norwegian civil society. He was released on July 31, but his license to practice was revoked.

When Reichskommissar announced the order establishing the People's Court on October 25, 1940, the Judges' Association issued a protest against this encroachment on the jurisdiction of the ordinary courts. There seems, however, to have been no protests from the judges when the Peoples' Court was inaugurated in February 1941. This was in contrast to the activities of the Bar Association, which sent repeated protests to the Ministry of Justice during the winter and spring of 1941, and again in March 1942.

The advocates were overall much more active in their protests against the attacks by the regime on the rule of law than the judges.[7] As we have seen above, the Bar Association had closer connections with the Supreme Court judges prior to their resignation, and it was more active in the protests against the Nazification attempts toward the trade associations. The Bar Association followed up the correspondence with the ministry after the resignation of the Supreme Court judges, and on February 8 wrote a letter voicing concern over measures by the occupying authority going beyond the competences granted under international law. In particular, it pointed to the establishment of the People's Court and an order extending the duty to give evidence to the police and limiting the scope of privilege for doctors, attorneys, and ministers and priests. It also pointed to an order empowering the police to hold accused persons in custody without seeking an order from a judge. The association also protested against the holding of trials in German courts without representation of the accused by council, and demanded Norwegian advocates to be appointed as public defenders. Both the German and the Norwegian authorities accommodated this demand.

The association also engaged in a legal discussion with the chairman of the People's Court over the correct procedure in cases under the jurisdiction of the court. The order establishing the court stated that apart from where explicitly stated in the order, the ordinary rules of criminal procedure should apply. This gave vast room for interpretation, and the association wrote detailed guidance to its members. This was followed by a lengthy comment from the president of the court, and finally by a circular by the ministry. The association followed up with commentaries to this circular to its members.

On March 31, 1941, the association wrote a letter to the Ministry of Justice and the Ministry of Police summarizing its views on the legal situation of the occupation. The content of these letters had been decided in a meeting of the supervisory

7 The description of resistance activities of the Bar Association is based on Bødtker (1958) and Poulsson (1958).

board. The measures enacted in the field of the administration of justice were criticized both for going beyond the rights of an occupying authority under international law, and for being contrary to established principles of justice and the rule of law. The ministries were also criticized for going beyond the scope of the orders of the Reichskommissar. There was never a reply by the ministries to this letter.

In the same meeting, the supervisory board concluded that the association had to be prepared for oppressive measures from the authorities against the association and its members. It decided to establish an action commission with an unlimited mandate to protect the interests of the association in case of measures inhibiting the normal operation of the association and its leadership. In July 1941, the association ceased its existence because of the measures taken by the regime against the trade organizations.

After this, the organized activities of the Norwegian bar entered into a new stage as an illegal organization. The first move of the action committee was to write a circular to all the members urging them to withdraw their membership of the Bar Association. Eighty percent of the members followed this call. The ministry replied by making membership compulsory for all members of the profession. The action committee continued to keep the members of the bar informed about developments within the field of law in illegal circulars.

Early in 1942 the ministry enacted a regulation making it compulsory for advocates to pay the membership fee to the Bar Association, with provisions on a right of distraint in the case of non-payment. The action committee wrote to the members of the bar urging them not to pay. It also wrote a letter addressed to the judiciary, stating that the regulation was contrary to international law, and that the courts therefore were obliged to deny distraint in any case against a member of the bar. The ministry subsequently gave up its efforts to enforce the compulsory membership.

The action committee continued to address members of the bar, informing them of important developments, commenting on events, and advising and urging on forms of resistance against measures by the regime. A striking feature in the writings of the action committee is the total silence concerning the legislative measures and deportations of the Jews in Norway. Hover, the committee cooperated with action committees of other associations and organizations, thus forming part of the organized civil resistance against the NS and the occupying authority. The Judges' Association as such was not part of this cooperation, but prominent judges held leading positions in the organized resistance movement.

Not only lawyers, but also civil servants formed a secret underground organization to gather and disseminate information about planned and enacted nazification measures and to encourage and abet resistance among civil servants. The organization was established after the coup in February 1942 and was active throughout the occupation (Støen 2013: 94–102).

The silence of the Norwegian judges is in contrast to the protests of the judges of the Netherlands. The Netherlands was also under German civilian administration under a Reichskommissar. In this country, the occupiers established special peace courts to deal with cases of political opposition. This led to widespread opposition by the judiciary, including the resignation of three members of The Hague Court of Appeal (Michielsen 2004: 144–145). The Supreme Court, however, by swearing in the members of the newly formed peace courts, quelled the opposition.

The ordinary courts continued their judiciary functions without protest, and applied legislation enacted by the new regime. They accepted the rules on the composition of the courts that had led to the resignation of the Supreme Court, and applied laws that were far outside the scope of the powers of an occupying force according to international law. In this, the regular courts of Norway fell into the general picture of courts under fascist regimes, applying their law irrespective of its origins and impact (Skinner 2015: 192).

One cannot explain the silence of the Norwegian judges as ignorance of either the law or the arguments against the legality of the regime. Due to the publicity around the resignation of the Supreme Court judges, the judiciary was well aware of the official view on measures taken by the occupying authorities and the NS regime outside the scope of international law. The judges had even expressed their support for this view in their letter supporting the resignation of the Supreme Court. Their silence must therefore have reasons other than ignorance.

4. Administration of Justice in Denmark during the German Occupation

An important aim for the Danish policy of cooperation was to maintain an autonomous legal order and to ensure jurisdiction for Danish courts in cases against Danish citizens (Tamm 1984: 35). This necessitated the enactment of substantial and procedural rules in Danish law to accommodate the interests of the occupying authority, as well as an active enforcement of the rules. The Germans would not accept ceding authority to the Danes in such cases if the Danish enforcement were lenient and half-hearted (Tamm 1984: 41). Consequently, the Danish authorities enacted changes in both the criminal code and criminal procedure. Public expression and dissemination of rumors that could harm the relationship of the country with other powers were criminalized and made punishable by prison. A special law was enacted that made all acts against the German forces or in favor of the forces of the enemies of Germany punishable with a prison or even a life sentence. The reforms eliminated any participation of lay judges, and the prosecutor had discretion to decide to direct cases to the City Court of Copenhagen, where one judge had the task of dealing with the political cases. The Ministry of Justice had to grant leave to appeal a case. The right to defense council was limited. The legal complex remained mostly silent over these changes in the law that abolished many of the traditional procedural rights of Danish law (Tamm 1984: 45).

The judiciary, however, remained intact and independent of interventions from the Germans and thus from attempts of Nazification. There was no Nazification of the judiciary, and only two judges gave their support to Nazism during the occupation (Tamm 1984: 570). The judges were, on the other hand, under strong pressure from the Danish authorities to support the policy of cooperation and to enforce the special legislation. The only Jewish member of the judiciary, District Court Justice Julius Moritz was deported October 1, 1943 to Theresienstadt, where he died. He refused to flee to Sweden, being of the firm conviction that a servant of the royal Danish Crown would be untouchable (Garde and Tamm 2000: 102).

The Danish authorities succeeded for the most part in maintaining jurisdiction over Danish citizens in Danish courts, even when the charge was a direct attack on German institutions or interests. The main factor in this seems to have been the negotiations by the Danish government and administration, and their flexibility in enacting legislation accommodating the demands of the Germans. The courts followed suit in applying this legislation in a strict manner.

One notable example is the case against a Danish officer, arrested in Berlin in 1940 for attempting to persuade Danish pilots to enter the war on the side of the British. The Danish authorities negotiated with the Germans to have him extradited to Denmark. The German authorities set as a condition for extradition that he should be sentenced to a punishment no less than life imprisonment. This was not possible under Danish law, but parliament passed a law in January 1941 that criminalized aid to enemy forces with a maximum punishment of life imprisonment. The officer was returned to Denmark the same day, and shortly afterwards was convicted and retroactively sentenced to imprisonment for life by the Copenhagen City Court (Tamm 1984: 44–45).

The Germans put pressure on the Danish authorities to enact legislation against Jews and Communists. The government refused to enact anti-Jewish legislation. After the German request, the king attended synagogue services in Copenhagen to demonstrate his solidarity with the Jews (Lemkin 2008: 160). There is no evidence that the legal complex played an important role in the government's refusal. On the other hand, sympathy for the Jews extended to the legal community. One of the leading legal scholars, Frederik Vinding Kruse, who after the war was accused of Nazi sympathies, wrote on the "Jewish question" in a textbook in 1943 in a way that after the war was commended by the chief rabbi of Denmark. The rabbi wrote that the professor with his writing had taken a brave stand against the Nazi doctrine, unsurpassed by any other publication during the occupation (Evald 2005: 309).

Measures against the Communists were another matter. After the German attack on the Soviet Union on June 22, 1941, the Germans approached the Danish authorities with a demand that all known members of the Communist party be interned (Tamm 1984: 52–59). The German police had a list of about seventy persons to be arrested. The Danish police did not stop with the people on the list, and interned over one hundred people.

The internments were all done on an administrative basis. When the Germans subsequently demanded that a law should be enacted prohibiting the Communist Party, the president of the Supreme Court, Troels G. Jørgensen, advised the minister of justice that the law should give a legal basis for the continued internment of the communists. Jørgensen offered his services in the drafting of the act, and later wrote a commentary to the act defending its constitutionality. When some of the interned later filed a case contesting the legality of their internment, the Supreme Court confirmed the validity of the act.

President Jørgensen also intervened in another case against a famous history teacher, Vilhelm La Cour, for undermining the status of the German army through a series of lectures he had held around the country. The Germans wanted to prosecute la Cour in a German court. This caused the Danish authorities to bring charges against him in the Danish court. There were some disputes between the German and Danish authorities over this, but the Germans dropped their charges after the questioning of la Cour by a German military judge. The Copenhagen City Court convicted La Cour and gave him a mild sentence, but he appealed to the Supreme Court, which made the punishment more severe. Before the proceedings in the Supreme Court, Jørgensen wrote a letter and later conferred with the ministry to ensure that La Cour was dismissed from his position as a teacher before the case was decided by the Supreme Court (Gamborg 1946: 628–632).

Until the political crisis with the breakdown of the Danish government's cooperation policy, Danish courts dealt with almost all cases involving Danish citizens. This even included cases of espionage against the Germans. At a meeting of April 12, the German negotiator demanded that a special prosecutor be appointed to deal with cases involving attacks on German interests (Andersen 1946:267). The Danes agreed to this and duly appointed a special prosecutor. At the same time, the government decided that a specially appointed judge at the Copenhagen City Court would try the cases. The provincial courts should deal only with minor cases. The Ministry of Justice had to give leave for appeal in these cases, and in 1942 the law was changed, so that appeals bypassed the Court of Appeals and went directly to the Supreme Court. In most cases where the Supreme Court took decisions, the level of punishment was increased.

The wartime cases included political cases, cases where German interests were involved (including prostitution and the spread of venereal disease), breach of rationing provisions, black market trading, and others. Altogether, the special prosecutor dealt with 5,684 cases in the period from April 9, 1940 to April 1, 1941 (Andersen 1946: 268–269). Approximately 20 percent of the cases investigated by the prosecutor may be characterized as cases of political resistance. In total 447 persons were sentenced. In the following year the number of convictions was 861, and in 1942–1943 the total was 868. In addition, German military courts sentenced eleven persons in 1940–1942, and another thirteen were sentenced in 1942–1943. From 1943, the German courts started using capital punishment, executing in total 113 persons after convictions by German courts.

The German authorities did not intervene directly in the operation of the Danish courts. As mentioned above, the Nazis did not resort to the "telephone justice" of the soviet system, a type of intervention into the judiciary that is prolific even today in many post-communist states (Nußberger 2012: 892).[8] On the other hand, the German military court followed the cases closely, and issued directives to the prosecutor to appeal the case if it meant that the defendant had been treated too leniently (Gamborg 1946: 629). As mentioned above, the Supreme Court regularly increased the level of punishment in these cases.

The effects of maintaining Danish jurisdiction over cases as compared to Norway depends on whether one looks at cases brought in German courts or in the Norwegian special courts. The sentencing in the German courts was by far much more severe than it was both in the Danish and Norwegian courts. To some extent, this is a consequence of the fact that the more serious cases were brought in the German courts. However, the level of punishment in German criminal law far exceeded the measure of proportionality in Danish and Norwegian legal opinion. Where, for example, the regular punishment in the SS court for illegally trying to leave the country was death, the Danish Supreme Court fixed the punishment at one-and-a-half year's imprisonment (Tamm 1984: 46). The Danish policy of national jurisdiction saved lives. Until 1943, no Dane received the death sentence. After the breakdown of the policy of cooperation this changed, and in total 113 Danes were executed. The corresponding number in Norway was 273.

If on the other hand we compare the sentencing of the Danish courts with the sentencing of the Norwegian People's Court, there are no notable differences. Cases involving the production and distribution of illegal printing were regularly punished with prison sentences up to a few years. The highest punishment for this in the People's Court was four years, whereas the Copenhagen City Court in one case reacted with eight years in prison. The Supreme Court reduced this term to six years. Vilhelm La Cour received seven months in prison for critical remarks toward the government and the Germans in a series of public lectures. The lecturer in law in Norway, Jens Christian Hauge, received one hundred days in prison for his demonstrations in favor of the government in exile in his lectures to law students at the University of Oslo.

There was not a single protest from the judiciary against the legislation criminalizing political actions, increasing the punishment, and introducing procedural measures contrary to the established principles of rule of law. The judges did not see it as their responsibility to depart from the policy of cooperation (Garde and

[8] For judicial independence in Nazi Germany see Graver (2015a: 39–45).

Tamm 2000: 97). There is only one example of judicial protest, and that was against the deportation of their Jewish colleague to Theresienstadt. The Judges' Association and members of the Court of Appeal protested to the Ministry of Justice, but to no avail (Garde and Tamm 2000: 102–103).

5. Conclusions

The occupation affected Denmark and Norway differently. Denmark maintained its political institutions and there were no systematic efforts toward turning Denmark into a national socialist state. In Norway, the Germans established a supreme German civilian rule with legislative powers. With the aid of the Germans the NS performed a *coup d'état* and tried to transform Norwegian political and social institutions in line with its ideology. This also led to the development of a national socialist legal theory, attempts at Nazification of the judiciary and other public institutions, and the establishment of special courts. A much larger number of Norwegian judges were supporters of the NS than their Danish colleagues. Eight of the judges appointed before the occupation joined the NS in Norway, whereas in Denmark only two judges turned to Nazism. The difference can be explained by the lack of official pressure on the judges in Denmark to support Nazism. In addition to the eight, the NS appointed about forty party members to judicial positions in Norway. Approximately 20–25 percent of the judiciary in Norway were members of the NS.

On the other hand, the high level of National Socialists among the judiciary in Norway does not seem to have influenced the jurisprudence of the courts in any significant way. In many of the collaborator cases held against judges after the war, the accused were commended for not having let their political sympathies influence their judging. Of course, there were cases where a National Socialist would rule differently, for example in cases of custody over children where one of the spouses was a member of Nasjonal Samling. It was an expressed view of the party that it was in the best interest of children to be raised in the national socialist worldview, and some judges based their rulings on this. In criminal cases, and in the more political cases, there seems to be no great difference between the People's Court of Norway and the City Court of Copenhagen. The caseload in the National Socialist People's Court was not particularly large, and the level of sentencing was comparable. To this picture must be added, however, that the more serious cases in Norway were dealt with by the German courts, and that an increasing number of cases were dealt with administratively by the security police under special provisions empowering the police to employ "security measures" against political opponents.

The attitude and actions of the Supreme Court presidents in the two countries are remarkably different. The Norwegian Paal Berg originally sought ways to cooperate with the Germans in the civil administration of Norway. When this failed he was firmly on the line of defending the independence of the judiciary, and he actively led the judges into the resignation of their offices. After his resignation, he was the leader of the secret Norwegian resistance movement. The Dane Troels G. Jørgensen, on the other hand, was instrumental in the drafting of the law against Communism in Denmark, and thus contributed to a blurring of the lines between legislation and adjudication. In his defense he argued that the Germans demanded the arrests, and that a failure to comply could endanger the status of Denmark, and that in any case it would not benefit the Communists to be interned by the Germans. Critics pointed out that it was the Danish government that was under pressure from the Germans, and that there was no particular reason why the Supreme Court president should engage himself in undermining the rule of law in this way (Evald 2005: 292–293).

The Supreme Courts therefore took very different lines over the question of limits to legislative powers to accommodate the demands of the occupier. Where the Norwegian Supreme Court drew a fixed line, the Danish courts never questioned the measures enacted by the legislator or the administration. In one way it might be said that this was more difficult for the Danish courts since the measures were all enacted by national institutions who had their powers firmly established in the constitution. There was therefore no question about their legitimacy. In substance, however, many of the measures that were enacted were questionable, under both Danish law and international law. The example of the Belgian courts shows that it is possible for the courts to set limits under such conditions. The Belgian court engaged in several fierce battles over their right to review measures enacted by the Belgian administration.

After the resignation of the Supreme Court, there was no controversy in Norway over judicial review. The other courts accepted both the German measures and the measures enacted by the government of the Nasjonal Samling without question. In the day-to-day dealings of the courts there were therefore no differences between Denmark and Norway. There was one notable exception to this picture. The Danish judges protested against the deportation of their one Jewish colleague. From neither the Norwegian judiciary, nor from the bar, for that matter, was there a single open protest against the measures taken against the Jews of Norway.

Lawyers, judges, and other legally trained professions often mobilize as a legal complex for political liberalism against authoritarian rule (Halliday, Karpik, and Feeley 2007). This mobilization was an important part of the rise of liberal rights and the rule of law in the eighteenth and nineteenth centuries of Europe and the United States. On the other hand, the legal complex has not always sided with political liberalism when those in control of the state are dismantling the rule of law. In such situations, the legal complex is often seen to slide away from the protection of liberal legal norms (Halliday and Karpik 2012). Even if we can presume that countries with a long-established liberal legacy have a higher probability of continuing along this path, this is by no means certain. Moreover, in countries well established within the Western legal tradition we have seen the dismantling of the rule of law with the consent and even active participation of the judiciary and other professions with legal training (Graver 2015a).

There are limits to the attacks that the legal complex can resist. Halliday, Karpik, and Feeley (2007: 36) point out that "some repression simply extinguishes the legal terrain." To what extent the terrain is "extinguished" depends on the type of rule and its historical and social circumstances. Rulers all over seek to ensure judicial compliance with their political aims. The measures differ, as do the reactions of the judiciary. At some point, judges in any legal system cease to act independently and become mere organs of the state. It is crucial to obtain better knowledge on how rulers seek judicial compliance with authoritarian measures, how judges react to such measures, and the conditions under which an independent judiciary breaks down.

The Nazi and fascist regimes of twentieth-century Europe, which developed in societies steeped in the Western legal tradition, had as an important trait the continuity between fascist law and what we regard as law in democratic, rule-of-law states (Skinner 2015: 191). These regimes were maintained and developed legal form, but operated in concordance with the prerogative state described by Ernst Fraenkel as the dual state, where the security police operated against opponents of the state outside the jurisdiction of the courts. The legal institutions and the law were for the most part taken over from the predecessor regime, without any radical break with the past. The legal terrain was not extinguished, but the conditions were radically changed. This also changed the operation of the judiciary and legal professions, who for the most accepted going about their legal business in the usual way, despite any lack of legitimacy of the new legal measures and despite a radical break with traditional legal values of the rule of law. To practice the law of the land, whether he or she personally approves of the result of its application, seems to be a stronger part of the judicial ideology than the recognition of inalienable rights and the rule of law (Graver 2015a: 208–212).

Fascism and Nazism were home-grown in many countries such as Italy and Germany. The scepter of fascism was imposed on other countries by occupation during World War II. Unlike most other countries that experienced fascist rule in the twentieth century, the Western European countries occupied by Germany had long and unbroken traditions of rule of law and democracy, with courts that had an active practice of judicial review of both legislation and administrative decisions. There was no previous tradition of authoritarianism that the rulers in power could draw upon and that the courts could refer to in an acceptance of authoritarian rules.

On the other hand, both the Danish and Norwegian legal traditions were, and still are, based in pragmatic realism where principled legal reasoning is not held in high regard.[9] The legal community comprised a small number of persons, where

[9] See on Scandinavian legal realism Graver (2015a: 233–236).

individual action and attitudes perhaps had more room to play, unstrained by the heavier institutional constrictions of larger societies. This may have left the legal institutions in these countries more susceptible to succumb to authoritarian pressure than countries with larger, more formalized, institutions less dependent on individual personalities.

The experiences of Denmark and Norway confirm that the legal complex is accommodating towards a breakdown of the rule of law at times of great threat to the national security. When under extreme authoritarian pressure the legal complex is silenced. The law, its institutions, and personnel for the most part acquiesce in becoming instruments for the oppression of individual rights and the rule of law.

References

Andenæs, Johs, Magne Skodvin, and Olav Riste. 1966. *Norway and the Second World War*. Oslo: Aschehoug.

Andersen, Arthur. 1946. "Fra domstole og Fængsler," in Vilhelm La Cour (ed.), *Danmark under besættelsen III*. Copenhagen: Westermann, 9–73.

Bohn, Robert. 2000. *Reichskommissariat Norwegen: "Nationalsozialistische Neuordnung" und Kriegswirtschaft*. Munich: Oldenbourg Wissenschaftsverlag.

Bødtker, Henning. 1958. " Den norske Sakførerforening 1933–juni 1941," in Rolf Christophersen (ed.), *Den norske Sakførerforening 1933–1958*, 11–90. Oslo: Den Norske Sakførerforening.

Curran, Vivian Grosswald. 2005. "Law's Past and Europe's Future," *German Law Journal* 6: 483–512.

Dahl, Hans Fredrik. 2004. "Innledning: Oppgjøret som rystet Norge," in Hans Fredrik Dahl and Øystein Sørensen (eds.), *Et rettferdig oppgjør? Rettsoppgjøret i Norge etter 1945*. Oslo: Pax Forlag.

Espeli, Harald. 2008. "Tilpasning og motstand. Okkupasjonen under 1940–1945, kapittel 6," in Harald Espeli, Hans Eyvind Næss, and Harald Rinde (eds.), *Våpendrager og veiviser Advokatenes historie i Norge*. Oslo: Universitetsforlaget.

Evald, Jens. 2005. *Frederik Vinding Kruse (1980-1963) En juridisk biografi*. Copenhagen: Jurist- og Økonomforbundets forlag.

Fraenkel, Ernst. 2010. *The Dual State: A Contribution to the Theory of Dictatorship*. New York: The Lawbook Exchange Ltd. Originally published by Oxford University Press 1941.

Gamborg, Leif. 1946. "Den retlige udvikling," in Vilhelm La Cour (ed.), *Danmark under besættelsen I*. Copenhagen: Westermann, 457–478.

Garde, Peter, and Tamm, Ditlev. 2000. "Dommerskæbner under besættelsen og retsoppgøret," in P. Garde, C. Larsen, and B. Pedersen (eds.), *Dommeren i det 20. århundre Dommerforeningens 100 års jubileum*. Copenhagen: Jurist- og Økonomforbundets Forlag, 97–120.

Graver, Hans Petter. 2015a. *Judges Against Justice: On Judges When the Rule of Law is Under Attack*. Berlin and Heidelberg: Springer.

Graver, Hans Petter. 2015b. *Dommernes krig Den tyske okkupasjonen 1940–1945 og den norske rettsstaten*. Oslo: Pax forlag.

Halliday, Terence C., and Lucien Karpik. 2012. "Political Liberalism in the British Post-Colony," in T. C. Halliday, L. Karpik, and M. M. Feeley (eds), *Fates of Political Liberalism in the British Post-Colony: The Politics of the Legal Complex*, 3–58. Cambridge: Cambridge University Press.

Halliday, Terence C., Lucien Karpik, and Malcolm M. Feeley. 2007. "The Legal Complex in Struggles for Political Liberalism," in T. C. Halliday, L. Karpik, and M. M. Feeley (eds), *Fighting for Political Freedom Comparative Studies of the Legal Complex and Political Liberalism*. Oxford and Portland, OR: Hart, 1–40.

Lemkin, Raphael. 2008. *Axis Rule in Occupied Europe: Law of Occupation, Analysis of Government, Proposals for Redress*, 2nd ed. Clark, NJ: The Lawbook Exchange, Ltd. Originally published by the Carnegie Endowment for International Peace, Washington, DC 1944.

Michielsen, J. N. M. E. 2004. *The "Nazification" and "Denazification" of the Courts in Belgium, Luxembourg and the Netherlands*. Maastricht: University of Maastricht.

Nissen, Gunnar. 1983. "Krigstid og Landssvikoppgjør i etterkrigstid," in Gunder Egge, Gunnar Nissen, and Johannes Dannevig (eds.), *Den dømmende makt. Domstolenes organisasjon og virksomhet*, Oslo: Universitetsforlaget.

Nußberger, Angelika. 2012. "Judicial Reforms in Post-Soviet Countries: Good Intentions with Flawed Results," in Anja Siebert-Fohr (ed.), *Judicial Independence in Transition*, 885–908. Heidelberg: Springer.

Poulsson, Erik T. 1958. "Den Norske Sakførerforening juli 1941–mai 1945," in Rolf Christophersen (ed.), *Den norske Sakførerforening 1933–1958*, 91–221. Oslo: Den Norske Sakførerforening.

Rüthers, Bernd. 2015. *Die unbegrenzte Auslegung Zum Wandel der Privatrechtsordnung im Nationalsozialismus*. Oxford: Mohr Siebeck.

Schjelderup, Ferdinand. 1945. *Fra Norges kamp for retten 1940 i Høyesterett*. Oslo: Grøndahl & Søn.

Skinner, Stephen. 2015. "Conclusion: Repression and Legality," in S. Skinner (ed.), *Fascism and Criminal Law History, Theory and Continuity*, 191–196. Oxford: Hart Publishing.

Støen, Ane Ingvild. 2013. *Justisdepartementet under okkupasjonen*, Masetoppgave i historie Institutt for arkeologi, konservering og historie, University of Oslo, available at https://www.duo.uio.no/

Tamm, Ditlev. 1984. *Retsopgøret efter besættelsen*. Copenhagen: Jurist- og økonomforbundets forlag.

Wyller, Thomas Christian. 1953. *Fra okkupasjonsårenes maktkamp*. Oslo: Johan Grundt Tanum.

Zezza, Stefania. 2015. "Norway: A Country Dealing with Its Past. Reflections on Civilian Resistance in Norway During the Second World War," *Trauma and Memory* 3(3): 98–109.

7
Finland
Lawyers In and Out of the Shadows of Political Liberalism

Esa Konttinen[*]

1. Introduction

According to the theory of legal complex, lawyers' actions that favor or resist political liberalism are closely connected with the positions, cultural character, and roles of their core institutions in society: the courts, bar, academic institutions, legal departments of state administrations, and legal firms. At the same time, liberal action implies the autonomy of the bar and the judicial system, even amid a general cleavage in political society pitting the state against society, such that lawyers can claim to be the spokespeople of the public. Allying the various parts of lawyers' collectives can improve the possibility that efforts to advance political liberalism succeed (Halliday 2010; Karpik & Halliday 2011; Feeley 2014).

Lawyers have made not only advancements into but also retreats from political liberalism. To Halliday and Karpik (2014: 6–7), such a dynamic has predominated in circumstances in which lawyers perceive society to be socially and culturally chaotic, conditions that threaten the very basis of lawyers' existence.

The relationships between lawyers and political liberalism are quite complex and specific to the society in question, meaning that careful historical analysis is necessary. In the following pages, we study how lawyers' sociocultural character, their institutions, and their positions in Finnish society influence their orientations and activities around issues of political liberalism. This research may produce especially interesting results given that lawyers have for more than a century constituted a core elite group within Finnish society. Indeed, it seems that in their privileged position of close ties with the state, they had quite limited aspirations to promote political liberalism—with the partial exception of legal academics. Their roles and fates in the Finnish Civil War (1918) even strengthened an orientation that turned against liberalism politically. Furthermore, the bar's exceptionally weak position undermined the probability of the emergence of an independent counterpower for the state, which in some societies, in some periods, could become an

[*] Professor (emeritus), University of Jyväskylä.

Esa Konttinen, *Finland* In: *The Limits of the Legal Complex.* Edited by: Malcolm Feeley and Malcolm Langford, Oxford University Press. © Esa Konttinen 2021. DOI: 10.1093/oso/9780192848413.003.0007 influential element in creating and defending political liberalism. Only during recent decades have there been consistent factors orienting lawyers in favor of political liberalism, and thus certain major changes occurred. These have been largely influenced by strong motives from outside the national legal complex.

We begin with a short review of a primary element of the issues concerning political liberalism in numerous societies: the historical character of the courts.

2. Courts: Born into a Political Shadow

Finland was a part of Sweden until 1809, when it was annexed to Russia as a grand duchy after the Finnish War. Finland remained in this state until gaining independence more than a century later, in 1917. As such, Finland originally maintained the social institutions of Sweden and conformed to its societal norms. One of the farthest-reaching elements of this remote heritage has been a broad stratum of free peasants[1]—broader in Finland than in the western coast of the Gulf of Bothnia—and the weak feudalism that resulted. Free peasants participated in local matters, including parish and community meetings, as well as in local court systems (*tings*). The peasantry was bound within this society by an inclusionary ideology of "law as for the good of the common man," which gave rise to a panel of laymen in local court processes (Letto-Vanamo 2014). In the old Swedish system, laymen represented local authorities, customs, and common sense. Modéer (2003: 157) has noted that the system was a marriage on the one hand between elitism and state control, and on the other, democracy and proximity to the local environment. In this context, a judge was an autocratic leader of the court process, and the position of any attorney was quite technical yet invariably secondary to that of judges. No educational qualifications were required in order to practice as an attorney, educated lawyers being particularly scarce in Finland. This system has remained strong in Finland, where major changes have occurred only in modern times (Pihlajamäki 2009; Letto-Vanamo 2014).

In Finland, the role of court actor did not encourage attorneys to pursue active political influence. Finnish courts never constituted the theater, where dramaturgical battles to capture the attention of the general public were waged. The situation was highly unlike that of France, where lawyers of the bar formed an independent and powerful political force (Karpik 1997).

This state of affairs more generally reflected the secondary position of the court system in society, where the representative system of politics and the bureaucracy

[1] Perry Anderson (1978: 176) locates the free peasantry's remote roots to Scandinavian Viking society, which was based on a system of slavery exploiting foreigners brought from abroad, whose influx made possible a broad stratum of free peasants in society. At the end of Viking societies in the eleventh century, this stratum was strong and steady enough to endure.

clearly dominated. It was typical of Sweden in the sixteenth to eighteenth centuries that coalitions between a king and the estates, as well as those between and within estates, often fluctuated, meaning that in this country with such weak feudalism, no stable power constellations could exist (Anderson 1980). This situation may have stifled the court's ability to develop into a powerful political institution. Complex changes in the political configurations of chief powers probably left insufficient space for the courts to evolve into a strong balancing institution and leading status group. On the contrary, given such volatile circumstances and attempts to stabilize society, a representative system with forms already established seems to have become necessary. The diet of the four Estates—the nobility, the clergy, the bourgeoisie, and the peasantry—formed the representative organ. These status groups were also the basis for social privileges.

Having outlined the history of the position of the early court system in Finland, we turn to the position of lawyers, the history of which has followed an entirely different route. For more than a century, lawyers formed the most prestigious and elite stratum of Finnish society, arguably due to the development of the bureaucracy in the early period of the grand duchy. Only then and in that context did educated lawyers surface in Finland.[2]

3. Lawyer–Bureaucrats at the Top of Society

Immediately after Finland was annexed from Sweden to Russia in 1809, an administrative bureaucracy began to develop in the new grand duchy. This bureaucracy was a highly hierarchical organ, with a senate as its leading body and a Russian governor general as its president. A great deal of power was concentrated in the hands of top bureaucrats in the Senate and in the Committee of Finnish Affairs in St. Petersburg, where the body introduced domestic affairs to the emperor. Finnish administration really wielded supreme power within the country, but, on the other hand, it was subordinate to metropolitan power and could only act within the limits imposed from above (Alapuro 2016: 4–5).

As part of Sweden, Finland had lacked its own central administrative apparatus, meaning that as a grand duchy, there was an urgent need for qualified administrative personnel to manage the new situation. New examinations for administrative functionaries were established as early as 1817 at the university in Turku (later moved to Helsinki), and notably, these examinations were legal in nature (Konttinen 1991a: 505–511, 1991b: 113–121). The bureaucracy thus became a locus of educated Finnish lawyers. The proportion of officials who had passed

[2] The requirement that some administrative officials pass a legal examination was established in 1749 (Ylikangas 1988: 190–191). However, in eastern Sweden, only a few administrative posts existed. A handful of educated jurists emerged at the Court of Appeal in Turku.

legal examinations was 74 percent in the Senate during the period 1809–1859, and grew to 84 percent between 1860 and 1909. In fact, by 1852, passing the legal examination had become compulsory for all lower officials in the Senate. Furthermore, during Finland's period as a grand duchy, a clear majority of members of the Senate and senators were lawyers by profession.

Also important from the perspective of our theme was that higher-level lawyer–bureaucrats became closely connected with the First Estate—that is, the nobility—which urgently needed new posts suiting their status.[3] Indeed, in addition to military officer, bureaucratic officer became the most important profession for the nobility. Of all higher-level civil officials, 50 percent were noblemen in 1820, a figure that by 1860 had dropped to only 44 percent (Mikkeli, cit. Konttinen 1991a: 505; see also Ylikangas 1996: 483). Czar Alexander I, who maintained the earlier Swedish practice, further secured positions for nobles by requiring that at least half of all members of the Senate be noblemen. By 1850, however, the proportion had increased to 76 percent (Konttinen 1991a: 503–504). Owing to these favors, the Finnish nobility felt deep gratitude toward Alexander, whose aim was to nurture a satisfied upper class as an added security against Western powers.

Lawyer–bureaucrats and military officers now held the core posts in the bureaucracy and formed the core status strata of Finnish society at the time.[4] The bourgeoisie was far from being able to challenge this bureaucracy-centered power system. In this undeveloped administrative political system, the highest court belonged directly to the bureaucratic complex. The Senate was divided into two departments: one for economics and one for the judiciary. As such, the legal department functioned as Finland's Supreme Court, and accordingly, the bureaucracy became an absolute instrument of rule for the czar. For those working at the top, it was also a locus of power and status within the grand duchy.

Table 7.1 shows that the public sector was the domain of lawyers in nineteenth-century Finland. Business remained weak, and independent attorneys formed only a narrow stratum. Lawyer–bureaucrats often performed the tasks of attorneys on the side.

[3] The Finnish nobility was in essence an office-holding class. Since the broad stratum of independent peasantry left little room for noble land ownership, state office furnished nobles with their primary source of income. According to some estimates (Wirilander 1974: 192), only three percent of Finnish noblemen during 1721–1800 held no office. Furthermore, only one office remained for the nobility: army officer. Accordingly, in 1730, 91 percent of all Finnish noble officials were in the service of the military, and by 1800, the figure grew to 93 percent. The Finnish nobility thus confronted a profound crisis following Sweden's defeat in the Finnish War in 1809, when Czar Alexander dismantled the Finnish army. However, lifelong pensions would not secure the future of the First Estate (i.e., the incomes of the sons of the noblemen). Following a 150-year absence from institutes of higher education, the knowledge from which proved unnecessary on the battlefield, noblemen returned to universities to study law. In effect, the bureaucracy became their stronghold.

[4] As a result, another traditional status-based group in Finland—that is, the clergy, also known as the learned Estate—dropped to a secondary position. As clergymen, schoolteachers, and university professors, the class became entirely dependent on the bureaucracy, though its members would again move to the forefront of society in the second half of the nineteenth century.

Table 7.1 Locations of lawyers in Finland, 1879 and 1898

	1879 (%)	1898 (%)
The court system	45	33
The Senate	14	14
Other administration	22	28
Business	4	6
Legal practice as attorney	3	5
Other	12	14
Total (%)	**100**	**100**
Total (number)	**667**	**992**

Source: Konttinen (1991a: 515).

At the dawn of the twentieth century, there were one thousand lawyers in Finland. The only major proportional change during the two decades was thus their concentration in administration and their decreased participation in the court system.

4. The First Liberal Wave: From Above

During the first decades of Russian rule, all opportunities for liberalism were rigidly curtailed. Censorship was strict, and nationwide civil society associations were prohibited unless they could demonstrate their political harmlessness. Furthermore, the Diet of Finland was not allowed to convene. This system encountered an initial break in the mid-1850s, however. Two liberal waves emerged during Finland's time as a grand duchy, the first following the ascension of Alexander II to the throne in 1855 and Russia's defeat in the Crimean War (1853–1856), and the second after Russia's defeat in the Japanese War (1904–1905).

Pressures for liberalization in Russia had increased, and when reform-minded Alexander II gained power during the Crimean War, circumstances were ripe for change. They were similarly ripe in Finland, where certain circles of the Finnish gentry—above all, Fennoman nationalists and liberals—hoped that more liberal circumstances would enrich Finland's economic and public life. The grand duchy's economic life had advanced, albeit slowly, due in part to numerous bureaucrat noblemen becoming involved in more modern economic activities. The liberal-minded emperor played a decisive role in ushering in some forms of liberalization. During his visit to the Finnish Senate in 1856, Alexander dictated in the minutes his proposals for social and economic reforms. Committees were established to plan reforms (Kekkonen 1998: 28–29; Viljanen 1988: 90–101) and ultimately, in 1879, full freedom to act was implemented, which gave citizens formal economic freedom (e.g., freedom of mobility). Unsurprisingly, the liberalization was supported by industrialists, the non-privileged bourgeoisie, and wealthy peasants, for all of whom liberalization would be profitable; and opposed by the privileged bourgeoisie and craftsmen.[5]

Some opportunities for political action soon occurred. Censorship was mitigated[6] and national associations allowed to an unprecedented degree. The Diet of Finland's system of four Estates began to resurface in 1863, after more than fifty years of marginalization. Women gradually earned rights such as plenipotentiary status (if unmarried and over 25 years old) in 1864, statutes of legacy in 1878, and the full right to university study in 1901. Of several other reforms realized, among the most important was the reform in Finnish municipalities in 1864 and in towns in 1873, which as similar reforms had done in Sweden, broadened remarkably the influence of locals in local matters. In this wave of reforms, the grand duchy also took the first short steps toward religious liberty. The Evangelical Lutheran Church was organizationally separated from the state, and the Church Act of 1869 paved the way somewhat for freedom in religious matters. Henceforward the right to separate from the Church would be allowed. The development, however, was slow. The Lutheran Church had long been an important instrument in keeping the population loyal, and that was the case not only during the Swedish period, but also during the grand duchy. Religious freedom would have weakened this function of religion for the rulers.[7]

[5] Finland and Sweden had a common outstanding early defender of liberalism, Anders Chydenius (1729–1803), born in the Sotkamo municipality in Eastern Finland. After having studied mathematics, natural sciences, Latin, and philosophy in the universities of Turku and Uppsala, Chydenius made his career as a rector in the town of Kokkola on the eastern coast of the Gulf of Bothnia. In his works and as a member of the Swedish diet, Chydenius, who was influenced by the Enlightenment, demanded the liberalization of economic life, classical liberal rights, democracy, and the abolition of gentry privileges. Among Chydenius' achievements in Sweden are said to be the limited freedom of the press (1766) and limited freedom of religion for foreigners (1799), and gradual liberalization in the nineteenth century. But in Finland, his practical influence was quite minor after Finland was detached from Sweden and annexed to Russia in 1809. Attempts to follow Sweden were made by bishop Jacob Tengström and later in the 1860s by members of the constitutional law committee (Viljanen 1988: 88–95), but without success. Today, Chydenius' works and political action have won much recognition. It has been stated that he presented much the same ideas on free trade as Adam Smith in his Wealth of Nations, but eleven years earlier.

[6] Censorship became stricter again at the end of the century during the so-called "years of oppression."

[7] Ruling through the Church was organized with the help of a broad stratum of clergymen, who kept the people loyal. The number of clergymen had increased in Sweden, mainly for the benefit of the king. Following this and efforts of the Church (Konttinen 1991b: 83–89), the profession formed in the nineteenth century the broadest educated professional stratum in Finland (Konttinen 1991a: 517). The clergy formed a representative Estate in the diet, which often allied with another conservative Estate, the peasantry.

The first liberal turn was essentially allowed, if not arranged, from above; accordingly, it took a direction heavily influenced by industrialism and cultural aristocracy. Unlike in Sweden, no pressure was required from the lower social classes (Alapuro & Stenius 1987: 34). Everything happened within the frames set and controlled by the Russian emperor. Alexander II converted two-thirds of the members of the Senate into more liberal political actors and even nominated as senator the leader of the Fennoman national movement, Hegelian philosopher J. W. Snellman. In this liberal wave, even bureaucrats at the highest level could change their stance and become proponents of liberalization. The reform was in fact what the Finnish gentry had sought: economic liberalization and freedom of speech, the press, and association (Pulkkinen 1987: 56). With very few exceptions, however, basic individual human rights were not yet established by law. Privileges were still based on the principle of Estates. The legal department of the Senate functioned as Finland's Supreme Court.[8] The diet remained undemocratic.

During this period of change, the role of lawyer–bureaucrats was chiefly that of agents of the bureaucracy. Reforms were given to lawyers in the Senate to both plan and execute (Kekkonen 1998: 25–32; Stenvall 2000: 81–82). As a result, the legal systematization of reforms advanced, bolstered by the advancement of legal education in the university. In the hands of educated lawyers, reforms became codified into legal acts. To some degree, the development of the roots of the legal justice state aligned with the development in Prussia in the 1800s, as described by Dietrich Rueschemeyer (1997: 216). There, Rechtsstaat roughly referred to a state in which the rule of law prevailed, state functioning was subordinate to the law, and laws were controlled by independent courts and challenged by an established bar. However, in the grand duchy, only the first aspect of this three-pronged ideal became a reality. Through German influences, including that of German legal thought, attempts to render the Finnish legal system predictable were made (Pihlajamäki 2004: 144–162). This doctrine, which later did become dominant in Finland, emphasized the mechanical application of law. It was the bureaucratic judiciary that developed in Finland, not challenges by the bar association nor controls by independent courts. Furthermore, legal codification and legal control were exercised in the frame set by the emperor (Pajuoja and Pölönen 2011: 41–42).

During the liberal turn, establishing nationwide voluntary associations became possible (Konttinen 2003: 111–116). As an organization harmless to Russian rule, Juridiska Föreningen i Finland was founded in 1862, and was in existence unofficially from 1856. This association seemed to focus on legal issues in a rather technical manner. Its members ranked among the very elite of society, as proven by

[8] Through initiatives in the diet, a committee was established in 1864 to plan a new constitution involving a limited form of parliamentarism and an independent supreme court. The proposed reforms were given no opportunity to proceed.

the composition of members in its central department in Helsinki.[9] Later in 1898, lawyers supporting the Finnish language founded Suomalainen Lakimiesyhdistys (Finnish Lawyers´Association), an act that exemplified the struggle between the Swedish and Finnish languages. Two presidents (K. J. Ståhlberg and P. E. Svinhufvud) of independent Finland served as chairs of this association during the grand duchy years.

Significantly, these judicial associations in Finland were characterized by their close relationships with the leadership of the emerging state. Many of their leading members represented the highest administrative political and academic elite of the country even into the 1960s, after which some major changes occurred (Pajuoja and Ervasti 1994: 103). This closeness has meant orientations aligned with those of the most elite of the state bureaucracy, and that Juridiska Föreningen and other judicial associations founded later encountered few opportunities to develop as spokespeople and representatives of citizens with viewpoints critical of the state. They were not collective actors with their own moral and political culture who operated distinctly from those of the bureaucratic elite.

Yet the close relationship of the emerging state and the leadership of civil society associations did not concern only lawyers, but was a general characteristic of the civil society in Finland, as it was in other Nordic countries (Sivesind and Selle 2010; Stenius 2010). This was particularly the case in Finland,[10] and even popular movements had leaders at the top of the bureaucracy. In light of later developments in Finnish society, such companionate relations of civil society associations and the state have clearly constituted one pillar of the corporatist model of Finnish governance.

In sharp contrast to certain other major associations of the period, Juridiska Föreningen was not a movement by character, but an elite club, whose distance from the common people was vast. To the majority of lawyer–officials who represented the most privileged elite of the nation and enjoyed great material rewards

[9] In 1862, a third were noblemen, more than half were officials in the Senate or other administrations, some were senators, and five were professors of law (Konttinen 1991a: 513).

[10] Fennoman leaders—so-called "Old Fennomans"—had won central positions in the leadership of the state apparatus by the end of the century. At the same time, they had led important movements, including the hierarchically structured mass organization Kansanvalistusseura (The Finnish Lifelong Learning Foundation), a robust temperance movement, and even a labor movement in its initial phase. With their Hegelian doctrines, these conservative Old Fennomans sought to suppress civil society associations under the auspices of the state. Though they ultimately did not succeed and the associations gained greater independence, the affiliation model became a continual one. The close relationships of the movements and Fennoman leaders in the late 1800s can be interpreted in the light of nation building as the most important effort of the Finnish gentry during the period. As a part of this effort, among the chief interests of these Fennomans were to improve the social position of Finnish laypeople by developing basic education and advancing the use of the Finnish language in public office. The Fennomans saw the free peasantry as the core of the Finnish nation. They were not, however, at the forefront of political liberalism or democracy, and they were not separatists. Their conservative social and ideological character was closely connected with that of the old gentry group: the learned Estate and the clergy. But differing greatly, for example, from judicial associations, they were major actors in mobilizing civil society, which brought about more associations than perhaps anywhere else at the time (Siisiäinen 2009).

(Nevanlinna 1907), inequality was a natural state of affairs. The conservative representative system and status-based privileges suited the broad ranks of these lawyers well, though individual lawyers were liable to participate in movements.

Other parts of the legal complex remained weak in this country of conservative representative organs and powerful bureaucracy. Though numerous reforms in the second half of the nineteenth century precipitated the need for educated attorneys (Pihlajamäki 2009: 126–142), their numbers remained scant.[11] As Table 7.1 shows, attorneys comprised only five percent of lawyers in 1898, and despite attempts in the last decades of the century, their own association was founded much later, in 1919. As stated earlier, purportedly democratic local court processes made it impossible to monopolize the advocacy of educated lawyers. Court processes were highly formalized and did not allow much room for the intervention of attorneys. In numerous cases, office-holding lawyers practiced advocacy as a secondary occupation. The bar was far from able to function as a challenger of the state. Considering all legal professionals together, office-holding lawyers dominated their ranks, and the fate of the bar was to linger in the shadows.[12] The legal department of the Senate continued to act as Finland's Supreme Court.

5. The Second Liberal Wave: From Below

Toward the end of the nineteenth century, after the period of Liberalism, Russia exercised still stricter control over Finnish political life and the political freedoms of citizens. Steps were taken to align Finland more closely with Russia and to reduce the autonomy of the grand duchy. But soon after the turn of the century, the situation suddenly changed.

Whereas the first liberal wave was arguably arranged from above by the emperor, the second wave essentially emerged from below, namely from the demands of Finnish movements. But as so often in Finnish history, this wave of political change generally revolved around changes in foreign relations. Russia's defeat in the Russo-Japanese War (1904–1905) opened the gate for political upheaval in Russia, and in the weakened state of Russian rule, opportunities emerged in the grand duchy for liberal reforms. Protests had already gathered steam among some circles of the Finnish gentry against Russia's attempts at more thoroughly integrating Finland into the motherland.

[11] There was one full-time attorney per 52,000 inhabitants in Finland at the dawn of the twentieth century, whereas in Prussia during the far earlier 1850s and 1860s there was one per 12,000 people, one per 1,970 in France, one per 1,240 in Great Britain, and one per 2,700 in Belgium (Rueschemeyer 1997: 210; Pihlajamäki 2009: 89).

[12] The founding of a bar association was discussed in Juridiska Föreningen as early as 1870 (Pihlajamäki 2009: 129–130). In those discussions, civil servants also sought to gain the opportunity to act as attorneys, and ultimately an independent bar association was not founded.

An essential new political factor, the political labor movement, had grown in Finland by this time and could now have encouragement from revolutionary events in St. Petersburg. The movement grew rapidly into a primary factor of political power that demanded democracy and the institutionalization of the principles of political liberalism (Laine 1946; Viljanen 1988: 106, 151; Kujala 2016).

As demands for autonomy, democracy, and civil rights became louder, in 1905 massive demonstrations were arranged in Helsinki and other cities. Various protest groups affiliated with others to render their protests influential, and alliances between political powers shifted (Alapuro 1988: 101–127; Kujala 2016). Conservative political parties were forced to acquiesce to many demands from the radicalized political labor movement, a defender of the principles of equality and political liberalism. But even from the elites came calls to broaden civil rights. The defense of autonomy of the grand duchy through organized protest presupposed rights such as press freedom and free assembly (Viljanen 1988: 105).

After a general strike in November 1905, the older undemocratic diet proposed both its own abolition and the establishment of a parliament. Without delay and without modification, Emperor Nicholas II accepted the proposal made by officials of the Finnish Senate (Apunen 1987: 203), and a modern—indeed, the most modern in Europe—unicameral parliament with common, secret, and equal elections was established. Freedom of assembly, association, speech, and the press were declared.

Legal academics Leo Mechelin, Robert Hermansson, and R. A. Wrede played decisive roles in formulating the new constitution (Viljanen 1988: 62–72; 107–117). Since the second half of the nineteenth century, European doctrines of liberalism had won support among the legal learned of the University of Helsinki. Toward the end of the century, their influence in politics became even stronger. Among lawyers, legal academics were the most willing and able actors to promote political liberalism. These academics did not act as an organized social collective, but as individuals who had internalized Western legal culture. To Rein (1915), Mechelin in particular represented a broader outlook of political science that encompassed more than only legal doctrines. Their influence also reflected the high esteem in which academic life was held in Finland, where the (only) university represented freedom of thought and academic authority. Like learned men more generally, these legal scholars were embraced by the elite and gained great political influence. As the Finnish solution of political liberalism followed measures taken in Prussia, Austria, and Belgium (Viljanen 1988: 112, 125–126, 165; Jyränki 1998: 178–179), for the first time Finland joined the Western liberal tradition of basic political rights. But certain regulations to ensure the privileged position of elite groups were included in the reform. The so-called constitutionalists, including liberal-minded legal academics, succeeded in their efforts to limit radical demands of the political labor movement. In this context strong protection of property was established (Viljanen 1988: 189–202). The greatest power remained in the hands of the emperor. During the remaining eleven years of the grand duchy, his veto made numerous reforms impossible, and the social democrats in the parliament (e.g., 80 of 200 in the first session) were rendered ineffective. Furthermore, the legal department of the Senate still functioned as the Supreme Court.

During these revolutionary years the political labor movement and some radical circles of intellectuals demanded religious freedom and the separation of the Church from the state. Religious freedom was broadened, but the separation failed. Only in the changed political conditions of 1918 did Jews gain full rights as citizens and non-Christians testify in court. A more comprehensive law of religious freedom was put in place in 1923. However, atheists, for example, were still mistrusted, and it was often difficult for them to get work. Since then (and mainly during the last few decades), religious freedom has advanced and the state and the Church have slowly and gradually been distanced from each other.

As Russification attempts intensified at the end of the nineteenth and beginning of the twentieth centuries—a period known as "the oppressive years"—legal arguments came to be used above all to protect the autonomy of the grand duchy. By appealing to Alexander I's promise to honor the autonomous position of Finland and earlier Swedish constitutional acts, critics stalled Russia's attempts to more inextricably integrate Finland into the empire. The issue of constitutionality even became a kind of super-ideology during those few years (Jyränki 1989: 453) when Mechelin played a central role among the elite in the fight against Russification. In the politically momentous year of 1905, all officials in the legal and economics departments interrupted their work to support the general strike (Laine 1946: 225). Protests were also arranged in the lower-level court system.[13] In effect, these collective organs of the legal complex now formed an element, though not uniform, in the fight to protect Finland's autonomy.

Legalists defending Finnish autonomy left their tracks in the country's legal and political culture. It has been noted (Tuori 2002: 66–67) that, owing to this period, constitutionalism has maintained a stronger position in Finland than in Sweden, which represents a more pragmatist orientation toward constitutions. The influence of Scandinavian legal realism also remained quite limited in Finland, where German legal deductivism has been the stronger doctrine.

[13] Russian Governor General Nikolay Bobrikov, a chief contributor to Russification attempts, even claimed that "the Finnish Court did all it could to cancel his policies," and therefore officials of the court could be removed when needed (Apunen 1987: 162). Protests against Russification emerged in the Courts of Appeal in Turku and Viipuri (Kekkonen 1998: 34), where dozens of court officials were removed and substituted with more moderate lawyers. In 1913, a total of twenty-three members of the Court of Appeal in Viipuri were sentenced to imprisonment. One of the leading legal figures, liberal K. J. Ståhlberg, was removed from his office in the Senate in 1903 due to "lack of respect and obedience" (Apunen 1987: 205). In 1914, another leading figure of passive resistance, P. E. Svinhufvud, was fired from his judge's office and expelled to Siberia (Kekkonen 1998: 39). Both were later elected president of independent Finland.

The position of lawyers in administration and political life, and particularly that of legal academics, together with the legalist fight for autonomy, brought legal political culture to the grand duchy. According to Rasilainen (2004: 312), the judiciary was present in the political rhetoric to such an astonishing extent that, "in all cases," desired political aims had to be justified by legal arguments. For him, Finnish legalism has essentially nurtured a culture of legitimation, and Finland's struggle against Russification was its purest manifestation.

6. Tragedy for Finland—How Were Lawyers Involved?

In 1917, when revolutionary chaos erupted in Russia, an opportunity surfaced for Finland, and the Senate declared independence on December 6 of that year. But when Russia's control over Finnish society broke and finally ended, only a few weeks into the new year, the nation plunged into civil war between the so-called "Whites" and "Reds." The political fight for power had intensified between social democrats and the bourgeoisie parties during the year, exacerbated by rapid revolutionary changes in Russia. Both sides had established armed cadres, which rapidly became more influential as no political solution was reached. The war led lawyers into situations and roles that profoundly influenced them in terms of political liberalism. In what follows, we closely review the circumstances that factored into this shift.

At the beginning of the Finnish Civil War, the country was divided into the south, dominated by the Reds, and the midlands and the north, where the Whites dominated. With the aid of German military units the Whites had called, they reached an advantage. Ultimately, in a decisive fight for the city of Tampere the Whites defeated the Reds, thereby ending the war a few weeks later on May 15, 1918.

In the areas they controlled, the Reds established legal codification that has been called "legalistic" (Pihlajamäki 2009: 147). In this system, a revolutionary court was set up in every municipality, the prosecuted were entitled to choose an attorney, and using an advisor was compulsory. However, the Reds had only a small number of educated lawyers at their service, as a large portion had either refused to serve them or had escaped into territory held by the Whites. In practice, these revolutionary courts were occupied by laymen with hardly any education in legal matters. Furthermore, the prestige of the courts among the Reds was not high (Siro 2009: 131–132). The possibility of arbitrariness outside the courts was bolstered in many cases by the longstanding oppression of crofters by estate owners. Red terror, often involving murder, had existed before the Finnish Civil War and persisted outside the battlefield during the conflict.

On the side of the Whites, commanders were initially given broad responsibility in dealing with captives and suspected Red sympathizers. Many Finnish generals, among them Chief Commander Carl Gustaf Mannerheim[14], had served in the Russian army and internalized Russian practices of warfare, including that which made the killing of civilians permissible (Jyränki 2014: 105–107). At the beginning of the war, Mannerheim's legal advisor prepared what became known as the "will be shot immediately" ordinance, according to which even armed civilians could be executed immediately and without court proceedings. The order also allowed the killing of those who surrendered on battlefields, which often occurred en masse.

Though the Whites' terror was most violent just after the war, the chief commander ordered more regulated, less inhumane behavior in dealing with prisoners of war. Field courts were established in every troop division, and educated lawyers were ordered to serve as chairs of these courts, as well as to perform secretarial tasks in some cases. Nearly all of the lawyers in Finland came to work in the special field courts and later in the state's criminal courts. However, their functioning was inconsistent. Court processes were variegated and did not fulfil legal demands. Swedish constitutional acts ratified in 1772 and still applicable in Finland in 1918 denied the establishment of this kind of special field courts. Furthermore, even capital cases were doomed by scant and biased testimony (Jyränki 2014: 164–204; Kekkonen 1998: 54–56, and 2016: 122–126). Far more deaths occurred outside legal practice, often in local settings, in acts of revenge and still more due to hunger in prisoner camps.[15]

Though some lawyers criticized the practices of these field courts,[16] they were not influential. Neither collective opinions nor organized, such criticism and opposition typically constituted the individual protests of a few attorneys and officials. The great majority participated and accepted legally poor procedures (Kekkonen 2016:149–150). Indeed, no collective part of the legal complex mobilized, which raises quite a few questions. The struggle against Russification had earlier proven lawyers' ability to mobilize, as had occurred even in the legal department of the Senate. However, such group-level protests against field court happenings never developed.

The dynamics of this situation played an important role. In Finnish society, now suddenly polarized and hierarchized, fierce competition for power produced leadership on both sides that urged absolute loyalty and submission under strict command. There was no neutral realm.

But situational factors allow only a partial and, as such, unsatisfactory explanation. As concerns the lawyers themselves, structural factors behind their

[14] Jyränki (2014: 125–127) has concluded that the Senate did not want to take the responsibility, but delegated it to Mannerheim in order to avoid criticism.

[15] The Civil War had approximately 38,000–38,400 casualties, with roughly five times more Reds than Whites (Kekkonen 2016: 98–99).

[16] Some lawyers refused to participate in field courts or else tried to bring about milder sentences; a few lawyers found to be "too gentle" were relieved of their jobs. A number of lawyers also petitioned the Senate to be excused from participating in the courts (Kekkonen 1998: 56, n. 44).

behavior can be detected, though research has only recently been able to address these factors with confidence. Our earlier analysis indicates that Finnish lawyers had strongly identified with the upper circles of Finnish society and shared attitudes characteristic of them. Indeed, a feeling of deep division between them and the common people prevailed. On the White side, the issue was not only about a simple class struggle in economic terms. This period of the coming of a new nation was also a period of rising nationalism. The need for a unified nation was something essential in the minds of a great number of the educated and upper class. To them, the revolution was a deception in this sense, something that seriously threatened their understanding of a healthy nation. Those who had broken ranks must be mercilessly suppressed. It was about restoring a healthy nation again. Jukka Kekkonen (1991) has posited that, by its very character, White terror was breaking the will of the enemy.

From the perspective of our topic, attention is directed to the relationships of the civil society associations of lawyers with the state. Given the close relationship of primary lawyer associations with state leadership in late nineteenth-century Finland, a strong continuity can be observed in their connections before, during, and after the Finnish Civil War.[17] In this context, the primary organs of the civil society of the legal profession formed an ideological and personally connected axis[18] with state powers on the side of the victors. It thus seems justified to conclude that the same structure also formed a hegemonic wall against the collective mobilization of any part of the legal complex advocating legality and humanity in post-civil war issues. For underdeveloped parts of the legal complex, it was still more difficult to mobilize collectively, for the primary organ of the entire profession as represented by its leading figures showed indifference to and offered no ideological support for protests. Founded only in 1919, the bar association limited strongly, if not completely, any political engagement. Furthermore, the leadership of the association and the majority of its members were ideologically linked to the Whites.

Much championed by those with advanced legal academic degrees in the highest political posts and allowed by the top legal authorities (Pajuoja and Pölönen 2011: 99–100), a general amnesty was granted in 1918 for those guilty of illegal executions on the White side.

[17] For instance, all the presidents of the Finnish Lawyers´ Association between 1914 and 1928 held the very top positions in Finnish politics during the last years of the grand duchy or the first years of the republic. Among them there were senators, government ministers, and members in the Supreme Court (Pajuoja and Ervasti 1994: 37–40). It should be added that some leading attorneys, both liberal and on the extreme right, have also held high political posts (Pihlajamäki 2009: 119–120). More recently, connections between political posts and membership of legal associations have decreased.

[18] However, as stated earlier, legal or other civil society associations in Finland were not strictly subordinated to the state, but acted as its affiliates, as is the case in Nordic countries in general.

7. Professional Trauma?

For scholars such as Jyränki (2014: 188), the situation described above raises the question of how court processes surrounding the Finnish Civil War and the involvement of lawyers influenced future Finnish society and lawyers. To him, it seems clear that what transpired corroded the trust of much of the Finnish population in the impartiality of the courts and their judges during the two subsequent generations. In addition to the fact that, for instance, several lawyers in the state administration who had participated in these wartime and postwar practices had successful careers, legal activity during and after the war passed without official criticism. Likewise, when extreme right-wing thinking spread in the early 1930s and civil rights became restricted—for example, the so-called "communist laws" rejecting the association of communists—no part of the legal complex mobilized, though there were known to be several judgments clearly in contradiction with the existing law (Jyränki 1989: 528–537; Pajuoja and Pölönen 2011: 116–120). As political expediency overcame legality, direct political violence against leftists was only mildly sanctioned by the courts (Eriksson 1970: 67–68). During the Continuation War (1941–1944) between the Soviet Union and Finland, prosecuted leftists faced difficulties in securing qualified legal aid for their defense (Pihlajamäki 2009: 201–202).

The long silence of Finnish lawyers on human rights issues becomes somewhat comprehensible in light of these occurrences and factors that allowed for the tacit approval of what happened and prevented open criticism within the legal profession. This silence furthermore was tolerated given the apolitical nature of German legal thought dominant in Finland at the time.

To seize an opportunity for a brief theoretical point, I would here like to introduce the concept of *professional trauma*. Smelser (2004: 37–38) states that as a collective phenomenon *cultural trauma* is the result of an acute discomfort entering into the core of the collectivity's sense of its own identity. For Smelser, cultural traumas are made, not born. In our case the trauma was made by lawyers themselves by participating in the inhuman treatment of the defeated Reds that went beyond the law. According to this line of reasoning, that participation wounded the core of their professional identity, particularly from the perspective of political liberalism. Since this cultural trauma is specific to a profession with their specific culture, we may call it professional trauma. Influenced directly or indirectly by their associations, practitioners became involved in poor practice in a way that made them prone to developing defenses that hindered the adoption of high ethical standards. Unethical practices were justified as unavoidable or even necessary. Other reactions might include a segment of practitioners withdrawing and becoming isolated.

For several reasons, this condition is unique to professionals. First, professionals serve certain functions in society considered to be of great value, if not necessity.

Second, professionals require an exceptional amount of trust from their clients in order to function effectively (Freidson 2001: 214–215), and if that trust becomes broken, then the consequences can prove disastrous to both the professionals in question and the profession in general. Third, direct, external control over professionals is difficult to achieve, given that they enjoy significant autonomy in their work.

In fact, given this last difficulty, indirect forms of control or of self-control, such as ethical codes, tend to be exercised by professionals and usually controlled by professional associations developed in part to oversee professional practices. Since these professional bodies control the functioning of the ethical code among their members, they play an important role in the context of professional trauma.

It seems that in Finland, professional trauma characterized the lawyer profession during and after the Finnish Civil War.[19] The silence on human rights in later decades may partly reflect the long-lasting impacts of professional trauma.

To conclude, it is necessary to mention that lawyers were not the only ones among the Finnish professions who were politically oriented to the right during this period. On the contrary, this was common in that stratum. Even extreme right-wing orientations could be found among, for example, teachers and clergymen.

8. Advance Constitutional Control in Parliament

During and just after the victory the Whites strongly leaned on Germany, but after Germany was defeated in World War I, Finland had to change its political course. Finland adopted the form of republic as system of government instead of monarchy, which had won broad support among the elites of the nation.

Tens of thousands of Reds were freed from prison camps at the end of 1918, social democrats were given the right to political action, and parliamentary elections were arranged in the spring of 1919.

Furthermore, the recent Finnish Civil War had created an urgent need to reintegrate the broken nation. A range of laws were passed to meet this goal, including laws (Lex Kallio) for the improvement of the position of crofters and the possibility of their acquiring farms, along with a set of laws to augment social care. In short, the country adopted a democratic representative course. However, to those in power, the victorious party of the Civil War formed a legitimate nation, and as a result, a great many members of the Finnish Parliament were quickly arrested and were no longer able to participate in parliamentary work.

[19] Issues of control and ethical codes have been widely addressed in the sociology of professions. An authoritative figure of the discipline, Eliot Freidson (2001: 214), has held that in the complexity of our present-day society, issues of trust and ethics have taken an even more central place, meaning that the control and guidance functions of professional associations have come closer to the forefront.

Later that year, a new constitution was passed, planned by a small group of lawyers (Jyränki 1989: 476–477; Kekkonen 1998: 58–59), as legal specialists and politicians. The separation of powers was realized, and a distinct Supreme Court and Administrative Supreme Court were established.

From the viewpoint of first-generation liberal rights, the new 1919 constitution basically concerned the systematization of 1906 regulations (Jyränki 1998: 179) according to the influence of nineteenth-century European and US traditions and Scandinavian models (Jyränki 1989: 487). The 1919 constitution consisted of statutes granting civic freedoms, equality, and social rights such as free primary education sponsored by the state, and of statutes protecting property. Viljanen (1988: 250) describes how Finland had now reached a level of basic rights typical in continental European constitutions in the middle of the nineteenth century. However, the political freedom of citizens was limited: the aim of safeguarding "legal order in society" now overcame the rights of individuals (Viljanen 1988: 179, 186). Constitutional legal rules occasionally lost their imperative position to normal laws.

The protection of property had been based on the Swedish constitution of 1772, according to which one's property cannot be taken without legal inspection and judgment. This principle of individual rights gradually advanced toward the end of the autonomy period (Viljanen 1988: 189–209). After the turbulent revolutionary period of 1905–1906, the principle of the protection of acquired rights meant stronger protection for property. As stated earlier, this issue, developed originally by legal academic Robert Hermansson, is interpreted as an achievement of the upper class to safeguard its social position. After the Finnish Civil War, the protection of property became still stronger—now it included a principle of full compensation in the case of expropriation—and has remained basically unchanged. Today, Finland is among the top-rated countries in the world (rated number one in 2015 on the International Property Rights Index) in terms of the strength of the protection of property.[20]

Despite the new constitution's liberalism, features supporting the societal order represented by the Whites were nevertheless included (Jyränki 1970: 23, 2014: 218–219; Viljanen 1988: 179–180). In effect, the political actions of Communists were restricted. The president of the republic was particularly empowered by the new constitution. As stated above, during the 1930s, the interpretation of law in Finnish courts shifted in a less favorable direction from the viewpoint of left-wing politicians and civic activists (Kekkonen 1998: 73–76). In numerous cases, the basic rights of citizens were subject to regulation by normal laws (Viljanen 1988: 213–217). Later in the 1930s, democratic tendencies

[20] See www.internationalpropertyrightsindex.org.

strengthened in governmental politics, and when fascist movements attempted to seize power, some fascist associations were forbidden and their leaders arrested.

Importantly for our purposes, control over lawmaking in Finland came to consist of the self-control of the lawmakers themselves. Finland thus took a different course from countries that had adopted US-style constitutionalism with judicial review (Feeley 2014: 495–497). The dominance of the Finnish Parliament over the court system can still be observed in the fact that the controling system, the Constitutional Law Committee, has been located within parliament and consists of its members. As a manifestation of the continuity of this representative principle, such had already been the case in the first parliament in 1906, its roots firmly set in the Law Committee of the Senate.[21]

The basic task of the Constitutional Law Committee is to ensure the legality of laws according to the constitution in advance. For Husa (2012: 15–16), the Finnish a priori form of controling constitutionality is one of the most strikingly different features compared with other Nordic systems. While judicial review was adopted in many European countries, most notably in Austria, Germany, and France, during the inter-war period (Feeley 2014: 496), the Finnish 1919 constitution prohibited judicial review of the constitutionality of parliamentary acts (Jyränki 1989: 516–519; Scheinin 2008: 137; Ojanen 2009: 195; Lavapuro et al. 2011: 511).[22] Only in the 2000 constitution was this prohibition abolished and restricted judicial review came into force to match the direction of other Nordic countries.

The 1919 constitution additionally established the new offices of legal ombudsman of the parliament, to be nominated by parliament, and of legal chancellor, to be nominated by the president, with origins dating back to the period of Swedish rule. Finland was the second country after Sweden to adopt the system of ombudsman as supreme controller of legality. The legal chancellor exercises legal control over the government; the ombudsman controls the courts, and other officials.

[21] In the late 1870s, Mechelin issued an initiative for the codification of constitutional acts, and in 1884, the Senate established a committee to prepare laws and codify them with the constitution (Rein 1915: 89–91). It thus seems plausible that advance control related to the position of the grand duchy in the Russian Empire allowing the investigation of the relationships of laws of the parties. Knowing Mechelin's strong interest in defending Finland's autonomy, it is no wonder that his persistent pursuit of codification were a part of that cause. In discussions held by Juridiska Föreningen i Finland about the position of courts in examining the constitutionality of statutes, various opinions were proposed (Jyränki 1989: 444–448).

[22] In 1931, Svinhufvud's government attempted to give the Supreme Court the role of examining the constitutionality of laws (Eriksson 1970: 71; Jyränki 1989: 9; Kekkonen 1998: 59, 63). The act did not pass, however, for the political center and left opposed it. Given their political stance, Svinhufvud and his government experienced how the "power of political parties" hindered their radicalized right-wing politics, as ideological uniformity prevailed in the government and the Supreme Court (Kekkonen 2012: 79). However, Svinhufvud was a man who honored legality and was in a decisive position to stop extreme right-wing movements from seizing power by anti-parliamentary methods (Silvennoinen, Tikka, and Roselius 2016).

The situation surrounding the adoption of the new constitution raises a critical question: If lawyers were at the very top of society and their position was strong, as we have seen, then why were courts left in a secondary position without control of constitutionality, and why did lawyers in high posts not make efforts to that end?[23] For one, lawyers had already lost some of their earlier power with the arrival of the parliamentary system, and by the Fennomans conquering a stronger position in the state, they were more likely to favor other areas of educated strata, like the humanities (Ylikangas 1996: 493–513). Second, it was not the courts but the bureaucratic lawyers who had been in a strong position. Above all, they had been accustomed to a bureaucracy-centered system; in fact, the Law Committee had been situated in the bureaucracy for decades. German legal doctrine, with its understanding of lawyers as mechanical users of the law and not as forces of political change, surely contributed to this state of affairs.[24] Third, the previous supreme court of sorts in the legal department of the Senate had lost much of its prestige during the last three decades of the grand duchy. Jyränki (1989: 519–520) has posited that this loss supposedly stemmed from the fact that the legal department of the Senate had been less consistent in its opposition to Russification, while lower-level courts had clearly been more consistent. Ambivalence on this matter had eroded the department's prestige, which in turn decreased the power of its actors.

In fact, in this Finnish system, the oversight of constitutionality and legality has been widely practiced by legal academics. The Constitutional Law Committee has continually consulted them, and they also quite often appear in public. This tradition is an old one and in practice means there is a remarkable dependence on learned legal scholars. In response, questions (e.g., Wiberg 2003) have been raised about who retains the real power of constitutional control: Members of parliament or the constitutional law experts who advise the committee?

9. Weak Bar Association

In several countries, bar associations have been significant actors in mobilizing for political liberalism (Karpik and Halliday 2011: 218–219; Halliday and Karpik 2014), though such has not been the case in Finland. The Finnish bar has been left in the shadows. During the period of Swedish rule, relatives and others trusted by the prosecuted depended on talented laymen employed by noblemen to act as their advocates. The court process was, however, dominated by a judge, and advocates played insignificant roles (Pihlajamäki 2009: 141, 222). The Finnish bar

[23] For comparison, in Norway at the end of the nineteenth century, the Norwegian Supreme Court succeeded in seizing the power to investigate the constitutionality of laws (Viljanen 1988: 40).

[24] Furthermore, the long tradition of favoritism during Russian rule (Ylikangas 1996) had strengthened this orientation.

modernized slowly during general societal modernization in the late 1800s. Educated lawyers specializing in advocacy emerged, along with private advocacy firms, the first of which was established in 1888. From that point on, a university examination in law was required for advocacy in higher courts, as advocacy began its slow separation from lawyer–bureaucrats.

Finland's national bar association, Suomen Asianajajaliitto, was founded decades later in 1919, after inflation had eroded the standard of living of advocates. Other motives for its founding included raising the diminished status of advocates, and achieving the status of a profession that can engage in the important task of critically challenging the liberal state (Pihlajamäki 2009: 115, 129, 135–139). By the end of 1919, 177 lawyers had joined Suomen Asianajajaliitto, and by the early 1930s, the association had more than five hundred members (ibid: 165, 179).

As stated earlier, the right of laymen to act as advocates has been conceived in Finland as a long-standing democratic tradition. This is why only 210 advocates had passed the university legal examination in 1954, and some were occupied serving in other offices (Pihlajamäki 2009: 216). Finnish advocacy was one of the freest in Europe, and even when the position of the Finnish bar association was promoted in the 1958 reform as a public legal association, the right of laymen to act as advocates remained safeguarded. Leftist members of parliament had particularly opposed the monopoly, for one of the principal changes in the new advocacy law was that advocacy could now be managed as a primary office only and solely by members of the bar association. Nevertheless, the situation continued to resemble that of two hundred years earlier; the court process was strongly centered on judges, and space for prosecutors and advocates was quite limited.

Accordingly, the silence of this professional group did not shift toward activism. On the contrary, the 1960s seems to have been the most silent period (Pihlajamäki 2009: 226) in the history of the association. The number of members at the time decreased to no more than 350, supposedly due to a 1958 reform. This silence was again backed by an understanding of the courts influenced by German legal doctrine as mechanical users or adopters of the law and not as political actors (Letto-Vanamo 2014: 224–226). To change the conservative silence of Finnish lawyers, a strong catalyst was needed from outside the old associations of the legal profession and their ranks. In the 1960s, one such catalyst emerged.

10. The End of Silence

The end of Finland's Continuation War with the Soviet Union in 1944 saw the liberation of all left-wing political associations—instead several war-related, right-wing ones were now forbidden—and the rise of stormy but peaceful competition between political powers. Despite the new political situation, no transformation concerning constitutional oversight arose in Finland, and changes were minor compared to those effected in 1906 and 1919.[25] Generally, the administrative and professional elites would keep their posts.

Minor collective ruptures in the sociopolitical mentality among Finnish lawyers at the level of civil society occurred in this new atmosphere. These changes date back to the founding of Ihmisoikeussäätiö (the Human Rights Foundation) in 1949 by Ihmisoikeusliitto (the Union of Human Rights)[26] in order to promote human rights, a democratic constitution, and democratic culture. There was a law bureau in the foundation whose lawyers acted as advocates to defend prosecuted leftists and trade union activists, for example, in the context of labor strikes. In 1954, these lawyers and a few others established Demokraattiset Lakimiehet[27] (Democratic Lawyers), an association closely connected with the political movement of the Democratic League of the Finnish People (Fredman 2008) and more left-wing than the social democrats.

Demokraattiset Lakimiehet developed as an association on the periphery of the core professional group of lawyers, which, according to Halliday (2010: 217–218), was common elsewhere at the time. However, the imminent rupture among lawyers was not due to any simple evolution of this association, but was essentially pushed by the cultural and societal radicalism of educated younger generations of the 1960s and 1970s, lawyers among them. Furthermore, the changes were closely connected with the development of the welfare state and, later, still more with Finland's international relations.

Common to the Western world, this radicalism in Finland was fed by rapid industrialization and economic growth in the 1950s and 1960s—only then did Finland develop into a modern industrial society—as well as a collective will to maintain distance from the so-called "war generation" and its values (Tuominen 1991). Among the young and educated, sustained economic growth had fed the optimism and values of cultural liberalization, social equality, and the defense of the positions and rights of minorities. So-called "one issue" movements emerged: a Russellian-type peace movement, a movement attempting to promote the social position of the poor, one demanding improvement for Roma, a movement for

[25] For Scheinin (2001: 245), as an exception to other Nordic countries, Finland's position on property rights was developed within the country's constitutional law during the late 1940s out of fear that Finland would fall into Soviet hands.

[26] This association in part dates back to 1934, when it was founded as a committee against death sentences, given the demands by the extreme right to restore death sentences (Kekkonen 1998: 73). The committee ultimately organized a petition that roughly 100,000 Finns signed. In Finland, death sentences during peacetime had been abolished as early as 1826 by Czar Nicholas I, who upon ascending the throne pardoned prisoners sentenced to death (Kekkonen 1998: 23). The goal of populating Siberia had been behind this policy. From this time onward, people condemned for serious crimes were sent to that remote region; from Finland, a total of 3,321 persons were sent to Siberia during the period 1826–1888.

[27] The association was named after the Union of International Democratic Lawyers (IADL) founded in 1946 by lawyers acting in the Nürnberg Trials (Fredman 2008). The first president of IADL, Rene Cassin, is known for having prepared the UN Declaration of Human Rights in 1948.

improving the position of prisoners, the sexual minority movement, the women's movement, the third-world movement, and the modern environmental movement. In pamphlets (Eriksson 1967), the poor legal position of marginalized groups was often stressed, and young professionals such as physicians, social scientists, humanists, and lawyers participated in and led the movements. Later in the 1960s and early 1970s, such radicalism broadened and became more closely connected to leftist political parties and Marxism.

In the early 1970s, Demokraattiset Lakimiehet evolved into a more influential association, partly due to the strong motivation provided by then-president Urho Kekkonen, a doctor of law himself, in his interview in 1970 in *Lakimies*, a periodical of Suomen Lakimiesliitto (the Association of Finnish Lawyers).[28] In what has been called a wedge for broad ranks of lawyers (Pajuoja and Ervasti 1994: 142–156; Fredman 2008: 6; Pihlajamäki 2009: 241–244; Salojärvi 2013: 340), Kekkonen openly stated that old ranks of lawyers represented a bygone world and values alien to common people. He also argued that legal science is biased in favor of conservative social circles. This is exactly what younger radicalized lawyers had insisted. Kekkonen also lambasted the action of courts in the context of the Finnish Civil War and the later political trials of the 1930s.[29]

As an authoritative figure in Finnish politics, Kekkonen's speech offered strong encouragement to radicalized lawyers and law students. In response, Demokraattiset Lakimiehet became activated and reorganized its ranks to form a collective body for reform-minded, liberal, and leftist lawyers in general, not only leftist advocates. Characteristic of the period, the board of executives of the association was elected by political principles: one third representing social democrats, one third people's democrats, and one third the political center. The long period of silent Finnish lawyers was coming to an end. As a conclusion of his comparative study Salojärvi (2013: 352) writes that the most striking difference between Scandinavian countries was that critical legal scholarship was more radical and political in Finland.

Opportunities for change seemed favorable. Though members of Demokraattiset Lakimiehet formed a small minority in the legal profession—no more than 10 percent in 1971—the political parties supporting them enjoyed a majority in the Parliament. The activity of the association grew and membership climbed to approximately 800 in 1982 (Fredman 2008). Contributing to the change was the rapid growth of a new generation of law professionals (Table 7.2).

[28] The interview was arranged by younger lawyers representing the left-wing radicalism of the period.

[29] At a broad political level, the interest of both Kekkonen and the general public in Finland focused on political security issues, which materialized in the Conference on Security and Co-operation in Europe in Helsinki in 1975. Human rights were firmly on the table, which surely strengthened consciousness about them in Finland as well.

Table 7.2 Number of lawyers in Finland, 1898–2003

1898	992
1939	2,323
1970	4,465
1975	6,766
1982	8,973
1988	11,290
2003	15,790

Source: Ervasti (2005: 359).

This intellectual radicalism of law students clearly echoed international shifts (Salojärvi 2013), but one can also suppose that national history played a part. As stated earlier, as a result of the Civil War, a great part of the Finnish people lost confidence in the impartiality of the courts. Distrust was also characteristic of the legal radicals at the beginning of the 1970s. The courts in particular became a target of the criticism (ibid: 294–298). Distrust can be clearly observed in the state committee report by Oikeuspoliittinen toimikunta (Legal-political committee, 1971) issued by the popular front government soon after Kekkonen's speech, and written by three prominent young lawyers representing the Social Democratic Party. The report stated that one of the decisive issues in the discussion about the system of courts was whether the courts themselves were to be integrated into the democratization process. The policy of control by the system of courts was not experienced equally, the report stated, and therefore the most important target in the long term was to make equality and democracy realities.[30] Numerous acts were proposed, including those that would strengthen the position of laymen in court processes, and it was recommended that higher judges' offices be nonpermanent. The renewal of legal education was also proposed by increasing the presence of social sciences in the curriculum.

The approach of the report, as with the entire criticism of legal matters, was strikingly sociological.[31] The need for change in the courts system was advocated

[30] It was stated in the report that 39 percent of Finnish lawyers came from the highest social strata, while their proportion in the general population was 1.6 percent. Only 7 percent of lawyers came from the lowest strata, which constituted 49.5 percent of the population (Oikeuspoliittisen toimikunnan mietintö 1971: 270). A starting point for criticism was a doctoral dissertation (Blom 1970) that revealed the attitudes of Finns toward lawyers, which were interpreted to suggest that a great deal of the Finnish people did not trust the impartiality of the courts. However, the dissertation did not reveal any major differences between confidence in the courts and that in other institutions.

[31] A close connection of legal thinking and social sciences had its institutional manifestation in the association of Oikeus- ja Yhteiskuntatieteellinen Yhdistys (the Association of Legal and Social Sciences)

by referring to the changes occurring in society (Oikeuspoliittisen toimikunnan mietintö 1971: 32–39), which reflected the more general frame of intellectual thinking at the time, holding that society and its structures were the basic units for change. Young leftist and liberal lawyers maintained close contacts with social scientists, and Demokraattiset Lakimiehet also ranked them among its members. This general intellectual frame was an important determinant for these lawyers and paved the way for new legal paradigms (and not vice versa) such as empirical emphasis of realism and, later, Marxism in legal thought. This social mentality can correctly be conceived as something quite opposite to the faith in judicial review.

Characteristic of 1960s' sociocultural radicalism in Finland was the emphasis on the principles of tolerance, social equality, democracy, and social justice. The rational optimism of influencing and planning through state structures was also typical, as was strong faith in modernity in general: in industrial and economic development, in steering social development through science, and in trust of the centralized state. This atmosphere had much in common with social engineering and social engineering projects, which Koivisto (2012: 168) has called part of the Nordic mentality of welfare state building. Generally, in this atmosphere academic legal thought began to abandon its deep-rooted principle of one correct legal solution, and this tendency strengthened in the 1970s (Salojärvi 2013: 267–282). Thus, more room appeared for broader principles in legal reasoning than was the case in the long tradition of Finnish legal thought. In the "sociological period" of the late 1960s and early 1970s, the principle of social rights won support among radicals, and later the more general principle of human rights.

From the viewpoint of our focus on lawyers and political liberalism, it is noteworthy that this radicalism and optimism produced a group of lawyers able to gain political influence and dedicated to social justice. As shown later, its greater importance materialized in the late 1980s and 1990s with the advent of attention to fundamental rights and human rights issues in the Finnish justice policy. Many proponents of these principles at that time were in the 1960s and the 1970s activists in the movements and were now holding influential posts in state administration and politics, in various professions, and as professors in universities.[32] To put the changes in the legal profession into a larger socio-historical context, one reason for the importance of the 1960s and 1970s radicalism in Finland lies in the fact that no major changes had occurred earlier. In a number of defeated European countries, political and administrative elites underwent a profound turn following the

founded in 1970. Many of the founders were activists in Demokraattiset Lakimiehet. The organizations together established periodical Oikeus (Justice).

[32] Although organized attempts at keeping radical leftist intellectuals from influential posts in society were made in the 1970s and later, as was the case in West Germany (known as Berufsverbot), no such broad prohibition occurred in Finland. The sharpest confrontations were over by the end of the 1970s.

outcomes of the World War. That happened in only a very limited way in Finland, and not in the courts and the legal profession. This is why the influences of two and three decades later were a remarkable break with the past.

11. The Welfare State

Changes in the character of this new generation of lawyers were closely tied to the building of the welfare state, which has occurred in Finland since the late 1950s, when welfare was pushed by the trade union movement and the political center and left. According to Hänninen (2001: 29–33), the Finnish welfare ethos surfaced in political battles in the process of mutual recognition. Once decided and realized, the reforms won support among large swathes of the population. Rapid industrialization, catalyzed by war reparations to and subsequent regular trade with the Soviet Union, produced economic resources for welfare reforms, promoted particularly by Popular Front governments during 1966–1971 and 1975–1982. Welfare reforms in Finland were justified not as the social rights of individuals, but as the "rights of citizen groups" or the "population," or else for "solidarity between citizens" or "societal justice and equality" (Kotkas 2014: 141).

It might be assumed that since welfare state building in Finland was a complex political process involving political parties and trade unions, the legal system—the courts in particular—as policymaking parties were left still further in the shadows. However, welfare reforms themselves influenced the legal profession as a whole. Following the Swedish model, an initiative of the Popular Front government in 1973 established public legal aid offices to help poorer citizens, though the measure was opposed by the Finnish Bar Association, which belonged to a conservative camp of lawyers. Advocates of these offices could join the Bar Association, and the bar as a whole thus started to shift ideologically toward embracing welfare state principles and practices. The reform also minimized the need for uneducated attorneys, who had tended to serve the poorest of society. The decrease in those practicing advocacy as a secondary occupation or as work on the side also contributed to the bar's professionalization (Pihlajamäki 2009: 236–240, 244–254).

In Finnish welfare state building, higher education expanded rapidly in the 1960s and 1970s, as did the number of lawyers, though those passing the examination in social science now occupied an increasing number of posts in public administration.

Introducing welfare state mechanisms particularly increased the need for regulation (Ervasti 2005: 357–358), which created a host of new tasks in the state machinery for lawyers to complete. So did the development of frequently established special courts, whose members included not only lawyers but also representatives of social interest groups, and where social conflicts were resolved before escalating (Nousiainen 1995: 66–67, cit. Ervasti 2005: 362). This inclusion of interest groups in the pre-political process is a cardinal characteristic of Finnish corporatism, manifested most readily in long-standing planning procedures of state committees.[33] Since divergent interests are reconciled and potential conflicts resolved before having to enter the courts, these procedures were among those that kept the courts from becoming a more central institution in Finnish society.

Furthermore, a developed governmental control system of legality erodes the possibility of the courts taking on this role. The system consists of the parliamentary ombudsman (since 1920), of specific legality controlling authorities like the office of Valvira in the social and health sector, of regional administrative offices, and of specific legality and interest ombudsmen[34] (Ylönen 2015: 1–2). A citizen has a right to choose an authority to appeal; the parliamentary ombudsman is a general one that includes the whole field. The position of the latter was strengthened during postwar decades, particularly in the 1990s and 2000s (Pajuoja and Pölönen 2011: 162–165, 341–342, 505). This role resembles greatly that which exists in Sweden (ibid: 186).

Among other forms of legal expansion, the number of planning personnel who had passed the legal examination increased. The body was thus no longer overwhelmingly of upper-class origin, as earlier lawyers had been. More noticeable, however, has been the decline of the social status of judges, who by the 1980s resembled other officeholders. In fact, judges have even planned strikes to advocate for their economic demands (Pajuoja and Ervasti 1994: 225–229).

Together with this expansion, legal education in the universities experienced a change from the late 1960s onward, when scholars representing modern legal paradigms, the analytical school and its realism, obtained teaching posts. Old deductive legal thought, German *Begriffsjurisprudenz*, gradually lost its grip (Tuori 2011) and the new generation of lawyers benefited from modernized legal education. Social science played a considerable role in the initial phase of change in the 1960s and 1970s.

We have seen that the political history of the Finnish nation and the national history of Finnish lawyers within their institutions have largely been different from those that contributed to the development of rights-based ideologies among lawyers in a number of other countries. However, certain rights-related solidarity ideologies emerged in the 1960s outside the legal complex, but penetrating its elements. The seeds then planted proved to be influential much later, when new internationalization and globalization forces intervened in Finnish legal life.

[33] Members of these state committees are appointed not only from political parties, but also from interest groups such as business, trade unions, and civil society associations. They also carry out empirical research work and deal with various interests and potential conflicts. Thus they prevent deeper conflicts from emerging. The system was largely given up in the 1990s as "too heavy and too rigid."

[34] Today there are ombudsmen of equality, data protection, consumers, patients, minorities, foreigners, non-discrimination, and children.

12. The Late Discovery of Rights

Duncan Kennedy (2006: 65) has outlined three broad, partly overlapping, long-term waves in the globalization of legal thought in the Western world: the rise of classical legal thought during 1850–1914, the rise of socially oriented legal thought during 1900–1968, and the globalization of human rights since 1945. The first period was very much a result of the work of economic powers shifting from mercantilism to liberalism, while the second was due to the rise of political powers in response to strengthening economic actors. In this sense, the coming of human rights has been the result of ongoing globalization, economic and otherwise, and of the changing principle of identity in today's world: the group loses its centrality as an identity category in favor of the individual. Kennedy has underscored that the development has not been mechanical, but instead a result of the interplay of economic, political, and institutional factors. Lawyers have important roles within this interplay: they participate in the continuous transformation of how society understands economic development.

Kennedy (2006) has posited that each of the above stages discovered a bundle of rights typical of the period. Classical legal thought brought about individual and property rights with the principle of formal equality, whereas the second period of the "social" founded group rights and social rights with the principle of social justice. The principle of human rights in turn is based on the principle of individual difference.

This overall development has occurred in Finland too. Mercantilism was pushed aside by ruling Russian emperors and the rising economic powers in the grand duchy, while later individual political rights were pushed forward in the 1906 and 1919 constitutions. The social circumstances of large groups of the population were also improved, largely owing to the need to reintegrate the broken nation after the Finnish Civil War. Then, from the 1950s onward, the social welfare needs of large numbers of the population were satisfied during the building of the welfare state, via political struggles. Political powers demanding these reforms appealed to the principle of solidarity, and their successes in these battles were accepted by large groups of citizens. Again, however, constitutional rights were not a mode of their establishment. As shown above, and as Kennedy has generally averred, with the thinking of an avant-garde group of lawyers, this period was strongly influenced by social policy and social science, with the principle of social justice at the center of the frame.

The third period—in the globalization of legal thought—in Kennedy's typification concerns human rights. In this schema, human rights play the same role in the contemporary legal consciousness that private rights played in classical legal thought and social rights played in the period of social-mindedness. Kennedy (2006: 59–62) has argued that this period was also built on the criticisms of the previous era—on the disappointment of "social." For him, beyond those foundations were criticisms of the ability of governments to master international relationships (e.g., the wars in Vietnam and Afghanistan) and of the state bureaucracy to deal with human needs. Above all, social-mindedness was unable to take individual difference into account. People today have a number of cross-cutting identities, which often contradict those of others, if not the majority of people. Thus, for Kennedy, the conceptualization of rights based on the principle of the group can no longer be valid.

The last decades have heralded the triumph of the dual principle of limited government through constitutionalism and judicial review. As an attempt at limiting the government and protecting individual liberties, this development has often been described as a "rights revolution" (Feeley 2014: 497). While the concept of social rights brought social science to the fore, the concept of human rights positions judges as heroic figures of the third globalization (Kennedy 2006: 65). Courts and judicial review thus have new opportunities to work themselves into the forefront. The principle of human rights makes judges political—those who do "politics by other means" (Feeley 2014: 497–498; see also Hirschl 2011: 459–460)—meaning that their task is to represent the law against legislative politics domestically and sovereign politics internationally.

In Finland, the concept of fundamental rights came to the fore quite late—in fact, only in the late 1980s—although some signs in the legal culture pointing in this direction can be observed in the doctrines of constitutional law prominent during the early 1970s, the Supreme Administrative Court being a forerunner in their application (Ilveskivi 2001: 234). Lavapuro, Ojanen, and Scheinin (2011: 511–512) and Scheinin (2008: 139–140) have argued that constitutional rights lacked all legal significance in Finnish court practice until the end of the 1980s,[35] as was also the case in Sweden, Denmark, and Norway, at least in part. They have posited that Finland's signing of the European Convention on Human Rights (ECHR) in 1989 and the incorporation of its provisions into the domestic legal order in 1990 represent one of the most important sets of events in Finnish constitutional history: "It was the European human rights system, with its extensive case law, that first convinced the reluctant national courts to regard human rights as legally binding and enforceable rights" (Lavapuro, Ojanen, and Scheinin 2011: 513; see also Scheinin 2008: 140–149; Krommendijk 2014: 20–21). An extensive bill of rights catalog was included in the constitution in 1995, both to make it consistent with international human rights treaties and to accommodate the ECHR. In this sense, the ECHR represents an ideological conception of the rights, based on the liberty of

[35] According to Lavapuro, Ojanen, and Scheinin (2011: 520), the Finnish Supreme Court never cited an international human rights treaty provision in its case law prior to 1990. Since 1990, the situation has changed, as those authors attest: "In view of the overall changes in Finnish constitutional rights and human rights culture, EU law emerges as one of the major reasons behind the shift in the legal reasoning from formal, rule-oriented reasoning toward a greater reliance on reasoning from principle" (p. 515; also see Ojanen 2012).

the individual (Scheinin 2008: 150). The rights concern everyone, not only Finnish citizens.

Finland's membership of the European Union since 1995 has been a major source of change in the Finnish legal regime. It was estimated in 2005 that roughly two-thirds of bills were affiliated with the European Union (Ervasti 2005: 366–371; Tala 2005).

Thus in Finland, a key factor was an effective transnational human rights regime in Europe, as Hirschl (2011: 462) has noted. But domestic factors were also at play. According to Lavapuro, Ojanen, and Scheinin (2011: 519, 530), the origins of the transformations derived from and were motivated "originally and in a large measure" by a liberal-leftist rights-based critique of the injustices of existing constitutional practices and as a result of pressure from below—that is, by the actions of practiced lawyers and non-governmental organizations and by media attention. Many of these lawyers and legal scholars were the same avant-garde legal minds who in the 1960s and later had been vocal defenders of the equality and rights of minorities and other marginal groups. In general, the subtext of their efforts has been moral. The association of Demokraattiset Lakimiehet (later Demla) also participated in the criticism (Fredman 2008: 19–20) by, for example, making a thorough appeal to the ombudsman of the parliament to improve the treatment and rights of foreigners in Finland. Among Finnish universities, researchers from the Swedish university in Turku (Åbo Akademi) are said to have been important catalysts during the years of change (Pajuoja and Pölönen 2011: 430). All told, it came to be understood that the courts in Finland have the competence and even the duty to apply a catalog of fundamental rights, even of a foreign origin, as a normative basis for reviewing decisions and other measures taken in the application of domestic law (Pellonpää 2008; Scheinin 2008: 141).

The influence of 1960s radicalism on the rights revolution occurred to a considerable extent through persons who had at the time internalized values important for them two decades later. Those values constituted a basic orientation that was now directed toward supporting individual liberties and rights. They also supported the promotion of the position of people belonging to disadvantaged and vulnerable social groups. At the same time, this radicalism changed the legal cultural space more generally and contributed to a new intellectualism among legal scholars and lawyers. The emergent cultural orientation distanced itself from the Finnish lawyer culture of decades earlier by being more open to rights principles. Of course, changes also occurred at a much broader cultural level. With the weakening and collapse of the Soviet Union emerged more political room for Finland to shift toward the West.[36] Part of Finland's willingness to adopt European Union standards perhaps becomes more understandable in light of these profound

[36] It is certain that some main driving forces behind the internationalization tendencies had for decades been the business interests of the export companies.

changes. No doubt these international changes would have influenced Finnish political and legal culture in human rights issues too had earlier catalysts, including the radicalism of the 1960s, not occurred.

The Finnish bar also developed amid these changes. Civil law processes in court were reformed in 1993, again following the Swedish model (Pihlajamäki 2009: 265). As a result, advocacy took a more central position in court processes, and advocates became independent parties instead of being legal assistants. More generally, changes in the 1990s have been called "a great transformation of the bar" that resulted from a set of tendencies, including internationalization, professionalization, and specialization, as well as the increased number of advocates and their elevated status. There were 564 members in the Finnish Bar Association in 1980, 966 in 1990, 1,539 in 2000, and 1,810 in 2007 (Pihlajamäki 2009: 271, 272–311). As late as 2002, educated lawyers had formed a virtual monopoly in advocacy—not as a result of the demands of the Finnish Bar Association, but instead due to legal matters becoming more complex.

In the 1980s, in the context of certain criminal events, issues of protection by law gained more attention among advocates, as the viewpoint of human rights would later (Pihlajamäki 2009: 289).[37] These advocates were individual lawyers, and not, for example, the bar associations that presented this kind of criticism. During recent years, the Finnish Bar Association has paid more active attention to human rights issues; for instance, to those concerning political refugees.

Changes occurred, and a main stage seems to have been the Finnish Ministry of Justice. Lavapuro, Ojanen, and Scheinin (2011: 519, n. 48) have noted that two ministers of justice—namely, Matti Louekoski and Tarja Halonen, both social democrats—at the end of the 1980s and early 1990s played a key role in "neutralizing the resistance," as they put it, inside the ministry. The Ministry of Foreign Affairs has also received positive commentary from a reviewer for its effectiveness in putting into practice the recommendations of UN Human Rights Treaty Bodies (Krommendijk 2014: 22–24). From 1995 to 2000 the head of the ministry was Tarja Halonen, a lawyer, former minister of justice, defender of minorities since the 1960s, and president of Finland 2000–2012. Officials in her ministry are said to have internalized the spirit of defending and promoting human rights treaties. The minister of justice following Halonen, Tuija Brax, a lawyer from the

[37] One such advocate was renowned public figure Matti Wuori (1945–2005), who bitterly criticized Finnish legal practices from a human rights angle and argued (Wuori 1995) that traditionally the strong position of state administration in practice had largely denied individual citizens' classical rights. For Wuori, the problems rested in the centrality of parliament's Constitutional Law Committee as the overseer of the constitutionality of basic rights. Earlier, he envisioned that joining the ECHR would change the situation dramatically. An authentic 1960s personality, Wuori defended in court those accused of refusing army service in the 1970s. He was chairperson of Greenpeace Finland (1989–1998) and Greenpeace International (1991–1993), a representative of the Green League in the EU Parliament, and he reported on human rights for the European Parliament 2000–2001. Wuori also participated in the work of South Africa's Truth Commission.

Green League, has been portrayed as an equally strong defender of rights-based principles. Initiatives of the ombudsman of parliament have also been recognized (Hänninen 2013: 214–215) as promoting a legal culture that prioritizes basic and human rights. In all, the changes seem to have coincided with strong personalities at the head of offices.

In general, Finland seems to have been quite responsive to EU proposals and demands concerning the incorporation of EU law into the Finnish legal system (Krommendijk 2014). However, Finland's reluctance to ratify ILO 169 Convention 169 on indigenous people's rights, specifically those of the Sami people, has been severely criticized.

The constitutional rights reform of 1995 did not alter the institutional arrangements and power constellations surrounding constitutional rights and human rights. Though the older doctrine prohibiting judicial review remained intact, the interpretive mandate corresponding to the principle of a human rights-friendly interpretation was again reiterated (Scheinin 2008: 142–143; Lavapuro, Ojanen, and Scheinin 2011: 517). Ultimately, the prohibition of judicial review was formally abolished five years later to allow for a weak form of judicial review.

The constitutional reform that entered into force in 2000 introduced a system of decentralized constitutional review. Consequently, courts are able to not apply national legislation that manifestly conflicts with the constitution. The constitution even contains an obligation for public authorities to guarantee the observance of basic rights and liberties as well as human rights (Krommendijk 2014: 21). The centrality of the parliamentary Constitutional Law Committee still prevails and observes the duty to "issue statements on the constitutionality of legislative proposals, as well as their relation to international human rights treaties."

The move toward rights-based constitutionalism has not proceeded without hesitation and argument. In particular, Finnish lawyers and legal academics[38] have recognized that changes in the direction of judicial review may increase the power of courts and judges. According to critics, the positions of parliament and politicians are thus possibly threatened. Among Finnish legal scholars, a vibrant discussion has addressed the position of Finnish courts and judges, in addition to possible dangers, such as juristocracy (Kekkonen 1998: 142–146; Aarnio 2002; Husa 2003, 2012: 14–16; Tuori 2003; Ervasti 2005; Pajuoja and Pölönen 2011: 518–525; Kotkas 2014: 146–151). Occasionally, proposals arise for establishing a distinct Constitutional Law Court, yet currently among politicians and law academics there seems to be somewhat broad support for preserving the system of the Constitutional Law Committee in parliament. The Human Rights Center was

[38] Lavapuro, Ojanen, and Scheinin (2011: 519, n. 48) have argued that, in terms of academic discourse, established private law scholars especially have argued against the rights-based judicial review of ordinary legislation, by defining rights as either subordinated to traditional private law paradigms or as merely representing standards of natural law.

established, though, in 2012 in the office of the parliamentary ombudsman. The role of civil society was strengthened through establishing the Human Rights Delegation, consisting of twenty to forty members, within this center.

References

Aarnio, Aulis. 2002. "Oikeusvaltio – tuomarivaltio?" in A. Aarnio and T. Uusitupa (eds.), *Oikeusvaltio*, 1–12. Helsinki: The Finnish Association of Lawyers.

Alapuro, Risto. 1988. *State and Revolution in Finland*. Berkeley, CA: University of California Press.

Alapuro, Risto. 2016. "Finnish Elites and Russia in the Nineteenth Century," *Petersburgskii istorichjeskii zhurnal* 12(4): 104–128.

Alapuro, Risto, and Stenius, Henrik. 1987. "Kansanliikkeet loivat kansakunnan," in Risto Alapuro, Ilkka Liikanen, Kerstin Smeds, and Henrik Stenius (eds.), *Kansa liikkeessä*, 8–52. Helsinki: Kirjayhtymä.

Anderson, Perry. 1978. *Passages from Antiquity to Feudalism*. London: Verso.

Anderson, Perry.1980. *Lineages of the Absolutist State*. London: Verso.

Apunen, Osmo.1987. "Rajamaasta tasavallaksi", in Paula Avikainen, Ilari Hetemäki, and Erkki Pärssinen (eds.) *Suomen historia* vol 6, 49–407. Helsinki: Weilin & Göös.

Blom, Raimo. 1970. *Luottamus oikeuslaitokseen*. Tampere: Acta Universitatis Tamperensis, Ser. A 34.

Eriksson, Lars D. 1970. "Tuomioistuinten poliittinen valta," in Heikki Karapuu (ed.), *Harvojen tasavalta. Perustuslakien epädemokraattisuus*, 66–77. Helsinki: Tammi.

Eriksson, Lars D. (ed.) 1967. *Pakkoauttajat*. Helsinki: Tammi.

Ervasti, Kaijus. 2005. "Tuomioistuinkulttuurin kehityslinjoja," *Oikeus* 34(4): 352–375.

Feeley, Malcolm M. 2014. "Judge and Company: Courts, Constitutionalism, and the Legal Complex," in Terence Halliday, Lucien Karpik, and Malcolm M. Feeley (eds.), *Fates of Political Liberalism in the British Post-Colony. The Politics of the Legal Complex*, 493–521. Cambridge: Cambridge University Press.

Fredman, Markku. 2008. *Demla r.y. – vähän yli 50 vuotta*. https://demla.fi.

Freidson, Eliot. 2001. *Professionalism. The Third Logic*. Chicago, IL: The University of Chicago Press.

Halliday. Terence C. 2010. "The Fight for Basic Legal Freedoms: Mobilization by the Legal Complex," in James J. Heckman, Robert L. Nelson, and Lee Catabingan (eds.), *The Global Perspectives on the Rule of Law*, 210–240. London: Routledge.

Halliday, Terence C., and Lucien Karpik. 2014. "Political Liberalism in the British Post-Colony. A Theme with three Variations," in Terence C. Halliday, Lucien Karpik, and Malcolm M. Feeley (eds.), *Fates of Political Liberalism in the British Post-Colony. The Politics of the Legal Complex*, 3–55. Cambridge: Cambridge University Press.

Hirschl, Ran. 2011. "The Nordic Counternarrative: Democracy, Human Development, and Judicial Review," *I•CON* 9(2): 449–469.

Husa, Jaakko. 2003. "Perusoikeudet ja vallanjako – suomalaisen perusoikeuskeskustelun sokea piste?" *Oikeus* 31(1): 4–26.

Husa, Jaakko. 2012. "Panorama of the World's Legal Systems – Focusing on Finland," in Kimmo Nuotio, Sakari Melander, and Merita Huomo-Kettunen (eds.), *Introduction to Finnish Law and Legal Culture*, 5–18. Helsinki: University of Helsinki, Publications of the Faculty of Law:.

Hänninen, Sakari. 2001. "Pohjoismaisen hyvinvoinnin poliittinen eetos," *Tiede & Edistys* 26(1): 19–33.

Hänninen, Sakari. 2013. "Tosiasioiden merkityksestä Suomen sosiaalioikeuden laillisuusvalvonnassa," in Marja Pajukoski, Sakari Hänninen, Toomas Kotkas, Eeva Nykänen, and Maija Sakslin (eds.), *Muuttuva sosiaalioikeus*, 193–215. Helsinki: Finnish Lawyers' Association.

Ilveskivi, Paula. 2001. "Fundamental Social Rights in the Finnish Constitution, with Special Reference to their Enforcement by the Administration," in Martin Scheinin (ed.), *The Welfare State and Constitutionalism in the Nordic Countries*, 219–244. Copenhagen: Nordic Council of Ministers.

Jyränki, Antero. 1970. "Kriittinen katsaus perustuslakiemme syntyvaiheisiin," in Heikki Karapuu (ed.), *Harvojen tasavalta. Perustuslakien epädemokraattisuus*, 1–24. Helsinki: Tammi.

Jyränki, Antero. 1989. *Lakien laki*. Helsinki: The Association of Finnish Lawyers.

Jyränki, Antero. 1998. *Valta ja vapaus*. Helsinki: The Association of Finnish Lawyers.

Jyränki, Antero. 2014. *Kansa kahtia, henki halpaa. Oikeus sisällissodan Suomessa*. Helsinki: Art House.

Karpik, Lucien. 1997. "Builders of Liberal Society: French Lawyers and Politics," in Terence C. Halliday, and Lucien Karpik (eds.), *Lawyers and the Rise of Western Political Liberalism. Europe and North America from the Eighteenth to Twentieth Centuries*, 101–123. Oxford: Clarendon Press.

Karpik, Lucien, and Terence C. Halliday. 2011. "The Legal Complex," *Annual Review of Law and Social Science* 7: 217–236.

Kekkonen, Jukka.1991. *Laillisuuden haaksirikko*. Helsinki: The Association of Finnish Lawyers.

Kekkonen, Jukka.1998. *Suomen oikeuskulttuurin suuri linja*.Helsinki: Publications of Finnish Lawyers' Association Ser. C 32.

Kekkonen, Jukka. 2012. "The Finnish Path to a State Based on the Rule of Law: From the 1850's to the Present," in Kimmo Nuotio, Sakari Melander, and Merita Huomo-Kettunen (eds.), *Introduction to Finnish Law and Legal Culture*, 75–84. Helsinki: University of Helsinki, Publications of the Faculty of Law.

Kekkonen, Jukka. 2016. *Kun aseet puhuvat. Poliittinen väkivalta Espanjan ja Suomen sisällissodissa*. Helsinki: Art House.

Kennedy, Duncan. 2006. "Three Globalizations of Legal Thought, 1850–2000," in David M. Trubek, and Alvaro Santos (eds.), *The New Law and Economic Development. A Critical Appraisal*, 19–73. Cambridge: Cambridge University Press.

Koivisto, Marjo. 2012. *Normative State Power in International Relations*. Oxford: Oxford University Press.

Konttinen, Esa. 1991a. "Professionalization as Status Adaptation: The Nobility, the Bureaucracy, and the Modernization of Legal Profession in Finland," *Law & Social Inquiry* 16(3): 497–526.

Konttinen, Esa. 1991b. *Perinteisesti moderniin. Professioiden yhteiskunnallinen synty Suomessa*. Tampere: Vastapaino.

Konttinen, Esa. 2003. "'Finland's route' of Professionalization and Lawyer-Officials," in W. Wesley Pue and David Sugarman (eds.), *Lawyers and Vampires. Cultural Histories of the Legal Professions*, 101–121. Oxford: Hart Publishing.

Kotkas, Toomas. 2014. "Suomalainen hyvinvointivaltio ja sosiaalisten oikeuksien lyhyt historia," in Olli Mäenpää, Dan Frände, and Päivi Korpisaari (eds.), *Oikeuden historiasta tulevaisuuden Eurooppaan. Pia Letto-Vanamo 60 vuotta*, 135–152. Helsinki: Finnish Lawyers' Association.

Krommendijk, Jasper. 2014. "Finnish Exceptionalism at Play? The Effectiveness of the Recommendations of UN Human Rights Treaty Bodies in Finland," *Nordic Journal of Human Rights* 32(1): 18–43.

Kujala, Antti. 2016. *Vastakkainasettelun yhteiskunnan synty*. Helsinki: The Finnish Society for Labour History.

Laine, Y. K. 1946. *Suomen poliittisen työväenliikkeen historia, part I*. Helsinki: Tammi.

Lavapuro, Juho, Tuomas Ojanen, and Martin Scheinin. 2011. "Rights-based constitutionalism in Finland and the development of pluralist constitutional review," *I•CON* 9(2): 505–535.

Letto-Vanamo, Pia. 2014. "Nordic Democracy Facing the EU: Traditions, Myths, and Challenges," in M. Fichera, K. Tuori, and S. Hänninen (eds.), *Polity and Crisis. Reflections on the European Odyssey*, 217–234. Farnham: Ashgate.

Modéer, Kjell Å. 2003. "From 'Rechtstaat' to 'Welfare State': Swedish Judicial Culture in Transition 1870–1970," in W. Wesley Pue and David Sugarman (eds.), *Lawyers & Vampires. Cultural Histories of Legal Professions*, 151–167. Oxford: Hart Publishing.

Nevanlinna, Ernst. 1907. *Virkamiesolomme. Millaiset ne ovat ja millaiset niiden pitäisi olla?* Helsinki: Suomalainen Kustannus Oy Kansa.

Nousiainen, Kevät. 1995. "Tuomioistuimet ja oikeusturva," *Lakimies* 93: 55–68.

Oikeuspoliittisen toimikunnan mietintö. 1971. Helsinki: Valtioneuvoston kanslia, KM B 112.

Ojanen, Tuomas. 2009. "From Constitutional Periphery toward the Center – Transformations of Judicial Review in Finland," *Nordisk Tidskrift for menneskerettigheter* 27(2): 194–207.

Ojanen, Tuomas. 2012. "The Europanization of Finnish Law – Observations on the Transformations of the Finnish Scene of Constitutionalism," in Kimmo Nuotio, Sakari Melander, and Merita Huomo-Kettunen (eds.), *Introduction to Finnish Law and Legal Culture*, 97–109. Helsinki: Publications of the Faculty of Law of the University of Helsinki.

Pajuoja, Jussi, and Ervasti, Kaijus. 1994. *Suomen lakimiesliiton historia*. Helsinki: The Finnish Association of Lawyers.

Pajuoja, Jussi, and Pölönen, Pasi. 2011. *Ylin laillisuusvalvonta*. Helsinki: Tietosanoma.

Pellonpää, Matti. 2008. "Euroopan ihmisoikeustuomioistuimen ja EY:n tuomioistuimen vaikutuksista Suomen valtiosäännön kannalta," in H. Kanninen, H. Koskinen, A. Rosas, M. Sakslin, and K. Tuori (eds.), *Puhuri käy*, 103–127. Helsinki: Edita.

Pihlajamäki, Heikki. 2004. *Johdatus varhaismoderniin oikeushistoriaan*. Helsinki: Publications of the Faculty the Law, University of Helsinki.

Pihlajamäki, Heikki. 2009. *Kansan ja esivallan välissä. Suomalaisen asianajajakunnan historia*. Helsinki: Edita.

Pulkkinen, Tuija. 1987. "Kansalaisyhteiskunta ja valtio," in Risto Alapuro, Ilkka Liikanen, Kerstin Smeds, and Henrik Stenius (eds.), *Kansa liikkeessä*, 54–69. Helsinki: Kirjayhtymä.

Rasilainen, Aki. 2004. *Oikeudellinen argumentointi politiikassa. Suomalaisen legalismin poliittinen historia*. Helsinki: Finnish Lawyers' Association, Ser. A 257.

Rein, Th. 1915. *Leo Mechelinin elämä*. Helsinki: Otava.

Rueschemeyer, Dietrich. 1997. "State, Capitalism, and the Organization of Legal Counsel: Examining an Extreme Case – the Prussian Bar, 1700–1914," in Terence C. Halliday, and Lucien Karpik (eds.), *Lawyers and the Rise of Western Political Liberalism. Europe and North America from the Eighteenth to Twentieth Centuries*, 207–227. Oxford: Clarendon Press.

Salojärvi, Juhana Mikael. 2013. *A Menace to Society. Radicalism and Legal Scholarship in the United States, Scandinavia and Finland, 1965–1980*. University of Helsinki: Faculty of Law.

Scheinin, Martin. 2001. "Protection of Economic, Social and Cultural Rights in Finland: A Rights-Based Variant of the Welfare State?" in Martin Scheinin (ed.), *The Welfare State and Constitutionalism in the Nordic Countries*, 245–285. Copenhagen: Nordic Council of Ministers.

Scheinin, Martin. 2008. "Constitutionalism and Approaches to Rights in the Nordic Countries," in Joachim Nergelius (ed.), *Constitutionalism: New Challenges: European Law from a Nordic Perspective*, 135–153. Leiden: Brill Academic Publishers.

Siisiäinen, Martti. 2009. "Differentia Specifica of Voluntary Organizing in Finland," in Annamari Konttinen (ed.), *Civic Mind and Good Citizenship*, 87–113. Tampere: Tampere University Press.

Silvennoinen, Oula, Marko Tikka, and Aapo Roselius. 2016. *Suomalaiset fasistit*. Helsinki: WSOY.

Siro, Jukka. 2009. *Tuomiovalta kansalle. Vallankumousoikeudet sisällissodassa 1918*. Helsinki: Finnish Lawyers' Association, Ser. A 295.

Sivesind, Karl–Henrik, and Per Selle. 2010. "Civil Society in the Nordic Countries: Between Displacement and Vitality," in Risto Alapuro, and Henrik Stenius (eds.), *Nordic Associations in a European Perspective*, 89–120. Baden-Baden: Nomos.

Smelser, Neil J. 2004. "Psychological Trauma and Cultural Trauma," in Jeffrey C. Alexander, Ron Eyerman, Bernhard Giesen, Neil J. Smelser, and Piotr Sztompka (eds.), *Cultural Trauma And Collective Identity*, 31–59. Berkeley, CA: University of California Press.

Stenius, Henrik. 2010. "Nordic Associational Life in a European and Inter-Nordic Perspective," in Risto Alapuro and Henrik Stenius (eds.), *Nordic Associations in a European Perspective*, 29–86. Baden-Baden: Nomos.

Stenvall, Jari. 2000. *Käskyläisestä toimijaksi*. Tampere: Acta Universitatis Tamperensis 759.

Tala, Jyrki. 2005. *Lakien laadinta ja vaikutukset*. Helsinki: Edita Publishing.

Tuominen, Marja. 1991. *"Me kaikki ollaan sotilaitten lapsia": Sukupolvihegemonian kriisi 1960-luvun suomalaisessa kulttuurissa*. Helsinki: Otava.

Tuori, Kaarlo. 2002. *Foucault'n oikeus: Kirjoituksia oikeudesta ja sen tutkimisesta*. Helsinki: Sanoma Pro.

Tuori, Kaarlo. 2003. "Tuomarivaltio: Uhka vai myytti?" *Lakimies* 101(6): 915–943.

Tuori, Kaarlo. 2011. *Ration and Voluntas: The Tension Between Reason and Will in Law*. Farnham: Ashgate e-book.

Viljanen, Veli-Pekka. 1988. *Kansalaisten yleiset oikeudet*. Helsinki: The Finnish Association of Lawyers.

Wiberg, Matti. 2003. "Perustuslakivaliokunta asiantuntija-areenana," *Lakimies* 101(6): 967–991.

Wirilander, Kaarlo. 1974. *Herrasväkeä. Suomen säätyläistö 1721–1870*. Helsinki: Finnish Historical Society.

Wuori, Matti. 1995. "Lakimiehen yhteiskunnallinen rooli," *Oikeus* 23(3): 280–287.

Ylikangas, Heikki. 1988. *Valta ja väkivalta keski- ja uudenajan taitteessa Suomessa*. Helsinki: WSOY.

Ylikangas, Heikki. 1996. "Autonomisen Suomen virkamieseliitti," in Committee of administrative history. Co-author: Seppo Tiihonen, *Suomen keskushallinnon historia 1809–1996*, 423–516, Helsinki: Edita.

Ylönen, Jussi. 2015. *Eduskunnan oikeusasiamiehen laillisuusvalvonta ja alemmat laillisuusvalvojat – päällekkäisen toimivaltajaon problematiikka*. Rovaniemi: University of Lapland.

8
Iceland
Lawyers, Politics, and Liberalism

*Ragnhildur Helgadóttir**

1. Introduction

Until Iceland gained sovereignty in 1918, questions regarding independence overshadowed all other considerations in Icelandic politics (Hálfdanarson 2001; Kristjánsdóttir 2011: 82). While certain political leaders in the nineteenth century, notably Jón Sigurðsson and Arnljótur Ólafsson, were political liberals, the independence movement was deeply conservative and the same can be said of Icelandic nineteenth-century politics in general. Indeed, it has been argued that the Danish government was the main protagonist when political liberalism came to Iceland in the nineteenth century.

This chapter aims to examine whether the theories of a legal complex—spanning trained lawyers working in all legal fields—mobilizing primarily, but not consistently, for issues that can be classified as classical political liberalism, aptly describe the political activities of Icelandic lawyers, from the late nineteenth century to our times. Political liberalism is then viewed as having three core attributes; a moderate state, civil society, and certain basic legal freedoms (Halliday and Karpik 1997; Halliday, Karpik, and Feeley 2007; Karpik and Halliday 2011).

This chapter therefore describes the activities of the Icelandic legal complex, which has been quite active, for example, in influencing legislation. The aim here is to focus as far as possible on agency, on individual events, and on the unanimity and influence of the Icelandic legal complex and then to consider the results in light of the theories of the legal complex formed on the basis of other stories from very different states.

In this introduction, the methodology of the study will be discussed and some background given regarding Icelandic history and the history of lawyers in Iceland, thus defining the time in which it makes sense to speak of a legal complex. The second part starts with a discussion of the longue durée example of the development of a relatively liberal and robust constitutional jurisprudence around 1900.

* Professor, Faculty of Law, Reykjavik University.

Ragnhildur Helgadóttir, *Iceland* In: *The Limits of the Legal Complex*. Edited by: Malcolm Feeley and Malcolm Langford, Oxford University Press. © Ragnhildur Helgadóttir 2021. DOI: 10.1093/oso/9780192848413.003.0008

We then move on to the crises of political liberalism in which the legal complex took no part ("the non-examples") and from there to the examples of the legal complex's mobilizing due to certain events: Its actions against arbitrary changes to the Supreme Court from 1930 to 1932 and wariness of constitutional changes from 2010 to 2013. A few other examples and non-examples are discussed for comparative purposes and to illustrate the workings of the Icelandic legal complex. In the final part of the paper, conclusions will be drawn and briefly compared to other scholarship on the legal complex.

In order to find examples of the impact of Icelandic lawyers on individual issues or events, newspaper archives up to about 1970 were searched for mention of the Bar Association and the Judges' Association as well as the Law Faculty. I then followed up on those issues where these associations seemed to have impacted or sought to impact anything other than their own organization by examining parliamentary records and other public documents. Those issues which were uncontested in society more generally (such as mobilizing in the late 1950s for more judicial positions) were dropped, although one illustrative example—a recent one concerning appellate courts—is discussed in Section 3.3. I also looked particularly for any signs of engagement of the legal associations on various controversial issues—the "crises of political liberalism" or "big challenges" mentioned above.

The individual events discussed in this chapter are those where the above-mentioned search showed that at least two and up to all parts of the legal complex engaged for a particular outcome. As for more long-term developments where lawyers have been key, there are primarily two possible candidates: The development of constitutional jurisprudence and culture in the decades after 1874, which will be described in Section 3, and the emergence of the regulatory welfare state after World War II. While it is uncontestable that lawyers played a great role in the emergence of the regulatory state, that will not be discussed any further here, since this was to some extent a shared western European and American phenomenon, there were no particular contra-indications or opponents, and agency is very hard to find. Regarding examples of more long-term developments, I relied primarily on secondary sources, to some extent my own as relatively little has been written on legal history of the twentieth century.

The choosing of "non-examples," where the legal complex could be expected to mobilize is methodically difficult, as it implies an evaluation of when the legal complex "should" have mobilized. Five examples in Icelandic history since the 1900s are prime candidates, based on being either important constitutional changes or well-known examples of violations of rights: Icelandic lawyers did not mobilize concerning parliamentarism in 1903, sovereignty in 1918, the jailing of socialist MPs during World War II, the postponing of general elections in 1941, or the different weight of votes in the twentieth century, but the discrepancy was fivefold in the 1979 elections and even greater in 1934. These "crises of political liberalism" where the legal complex might perhaps have been expected to act, but did not, will be discussed further in Section 3.2.

2. Setting the Stage

2.1 Iceland: Constitutional and Political Background

Iceland was part of the Danish state until 1918, when it became a sovereign state united with Denmark in the person of the Danish monarch, much as Norway had been with Sweden from 1814 to 1905.

In 1874, King Christian IX gave Iceland a constitution concerning the country's special affairs, which will be discussed in more detail below. It vested legislative power in those matters pertaining especially to Iceland in Alþingi (the Icelandic Parliament) and the king but was otherwise very similar to the 1866 Danish constitution. Constitutional changes have been frequent in Iceland since 1874, but until 1944 most of them were stepping stones to greater independence and did not change the constitutional structure. In spite of those changes, and the founding of the republic in 1944, the Icelandic constitution is still largely based on the Danish constitution of 1849. That constitution was very liberal by the standards of the times; it guaranteed rights including the right to free speech and to property, as well as habeas corpus and others. It was largely based on the Belgian and Norwegian constitutions of 1830 and 1814, respectively.[1] However, Icelanders categorically denied that this constitution (and the succeeding one of 1866) applied to them; arguing that they had in 1262–1264 entered into a personal union with the king and that the status of Iceland within the Danish state was only for Icelanders and the Danish king—not a constituting assembly or any other government bodies—to decide. While emphatically rejecting that the constitution applied to them, Icelandic political leaders variously resisted all liberalization (including freedom of religion—which the majority of Alþingi rejected in 1863 and 1865) or argued that basic civil freedoms were so obviously to apply to all that they needed no further discussion: "That any man has the freedom to believe what he will, write what he will and have whatever he will printed—while not injuring anyone—is by all in Iceland accepted as by no means excessive freedom," wrote Jón Sigurðsson, the leading (and relatively liberal) politician of the age (Hálfdanarson 2001: 83). Jón Sigurðsson also stressed the importance of the right to property (ibid.: 87, 95–96).

As mentioned at the outset, the status of political liberalism in nineteenth-century Iceland is not a simple matter. In his book on the emergence and limits of

[1] It is generally acknowledged that this basic law was very liberal and very democratic by the standards of the times. (See general discussions e.g., on http://danmarkshistorien.dk/historiske-perioder/det-unge-demokrati-1848-1901/grundloven-1849/)

the Icelandic national state, Guðmundur Hálfdanarson noted that the "freedom" Icelanders argued for was national, not individual (ibid.: 75): Nineteenth-century Icelanders wanted independence from Denmark, but resisted all attempts at liberalizing society, for example by allowing paupers to marry or by allowing people to be domiciled in towns by the sea instead of on farms.

> According to the nation's view of itself, the battle for independence was a battle for freedom and equality for the Icelandic nation and against foreign oppression and limits to freedom. One can point to the fact that Icelanders generally resisted when the Danish government wanted property to be a prerequisite for the franchise in 1843 ... When it came to the organization of Icelandic society, this love of freedom was less evident, or at least it was layered. Whether it concerned the marrying of paupers or the freedom of enterprise of servants, the parliament supported the interest of farmers against those who wanted to rebel against the rules of traditional farming society. [/] In the first years of the battle for independence, it looks like the leaders of Alþingi thought that the key issue for Icelanders was to preserve this layering of freedom.
>
> (Hálfdanarson 2001: 69 and more generally 51–76)

Hálfdanarson argues that Icelandic farmers in the nineteenth century simply did not have the *outillage mental* to be politically liberal and that generally speaking, the Danish government and its members in parliament were the main force driving the emergence of political liberalism in Iceland in the mid-nineteenth century, noting that it argued for freedom of enterprise, for example, but had to compromise given the massive resistance it met on the issue (Hálfdanarson 2001: 72).

The Constitution of 1874 guaranteed the freedom of religion, speech, enterprise, association, and assembly; it had provisions on juridical rights, habeas corpus and so on, the inviolability of the home including a provision on searches and seizures, and it protected the inviolability of property, noting that any taking of property for the common weal would be compensated. It also forbade any special privileges and nobility and provided for social assistance and general education.[2]

Constitutional and political continuity have characterized the period from 1870. Important periods and events to keep in mind for our purposes are: The move toward full independence, lasting from 1848 to 1944; the British occupation and later the stay of American armed forces 1940–1945; industrialization (which came late); and the emergence of the labor unions and the welfare state 1916–1960 and of the regulatory state after 1945. More recently, growing internationalization of the legal system and of trade (from 1980 onwards) and the financial crisis of 2008,

[2] This is very much the same catalog of "core legal rights" as is viewed as inherent in political liberalism. See Halliday, Karpik, and Feeley (2007: 10).

which also caused a constitutional crisis in Iceland, are key, and will be discussed in Section 3.3.

It should be noted at the outset that Iceland has about 320,000 inhabitants and its government and legal circles are commensurably small. Very few people can therefore have great impact, but criticism is also more costly for the criticizing individual than in larger societies where there are more people and more disparate elites.

2.2 The History of Lawyers in Iceland

The legal profession in Iceland is quite young and, until recently, quite small. In 1882, 134 Icelanders had earned a law degree from the University of Copenhagen. By 1910, a total of 202 Icelanders had earned a law degree but 133 of those had died prior to the year 1900. By 1950, the total number of law graduates, living and deceased, was 497 and it has since grown exponentially (Haraldsson 1993–1997: 11–12). If the year 1900 is taken as an example, the total number of living Icelandic lawyers was forty-eight. This was a small group of people, partly by design as few "secure" appointments were available to lawyers (Sigurðsson 1989: 34). In the 1890s, seventeen district commissioners and chiefs of police formed the first judicial instance, as well as being the holders of highest executive power in the various districts. Their judgments and decisions were appealed to the High Court, composed of three judges (Karlsson 2009: 105).

According to a decree from 1832, every man could argue before the lower courts, since legally trained advocates were scarce (Líndal 1993–1997: 62). In the first years after the High Court for Iceland was established in 1800, there were very few legally trained advocates, so "generally informed and reasonable men" could argue cases before the court (Þórðarson 1947: 67). In criminal cases, it was determined that district commissioners or other "legally knowledgeable" men should speak for the accused. Similarly, someone should be appointed to argue the case when parties to civil cases had legal aid or could for some reason not argue their own case. Usually, either the district commissioner for Gullbringusýsla or the Chief of Police in Reykjavik were appointed as spokesmen in such cases (Líndal 1993–1997: 62).

In practice, most cases before the High Court in the first half of the nineteenth century were argued by young, educated men clerking in the offices of those in highest power (Þórðarson 1947: 157). Finding a legally trained advocate remained difficult. In order to remedy that, a royal decree from March 19,1858 permitted the appointment of two barristers to the High Court and awarded them a fixed yearly salary. They had a monopoly on arguing civil cases before the court, but were seriously underpaid, so this occupation continued to be a stopgap for law graduates waiting to become public officials.

Being a barrister before the High Court did not become full-time employment for the two barristers until 1897–1898. Soon afterwards, in 1905, it was decided by law that all those who could become public officials could argue civil cases before the High Court, by applying once for such a license, but that only the two appointed barristers could defend criminal cases. This was partly due to an increased number of law graduates and partly to discontent with the two barristers' monopoly. Thirty-nine lawyers obtained a license to practice law under this statute.

The Bar Association was established in 1911, by which time a relatively independent bar had emerged (Líndal 1993–1997: 61). In its charter, the role of the Bar Association was defined as "Protecting the interests of its members, support their cooperation and ensure that they follow the same rules regarding remuneration for their work" (Pálsson 1981: 180). According to a festschrift written on the twenty-fifth anniversary of the association, the association proved instrumental in improving judicial processes since:

> When the Association was formed, it was acknowledged that attorneys did what they could to make work harder for their colleagues. Minor formal faults led to requests for cases to be thrown out of courts. A great part of legal documents were personal insults, sarcasm and irony. The public did not view a case as having been duly argued before the courts unless the attorneys were fined for defamation. An unfined attorney had very few clients. The Association changed all this.
>
> Pálsson (1981: 179), citing Líndal 1937.

There are no sources to suggest how this was framed to lawyers themselves: But they seem to have seen the "civilizing influence" of the Bar Association as benefiting themselves as well as the general good.

The Lawyers' Association (open to all law graduates) was established in 1958. It has not been politically active, but organizes seminars and other such activities. The Judges' Association was established in 1941 and the Association of District Commissioners in 1924, but it changed names frequently in the first decades of its existence (Björgvinsson 1991, 1998).

Changes in legal training took place at around the same time as the Bar Association was being established. Until 1908, lawyers trained at the University of Copenhagen. A Faculty of Law was established in Reykjavík in 1908 and in 1911, it merged with the Faculties of Theology and Medicine, as well as the newly established Faculty of Philosophy to form the University of Iceland (Jónsson 1993–1997).

Legal academics thus existed in Iceland from 1908, and as part of a national university from 1911. The establishment of a faculty of law and, later, an Icelandic university, had been discussed since 1850 and had been a bone of contention between Alþingi and the government in Copenhagen since 1867, when Alþingi first adopted a motion asking for such a faculty. The establishing of a law faculty was discussed at every single Alþingi from 1855 onwards and Alþingi adopted numerous bills on the matter, all of which were vetoed by the king (Sigurðsson 1989: 20–22). In 1903, Alþingi adopted such a bill (no. 3/1904), which the king then signed, as Iceland's constitutional status and its financial relationship with Denmark were changing at the time (ibid.: 71). Having a faculty of law in Reykjavik was viewed (in Parliament) as important in order to teach Icelandic law, as distinct from Danish law;[3] to enable those who were to become civil servants in Iceland to study in that country; and to emphasize practical education (ibid.: 72–73). In addition, having higher education in the country (both in law and in general) was viewed as important per se. The bill in 1903 was based on "the new University Act of the Norwegians" (ibid.: 81) and it was frequently noted that the University of Copenhagen should not be the only model for the University of Iceland and that notably the University of Kristiania should be considered as well.

Women came to legal studies relatively late; Auður Auðuns, the first woman to graduate, finished university in 1935, but until the beginning of the 1960s, fewer than ten women had graduated with a law degree. The first female full-time faculty member was appointed in 1978 and the first woman on the Supreme Court was appointed in 1986. From about 1980, women have been half or over half of all law students, but even today, they make up only 22 percent of the members of the Bar Association.

Another great change in the profession came when universities other than the University of Iceland got permission to educate lawyers, around 2000. As of now, four faculties with a combined number of thirty to thirty-five faculty members offer study programs in law or business law. The first few years of multiple universities were marked by a great increase in the number of law graduates, but the numbers have since dwindled. In 2016 about 170–180 students were expected to enroll in first-year law studies but only some of those will graduate after five-years of law study. But compared to the numbers around 1900, lawyers now are numerous. However, the number of those in non-legal jobs remains relatively low (Lögfræðingafélag 2014).

The establishing of the Law Faculty and the Bar Association would suggest choosing 1910 or thereabout as a starting point for this inquiry, since it marks the origins of both a relatively independent bar and legal academics. However, it may be necessary to look also at the preceding period because of the relatively progressive constitutional jurisprudence stemming from the constitution of 1874. Judicial review of an administrative (royal) decree had already been exercised in 1877 and judicial review of legislation existed from 1900 onwards (Helgadóttir 2006: 1). The development of a relatively robust constitutional culture at a time when lawyers

[3] Parliamentarians and other politicians described this well, naming differences in sources of law and influences as well as areas of the law where the difference was greatest.

were very few and there were only two barristers who argued those cases before the High Court, hired by the state and waiting for better public office, is interesting. This will be discussed in more detail in Section 3.

3. When Has the Icelandic Legal Complex Mobilized?

3.1 Longue Durée: Constitutional Jurisprudence (1874–2016)

The 1874 "Constitution on the Particular Affairs of Iceland"[4] was based on the 1849 and 1866 constitutions of Denmark and was an important milestone in the battle over Iceland's constitutional status. That battle lasted from about 1849, when Icelanders flatly refused that the 1849 Basic Law applied to them, until 1918. The 1874 Constitution granted the wish of the Icelanders to have a legislative assembly but not that of also having a one minister cabinet in Iceland (Karlsson 2014: 41). It was based on an Act of 1871, in which the Danish Parliament had unilaterally declared which issues were particularly Icelandic. This—along with the fact that the constitution was also unilaterally adopted by the king—angered Icelanders (Líndal 2011: 13).

Politically, the years after 1874 were relatively calm; Icelandic politicians were slowly getting used to the legislative and budgetary power that Alþingi had been granted by the 1874 Constitution. But the courts applied the new constitution right away. As early as 1877, the High Court found that a royal decree, in which a particular sheriff was appointed judge in all cases concerning sheep scab (a disease in sheep which required cleansing and eventual elimination of all stock in parts of the country) was unconstitutional. This sheriff had fined a farmer for refusing to obey his orders. The High Court found that the constitution's Article 42, which provided that the judicial system should be set down by law, prohibited giving power over a category of cases to one person by royal decree, since court jurisdictions were otherwise geographically determined.[5] The High Court thus held right away that the constitution was judicially enforceable, also vis-à-vis the king and other authorities.

It may be argued that the High Court was relatively progressive regarding the role of the courts: After the 1877 case—which was discussed in the newspapers as "important"—it reviewed the constitutionality of, for example, church taxes;[6] sanitary installations in Reykjavik; licensing fees on previously licensed pubs;[7] and the loss of liquor licenses due to prohibition.[8] In some of these cases, the cost of

4 Stjórnarskrá um hin sjerstaklegu málefni Íslands, no. 1/1874.
5 Lyrd. I: 249 at 255 (1877).
6 Lyrd. II: 455 (1885).
7 Lyrd. VI: 176 (1900).
8 See e.g., Lyrd. IX. 809 (1909) and Lyrd. X. 20 (1917).

the litigation was split, which has traditionally been the Icelandic courts' way of awarding a half-point to the losing party: It generally means that the court viewed the litigation as justified and the outcome doubtful. However, the High Court, and later the Supreme Court, upheld legislation in all cases until 1943, when it struck two laws before doing so again in 1946.

It may therefore be argued that between 1875 and 1940, the courts were quite progressive regarding their own role—reviewing administrative and legislative action—while not particularly progressive in protecting rights. The role they carved out for themselves concerning judicial review was important compared to most European countries at the time; equaled (up to 1918 at least) only by the courts in Norway. As I have argued elsewhere (Helgadóttir 2006), Icelandic constitutional developments in this period built on a legal-philosophical foundation which was shared with Norway and the United States, corresponded with similar developments in Norway and shared some traits—and intellectual ancestors—with pre-World War II constitutional jurisprudence in the United States, emphasizing vested rights and an abhorrence of special legislation. The courts, also in Iceland, thus positioned themselves as the guardian of a neutral state—which, it has later been argued, was anything but neutral (Helgadóttir 2006: 11–103). The important part for our purposes is that the Icelandic courts seem to have followed Icelandic and Nordic theory and not vice versa. The courts were, in fact, not innovative themselves, since they followed legal theory.

In the context of analyzing the Icelandic legal complex, therefore, the most important point regarding the development of constitutional jurisprudence is this: No real agency can be seen in these constitutional developments. Certainly, in 1885, a lone judge in the Eastern fjords found that an atheist farmer in his district should not pay any church tax—due to the freedom of religion clause in the constitution.[9] However, it seems that the farmer argued his case himself. And the High Court overturned the decision and had the farmer pay the cost of litigation for the priest in his parish, even though it refused to fine the lower court judge for his decision. Similar stories can be told of other constitutional cases of the period. Many cases concerned licensing fees and were thus quintessential vested rights cases, but the constitutional cases that were not were often argued by the plaintiffs themselves. We thus see no activist advocates. The courts, although this is perhaps primarily true of the High Court, were influential and progressive in how they defined Icelandic constitutionalism and the judiciary's role, but they were not particularly progressive with regard to individual rights.

It is therefore likely that jurisprudence and constitutional theory did the real work here; it was viewed as evident (also by judges and the bar) that the 1874 Constitution would be robustly applied, according to nineteenth-century

[9] Lyrd. II: 455 (1885).

constitutional theory. As previously mentioned, two laws were struck down as unconstitutional in 1943 as well as one taking property, which had a statutory basis, but was struck down as inconsistent with the protection of private property in 1946. One of the 1943[10] cases concerned prior restraint on speech: A blanket prohibition on publishing the sagas (written before 1400) unless under license and with a specific modern spelling. This was struck down as unconstitutional. The other case[11] concerned the repeal of an act granting tax exemptions to filmmakers. A filmmaker held that having been granted a three-year exemption while the act was in force, its repeal could not change his tax status for the worse, and the Supreme Court agreed. The argument that the real work was done by legal theory becomes even more persuasive when we see that in the 1943 free speech case (which is celebrated as the first case where a law was found unconstitutional), there are no mentions of judicial review or standards of review in the documents or arguments as noted. In other words, there is no evidence of the attorney for the accused (whose conviction was overturned) arguing the statute's unconstitutionality. This limited (or at least poorly documented) role of attorneys in constitutional cases seems to be the norm until the 1970s. This is strange, for attorneys who bring cases before courts are generally immensely influential in the development of jurisprudence. But the decision in the 1943 case on the prohibition of prior restraint on speech seems to have been made more or less *ex officio*. And there are no particular attorneys who focus on this field or argue many such cases, until the 1970s and 1980s. Up until the 1970s, therefore, according to the sources we have, judges implemented constitutional developments while members of the bar were relatively passive and other state actors gave tacit consent.

So while Icelandic constitutional jurisprudence, especially after 1874 and in the first half of the twentieth century, was very influential, especially in drawing up the constitutional order of the country—because of how it defined the role of the judiciary—and was based on the work of legal academics and judges, it is not a particularly good example of the legal complex mobilizing. The reasons for this are numerous: Firstly, the importance of constitutional theory in this predefined constitutional sphere and the corresponding lack of agency matter: In the absence of activist attorneys, it cannot be said that anyone chose or pushed this agenda, instead, it came to all involved as part of their official duties, which they fulfilled in accordance with the dominant legal theories at the time. Secondly, civil servants are largely missing from this narrative and thirdly, attorneys were more or less passive.

Like in the other Nordics, the emphasis in the decades after World War II was on building the welfare state. This is true even though Icelandic politics have been

[10] Hrd. 1943: 237.
[11] Hrd. 1943: 154.

more fragmented than the politics of its neighbors and there has not been the same Social Democratic Party dominance as, for example, in Sweden. The building of the welfare state had started earlier; the labor unions had already formed ASÍ in 1916 and social security existed, although it was unified and defined as a key feature of the state only after World War II. There were, however, a few waves of litigation due to the reorganization of the economy after the war. In practical terms, this entailed the devaluation of the currency and a prohibition on bypassing that (e.g., by linking payments to another currency) as well as heavy taxes on certain kinds of property. All of this was challenged before the courts, and the Supreme Court administered the government a slight slap on the wrist by holding minor provisions to be unconstitutional, while the legislation was for all intents and purposes upheld. These decisions were based on a very deferential stance to the legislature, so that even though the legislation was criticized by the Supreme Court, the legislature's leeway to reorganize the economy after the war was held to be more important.[12]

Judicial review of legislation and constitutional jurisprudence more generally was always a living part of Icelandic constitutional law throughout the twentieth century, but there was an important renaissance after 1990. Up to the late 1980s, the Supreme Court always held that international obligations (most often the European Convention on Human Rights [ECHR]), while binding on the state, could not be applied in domestic courts. This changed in 1990[13] when the Supreme Court changed prior constitutional interpretation to better fit the requirements of the ECHR. Since then, the ECHR has been widely used in constitutional jurisprudence, was incorporated into Icelandic law in 1994, and has been one of the main models for a new human rights chapter in the constitution.[14] The ECHR—and other human rights conventions—are now cited constantly in Icelandic courts and international judgments are frequently part of the arguments. Constitutional jurisprudence has therefore undergone a "rights revolution" and an internationalization; international law and international courts are an integral part of the constitutional order.

As will be discussed further in Section 3.2, there was no unanimity amongst lawyers about the constitutional amendments in 1995, nor do we see any kind of general mobilization for the rights revolution around 1990. Due to the lack of general mobilization and perhaps the fact that this history is shared with the other Nordics, constitutional developments are not a particularly good example of the workings of the legal complex.

[12] See e.g., Hrd. 1952: 434 and Hrd. 1958: 753.
[13] Hrd. 1990: 2.
[14] Act no. 97/1995.

3.2 Non-examples: Crises in Political Liberalism

As mentioned above, it is interesting to examine whether it is possible to approach the legal complex from a "negative" point of view. The five examples in Icelandic history since the 1900s that seem to lend themselves best to the exercise are the following: Icelandic lawyers did not mobilize concerning the introduction of parliamentarism in 1903, sovereignty in 1918, the jailing of socialist MPs during World War II, the postponing of general elections in 1941, or the different weight of votes in the twentieth century, but the discrepancy was fivefold in the 1979 elections and even greater in 1934.

A closer look at the first two instances reveals that they were at the time primarily viewed as political battles between Iceland and Denmark. There was unusual unanimity in Iceland regarding these issues and they were seen primarily as steps toward full independence. It is only recently, with the centenaries of these changes that they have come to be viewed as milestones in constitutional development as well as milestones in the fight for independence. However, there were other possibilities (a presidential-style government or a different political solution regarding the union of Denmark and Iceland), so this also fits the theory of the legal complex, these being some of the most important political questions of the day. But while we may now look at them as milestones in the development of a robust constitutional order they did not have strong links to political liberalism.

The jailing of socialist MPs during World War II and the postponing of the general parliamentary elections in 1941 are linked (Benediktsson 1959: 15). The British armed forces invaded Iceland in April 1940. In the winter of 1940–1941, British involvement in Icelandic politics increased, culminating in late April when the armed forces forbade the publishing of the socialist newspaper *Þjóðviljinn* and arrested Einar Olgeirsson, MP and *Þjóðviljinn's* editor, his co-editor, and one of the paper's employees and sent them to Britain where they were held in custody. However, a unanimous Alþingi as well as the government protested strongly, citing inter alia the constitution's provisions on parliamentary immunity (*Alþingistíðindi* 1941 D: col.5–6). General parliamentary elections should have been held at the end of June 1941, but were postponed. According to the motion of Parliament extending its own mandate past the constitutionally determined four years and thus postponing the election, this was necessary due to the uncertainty reigning in the country, the risk of escalation of armed conflict in and around the country, the effects of British occupation ("however considerately executed" as one MP put it) and the banning of the main opposition paper *Þjóðviljinn,* although the remaining Socialist MPs mocked the idea of the postponement being for their benefit (*Alþingistíðindi* 1941 D: col. 34–42) and voted against it. The motion to postpone elections was adopted with thirty-nine in favor and four against (ibid.: 49). The postponing of the elections was clearly unconstitutional but Parliament openly based its decision to adopt the motion on unwritten emergency powers

(Benediktsson 1959; Helgadóttir 2013). The silence of the legal complex on both issues can persuasively be explained by the fact that these were unquestionably war and emergency measures, all representatives of the state had protested regarding the jailed MPs and the postponing of the elections was based on an evaluation of risk during wartime, undertaken and discussed by elected officials (MPs). The inaction of Icelandic lawyers under such circumstances also fits with the theory of the legal complex as set out by Karpik and Halliday (2011).

There remains only the inequality of votes during much of the twentieth century. The legal complex's silence on the subject may perhaps best be explained by the fact that questions regarding the electoral system and the weight of votes in different districts have been viewed as the quintessential political question. Indeed, many constitutional amendments have been concerned primarily with election rules and the inequality of votes was much discussed during, for example, the drafting and adopting of the 1995 constitutional amendments. So this is a "living" area of constitutional law—under constant revision by politicians and, as such, not a likely area where lawyers of differing political persuasions might unite. Other accounts of the legal complex show that the legal complex is rarely active regarding voting rights. However, a fivefold difference in the "weight" of votes can easily be conceptualized as an equality matter, one that skews all political processes and thus the rights of a group of people. In other words, it could be viewed as the sort of neutral state issue around which lawyers have historically mobilized, according to various accounts of the legal complex. But this has not been the case in Iceland.

Selecting "non-cases" is methodologically difficult, as previously described, and the cases that seem obvious candidates for such status—and have been discussed in this section—are not really illustrative of the legal complex's activity or inactivity. Some are political developments and questions, while others concern wartime emergency measures. All in all, however, there is nothing exceptional (in terms of other accounts of the legal complex) in the silence of the Icelandic legal complex on those matters.

3.3 Mobilization by the Bar Association and Other Legal Bodies

One of the activities of the Icelandic Bar Association has traditionally been to "impact legislative activity, primarily regarding the judicial process in the country, but also to take the initiative regarding legislation." The Bar Association has been immensely active in sending opinions to Parliament regarding proposed legislation. Sometimes such opinions stem from a full meeting of the association, sometimes from its board and sometimes from its "legislative committee." Other associations of lawyers have been less active, but they still tend to react whenever legislation concerns civil and criminal procedure, the organization and duties of the judiciary and prosecutors, bankruptcy, and family law. The Bar Association has thus presented an opinion to Alþingi on close to 300 bills from 2001, compared to thirty-five opinions from the Association of Judges and the Association of Prosecutors, and these opinions are by no means limited to bills concerning judicial procedure. From 1981, the various associations of legal professionals have joined forces to organize a yearly conference for all lawyers. Obviously, topics that are viewed as important at the time are discussed at these conferences, as have the "events" mentioned below.

The individual events discussed below are those where the above-mentioned search showed that at least two and up to all parts of the legal complex engaged for a particular outcome.

A new Supreme Court 1930–1933

In 1930, Chairman of the Progressive Party and Justice Minister Jónas Jónsson submitted draft legislation for a new Supreme Court to the Alþingi. The bill proposed shutting down the current Supreme Court (Hæstiréttur) and establishing in its place a new court, which was to be called Fimmtardómur in Icelandic and Supreme Court in English (*Alþingistíðindi* 1930 A: 161). Apart from introducing an open system of discussion between the justices, which went somewhat further than the Norwegian one, and an upper age limit of 60 years, which would have required the retirement of all Supreme Court Justices in post and hence the appointment of a new court, as well as removing all influence of the court itself on new nominations, no major changes were proposed to the law on the Supreme Court. The comments to the bill (*travaux préparatoires*) said clearly:

> It is completely safe to say, that the Supreme Court has not, in the last few years, enjoyed the confidence that it should. And as has been stated before, many attempts have been made to change the organization of the court, and many are unhappy with the current organization. . . Based on all this, it is by no means erroneous [literally 'without fault'] or for no reason, that it is now attempted to organize the highest court in the country, so that it is as safe as possible and to make the highest court instance such, that it may enjoy as much confidence as possible from every person in this country.
>
> (*Alþingistíðindi* 1930 A: 179)

The reasons for the bill were given as "loud voices in Alþingi and beyond [requesting] the amendment of this Court" (ibid.: 177). Another reason that was given was nationalistic: To revive the name fimmtardómur—used from the year 1000 to 1262 for the appellate judicial and legislative body of Alþingi. The minister argued that the name "Hæstiréttur" had been borrowed from Denmark and was grammatically incorrect as there were only two court instances. The *travaux* stated:

> This alone justifies completely changing the name of the highest judicial instance, at the same time as it is changed drastically. Secondly, everyone knows that in the golden age of the Icelandic Republic the highest judicial instance was named fimmtardómur. It is therefore very appropriate, on the 1000 year anniversary of Alþingi and the Icelandic state, to adopt the ancient name for the last judicial resort and thus show full fidelity to the ancient memory, while at the same time purging from Icelandic legal language a semi-foreign word, which cannot be united with the strict and logical thinking of the Icelandic language.
>
> (*Alþingistíðindi* 1930 A: 180)

The arguments went on in that vein. In political debate in the Alþingi in the spring of 1930, the minister argued:

> The honorable member did not want to change the name of our key court. He did not want a name from the times of the Republic. He did not want to abandon a name, adopted in the period of our submission, a name, which is foreign and grammatically incorrect. It looks like he is afraid of the beautiful name of the key court of the Icelanders from the period of the Free State, from the nation's era of liberty. This pitiful way of thinking exists in old annexationists, who have never believed that Iceland could be anything but a Danish backwater. When the Act on the Supreme Court was drafted in 1919, those who authored the bill were in some respects at the same stage as the honorable member. They went to Denmark and only to Denmark and borrowed a model and a name for the final court of Icelanders. None of these leaders thought of Norway, Sweden, Switzerland or Germany or of the experience of those nations. They knew nothing of those countries. Those who drafted the Act knew nothing of public voting.
>
> (Tíminn 1930b, 3. May: 96)

Even at the time, the draft was viewed by many as the justice minister's vengeful reaction to prior judgments (see e.g., Íslendingur 1930) and most agreed that the substantive changes introduced in the draft could easily be attained without dismantling the current Supreme Court (see e.g., *Vísir* 1930a). Even the relatively party-neutral newspaper *Vísir* wrote:

> Everyone knows why this bill was submitted. The Minister of Justice wants to decide who sits on the highest court in the country. The current Supreme Court justices are no means to an end for him. They are established and experienced men, who do not differentiate based on who is party to a case. The Minister wants a new court – composed of men of his ilk.
>
> (*Vísir* 1930b: 2)

There seems to have been no particular theory or support behind the bill. The criticism referred to by the minister came mostly from himself and his party's supporters—lawyers had not complained and refuted all such claims categorically.

Alþingi split on the issue, but the legal complex did not. The Supreme Court wrote a letter to Alþingi, which was published in the parliamentary documents as well as in at least one newspaper in the early spring of 1930 (*Morgunblaðið* March 2, 1930: 9–10). The Court noted that the proposed changes were unimportant in substance, stated that some novelties were clearly unconstitutional, pointed out fallacies in most of the citations in the *travaux*, and "advise[d] against adopting the bill, which tends very much to weaken the judiciary and increase the influence of politics on the judicial power, even to the degree of violating the constitution" (printed in Committee report, *Alþingistíðindi* 1930 A: 1004). The Bar Association also sent an opinion, drafted by a sub-committee of three and adopted in a meeting by eighteen out of the twenty barristers residing around Reykjavik (ibid.: 1008). It opposed the bill strongly (ibid.: 1009). It noted in particular the "distressing" comments in the *travaux* on the lack of confidence in the Supreme Court.

> This is noted often, directly and indirectly, without any rationale. Even though the committee sees no reason to spend many words on these imputations, it finds it necessary to protest against these unreasoned comments. According to Icelandic Barristers, the Supreme Court enjoys full confidence and respect.
>
> (ibid.: 1011)

Finally, the Professors of the Law Faculty of the University of Iceland wrote an opinion, dated April 7, 1930, which was published in the Parliamentary proceedings (*Alþingistíðindi* 1930 A: 1206–1209) and in *Morgunblaðið* (April 17, 1930: 5). The Faculty agreed that it would have been perfectly feasible to accomplish the desired changes with amendments to the law of the Supreme Court and noted that "no amendment of consequence is intended to the procedure in the Supreme Court" (*Alþingistíðindi* 1930 A: 1209). It argued that the Act on the Supreme Court had functioned well and that there was no discontent amongst judges or lawyers (ibid.). In addition to these formal opinions submitted to the Alþingi and heated debate in the Alþingi, there was a lot of newspaper commentary[15] both times the bill was submitted, student meetings where lawyers gave speeches, and so on. The bill did not pass in 1930 and was resubmitted in 1932, but was not passed then either. In the manner of Icelandic bills with insufficient support, it did not come to

[15] In addition to the cited discussion and data in *Morgunblaðið* (which was the paper of the Conservative bloc) and *Vísir*, see e.g., *Lögrétta* (February 5, 1930: 4); *Vikuútgáfa Alþýðublaðsins* (February 5, 1930: 3). On the other hand, *Tíminn* (the paper of the Progressive Party, the party of the minister of justice) somewhat timidly argued the case of the justice minister, see e.g., *Tíminn* (February 1, 1930: 18). *Tíminn* never published anything from the Bar Association, Supreme Court, or the Law Faculty while this was going on.

a vote before the end of the Parliamentary session. Amendments to the Act on the Supreme Court, drafted by a committee, were then adopted in 1935.

The Justice Minister, Jónas Jónsson, had a tumultuous career, entering politics in 1922 and a minister from 1927 to 1934. While he is remembered for being an educator and reformer; as one of the instigators of the Icelandic party system; and for introducing the Progressive Party as a liberal center party, he was by the 1930s described as "fascist" by his more fiery political opponents in *Verkalýðsblaðið* and *Þjóðviljinn* while even those who were milder and his fellow party members noted his paranoia and bullying tendencies (see e.g., Íslendingur 1930). He engaged in various legal battles around 1930, fired numerous public officials, and was frequently deemed to have gone beyond his authority by the courts; he was compared to Nero and Caligula in Parliament and more or less declared insane (megalomaniac) by the chief physician at the country's only mental hospital, who discussed the minister's health with inter alia the Prime Minister and the Speaker of Parliament and was fully supported by the Association of Icelandic Physicians. Even a very laudatory article about him soon after his death noted that:

> It is far from true that everyone approved of Jónas and his work as minister. . . Jónas' opponents used of course the fact that many of his projects were disputed. The opposition in Iceland has seldom been rougher or less forgiving than in this period and the main thrust of it was against Jónas. . . The unlimited attacks on Jónas made him a power-hungry villain in the eyes of his opponents but a semi-saint in the eyes of his followers. It is probable that no Icelandic politician has been as controversial as Jónas in this period. . . Of course, the harsh attacks of his opponents on Jónas Jónsson affected his fellow members of the Progressive party, as some of them thought he went too fast and was rougher in dealing with his opponents than was appropriate. Jónas also made various important decisions without consulting the party. Some of them were questionable. He became much more influential in the party and did not welcome criticism or complaints from his fellow members. There were therefore often serious controversies between him and individual members of the party . . .
>
> (Þórarinsson 1970: 40–41).

It is also noted in the article that Ásgeir Ásgeirsson, later prime minister for the Progressive Party and president of the republic, and Jónas did not get along, as Ásgeir "thought Jónas too merciless and unfair a politician" (ibid.).

From a cynical point of view, this example of the entire legal complex mobilizing might be viewed as an example of lawyers defending their own institutions and their own reputation. However, the bill on Fimmtardómur was clearly unacceptable from a constitutional standpoint and seems to have been the culmination of attempts to politicize the state administration as well. The legal complex thus mobilized for an independent judiciary and the separation of powers as well as for a non-political state machinery more generally.

The real question in this example is whether the bill and its fate should be seen only as the expression of an ugly fight between the Supreme Court and the justice minister in which the Supreme Court was supported by other lawyers, or as an attempt to grab more executive power and move Icelandic politics in an illiberal direction, which was successfully thwarted by the legal complex and other politicians. It is generally viewed as one of the decisive battles in Jónas Jónsson's career. He quit as minister in 1934 although he stayed in Parliament until 1949 and lived until 1968. Based in part on the overtly nationalist reasoning behind the bill, and the lack of self-control shown by the minister in his dealing with the Supreme Court, I tend toward the latter explanation but, in any case, this is a clear example of mobilization by the legal complex.

The constitutional amendments of 1995 and the limits of the engagement of the Bar Association

The Icelandic Human Rights Center was founded in 1994 and to begin with, the Bar Association was part of it along with the University of Iceland and seven other non-governmental organizations (NGOs). At the same time—around the fiftieth anniversary of the Republic in the summer of 1994, the constitution's chapter on human rights was rewritten. In that process, the Bar Association, represented by not only the "legal advisory committee" but also the board, sent in a fifty-four-page opinion on the draft bill to the Alþingi (Lögmannafélag Íslands 1995). The opinion was encouraging in general, although critical regarding individual matters. One of the key criticisms was the division of human rights into civil and political rights on the one hand and economic, social, and cultural rights on the other hand, even as the draft bill declared that its aim was to bring the constitution into accord with international agreements to which Iceland was party. The critique thus rested mainly on a comparison of the draft and international agreements and its general tenor was a request for more robust rights protection or at least for a conscious decision on the part of the legislature if economic, social, and cultural rights were to enjoy less protection under the constitution than those international agreements (ibid.: 6, 12, 14). The Icelandic Human Rights Center submitted a thirty-page opinion along the same lines but somewhat less diplomatic:

> The treatment of these rights [ESC] puts Icelanders – contrary to what has hitherto been their stance – in the company of those nations who have been criticized internationally for cherry-picking from human rights, in spite of international obligations.
>
> (Alþingi 1995: 6)

The Judges' Association and the Association of District Commissioners also sent in opinions, but legal academics were largely silent.[16] The opinion of the Bar Association caused serious uproar within that organization. Lawyers argued the matter openly in the media and the Bar Association's annual meeting in 1995 was mostly taken up by discussion of this (Tímarit lögfræðinga 1995). A motion was adopted, stating that:

> The Annual Meeting of the Bar Association believes that it is incompatible with the nature and the goal of the Bar Association under its statutes and legal provisions ... mandating membership in the Association for all attorneys, for the Association to own or take part in the workings of NGOs on social affairs, or to publish opinions, motions and results where a political stance on controversial social issues is taken in the name of the Association. The Meeting therefore adopts a motion to cease taking part in the Icelandic Human Rights Office and for the Board of the Bar Association to take care, from now on, to not offer political opinions in its name.
>
> (*Tímarit lögfræðinga* 1995: 305–306).

A middle-ground motion was put to a vote, stating that a policy would be worked out concerning participation in other NGOs and that:

> The Meeting directs the Board and the committee on new legislation to take care to be careful in opinions, motions and results given in the name of the Association on controversial social affairs, when those opinions etc. may be construed as political statements.
>
> (ibid.: 307)

The motion was defeated (Gunnlaugsson, January 31, 1995: 26–27; February 22, 1995: 22.).

> It is thus clear, that the majority of the Meeting found that the Board had gone too far in the directions of politics in its opinion of the constitutional bill. A new chairman was elected and the old one argued in the media, that the Icelandic Bar Association was the only such association outside dictatorships that would not engage in questions of human rights.
>
> (*Morgunblaðið* 1995b)

In retrospect this decision (and the Bar Association's decision to opt out of the National Human Rights Institute, which still stands) are questionable when viewed

[16] The one exception is Eiríkur Tómasson 1995. It is clear from newspaper commentary that legal academics had a hand in drafting the amendment. See e.g., Morgunblaðið (1995a).

in light of the many other motions and opinions adopted by the Bar Association before and since, including, for example, concerns regarding the rule of law after the 2008 financial crash, when bankers suspected of criminal activities were submitted to the same police procedures as other suspects had been for years, without any comment from the Bar Association (2009) and arguing with courts' conclusions regarding meetings with witnesses prior to judicial proceedings (2014). Indeed, it can persuasively be argued that there is a political decision inherent in defining "politics" so broadly that human rights as described in international instruments to which Iceland is party fall beyond the scope of what the Bar Association can legitimately engage in. However, all these examples are in harmony with theories on the legal complex: The Bar Association agreed on civil rights but split on social, economic, and cultural rights, characterizing them as "controversial social issues," even though Iceland had already acceded to human rights treaties protecting them. This is in full accord with what studies on the legal complex have shown in other countries (Halliday, Karpik, and Feeley 2007: 4; Karpik and Halliday 2011: 219–220).

It needs to be noted that the draft bill was changed, including some of the paragraphs most criticized by the Bar Association, although no fundamental changes were made regarding economic, social, and cultural rights. It was then adopted unanimously in Parliament. So even as the Bar Association scolded its Board, the association's intervention was effective. It should also be noted that while the Bar Association had many suggestions and criticisms regarding the constitutional draft of 2011, none of them was based on the differences between the different kinds of human rights (Alþingi 2013b).

Constitution-drafting 2010–2013

The other clear example of mobilization concerns the constitution-drafting of 2010–2013 (Ólafsson 2014; Thorarensen 2014; Helgadóttir 2016).[17] Much has been written about the process, which has been widely lauded as an experiment in participatory constitution-making (Ginsburg 2011; Elkins, Ginsburg, and Melton 2012). However, the draft constitution was not adopted before the general election in 2013. According to philosopher Jón Ólafsson, who edited a book on the process and its legacy, that was in part due to the negative influence of legal academia and lawyers more generally. The new constitution's fate is still unclear.

The constitutional bill, drafted by a Constitutional Council in 2011, intended an increase in constitutionally protected rights and a considerable increase in

[17] Full disclosure: I was involved in this process at all stages. I advised the Constitutional Council to the best of my ability while the constitution was drafted in the summer of 2011. However, I also stated before a parliamentary committee, the Venice Committee delegation and in the seminar series (which I helped organize) that I believed many articles of the draft were seriously flawed and most importantly that the workability of the proposed system was questionable at best. The same risk was identified by other legal academics and the Venice Commission.

public participation in governance. Once it came to be discussed in the Alþingi in 2012 and in parliamentary consultations, the legal complex intervened just as it had concerning prior constitutional amendments. This time, however, certain legal associations, the Association of Judges and the Judicial Authority, wrote that they could not comment in the very short time allotted (two weeks) while the Bar Association explained in its opinion that serious rewriting of the draft would be needed and advised that the draft not be adopted (Alþingi 2013b). The Parliamentary Ombudsman pointed to serious defects but the Supreme Court did not answer a request to comment, probably due to the short time period in which to answer. Legal academics submitted all in all thirty-six opinions on various matters in the draft, many of them critical and many pointing to the need of more discussion and more time for workability tests of the proposed constitutional order. The fear of non-workability was a key element in the criticism from Icelandic academics. The Venice Commission came to similar conclusions:

> 181. The Venice Commission notes in particular that numerous provisions of the Bill have been formulated in too vague and broad terms, which, despite the clarifications that might be provided by the Explanatory Notes, may lead to serious difficulties of interpretation and application, including in the context of the adoption of the implementing laws.
>
> [182. . . .]
>
> 183. The many possibilities for the people's intervention, through referendums, in decision-making, may in principle be welcomed. This being said, like other decision-making mechanisms provided by the Bill, these appear too complicated in the constitutional provisions, which would need a careful review, both from legal and political perspective. Overall, there are reasons for the Venice Commission to see the risk of political blockage and instability, which may seriously undermine the country's good governance. Similar considerations have been raised by the proposed electoral system, which would also need more careful consideration.
>
> (European Commission on Democracy through Law [Venice Commission] 2013)

Perhaps most importantly for public opinion, the four law schools in Iceland united in holding six seminars, open to the public, on the draft in the winter of 2012–2103. All speeches by legal scholars were critical, but commentary from a number of other faculties was more positive (Ólafsson 2014: 16). These seminars were widely discussed in the media and had considerable impact. As mentioned, all the legal faculty and political scientists who spoke were critical ("downright hostile" according to Jón Ólafsson) and so were most philosophers and historians. This unanimity led some who had formed the Constitutional Council in 2011 to complain in the media that the seminars were one-sided (*Morgunblaðið* 2013).

Both the bar and legal academics were accused of being self-serving (Bjarnadóttir 2012) and too late with its criticism:

> This is all a question of power. There are powerful elites in all societies, including in our small one. Politicians are not the only one with power, civil servants and academics are powerful. And those who have power do not want to let go, they believe they are fit to decide our fate.
>
> As far as I understand, they believe ordinary people have neither the necessary intelligence nor interest in deciding their own fate. The powerful classes do not want to let go, things are that simple.
>
> (Bjarnadóttir 2013).

Similarly, one of the participants in the Constitutional Council still argues, concerning legal academics, the bar, and those associations who commented, that "Their criticism, sometimes dressed up in legal jargon, was political – and irrelevant, i.e., it came too late" (Gylfason 2015). The focus is thus on participation during the initial phase—comments (including on wording and legal certainty) that did not arise then can, according to this view, have no place later. In any case, it has been argued that the seminar series was a game changer in that the general public started to doubt the workability of the proposed constitutional arrangement. All groups of legal professionals participated and the mobilization had some effect. As previously mentioned, the draft constitution was not adopted before the general election in 2013, where voters—who seven months previously had voted in a referendum that the draft constitution should be the basis for a new constitution—gave the majority in Parliament to parties who openly opposed the constitutional project.

This is therefore an example of the legal complex mobilizing but it can convincingly be argued that it mobilized in favor of legal certainty and rule of law considerations (which struck many as conservatism), even though that meant mobilizing against changes which (if successful) would have entailed more direct democracy, democratic experiments, and transparency in government.

Appellate courts 2011–2014

Finally, one typical instance of influence of Icelandic lawyers should be mentioned. In 2010, the four associations of lawyers (the Associations of Judges, Prosecutors, and Lawyers and the Bar Association) held a seminar on a possible appellate court system, but as of now, the Icelandic court system is two-tiered with regional district courts and one Supreme Court. There was consensus on the need for a third level of judiciary and an entreaty was sent to the minister of justice, who appointed first a special committee to make recommendations and then a committee to prepare a draft bill on the issue. One was headed by a legal academic while all legal groups were represented and the other composed of a judge, a barrister, and a legal academic. A bill was then passed in the spring of 2016.

This is not an example of protecting rights and arguably more of a technical issue than an idea regarding political liberalism, but this is clearly an example of the legal complex mobilizing for certain procedural safeguards—good judicial governance, as it were. Given that there was general consensus on the issue in political circles and the general public (to the extent that people care) this example should maybe be categorized with the battles for better funding and more manpower, as well as some changes in procedure in the 1950s and 1960s. Even though, as described above, I have not discussed those issues that were uncontested in society more generally, such as the lobbying for funding for more judicial positions in the 1950s and 1960s, I include this example here for its illustrative effect, for the modus operandi of the legal complex in other such cases was much as the one described here.

4. Conclusions

The Icelandic legal complex is very active in influencing legislation, through everyday methods such as parliamentary consulting, seminars, discussions, and motions adopted at meetings as described above regarding the appellate courts. The Bar Association, which is the most active body, submits a couple of dozen opinions on prospective legislation every year, and as a group, legal academics are not far behind. The same is probably true of civil servants, who draft legislation or regulation and appear frequently before parliamentary committees.

Based on the 1995 example concerning the Bar Association's opinion on constitutional amendments, the activism of at least the Bar Association is still very formal and quite limited. In that case, as we saw, even comparing the suggested protection of economic, social, and cultural rights to that of the international instruments *which were cited in the* travaux *as models*, was held by a general meeting of the Bar Association to be so political that a censoring motion was adopted, the Association disassociated itself from the Human Rights Center and a new board was elected. As already indicated, this author is of the view that taking such a circumscribed view of what the Bar Association may legitimately involve itself in is a very political decision. However, this decision of the Bar Association—which we cannot be completely certain would be the same today—is fully in line with theories on the legal complex and political liberalism, which argue that the legal complex generally does not involve itself in social and economic rights (Halliday, Karpik, and Feeley 2007).

The longue durée example—that of the development of constitutional jurisprudence—has to some extent the same characteristics as the influence of the legal complex on legislation. It happened peacefully, with no known opponents or protests, and it was part of a day's work for all the lawyers involved. It has proven immensely important for the development of the country and its constitutional and legal system, but agency is hard to find.

In addition to these developments, Icelandic history has two clear examples of the legal complex abandoning its everyday working methods and mobilizing in unusual ways for a particular purpose: From 1930 to 1932, the legal complex's input mattered for putting a stop to illiberal tendencies. A minister, frequently held by the courts to have violated procedure and other laws, was very antagonistic to the Supreme Court and attempted to increase the power of the executive over that court. The legal complex was as close to unanimous as possible in that case; I have found no evidence of any lawyers (outside possibly Progressive Party MPs) supporting the Fimmtardómur bill. The activity of the legal complex here fits with theories of the legal complex; not only is the organization of the judiciary a very "legal" matter, but this issue was one of executive overreach, a common trigger for legal complex mobilization.

In the case of the constitutional project of 2010–2013, the legal complex's influence was also arguably "legalistic" in the sense of being primarily concerned with the workability of a proposed system and less with the ideas that were being put into action. Again, we have a case where the overwhelming majority of lawyers, from all walks of legal life, agreed. Along with the Supreme Court battle of 1930–1932, this is the clearest case of the entire Icelandic legal complex mobilizing and having an effect.

We thus seem to have two good examples of events where the legal complex seems to have played an important role (1930–1932 and 2010–2013) and a suggestion of a longer period (constitutional culture 1874–1943). Finally, there are periods during which the legal complex was silent but which may illustrate which conditions need to be met before the legal complex engages. That is clearest in the case of the unequal voting rights: Most, if not all, lawyers agree that this is in contravention of international instruments to which Iceland is party, that it skews democracy and is (in spirit) against the equal protection clause of the constitution. But they also leave well alone, as this is a key political question, constantly under revision by the legislature. This is in harmony with theories on the legal complex, developed based on the history of other states during different times.

References

Alþingi. 1995. "*Umsögn Mannréttindaskrifstofu*." See *Alþingistíðindi* 1994–1995, þskj. 1039: 6. http://www.althingi.is/altext/erindi/118/118-1039.pdf.

Alþingi. 2012a. "Frumvarp til stjórnarskipunarlaga, 415. mál" www.althingi.is/pdf/erindi/?lthing=141&dbnr=1107.

Alþingi. 2012b. "Frum varp til stjórnskipunarlaga, 415.mál" www.althingi.is/pdf/erindi/?lthing=141&dbnr=1054.

Alþingi. 2013a. "Stjórnskipunar- og eftirlitsnefnd Alþingis Nefndasvið Alþingis" www.althingi.is/pdf/erindi/?lthing=141&dbnr=1276.

Alþingi. 2013b. "Umsögn laganefndar LMFÍ um frumvarp til stjórnarskipunarlaga um stjórnarskrá." Comments of the Bar Association to Alþingi, þskj. 1281 https://www.althingi.is/altext/erindi/141/141-1281.pdf.

Alþingistíðindi 1930 A: 1004. www.althingi.is/altext/althingistidindi/L042/042_thing_1930_C_umraedur_fallin.pdf

Alþingistíðindi 1941, D. www.althingi.is/altext/althingistidindi/L056/056_thing_1941_D_umraedur_thingsalyktanir_fyrirspurnir_vidbaetir.pdf

Bar Association Meeting's Resolution on relationship to witnesses, adopted on 26 November 2014. See *Lögmannablaðið 20:4 (2014), 10-11.*

Bar Association's Board's resolution on the rule of law after the financial crash: See *Lögmannablaðið* 15: 2 (2009), 7.

Benediktsson, Bjarni. 1959. "Stjórnskipulegur neyðarréttur," *Tímarit lögfræðinga* 9(1): 4–22.

Bjarnadóttir, Valgerður. 2012. "Professorene alene vider" http://blog.pressan.is/valgerdur/2012/11/09/strjornarskra-folksins-skotin-i-kaf/.

Bjarnadóttir, Valgerður. 2013. "Allt snýst þetta um völd" http://blog.pressan.is/valgerdur/2013/03/24/allt-snyst-thetta-um-vold/

Björgvinsson, Davíð Þór. 1991. "Saga Dómarafélags Íslands," *Tímarit lögfræðinga* 41(3): 164–211.

Björgvinsson, Davíð Þór. 1998. "Ágrip af sögu lögfræðingafélags Íslands," *Tímarit lögfræðinga* 48(4): 258–278.

Elkins, Zachary, Tom Ginsburg, and James Melton. 2012. "A Review of Iceland's Draft Constitution from the Comparative Constitutions Project" www.iconnectblog.com/2012/10/a-review-of-icelands-draft-constitution-from-the-comparative-constitutions-project/

European Commission on Democracy through Law (Venice Commission). 2013. *Opinion on the Draft New Constitution for Iceland*. Adopted at its 94th Plenary Session, March 8–9. http://www.venice.coe.int/webforms/documents/?pdf=CDL-AD%282013%29010-e

Ginsburg. 2011. "The Wisdom of Crowds: Iceland Citizen's Commission Submits Draft" www.iconnectblog.com/2011/07/the-wisdom-of-crowds-iceland-citizens-commission-submits-draft/

Gunnlaugsson, Jón Steinar. 1995. "Ásættanlegt frumvarp um mannréttindi," *Morgunblaðið*, January 31, 26–7.

Gunnlaugsson, Jón Steinar. 1995. "Misnotkun á stöðu' [Abuse of power]," *Morgunblaðið*, February 22, 22.

Gylfason, Thorvaldur. 2015. "Constitution on Ice." Presentation at a workshop on *Democratic Changes and Citizens' Participation in the 21st Century—Theory and Practice* at Institut d'Estudis Autonomics (IEA), Barcelona, 12 June https://notendur.hi.is/gylfason/lectures.htm

Hálfdanarson, Guðmundur. 2001. *Íslenska þjóðríkið – uppruni og endimörk*. Reykjavík: Hið íslenska bókmenntafélag.

Halliday, Terence C., and Lucien Karpik (eds.). 1997. *Lawyers and the Rise of Western Political Liberalism: Europe and North America from the Eighteenth to Twentieth Centuries.* Oxford: Clarendon Press; New York: Oxford University Press, 1997.

Halliday, Terence C.; Lucien Karpik, and Malcolm M. Feeley. 2007. "Introduction – The Legal Complex in Struggles for Political Liberalism," in Terence C. Halliday, Lucien Karpik, Malcolm M. Feeley (eds.), *Fighting for Political Freedom: Comparative Studies of the Legal Complex and Political Liberalism*, 1–42. Oxford: Hart.

Haraldsson, Gunnlaugur. 1993–1997. "Fylgt úr hlaði," in Gunnlaugur Haraldsson, Dögg Pálsdóttir, Garðar Gíslason, and Skúli Guðmundsson (eds.), *Lögfræðingatal 1736–1992*. Reykjavík: Iðunn.

Helgadóttir, Ragnhildur. 2006. *The Influence of American Theories on Judicial Review in Nordic Constitutional Law*. Leiden: Martinus Nijhoff Publishers.

Helgadóttir, Ragnhildur. 2013. "Nødret i Island og betydningen af den Europæiske menneskerettihedskonventions artikel 15," in Dag Michalsen (ed.), *Unntakstilstand og forfatning - Brudd og kontinuitet i konstitusjonell rett*, 382–401. Oslo. Pax Forlag.

Helgadóttir, Ragnhildur. 2016. "Une théorie du picorage constitutionnel - leçons du projet constitutionnel islandais de 2011," *Revue Internationale de Droit Comparé* 68(2): 495–514.

Íslendingur. 1930. "Hæstiréttur og dómsmálaráðherra: Stofnun Fimmtardóms," January 31, 1.

Jónsson, Agnar Kl. 1993–1997. "Inngangur," in Gunnlaugur Haraldsson, Dögg Pálsdóttir, Garðar Gíslason, and Skúli Guðmundsson (eds.), *Lögfræðingatal 1736–1992*, 11–44. Reykjavík: Iðunn.

Karlsson, Gunnar. 2008. "Upphafsskeið þjóðríkismyndunar," in Sigurður Líndal (ed.), *Saga Íslands IX*, 167–374. Reykjavík: Bókmenntafélagið, Sögufélag.

Karlsson, Gunnar. 2009. "Atvinnubyltingin og ríkismyndun 1874–1918," in Sigurður Líndal (ed.), *Saga Íslands X*, 5–312. Reykjavík: Bókmenntafélagið, Sögufélag.

Karlsson, Gunnar. 2014. *Brève histoire de l'Islande*. Reykjavík: Mál & Menning.

Karpik, Lucien, and Terence C. Halliday. 2011. "The Legal Complex," *Annual Review of Law and Social Science* 7: 217–236.

Kristjánsdóttir, Ragnheiður. 2011. "Drög að þjóðríki á 19. öld og þingræði 1904," in Ragnhildur Helgadóttir, Helgi Skúli Kjartansson, and Þorsteinn Magnússon (eds.), *Þingræði á Íslandi - Samtíð og saga*, 5–312. Reykjavík: Forlagið.

Líndal, Sigurður. 1993–1997. "Málflytjendur og lögmenn á Íslandi, Söguágrip," in Gunnlaugur Haraldsson, Dögg Pálsdóttir, Garðar Gíslason, and Skúli Guðmundsson (eds.), *Lögfræðingatal 1736–1992*, 57–71. Reykjavík: Iðunn.

Líndal, Sigurður. 2011. "Grundvöllur stjórnarskrár lýðveldisins Íslands," in Guðrún Pétursdóttir et al (eds). *Skýrsla stjórnlaganefndar, pp. 12-24*. Reykjavík. Available at http://www.stjornlagarad.is/other_files/stjornlagarad/skyrsla-stjornlaganefndar/skyrsla_stjornlaganefndar_seinna_bindi.pdf

Lögfræðingafélag. 2014. "Declaration by the Lawyers' Association 2014," http://www.logfraedingafelag.is/um-felagid/frettir/nr/414/.

Lögrétta. 1930. 5 February, 4.

Morgunblaðið. 1930. March 2, 9–10

Lögmannafélag Íslands. 1995. "Mannréttindaákvæði stjórnarskrárinnar - Umsögn Lögmannafélagsins," Reykjavík.

Morgunblaðið. 1930. "Fimmtardómurinn" April 17, 5.

Morgunblaðið. 1995a. "Deilt um skilgreiningu á mannréttindahugtakinu," February 11, 34–35.

Morgunblaðið. 1995b. "Úrsögn úr mannréttindaskrifstofunni samþykkt," March 11, 4.

Ólafsson, Jón. 2014. *Lýðræðistilraunir - Ísland í hruni og endurreisn*. Edda. Háskólaútgáfan.

Pálsson, Páll S. 1981. "Lögmannafélag Íslands 70 ára," *Tímarit lögfræðinga* 31(4): 178–183.

Sigurðsson, Páll. 1989. *Háskólamálið og Lagaskólamálið - Úrval heimilda um aðdraganda að stofnun háskóla á Íslandi*. Háskóli Íslands: Háskólaútgáfan.

Thorarensen, Björg. 2014. "The Impact of the Financial Crisis on Icelandic Constitutional Law: Legislative Reforms, Judicial Review and Revision of the Constitution," in Xenophon Contiades (ed.), *Constitutions in the Global Financial Crisis: A Comparative Analysis*, 263–283. Farnham: Ashgate.

Tíminn. "Fimmtardómurinn " 1930a. February 1, 18.
Tómasson, Eiríkur. 1995. "Mannréttindafrumvarp fimm þingflokksformanna - Ótvíræð réttarbót," *Morgunblaðið*, January 25, 21.
"*Fimtardómur*". *Vikuútgáfa Alþýðublaðsins*. 1930. February 5, 3.
Vísir. 1930a. "Frá Alþingi í gær" 28 January, 2.
Vísir. 1930b. "Fimtardómur hinn nýi" 17 February, 2.
Þórarinsson, Þórarinn. 1970. "Jónas Jónsson frá Hriflu," *Andvari* 1. tbl.: 3–52.
Þórðarson, Björn. 1947. *Landsyfirdómurinn 1800–1919*. Reykjavík: Sögufélag, Ísafoldarpre ntsmiðja.

9

Revisiting the Theory of the Legal Complex

*Malcolm Langford**

1. Introduction

The idea of a "legal complex" working for political liberalism has gained traction through a considerable body of work led and inspired by Terrance Halliday, Lucien Karpik, and Malcolm Feeley. The theory of the legal complex posits that lawyers are primed to advance collectively core civil rights, a moderate state, and the space for a vibrant civil society (for an overview, see Karpik and Halliday 2011). Political liberalism is a *discrete* but professionally *valued* good to which lawyers may act as guardians, speaking on behalf of the people for the rule of law and political liberalism.

Across a diverse range of jurisdictions, exploratory and qualitative studies have found that lawyers do mobilize in legal complexes and sometimes in spectacular fashion (Halliday and Karpik 1998; Halliday, Karpik, and Feeley 2007a; Halliday, Karpik, and Feeley 2012; Rajah 2012; Massoud 2013; Gobe and Salaymeh 2015).[1] The body of research finds though that lawyers do not always respond to threats to political liberalism or constitute its active vanguard; and in some cases represent its very opposition. Nonetheless, the leading scholars claim that when one finds struggles against political repression, politics of the legal complex are frequently part of that struggle, with powerful evidence that the nexus of bar and bench is a powerful core alliance in many transitions toward *or away* from political liberalism (Halliday, Karpik, and Feeley 2007b: 3).

However, the largely contrary findings in this Nordic volume provides a fresh opportunity to revisit the theory and findings of the legal complex. The Nordic paradox of legal presence but non-mobilization should prompt us to question the Halliday and Karpik vocational or "guardian of the law" explanation as to why legal complexes emerge. Moreover, we might also question whether the Nordics are not exceptional (which is a key line of inquiry in the opening chapter) and instead

* Professor, Faculty of Law, University of Oslo and Co-Director, Centre on Law and Social Transformation. He leads the project *Nordic Branding: The Politics of Exceptionalism*. Sincere thanks to Terry Halliday for comments on an earlier version of this chapter.

[1] It is also taken up in individual chapters or discussions in other works (see Wesley Pue and Sugarman 2003; Couso, Huneeus, and Sieder 2010; Cummings 2011; Kapiszewski, Silverstein, and Kagan 2013; Graver 2014; Ghias 2015).

Malcolm Langford, *Revisiting the Theory of the Legal Complex* In: *The Limits of the Legal Complex*.
Edited by: Malcolm Feeley and Malcolm Langford, Oxford University Press.
DOI: 10.1093/oso/9780192848413.003.0009

ask whether they are ordinary, and thus similar. What if Nordic exceptionalism is simply based on over-optimistic findings from elsewhere? In any case, and regardless of the empirical nuances, the scholarship on the legal complex is arguably a field ripe for re-examination. This reflection sets out some criticisms and attempts to offer a complementary theory of the legal complex.

2. Four Critiques

In engaging with the legal complex literature and its application in this research project,[2] I began to consider four potential critiques of a theoretical and methodological nature. These concerned its historicity, explanationary theory, disciplinary foundation, and summative interpretation.

First, as discussed in the Introduction, legal complex research has a particular *historicity*. The origins of the project lie in challenging an earlier debate in the sociology of the professions. Halliday and Karpik resisted the prevailing realist 1980s view of the legal profession, which depicted lawyers in solely materialist terms, dedicated to the maximization of income and maintenance of a self-regulated monopoly, and offered a moderated vision that carved out a space for collective action for political liberalism. However, since that time there has been considerable advances in thinking about *collective mobilization*, particularly through ideas of collective action theory, opportunity structures, and the new institutionalisms, which are less blunt than traditional realism or costructivism and are not so far reflected in the legal complex scholarship.

Secondly, seemingly little attention has been given to the *explanation* of the legal complex beyond the identification of a range of conditioning or mediating factors. The scholarship has focused on identifying whether various political conditions (e.g., levels of democracy) or level of organizational capacity (e.g., law associations) shape the likelihood and breadth of a legal complex. Only occasionally are the reasons that motivate individual lawyers discussed. The most commonly repeated idea is that of Karpik (1998): lawyers view themselves as self-appointed guardians of the people. However, he does note that this representation may be moderated by the logic of class and the situated pull of strong class alliances (Karpik 2007: 475). Others suggest in passing that the structure of the legal practice profession, the semi-autonomous and quasi-oppositional political space created by the lawyer–client relationship and the adversarial legalism of the courtroom, may orient lawyers toward a particular form of mobilization (Rueschmeyer 1998: 223).

Thirdly, the current research program on the legal complex has been strongly shaped by *historical sociology*. This sub-discipline can be described as a "two

[2] See Chapter 5 of this volume.

centuries old attempt by economists, philosophers of history and nascent sociologists" (and many doctrinal lawyers) to "provide a historically sensitive, yet generally applicable, account of the emergence of industrial capitalism, the rational bureaucratic state, novel forms of warfare and other core features of the modern world" (Hobson, Lawson, and Rosenberg 2010: 3357). The field of historical sociology is certainly diverse and always in flux (Deflem 2007: 13–14), but its traits are unmistakable. It is marked by a certain sociological sensibility that gives preeminence to social relationships and structures as research objects and a qualitative methodology that is inductive, historically attuned, and oriented to identifying necessary and sufficient conditions for social change.

The potential weaknesses of the legal complex project become clearer if we examine some of the common critiques of historical sociology. The first is that the role of individuals is often shrouded by the focus on the systematic relationships among legal actors and diverse historical institutions. While "biography" is the third pillar of historical sociology alongside "social structure" and "history" (Mills 1959), it seems to be the proverbial third wheel that is easily lost as historical sociology moves into its comparative and international modes.[3] In many leading historical sociological works on law and rights, individual experience and agency are simply absent (see Nonet and Selznick 1978; Teubner 1983; Kennedy 2006, 2013).

In the literature on the legal complex, it is striking that almost all of the attention is devoted to establishing the exogenous factors for lawyerly activism, with individual motivation relegated to a mysterious black box. The exception is Lucien Karpik, who regularly raises the question of motivation. Yet, his answer, oft-repeated by others, is always in the singular: it is the theory of the public spokesperson. On account of their symbolic legitimacy, lawyers can easily lay claim to speaking on behalf of the amorphous public.[4] However, even this notion tells us very little about the individual motivation—it is primarily an account of self-representation. On the precise issue of inner motivations, Karpik (2008: 488–489) simply throws up his hands:

> How is it that lawyers doing their work, which sometimes means opposing arbitrary power, are ready to take risks and sometimes extreme risks? Why are they not more neutral? More cautious? Of course risk varies with countries, with periods, with individuals. Depending on the countries/periods/issues, they will be few or numerous, they will be isolated or be part of collective action. In every case, the question remains.

[3] Hobson, Lawson, and Rosenberg (2010) acknowledge for instance that "biography" and "agency" may be lost when historical sociology moves into the international realm.

[4] See, e.g., Karpik (1998) and Karpik and Halliday (2011: 226).

This neglect of individual motivation is puzzling. Social and natural scientists have struggled to explain collective action for almost half a century (see, e.g., Ostrom 2000; Pinker 2002, 2015; Persson, Rothstein, and Teorell 2013).[5] Moreover, answering the question of motivation seems essential in validating the theory of the legal complex for political liberalism. If we cannot explain why lawyers mobilize, any findings must remain highly contingent. Facts do not a theory make.

The final problem with legal complex theory is the slippage between the *empirical findings* and communicated theory. The empirical studies and lengthy meta-analyses display nuance, tilting toward findings that legal complexes do emerge in quite diverse circumstances but that the struggles are often reactive, rest on fragile organizational capacity, and are vulnerable to silencing by political authority. Moreover, lawyers can remain silent, sometimes mobilize against political liberalism, and are often divided as a collective.

Yet, the general summary of the findings is often more upbeat. There is a tendency to restate initial hypotheses as a grand theory without the accompanying conditions. One constantly stumbles across grand statements that "lawyers more or less intensively fought in favor of civil and political rights" (Karpik and Halliday 2011: 219); "Since the eighteenth century, Western lawyers have been activist in the creation, defence and development of individual rights" (Karpik 2008: 463); or that "lawyers could often be found leading the charge towards a new kind of politics – political liberalism" (Halliday 2011: 52).

The dissonance is also marked by a peculiar, but perhaps telling, grammatical proclivity in the literature. Collective legal mobilization is frequently referred to in the *singular* not plural. Despite the carefully defined temporally and relationally contingent organizational networks of lawyers (suggesting a plurality—legal complex*es*), authors repeatedly refer to "the" legal complex, conjuring up a stronger and stable image of political lawyering and organization. However, if we could develop a theory that places causation rather than historical incidents at the center may help in providing a framework for nuanced generalizations of the legal complex.

To be sure, this criticism is meant neither to discredit the endeavor to extrapolate and generalize nor the reliance on inductive method. Indeed, the careful and sustained attempt within the legal complex research project to universalize is a welcome break from the resistance to general theorizing in historical sociology that was dominant in the 1970s and 1980s (for an overview of this trend, see Kiser and Hechter 1991).[6] Instead, the problem may lie in the under-articulation of the

[5] I will leave for now my speculation as to why the research program has developed in this direction but it is mostly due to its reaction against market-based theories of lawyers (which were nascent rational choice in orientation) and its emergence at a time when historical sociology was largely allergic to general theorizing and cross-disciplinary impulses.

[6] Karpik (2008) engages explicitly with those who might claim the results are too fragile for such extrapolation.

theory, initially or in light of the findings. This theoretical lightness makes it difficult to provide a coherent restatement of the hypotheses in light of the identified exogenous factors. The end result may be a problem identified by others with comparative historical sociology:

> Instead of relying on necessary explanations, historians are willing to use sufficient ones, in which an event is taken to be a natural outcome of a sequence. The structure of the arguments, therefore, tends not to be implicative (involving deductive logic), but conjunctive (involving the use of coherent narrative).

While legal complex researchers have demonstrated a heightened awareness of this causal trap, it may represent an embedded risk in the methodology—dominated as it is by historical sociology.

3. A Political Theory

This chapter suggests that the legal complex theory needs reframing but without doing violence to its basic concepts. The reframing proceeds in three steps, by identifying (a) the nature of the public good; (b) the form of lawyerly demand; and (c) the structural supply choices. Some examples are given along the way.

3.1 The Public Good: Political Liberalism in Context

In my view, it is reasonable to *assume* that lawyers would be inclined to support, and even struggle for, a limited public good such as political liberalism. As the Norwegian case study reveals, this discursive consensus emerged amongst many lawyers in the nineteenth century and is entrenched in the Bar Association objectives from the middle of the next century. The secretary-general of the association stated that the "social responsibility" of advocates is to "defend and develop" political liberalism (Smith 2015: 13). However, the idea or analytical category is too rigid in its expression. It is both overstated and understated, and unnecessarily static.

First, one can question Halliday, Karpik, and Feeley's (2008b) packaging of a diverse group of rights and principles under the umbrella of political liberalism. Within this notion, there are certain civil rights which have been subject to fierce contestation. It is more common to find lawyers wrestling over rights to property and religion than struggling collectively for them. Indeed, it seems odd to expect lawyers to view torture and property expropriation as equally morally repugnant, particularly in the post-Lockean nineteenth and twentieth centuries in which property rights occupied the center of ideological contestation.

Second, there is a sharp distinction to be made between rights as articulated in moral theory (abstract and often unencumbered) and rights as materialized. Once we move beyond a thin conception of rights, disagreement over their content rights might be reasonably expected amongst lawyers. This is evident in legal expression (in which rights are regularly qualified); coverage (which individuals and groups are to benefit); and institutional embedment (policy choices over the best way to protect rights). Indeed, one reason rights are constitutionalized in the abstract is that it widens support—so-called strategic ambiguity—as well as making them more adaptable to historical change. Thus, we might expect that lawyers may disagree more regularly on the substance of political liberalism when it moves beyond abstract notions of the selected civil rights. Conversely, we might surmise that many lawyers could be sensitive to the inner core of many social and political rights, for example freedom from hunger or blatant vote tampering. It is notable that English courts constructed a basic right to subsistence in the face of severe limitations to asylum seekers' rights.[7] Elsewhere, constitutional and supreme courts have melded social rights onto core civil rights substantively and procedurally, especially in Germany, Switzerland, Colombia, and India.[8] The right to life and dignity is interpreted to encompass a minimum level of existence and in Latin America the *tutela*, the powerful writ of fundamental rights that permits a guaranteed remedy within a very short period, has been interpreted to include the minimum core of a range of social rights.[9]

Third, the abstract concept of political liberalism ignores the role of law in shaping social and professional norms. Statutes, constitutions, treaties, and judgments may sociologically legitimize certain rights and, through omission or heavy qualification, delegitimize others (Tushnet 1995; Stoutenborough, Haider-Markel, and Allen 2006; Arbor 2008). Producing symbolic effects is often a key objective of legalized norm production. For example, it is not radical to suggest that the European Convention of Human Rights has *expanded* the *notion* of political liberalism amongst European lawyers. The adoption of the very liberal 1814 Norwegian Constitution may also partly explain the greater mobilization of Norwegian lawyers in comparison to their Nordic counterparts. In other words, conceptions of political liberalism are legally determined as much as they are morally fixed.

[7] *R v. Secretary of State for the Home Department ex p Adam; R v. Secretary or State for the Home Department ex p Limbuela; R v. Secretary of State for the Home Department ex p Tesema* [2005] UKHL 66 (House of Lords, United Kingdom).

[8] See BVERFGE 1, 97 (104), 1 BvR 220/51 (1951) (Federal Constitutional Court of Germany); *Hartz IV*, 1 BVL 1/09, 1 BVL 3/09, 1 BVL 4/09 (2010) (Federal Constitutional Court of Germany); *V. v. Einwohnergemeinde X. und Regierungsrat des Kantons Bern* BGE/ATF 121 I 367 (Federal Court of Switzerland); T-002/92 (Constitutional Court of Colombia); *Sunil Batra v. Delhi Administration* 1978 SC 1675 (Supreme Court of India). For a comparative discussion of this jurisprudence see Langford (2008).

[9] Cepeda (2004).

Equally, the repressive law codes enacted during fascist occupations and influence may have shrunk, for some lawyers, the legitimate sphere of political liberalism.

These caveats suggest that political liberalism might be thought of as a *construct* as much as an *idea*. It may be less generalizable and more contextual (at the individual and national level) than previously imagined. As we shall see, these shades of grey are also important in understanding the level of lawyerly demand for political liberalism—the next plank in a reconstruction.

3.2 Demand for Political Liberalism

A central question to ask is why lawyers would be willing to engage in collective action for a public good in situations that are contrary to self-interest or would involve costs that would incentivize free riding.[10] A way to proceed is to re-express this puzzle as a simple cost inequality or trade-off: The degree or intensity of collective mobilization by lawyers is a function of: (1) their individual motivations or preferences for political liberalism; and (2) the costs of mobilization, particularly of a financial and reputational nature.

Motivations can be loosely grouped into three categories: utilitarian interests, normative preferences, and identity markers. In the discussions about political liberalism, the most constantly named motivation is normative. So, I will begin there and flesh out the account with the other two more elements.

In experimental and other studies, normative concerns figure prominently in the decisions of individuals to contribute to the public good (Knoke 1988). In the case of lawyers, such preferences may be grounded in their individual ideological views or socially instilled values (including through the legal profession). In the case of practicing advocates, these values may be more deeply embedded if, through their work for clients, they encounter the darker and arbitrary side of state power.[11] However, the scholarship demonstrates that the *intensity* of such normative preferences varies dramatically amongst individuals. Even if we believe that social, instilled values are the prime normative determinant of individual behavior, their transmission may vary considerably between families, social groupings, and legal communities within which an individual lawyer finds herself or himself. Thus, we need to consider biography, the role of individual agency. This variance in normative outlooks affects arguably the propensity of an individual lawyer to engage in action for political liberalism.

[10] Strikingly, the first era of collective action theory would not even necessarily accept the realist depiction of lawyers since rational, self-interested individuals were only expected to mobilize to achieve their common interests under strict conditions.

[11] This observation was made by Merete Smith, Interview of January 6, 2016. This idea is partly confirmed in Voeten's (2008) analysis on the role of professional background in influencing judicial behavior in the European Court of Human Rights.

However, normative preferences are moderated in varying degrees by self-interest. Turning to a second motivational explanation, *utilitarian* or rational choice approaches would point to strategic or personal costs and benefits that lawyers might obtain by struggling for political liberalism—which determines the essential acceptable price for their normative preference. These costs might be financial and include loss of working time or dismissal from employment—a salient risk for judges and civil servants. Cynically, we might think that championing political liberalism provides more space for remunerative legal work—particularly through greater civil society and market freedoms or the passages of new laws. However, self-interest might well—and more frequently—point in the opposite direction. Lawyers might worry that greater civil society freedoms and civil rights could permit other actors to encroach on their monopolies (in the market or in social stratification). Self-interest is thus highly contextual and historically contingent.

Another utilitarian motivation is reputational. The public championing of political liberalism generates favorable publicity for the lawyers involved—and Karpik (1998) certainly hints in this direction. However, participation in collective mobilization may also generate negative publicity if lawyers are required to advocate for a highly unpopular cause without significant elite support. We know that status is a significant driver of human behavior (Weiss and Fershtman 1998; Rege 2008). A final utilitarian interest might only work in a positive direction. Many lawyers may derive satisfaction in working for an altruistic cause, having a break from their standard instrumentalized work routines.[12] A significant body of research demonstrate that sacrificial acts are often utility-enhancing (Pinker 2015: 73).[13]

Putting normative preferences and the overall costs together, we would expect that on average for a group of lawyers that the intensity and/or breadth of interest in (i.e., demand for) championing political liberalism—generally or for a specific case—will be a function of their normative preferences and the extent of costs and benefits. Thus, as the overall costs of mobilization increase, we would expect fewer lawyers to be involved or more tepid forms of mobilization by a larger group (i.e., less demand). As the overall costs of mobilization decrease, we should see more lawyers mobilizing or more intense forms of mobilization (i.e., more demand).

The result is that the nature of *commitment*—and tolerance of costs—may vary considerably across the lawyerly spectrum.[14] We can illustrate this commitment trade-off in a simple demand curve (1) in Figure 9.1. As the costs of mobilization

[12] Merete Smith pointed this out to me in her interview.

[13] This is also a standard assumption in corporate social responsibility scholarship. Corporations that do not engage in responsible behavior or provide space for the employees to do so risk losing talented staff.

[14] I think *committed* describes well the most active lawyers. Karpik (1998) also uses this term, though to describe all lawyers who mobilize. The idea of a committed lawyer provides a nice distinction from cause lawyers who focus on particular issues for sustained periods. We would expect there to be more lawyers deeply committed to political liberalism than cause lawyers devoted to this issue.

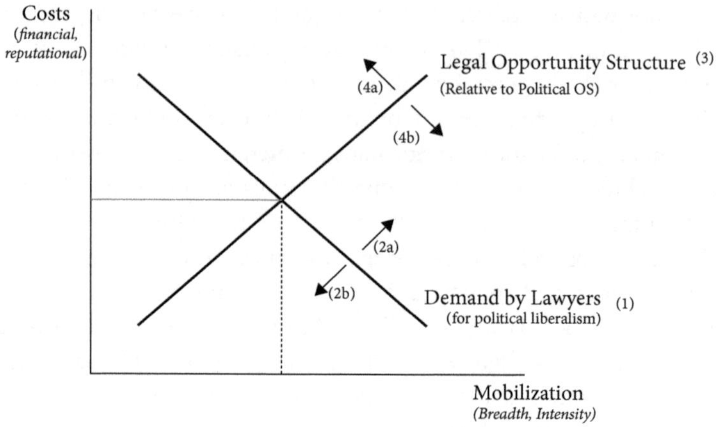

Figure 9.1 Depicting a Political Theory of the Legal Complex

increase (Y-axis), the degree and/or intensity of mobilization amongst lawyers falls (X-axis). This curve thus predicts many of the findings in the legal complex literature. It is very rare to find a fully united legal profession on political liberalism. With some important exceptions, legal complexes are either small or moderate and lawyers are often divided.

However, this demand curve may be sensitive to a final important motivation that may shift the curve outwards or inwards (2a and 2b in Figure 9.1). *Identity-oriented* motivations—primarily based on group membership—may inflect the demand curve. This factor may be partly affective. Individuals are more likely to engage in collective action when "people experience fraternal, or group-based, deprivation" (Zomeren, Postmes, and Russell 2008: 505) or when they have established 'affective bonding' through different activities (Knoke 1988: 316). Group action may also be partly strategic. Individuals engage in social competition in order to lift or maintain the status of the group (Zomeren, Postmes, and Russell 2008: 507). Thus, we might expect lawyers (as a whole) to be more committed to political liberalism struggles when members of their own profession or their elite grouping or class, or family/community are affected; and less engaged when other groups are the beneficiaries. The Norwegian case certainly provides some evidence. In moments of significant legal mobilization for political liberalism, the basic civil rights of Jews were overlooked or denied by the vast majority of lawyers. Moreover, the most high-profile and broad-based campaign by Norwegian lawyers in recent years involves contesting the low payments to lawyers working with free Legal Aid. The campaign is driven by notions of fairness and liberalism, but raising salaries is also in the self-interest of lawyers and builds heavily on group identity.

However, identity attributes are not static—and have feedback effects on normative preferences. *Engagement* in political action or *exposure* to concrete injustice may transform an individual's *personal* identity or connect them to the plight of the structural disadvantaged (Zomeren, Postmes, and Russell 2008). Some lawyers are particularly exposed to social realities and injustices, especially criminal defense lawyers and judges, who have less control over their caseloads. The Marcus Thrane trial of 1855 in Norway reflects precisely such an individual transformation of a criminal defense lawyer (Østvedt 1940).

3.3 Supply of Opportunity Structures

Turning to the supply side, various chapters in this volume point to the role of strategic decision-making in the context of varying legal and political opportunity structures. In his chapter, Karlsson Schaffer concludes that "legal professionals acting as defenders of liberal rights may be a product of just as much as a causal force for political liberalism." Thus nineteenth-century Swedish liberal reformers confronted authoritarian rule but rarely in courts because the existing legal–judicial system was part of the problem rather than of the solution, while the expansion of individual rights since the 1980s was in part caused by the changing nature of European human rights law. In Norway, however, a more favorable and open legal opportunity structure existed in the nineteenth century, and this may explain the slightly higher likelihood of legal complexes in that state. The key point is that the legal opportunity structure may vary over time and space.

Lawyers must therefore choose which strategies or repertories of action they will use to advance or defend "political liberalism." We can define legal strategies or mobilization in legal complexes as those which are lawyer-centric: lawyers make use of their professional role or organize with other lawyers.[15] These would include:

- *litigation* (case or trial is used by lawyers as a vehicle to advance political ends);
- *direct action* (e.g., protests/marches, judicial/prosecutor resignations, strikes, work boycotts);
- *lobbying* (e.g., petitions, submissions, opinion editorials);
- *legitimation* (e.g., mediation, strategic presence of lawyers in action by others, third-party opinions, strategic use of legalistic discourse);
- *awareness-raising* (e.g., education, materials, public speaking).

Yet, this choice of such legal mobilization is conditional and relative. It is dependent on the openness of the alternative political opportunity structure (Hilson 2002). If the political opportunity structure is open and less costly, it is likely that lawyers will utilize these opportunities and forgo collective legal mobilization. Indeed,

[15] This framework is partly drawn from political sociology of legal mobilization but is broader since it draws on the findings in the legal complex project and this study and seeks to incorporate all lawyers.

one explanation for any Nordic exceptionalism might be precisely that: a relatively open political space has obviated the need for lawyer-centric strategies. Figure 9.1 therefore plots a relative legal opportunity structure as a supply curve. If legal mobilization provides a relatively less "costly" form of collective action, the curve will be further to the right and will be likely to envelop more lawyers (and vice versa).

But what determines the costs in this relative opportunity structure for any particular issue? Three key elements can be named although it is unlikely that they are ever full objectively determined.[16] First, from the perspective of self-interest, there are the relative costs and benefits for those who engage in the action, such as financial (including time) and reputational. Second, from a normative perspective, we can surmise that all actors would prefer legal and political mobilization to be *successful*. Costs will be weighted according to likely outcomes. Lawyers are likely to be concerned with at least a narrow conception of success: for instance, a judicial victory or new legislation. They may also take into account the likelihood of implementation and avoidance of backlash. Third, the level of *resources* (legal, financial, organizational, and human) and presence of *allies* may vary considerably between the legal and political spheres and across specific issues (see also Epp 1988). Available resources and alliances are not only critical in determining costs and success, they may operate as condition precedent to any action: for example, the existence of the right to judicial review or a relevant coordinating organization.

It is worth focusing briefly on this third aspect and the organizational resources of a lawyer. Action through collective *structures* is a central concern of standard legal complex theory. A key question we should ask is whether organizational resources exist to mobilize lawyers, particularly reluctant lawyers (those with very modest and/or elastic demand curves). Nobel Prize winner in Economics, Ellin Ostrom (2000), argues that an important condition for collective action is the presence of "conditional co-operators" who invest in accessing information and build inter-group trust. This "activist" group in turn needs support from "willing punishers," who are willing to invest time and reputation to enforce the group consensus. If individuals of both psychological stripes are prominent or dominant in the legal profession, we would expect legal opportunity structure to be more open. Such intra-group solidarity is particularly critical when lawyers engage in high-risk actions such as strikes, resignations, or petitions, or when judges depart from strict legal positivism. Individual advocates, judges, and civil servant lawyers can otherwise easily defect or dissent.

It is also at this juncture that the constructivist approach toward political liberalism (Section 3.1) may be particularly salient. My general sense, although I may be

[16] It is thus preferable to speak of "constructed opportunity structures" (Langford, Vibe, and Kirkebø 2016). The assessment of respective choices by lawyers may be swayed by the paucity of information, individual biases, and the challenges of commensurability in weighing arguments (Benford and Snow 2000; Meyer 2004; Lobel 2006: 17; Blandhol 2011).

overly pessimistic, is that the influence of university legal training and professional ethics on lawyers' pre-professional commitment to political liberalism is not particularly significant. However, the social norm of political liberalism may provide a powerful force in helping mobilize and draw support amongst otherwise reluctant lawyers. If the social norm of political liberalism has been used to legitimate the legal profession or is part of the mandate of a lawyers' association, this process of reminding, if not shaming, may be quite effective. Thus, invoking political liberalism may provide a way of embarrassing lawyers into action (or strengthening the underlying "logic of appropriateness" [March and Olsen 1984]). Karpik's idea that lawyers view themselves as guardians might be instead reconceived as a latent discourse, capable of strategic and purposive invocation.

A final point to note is the choice between legal strategies. Bouwen and McCown (2007: 429–430), in their study of choices of European companies between litigation and lobbying, found the counterintuitive result that large companies and associations preferred lobbying while small companies preferred litigation. The cost–success ratio, however, made both choices rational. Based on this finding, we would expect well-organized law associations of judges and advocates to leverage their power directly with the state through direct action and lobbying. Where this is not present, we would expect more litigation, legitimation, and awareness-raising activities that reflect a more diffuse and decentralized profession. However, where gains cannot be made through lobbying, we would expect advocate associations to consider engaging in litigation. Indeed, the declining influence of lawyers in the Nordic states in the past two decades in the wake of neoliberalism and counterterrorism may indicate why we are seeing law associations turning more often to litigation.

4. Conclusion

This short chapter has argued that previous studies on the role of lawyers may have been under-theorized and findings partly overstated. Taking a departure point in the choices of lawyers in context, it has argued that the motivations of individuals to suffer costs in the struggle for political liberalism vary greatly (a question of agency) and lawyers are often rational in choosing whether to engage in the legal or political terrain (a question of structure). By focusing on costs to lawyers and alternative avenues for influence we may better understand why legal complexes are highly contingent and are more likely to emerge in particular times and particular countries.

This perspective may help to better explain existing literature and the Nordic case. It is possible to argue, as we have done partly in the introductory chapter, that Nordic exceptionalism can be accounted for by static structural features: a lack of an independent bar, strong state-led development of the rule of law, and the engagement of other actors. Nevertheless, the variance across time and space in the emergence of legal complexes suggests that other factors may also be at play. They emerge arguably when political opportunity structures narrow (Norway in the 1890s and 1940s and the Nordics generally in the 1970s) and material and reputational costs are diminished. The question to ask is whether the same features may also be present in other countries and periods previously studied. It is not that the lawyerly idea of being the guardian of the people is foreign to lawyers, it is that this idea is insufficient in itself to ground collective action.

References

Arbor, Louise. 2008. "Human Rights Made Whole," *Project Syndicate*, 26 June.

Benford, Robert D., and David A. Snow. 2000. "Framing Processes and Social Movements: An Overview and Assessment," *Annual Review of Sociology* 26: 611–639.

Blandhol, Sverre. 2011. "Valget mellom forlik og rettssak. Hvor gode er advokater til å bedømme prosessrisiko og hvorfor går det ofte galt?" *Lov og Rett* 10: 596–617.

Bouwen, Peter, and Margaret McCown. 2007. "Lobbying Versus Litigation: Political and Legal Strategies of Interest Representation in the European Union," *Journal of European Public Policy* 14: 422–443.

Cepeda, M. 2004. "Judicial Activism in a Violent Context: The Origin, Role, and Impact of the Colombian Constitutional Court," *Washington University Global Studies Law Review* 3: 259.

Couso, Javier A., Alexandra Huneeus, and Rachel Sieder (eds.). 2010. *Cultures of Legality: Judicialization and Political Activism in Latin America*. New York: Cambridge University Press.

Cummings, Scott (ed.). 2011. *'The Paradox of Professionalism: Lawyers and the Possibility of Justice*. Cambridge: Cambridge University Press.

Deflem. 2007. "Comparative and Historical Sociology," in Lecture Notes, University of South Carolina.

Epp, Charles. 1998. *The Rights Revolution: Lawyers, Activists and Supreme Courts in Comparative Perspective*. Chicago. IL: University of Chicago Press.

Ghias, Shoaib. 2015. "Defining Shari'a: The Politics of Islamic Judicial Review," in PhD thesis, Jurisprudence and Social Policy Program, University of California, Berkeley.

Gobe, E., and L. Salaymeh. 2015. "Tunisia's 'Revolutionary' Lawyers: From Professional Autonomy to Political Mobilization," *Law and Social Inquiry*.

Graver, Hans Petter. 2014. *Judges Against Justice: On Judges When the Rule of Law is Under Attack*. Berlin: Springer.

Halliday, Terence. 2011. "'The Conscience of Society?' The Legal Complex, Religion, and the Fates of Political Liberalism," in Scott Cummings (ed.), *The Paradox of Professionalism: Lawyers and the Possibility of Justice*. Cambridge: Cambridge University Press.

Halliday, Terence, and Lucien Karpik (eds.). 1998. *Lawyers and the Rise of Western Political Liberalism: Europe and North America from the Eighteenth to Twentieth Centuries*. Oxford: Oxford University Press.

Halliday, Terence, Lucien Karpik, and Malcolm Feeley (eds.). 2007a. *Fighting for Political Freedom: Comparative Studies of the Legal Complex and Political Change*. Oxford: Hart, 463-494.

Halliday, Terence, Lucien Karpik, and Malcolm Feeley. 2007b. "The Legal Complex in Struggles for Political Liberalism," in Terence Halliday, Lucien Karpik, and Malcolm Feeley (eds.), *Fighting for Political Freedom: Comparative Studies of the Legal Complex and Political Change*, 1–40. Oxford: Hart.

Halliday, Terence, Lucien Karpik, and Malcolm Feeley (eds.). 2012. *Fates of Political Liberalism in the British Post-Colony: The Politics of the Legal Complex*. Cambridge. Cambridge University Press.

Hilson, C. 2002. "New Social Movements: The Role of Legal Opportunity," *Journal of European Public Policy* 9: 238–255.

Hobson, John, George Lawson, and Justin Rosenberg. 2010. "Historical Sociology," in Robert A. Denemark and Renée Marlin-Bennett (eds.), *The International Studies Encyclopedia*, 13–23. Oxford: Wiley-Blackwell , https://www.oxfordreference.com/view/10.1093/acref/9780191842665.001.0001/acref-9780191842665-e-0180?rskey=2jWF1G&result=201.

Kagan, Robert. 2013. "A Consequential Court: the U.S. Supreme Court in the twentieth century," in Diana Kapiszewski, Gordon Silverstein, and Robert A. Kagan (eds.), *Consequential Courts: Judicial Roles in Global Perspective*, 199–232. Cambridge: Cambridge University Press .

Kapiszewski, Diana, Gordon Silverstein, and Robert A. Kagan (eds.). 2013. *Consequential Courts: Judicial Roles in Global Perspective*. Cambridge: Cambridge University Press.

Karpik, Lucien. 1998. "Builders of Liberal Society: French Lawyers and Politics," in Terence Halliday, and Lucien Karpik (eds.), *Lawyers and the Rise of Western Political Liberalism: Europe and North America from the Eighteenth to Twentieth Centuries*. Oxford: Oxford University Press.

Karpik, Lucien. 2007. "Postscript: Political Lawyers," in Terence Halliday, Lucien Karpik, and Malcolm Feeley (eds.), *Fighting for Political Freedom: Comparative Studies of the Legal Complex and Political Change*. Oxford: Hart.

Karpik, Lucien, and Terence Halliday. 2011. "The Legal Complex," *Annual Review of Law and Social Science* 7: 217–236.

Kennedy, David. 2013. "Law and the Political Economy of the World," *Leiden Journal of International Law* 26: 7–48.

Kennedy, Duncan. 2006. "Three Globalizations of Law and Legal Thought," in David Trubek, and Alvaro Santos (eds.), *The New Law and Economic Development*, 19–73. Cambridge: Cambridge University Press.

Kiser, Edgar, and Michael Hechter. 1991. "The Role of General Theory in Comparative-Historical Sociology," *American Journal of Sociology* 97: 1–30.

Knoke, David. 1988. "Incentives in Collective Action Organization," *American Sociological Review* 53: 311–329.

Langford, Malcolm (ed.). 2008. *Social Rights Jurisprudence: Emerging Trends in International and Comparative Law*. Cambridge: Cambridge University Press.

Langford, Malcolm, Vegard Vibe and Tori Kirkebø. 2015. *International Legal Mobilisation and LGBT Rights*, Law and Society Association Annual Conference, June, Seattle.

Lobel, Jules. 2006. *Success Without Victory: Lost Legal Battles and the Long Road to Justice in America (Critical America)*. New York: New York University Press.

March, J. G., and J. P. Olsen. 1984. "The New Institutionalism: Organizational Factors in Political Life," *American Political Science Review* 78: 734–749.

Massoud, Mark. 2013. *Law's Fragile State: Colonial, Authoritarian, and Humanitarian Legacies in Sudan*. New York: Cambridge University Press.

Meyer, David. 2004. "Protest and Political Opportunities," *Annual Review of Sociology* 30: 125–145.

Mills, C. W. 1959. *The Sociological Imagination*. New York: Oxford University Press.

Nonet, Philippe, and Philip Selznick. 1978. *Law and Society in Transition: Towards Responsive Law*. New Brunswick: Transaction Publishers.

Ostrom, Ellinor. 2000. "Collective Action and the Evolution of Social Norms," *The Journal of Economic Perspectives* 14: 137–158.

Persson, Anna, Bo Rothstein, and Jan Teorell. 2013. "Why Anticorruption Reforms Fail—Systemic Corruption as a Collective Action Problem," *Governance: An International Journal of Policy, Administration, and Institutions* 26: 449–471.

Pinker, Steven. 2002. *The Blank Slate: The Modern Denial of Human Nature*. London: Penguin Books.

Pinker, Steven. 2015. *The False Allure of Group Selection*. Edge.org Essays.

Rajah, Jothie. 2012. *Authoritarian Rule of Law: Legislation, Discourse and Legitimacy in Singapore*. New York: Cambridge University Press.

Rege, Mari. 2008. "Why Do People Care About Social Status," *Journal of Economic Behaviour & Organization* 66: 233–242.

Rueschemeyer, Dietrich. 1998. "State, Capitalism, and the Organization of Legal Counsel: Examining an Extreme Case: the Prussian Bar, 1700–1914," in Terence C. Halliday, and Lucien Karpik (eds.), *Lawyers and the Rise of Western Political Liberalism. Europe and North America from the Eighteenth to Twentieth Centuries*, 207–227. Oxford: Oxford University Press.

Smith, Merete. 2015. "Advokatenes samsfunnansvar," in Sigurd Knudtzon (ed.), *Å Være Advokat*, 13–23. Oslo: Universitetsforlaget.

Smith, Merete. 2016. Interview of January 6, 2016 by author.

Stoutenborough, James, Donald Haider-Markel, and Mahalley Allen. 2006. "Reassessing the Impact of Supreme Court Decisions on Public Opinion: Gay Civil Rights Cases," *Political Research Quarterly* 59: 419–433.

Teubner, Gunther. 1983. "Substantive and Reflexive Elements in Modern Law," *Law & Society Review* 17: 239–286.

Tushnet, Mark. 1995. "Policy Distortion and Democratic Debilitation: Comparative Illumination of the Countermajoritarian Difficulty," *Michigan Law Review* 94: 245–301.

Voeten, Erik. 2008. "The Impartiality of International Judges: Evidence from the European Court of Human Rights," *American Political Science Review* 12: 417–433.

Weiss, Yoram, and Chaim Fershtman. 1998. "Social status and Economic Performance: A Survey," *European Economic Review* 42: 801–820.

Wesley Pue, W., and David Sugarman (eds.). 2003. *Lawyers and Vampires: Cultural Histories of Legal Professions*. Oxford: Hart Publishing.

Zomeren, Martijn, Tom Postmes, and Spears Russell. 2008. "Towards an Integrative Social Identity Model of Collective Action: A Quantitative Research Synthesis of Three Socio-Psychological Perspectives," *American Psychological Association* 134: 504–535.

Østvedt, Einar. 1940. *Bernhard Dunker: juristen, politikeren og kulturmennesket*. Oslo: Gyldendal.

Index

For the benefit of digital users, indexed terms that span two pages (e.g., 52–53) may, on occasion, appear on only one of those pages.

Tables are indicated by *t* following the page number